War Stories

War Stories
A GI Reporter in Vietnam, 1970–1971

Conrad M. Leighton

McFarland & Company, Inc., Publishers
Jefferson, North Carolina

LIBRARY OF CONGRESS CATALOGUING-IN-PUBLICATION DATA

Names: Leighton, Conrad M., 1948– author.
Title: War stories : a GI reporter in Vietnam, 1970–1971 / Conrad M. Leighton.
Description: Jefferson, North Carolina : McFarland & Company, Inc., Publishers, 2016 | Includes index.
Identifiers: LCCN 2015051022 | ISBN 9781476663982 (softcover : acid free paper) ∞
Subjects: LCSH: Leighton, Conrad M., 1948—Correspondence. | Vietnam War, 1961–1975—Personal narratives. | War correspondents—United States—Biography. | United States. Army. Cavalry Division, 1st.—Biography. | United States. Army—Military life—Anecdotes. | Vietnam War, 1961–1975—Regimental histories—United States.
Classification: LCC DS559.5 .L448 2016 | DDC 959.704/3092—dc23
LC record available at http://lccn.loc.gov/2015051022

BRITISH LIBRARY CATALOGUING DATA ARE AVAILABLE

ISBN (print) 978-1-4766-6398-2
ISBN (ebook) 978-1-4766-2344-3

© 2016 Conrad M. Leighton. All rights reserved

No part of this book may be reproduced or transmitted in any form or by any means, electronic or mechanical, including photocopying or recording, or by any information storage and retrieval system, without permission in writing from the publisher.

Front cover: (inset) the author at the door of a bunker on the edge of Bien Hoa Army Base; (foreground) a 105mm howitzer crew in the midst of a fire mission (photographs from the author's collection)

Printed in the United States of America

McFarland & Company, Inc., Publishers
 Box 611, Jefferson, North Carolina 28640
 www.mcfarlandpub.com

Table of Contents

Acknowledgments   vi

Preface   1

1. In Country: August 15, 1970, to September 30, 1970   3
2. On Assignment: October 1, 1970, to December 31, 1970   37
3. Into the Jungle: January 1, 1971, to February 27, 1971   157
4. The Audience Shrinks: March 1, 1971, to April 30, 1971   213
5. Nearing the End: May 1, 1971, to June 30, 1971   260
6. Being Short: July 1, 1971, to August 15, 1971   298

Index   323

Acknowledgments

Kevin Perrier, Tom Preece, and Bruce Gottsche were invaluable in writing this book; I am grateful to them for their help and encouragement in tackling this project.

The men of Echo Recon, 1st Battalion, 7th Cavalry in our many emails and several reunions helped bring back that time for me. They made the war experience more human to me, making this a better book.

My now-departed parents, Frederick and Janet, were my most critical supporters. I sent them letters and they saved them. They were an invaluable sounding board and gave rock-steady support. They provided an upbringing that nourished me as a writer and their love carried me through Vietnam.

I write this for the most important people in my life now, my wife Anita and our children Tiffany, Tabitha, Linnea and Isaac, as well as their families—these writings will bring my wild stories and improbable claims into better focus.

And finally I must recognize my 22-year-old self. As I incorporated my letters home into this book, a total stranger confronted me. I repeatedly thought as I typed away: "I don't remember that," or worse, "that's not how I remember it." I'll never understand why he wrote so much but I'm glad now that he did.

Preface

I was a journalist in Vietnam from August 1970 to August 1971 while in the 1st Air Cavalry Division. I didn't approve of the Vietnam War even then—it was a foolish war—and yet ended up a GI reporter publicizing it. My primary mission was chronicling the life of the combat soldiers.

What I wrote for our division's newspapers and magazines were the Army's version of combat events sprinkled with human-interest stories. I would highlight what we—the troops—were doing and our successes, a cheerleader of sorts. I was allowed to make people laugh—war can be funny. I was encouraged to show curiosity, run down leads, take pictures, range around the division area in helicopters, and stick my nose in other people's business.

I've organized this book based on my many long letters home to my parents. I've also included stories I wrote for the Army. I've dared to write a little from my memory but I'm giving precedent to my writings and photographs from the time. Later additions appear in italics (and brackets, when they are inserted into letters for clarification). After reading my articles and letters home, I feel fortunate to remember half of what went on then.

I was an enlisted man writing primarily for enlisted men. What I can provide here is a record of some of our struggles, views of what it looked like, and the stories of a motley collection of GIs.

Kevin Perrier—a fellow 1st Cav veteran from the time I was there—found me in 2005 and hooked me up with my old friend Tom Preece from the unit I'd tramped with in the jungle. Tom, using old orders and Internet searches, tracked down the other men from Echo Recon, which I patrolled with in the jungle for a total of 12 days.

I have changed a few names and left out some others when what I say is unflattering or worse.

I've heard complaints that my photographs don't show sufficient violence and blood. I wrote many stories about combat but other than my two outings with the troops, lived it only vicariously. I didn't experience major war traumas personally—I was darned lucky—so my pictures reflect my experience.

I hope you enjoy the myriad stories of the place and time. For those who share the Vietnam War experience, maybe this will bring back memories—a few of you might even find yourself in a picture. For the rest of you, this should give you a better view of how the Vietnam War looked and felt to one soldier (me).

Chapter 1

In Country: August 15, 1970, to September 30, 1970

When I arrived in Vietnam, I was assigned to a unit and lived on a small base—Song Be—near the Cambodian border. I adapted to GI life and started roving around the "Black Horse" brigade in helicopters. Later I was reassigned to Bien Hoa Army Base, a huge installation near Saigon where the rest of my tour was spent.

How I Ended Up in Vietnam

I was technically a volunteer—I enlisted—but this was under duress. I had dropped out after two unhappy years at Ohio Wesleyan University and lost my draft deferment. I was a loser in the draft lottery of 1969—my number was 56 and men were taken with much higher numbers in 1970. Although I didn't consider myself much of a physical specimen, I passed my military physical easily.

I was already against the war but felt that if I didn't go, some other poor bastard would go in my place. I was no conscientious objector and although I like Canada, I couldn't see abandoning the United States. I was concerned about being stuck in a military job I didn't want so I enlisted to be an army journalist and haven't regretted it.

I endured basic training and after that, went to the Defense Information School (DINFOS) studying journalism. I graduated from DINFOS, giving me the military occupational specialty (MOS) of 71Q20, an information specialist—a writer. I was allowed also to be a photographer—this was a voluntary role that I embraced. I had been the yearbook photographer at my first high school in Mt. Vernon, Iowa, so I knew how to use a camera.

Following a short leave in Fremont, Nebraska, where my parents then lived, I flew to Vietnam. My letters were written to my parents and the younger of my two sisters, Becky. Both my parents were English majors in college and dad had a master's degree in journalism so they appreciated writing and wrote well themselves. The first note I sent home on the back of a postcard. I had landed in Cam Rahn Bay with no idea where I would end up.

My inexperience shows here, particularly in my slur about the Vietnamese. I quickly found that Vietnam wasn't that simple.

First Letter Home

August 17, 1970

I made it, though I lost Sunday altogether. My address is still temporary—please don't write to Cam Rahn Bay. This afternoon I move to another replacement center farther south in Bien Hoa near Saigon. I should know in a day or so where I'm to be stationed. That plane flight—2 hours to Alaska, 7 hours to Japan and 7 hours here—was not as bad as I expected. We had long stops along the way. The shear bulk of time lost still is staggering. The weather is not as hot as it could be but it's still sweltering. The humidity is very high and I never can dry off completely. I've seen my first natives. They are small, have good posture, are strong, and their honesty is not above suspicion. They look fascinating. Sandbags, helicopters and wooden barracks

An artillery crew is at work on Fire Support Base Green or perhaps Owens in October 1970. Keeping artillery pieces in good working order amidst the mud and dust required fussing over the guns constantly.

1. In Country: August 15, 1970, to September 30, 1970

appear in almost endless supply. I am in little or no danger. For a typical American with a fetish about cleanliness, Vietnam is bothersome. Showers are primitive, latrines don't have running water, and sand is everywhere. I brought too much junk with me.

First Team Academy

August 20, 1970

I am now a member of the 1st Cavalry Division, going through orientation at Bien Hoa not far from the airport. Yesterday I was flown up from Cam Rahn Bay in a noisy uncomfortable flying boxcar at 2 a.m. I slept little needless to say. Last night I got plenty of sleep.

Today I learned where in the country my division wants me. I'm staying in Bien Hoa during orientation but I'm assigned to the 15th Administration Company where I'll work in the Information Office. I don't know much more about this yet.

I'm at the "First Team Academy" for all new folk coming into the division. It is amid helicopter pads and there is an endless stream of copters overhead. I've seen all kinds of them.

The base is huge. The quarters are poor by stateside standards but otherwise it could be a U.S. base in the States. An airbase is next door with all kinds of antique aircraft. Surprisingly, I've seen no modern jets.

Now to complain. Fort Lewis just doesn't like me and lingers. You remember the cold I caught there in basic training? Well, it's attacked me again—I've got a dandy cold now despite it being hot here.

The only critter I've stepped on, Becky [*my younger sister*], was an oversized cockroach. There are no jungles here, just a few stunted palms.

Dad, you should receive a government check—I've decided I only need so much. The rest will be sent home to you, once or twice a month.

Please don't write yet—I should know my address in six days or so. I just can't believe how big our bases are.

Drug Users

August 21, 1970

I keep tripping merrily over happy contented drug users—they're everywhere. They are friendly, seem sane and are outspokenly pro-drugs. American drug laws seem ineffectual here.

Bien Hoa is colder than Cam Rahn Bay—I think I can get used to conditions here. Such old standards as warm and cold water, flush toilets and electric sewing machines are absent. I wish the Army would stop wasting my time with this orientation and allow me to get to work.

A Vietnamese who unfortunately speaks passable English has stopped me twice today, trying to sell me a Kentucky-made $46.00 Bible at $10.00 a month. He said my Mom would love to have me send her a Bible. I told him, trying to be polite, that my Mom would question my sanity, that she would wonder what had come over me. Mom, I can send you something better than that.

Vietnam is an attractive country at sunset. I can almost imagine I was in Nebraska except for the lulling put-put of a Huey's engine or the outline of a Chinook carrying a load like a giant locust silhouetted against an approaching thunderhead.

The sun is out of sight and the time is only 7:15 p.m.—that's the tropics for you.

I saw a monarch butterfly today but he had a white racing stripe, almost looking familiar. I also saw a lizard: [*I drew a picture*] That's rough. He was a little larger than a chameleon, a gecko maybe?

Tomorrow I begin actual training after three days of details. It will last four days and then off I go to my job.

I get to jump off a 50-foot tower on a rope, rappelling or something similar. You know how much I like heights—it will be a wee bit tense. But if a chubby E-6 can do it, so can I.

Hanoi Village

August 22, 1970

Today I was finally out in the jungle, a 6 acres second growth of shrubs—no canopy—in the middle of the large base. Called Hanoi Village, it was more interesting than I expected.

It wasn't the booby traps or lectures that fascinated me but the little jungle itself. It was crawling, scampering and leaping with life. Becky, if you stay hip on critters, you just have to see a jungle.

The first creatures I encountered were an orderly column of ants. They stopped for no obstacle. I picked one up, trying to give it a comprehensive examination but it must have been a warrior or something. He jabbed a small deep cut on one of my fingers. I dropped him instantly in surprise. He drew more blood than anything that small managed before although I made it worse when I ripped my skin pulling him off.

The butterflies are huge—a collector's dream. I saw strange grasshoppers, walking-stick-like leafhoppers, snails, chameleons and a spider. I had time to look but there was so much to see. Plant varieties were endless. There was crabgrass that climbed like a vine. I picked up two dead butterflies to send home but they were granulated in my fatigue pockets.

It's the hottest I've seen anyplace. It was so humid and the sun so merciless that I was thankful for the nearly total cover of my army fatigues. It

must have been nearly 100 degrees and wet. Now it's only 80 degrees and damp. P.S. I just saw a bat, you know, the ones that fly.

First Impressions

August 23, 1970

I have enclosed a Vietnamese moth—notice how similar he is to a butterfly. I'll attempt to mount some specimens and ship them home. Tomorrow we're to see a general and rappel off a tower. It's the monsoon season and raining hard now.

They have an outfit, part of the 1st Cav, called Kit Carson Scouts. The men of this group are all ex–Viet Cong or North Vietnamese soldiers who've volunteered to scout for the Americans. They all have prices on their heads. They are uniformly small, thin, and usually young. We had one of them, an ex–North Vietnamese lieutenant, show us what he could do going through wire. It took him twenty minutes to complete the course—his patience was astounding.

At Phuoc Vinh last night we suffered 27 KIAs (killed in actions). The enemy attacked and a medevac helicopter, a Huey, was flying out the dead and wounded. Chilling.

I saw a PFC lose his cool and tell off a tough-looking E-6 (staff sergeant). I respected him some for the generalizations he made on the foulness of the Army but he insulted the E-6 grossly in the process. He will probably be court marshaled.

Everyone, even the E-6 and E-7s, like my glasses. They shall become part of me yet—that's my vanity talking.

Rappelling; General Speaks

August 24, 1970

I rappelled today from this 40-foot tower by jumping off backwards on a rope while wearing a Swiss seat. Whee! It was funny, really. I felt like an airborne ranger for a 10 second period, even had a brief free fall. It was easy; everyone did it, including a platoon of Kit Carsons.

We had the Division CG (Commanding General), Major General Putnam. I can't remember much of what he said although he was a good speaker. The division was one that was in Cambodia and, to hear him tell it, was a roaring success. He said we have the enemy on the run. With all the helicopters, 400 Hueys and 80-some Cobras, the division must indeed be tough. He said that a lot of help for the troops could be trained on a small area.

I want to see the war from the view of a good fighting. I'm told the 1st Cav is one of the best.

We had a lecture on drugs by an army doctor. Although coming out against using anything in a combat zone, he was still somewhat liberal. His definition of using drugs, to change a mind in a hopefully favorable way, was one of the best I've heard.

Helicopter Crash

August 25, 1970

We had quite a day of using weapons and watching demonstrations. In one demonstration, two men died.

It was our last demonstration. Two Cobra helicopters, commonly known as snakes, gave us a view of the prowess of their rockets. Their firepower is fantastic; I'm glad they're supporting us.

After they'd expended their rockets, they made a low dive over our stands. They are small targets when they flew straight at us and the whole crowd was impressed. One snake came very low, just pulling out in time.

The pilot of this copter decided to take a pass out in an area near the dirt wall enclosing our firing range. He dived low. As I watched, he came in at what appeared to be too steep an angle. I didn't know much, I thought he could make it.

He went behind the dirt wall about 400 meters from where I stood. Instead of a copter coming back into sight, a ball of fiery metal scattered back to ground.

A copter crew, standing by after their demonstration, suddenly leaped into action, obvious upset. They called the medevac copter. Copters converged on the disaster scene.

My first thought was that no one could have lived through it. Finally some very sober soldiers who had run to the scene walked back. They'd been able to find only one charred body. The helicopter was a twisted mass of wreckage, they said. There were two men in the chopper when it crashed.

They pulled us together as best they could and marched us back to our hooches. As we walked back, a number of jeeps passed by, including one carrying Major General Putnam, obviously unhappy. The 1st Cav is accident prone, one guy told me. I believe it.

First Phuoc Vinh Visit

August 26, 1970

I flew up to Phuoc Vinh by Chinook early this morning and got a glimpse of the countryside. I found it indescribable. Helicopters were all over. Phuoc Vinh has the Chinooks—there were at least 20 of them at the airport.

I am in a hooch in a rubber plantation.

1. In Country: August 15, 1970, to September 30, 1970

I was given my own personal M-16 A1 rifle and a gas mask. I'm ready for anything now. I still don't know what I'm going to do though. This is the first place I've come where the fearless leaders didn't immediately grab me. Where are they?

Assigned to Song Be; Jeep Ride

My first posting was to Song Be, also called Fire Support Base Buttons, not far from the Cambodian border. I didn't mention it in this letter but I'd flown from Phuoc Vinh to Song Be. I remember this being my first ride in a Huey. I hopped up into it, took a seat and strapped myself in, and the chopper went up, raised its tail, and headed up and forward. It was exhilarating, something I came to do often and enjoyed.

August 27, 1970

After barely 24 hours, I changed places again; same address. I'm in the "Black Horse" second brigade of the 1st Cavalry Division, about 20 miles from Cambodia and the only brigade whose territory borders Cambodia. This is where I expect to be stationed for some time. My situation is good—even great.

The ranking man is a Specialist 4. I'm the only PFC around. There will be five or six of us here. I turn in five stories a week, get a press card, and go everywhere.

Today was indoctrination in good enlisted man style, we hopped in our office's decrepit jeep and drove around our local mountain, Nui Ba Ra, which looms over the base. I saw all sorts of things along the dirt road but didn't have a camera. The day sights included Montagnard village, hundreds of kids, Vietnamese, a Catholic mission, a market place, flying up to the base in a Huey helicopter, drinking cold cokes, introduction to my makeshift tent home, watching illegal money changing, buying two cases of cokes, seeing an abandoned-bullet-and-rocket-pitted two-story concrete structure, and generally goofed off.

The living is entirely different from what I know; humans don't hold up as well here. Many are small with rotten, golden, black-juiced teeth and naked or nearly bare bodies. They really look old.

The Montagnards are very interesting. I saw them weaving, separating rice by throwing it into the air. I saw them with crossbows and playing flutes. Ducks, dogs, and cows were in profusion. Huts were bamboo, metal, and grass. The people have darker skin than the Vietnamese, looking more Cambodian I'm told.

The photographic possibilities are endless—I wish I'd had a camera and film today. Take some money out of my account and send me some color and black-and-white film. Write in big bold letters that it's film so some yoyo doesn't x-ray it. My base hasn't been hit much since the Cambodian incursion. One guy was blown away two hooches down from here two and a half months ago but that was an exception.

I'll live in a tent with a bunker inside where I work and sleep. It's very hot in the day, I'm told.

Selling Books

August 29, 1970

The 1st Cav put out a history book about itself, *The First Team* and ordered WAY too many copies. So General Putnam has ordered the PIO section to sell all these copies, or most of them at least. I, along with 2 other unfortunates, have been picked to go out to the brigades to sell books and do home towners, news releases that go to soldiers' hometowns. Selling books is one of the stupidest things. Because I am up at Buttons, they haven't caught up with me yet. Maybe my bosses don't want to catch up with me.

We had a big firefight last night up near the Cambodian border with a company-sized force. It was a roaring battle with a lot of helicopters and artillery thrown in. It appears we won the battle. I was nice and safe.

Every night the artillery fires off rounds. To my green ears, they all sound

Dave Lewis, a fellow writer, stands outside our humble quarters, our Song Be home.

1. In Country: August 15, 1970, to September 30, 1970

The dirt road has our tent hooch and a number of others on the left side, the fence around the brigade tactical operations center (TOC) on the right. A group of handlers with their dogs lounge on the road.

like incoming. Flares go off through the night. My office, by virtue of putting out a newsletter every night before the next morning, doesn't have to stand night guard.

This country is beautiful. The cloud formations are breathtaking in the late afternoon. A 155mm howitzer just went off, god what a sound. But as I was saying, the thunderheads are magnificent and because we're at the top of a rise in the Central Highlands, you can look out at a lush green landscape with strange vegetation everywhere.

The mud and dust around here is from a reddish clay and is all over everything, including this poor typewriter I'm working on. It reminds me of the soil I saw going through Georgia when I went to Florida.

I jeeped it down to the Notra Dame des Mission, which sells all kinds of wondrous crossbows from beautiful native woods, elaborate weavings, spears, and bells from Montanyards, who are skillful craftsmen. Few know about their handiwork. I'll buy some tomorrow and send them home.

These people have some of the ugliest teeth in the world. Dad, I am sure you noticed the same thing when you were stationed in India. Some eat beetle-nut or some similar herb that dye their teeth an ugly black. I have seen some of the ugliest scars and emaciated bodies. It's so different. Nonetheless, they are human, though they probably couldn't imagine the way we live.

Nui Ba Ra Mountain behind the central Song Be helicopter pad with a Cobra gunship flying by, the effects of the monsoons apparent.

Uses Lots of Oil

I wrote many stories that didn't get printed—this was the first that did. There was invariably a delay from the writing to the printing, usually a few weeks. I only have clippings, not the full paper, from my early stories and I didn't date this clipping—it was printed in the Cavalair, *our division's newspaper, around September 26, 1970.*

FSB BUTTONS—The ponderous machine lumbered along, its diesel fuel exploding in the morning air, adding to the clatter as the man-sized tires bounced down the dirt road. Spec 5 Willy C Stroman drove the machine, seemingly enjoying the noise and the dust.

The giant earthmoving machine, officially known as the 290M tractor and scraper, is taking part in the preparations for the relocation of Troop A, 1st Squadron of the 9th Cavalry from Phuoc Vinh to Buttons here. Specialist Stroman was hauling laderite, a mineral substitute for asphalt, for surfacing a helicopter flyway.

According to Capt. William E. Mulligan, the commanding officer of the 557th Light Equipment Company, "this is the only light equipment company in the Cav's AO (area of operations). To move our equipment, the machines have to be convoyed." The cab of a 290M alone weighs 27 tons, too much to carry by air.

This weight sometimes is an advantage. "We hit 16 mines in Cambodia," explains Mulligan, "yet I never lost a man or a machine. Stroman alone hit four mines.

Eleven men, headed by Sgt. Brian T. Nagamine, maintain the eight 290Ms, four road graders, three bulldozers and a number of trucks in the company. Nagamine has an open secret for keeping the machines running: We use a lot of oil, two to four drums a day."

Flat tires, a rarity, are easy enough to handle in the field but a flat tire from a mine complicates the problem. "Because mines often blow up the hubs of the tires," states Sgt. Nagamine, "we can't always put a new tire on the spot."

Capt. James R. Parker, the officer in charge of the whole relocation project, said, "I don't know how much laderite will have to be moved in because the soil shifts as it is filled. The Monsoons permitting, I expect the relocation project to be completed shortly."

INFILTRATION BECOMES EVIDENT

Most of my subsequent articles were about enlisted men with enlisted man sources. I'm quoting a general here and am struck now by what a dull and plodding effort this was. My early writings were heavily rewritten and maybe I can credit the editor with squeezing the life out of this one. This was in the Cavalair *in late September 1970.*

FSB BUTTONS—"This is significant," stressed Maj. General George Putnam, Jr. "It's the first time we have had positive identification of infiltration in recent months."

"When they come in," the 1st Air Cav's Commanding General explained, "we're in a good posture to beat the hell out of them."

General Putnam, speaking to Alpha Troop, 1st Squadron, 9th Cavalry, was referring to two air-ground firefights recently, one of which the 1st of the 9th started barely 5,000 meters from the Cambodian border north of FSB Buttons. The other fight belonged to Bravo Company, 1st Battalion, 8th Cavalry.

WO Joseph Schlein, awarded a Silver Star for Gallantry in Action, was in charge of the LOH trying to find a 37mm anti-aircraft gun that had shot at a Chinook. In the process, they became the target for an enemy hornet's nest.

WO John Bartlett, also awarded a Silver Star, acted as a coordinator of artillery and air strikes besides firing off rockets from his Cobra.

WO Geoffrey Bookelaar, WO Tyrone Graham, and Sgt. Joseph Anderson all were awarded the Distinguished Flying Cross.

1st Lt. Robert Gromar, feels his squadron's job is clear cut: "Our job is to start a fight, then call in the division."

FSB Buttons Artillery; Brigade Briefing

August 30, 1970

I was just over collecting notes for a story on the artillery on Buttons. They have six 155mm recoilless howitzers, five of which are now in action. They can fire a 90-pound projectile 9 miles and make a big noise when they go off. They are the guns that have been keeping me up at nights. They are fairly inactive now. Before the Cambodian operation, they would have to fire as many as 100 rounds a day.

You can disagree with the Cambodian operation on judgment grounds in the context of the whole war being a mistake but from a purely tactical standpoint, it was a roaring success. It took a lot of pressure off the base I'm at, the whole area in general for that matter. This base was previously informally referred to as "Rocket City" for obvious reasons but it's quiet now. My life is much safer, that's for sure. I'm wondering how long it will take the North Vietnamese Army to resupply their camps in Cambodia.

We had an acting sergeant telling how inadequate our hooch was as far as incoming rockets were concerned. We had to agree with him. We are in a poor position because the post command bunker is next to us but then there aren't any really good positions. But rockets just aren't coming in these days.

My hair is growing without being hedged in the army fashion. I am human again.

I went to the afternoon briefing that the Colonel has for himself in the command bunker at 6 p.m. yesterday. I always feel kind of silly there. It's so serious. The Colonel wants just the facts, unabridged with humor or even human emotion. The only emotion shown is the fear from the personnel giving the briefing when they are asked a question. I suppose you have to know what is going on but there must be a better way. It is all secret, of course. Big deal. All the information is so mundane that I am almost yawning before the end. I don't want to draw attention however because I am by far the lowest ranking man in the room. We PIO men have status of sort—everyone wants to be in the paper. They go out of their way to make a good story for me, especially the important men.

Killer Helicopters

August 31, 1970

I just discovered, being an industrious reporter, that the new helicopter group being moved into Buttons is really a gung-ho bunch of guys. It shows on their record. They maintain the highest individual kill record for the Cav—it averages at about 37% of the Cav's entire total and they comprise less the 5% of the Cav's manpower. Isn't that rosy?

It appears that I'm in the province that is likely to be the coming battlefield. We had General Putnam up here today. He feels that the enemy is beginning to resupply our province because of two big firefights they had up here. The 1st of the 9th was in both of them and started one of them. It appears, however, that this unit is so good that it hasn't lost a man in a long time. As I understand it, they use Hueys, Cobras and LOHs predominately. They have four men today getting distinguished flying crosses and such big awards. They were for that big firefight August 27th. These guys earned their medals as far as I am concerned.

Last night I was watching some cargo handlers attaching loads to the underside of Chinooks to carry out. It might sound easy until you realize that the cargo has to be attached while the Chinook is actually in the air. The windblast is tremendous—it's been known to knock down trees. The handlers are surprisingly confident in their profession; I'm not sure I could have that kind of faith in a pilot. I saw one handler nearly get crushed when the copter dropped too low. But the guy made it. The whole operation was impressively backlit against a huge thunderhead and the sunset.

We have a constant stream of not only aircraft but also PIO people going through selling books. They don't seem to be trying to sell very hard. I can't see that I would try very hard in their place.

I've got to end this letter and start writing the 6 o'clock news.

Montagnards

September 2, 1970

I bought two Montagnard pieces of handiwork, a large woman's wrapping cloth and a crossbow of a wood resembling teak. The crossbow was brought in by the man who had just finished making it. I'll send them home as soon as I figure out how to do it. I'll probably buy some more before long. It has several modern touches, the M-16-type stock and a figure on the front.

There is a feeling that the Vietnamese are using us for their own gain. Among soldiers there is a general feeling of contempt for the "gooks" who are always after the serviceman's money. The Montagnards are more respected; they are only being hurt by this war. One of the PIO guys was a grunt at one time. His platoon set up an automatic booby trap [*claymore mines, probably*]. Montagnards tripped the booby trap and six were killed, a number of others seriously wounded. The Americans could have cried, feeling infinitely sorry for their mistake. They were very unhappy GIs. The Montagnards had been told to stay out of the jungles but it was their country, where they'd lived for centuries.

The money system over here is all screwed up. In the black market, you can get 300 peastres for a dollar. The Army gives the serviceman a little more than one to one. The black market thrives needless to say.

I've been getting to know the psychological operations (S-5) boys a couple of tents down. They have given me several story leads plus they are just good and intelligent. Their office is as much like ours as any on Buttons.

Tomorrow I plan to go to Snuffy or another of the firebases.

It is Uncle Ho's death anniversary. We expect something to happen tonight. Phuoc Vinh is the division headquarters, a bigger place than FSB Buttons where I am. Surprisingly, they get rocketed more often.

I Need...

September 3, 1970

Would you send me my Mamiyaflex and light meter along with some film? Also, how about a big roll of packing tape and plastic bags? I can't find a way to pick up a camera here or buy film, tape is hard to come by, and I need bags to protect my stuff.

Nobody attacked last night—with the 1500 people and vast quantities of ammo on Buttons I wouldn't want to attack either.

FSB Sally; MEDCAP Mission

September 5, 1970

Our typewriter is in use—my scrawl will have to do.

I had my first look at a true firebase yesterday. Called "Sally," it had been in place six days. It

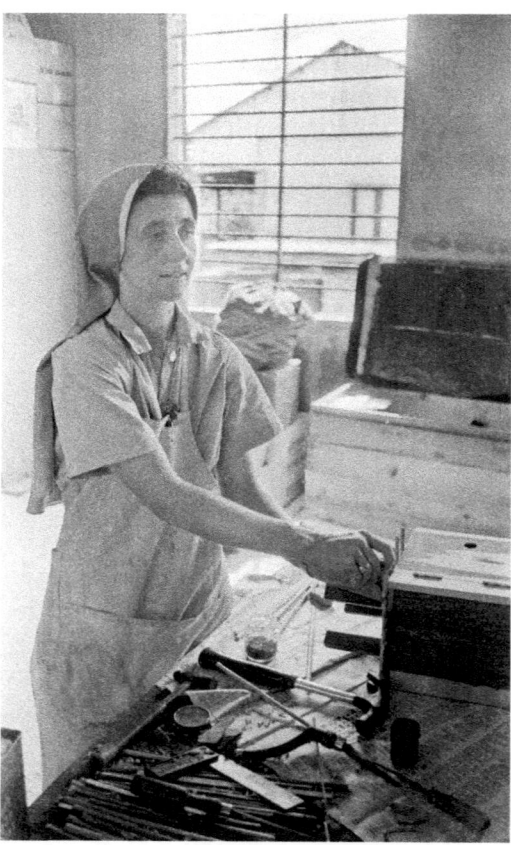

A Catholic mission a few miles from Song Be ministered to the Montagnard tribesmen, a poor minority group who found themselves in the middle of the war and too often its victims. A nun is in her workshop.

1. In Country: August 15, 1970, to September 30, 1970

was about the size of two football fields, surrounded by woods. It was muddy with leeches nearby—I saw the wounds from two of them on one guy.

I flew up and back in a Chinook. My ears are still ringing a day later. I could have had some great photos if only I had a camera. The photo possibilities are endless.

I watched a convoy going into Phuoc Vinh from the air yesterday. A Cobra was flying shotgun so heavy artillery support would have been momentary if the trucks had been attacked.

I also went out on a MEDCAP mission to give medical help to people in a Vietnamese village. The kids, more for such a small area than I've ever come across before, held us under siege most of our stay. A Polaroid camera went over big with the villagers. The interpreter played an important role. And our American eyeglasses fascinated them. The village chief swapped pens with me—I think I got the raw end of the deal.

Bien Hoa Jaunt

September 8, 1970

I flew down to Bien Hoa yesterday semi-illegally. I picked up some tape to mail the Montagnard stuff. It was strange walking around in Bien Hoa with men in civilian clothes and no mud. The 1st Cav has no one who can wear civilian clothes out here. It's not that bad because there is nothing to do if you do put on civilian clothes except get them dirty.

I haven't done much writing for the army recently. It's harder work than I expected because I don't know this area very well.

The lifers are really having fun now that there isn't much fighting. They are getting strict with the rules. It's funny, when we are actually fighting, I'm told the rules don't mean much. Rank is less important,—first names are the rule. This is one reason some places in 'Nam are better. You don't get hassled like you do on peaceful tours. This is a hardship tour supposedly. The lifers may ruin 'Nam for the rest of us.

It takes only a day for the mud to dry. It all dried up yesterday although everything in the countryside is still green. It's growing cloudier; maybe we will return to the mud.

Helicopters; Airplanes

September 8, 1970

I'm handwriting this letter because Dave Lewis, my cohort, is writing the nightly newsletter on the typewriter.

The helicopter is a marvelous invention that may have saved the war for the U.S. It makes air surveillance easy and air support a mobile threat. It is the center of the war effort, at least in our division. Bases can be moved and supplied completely by air; fire support bases in fact are moving constantly in search of the enemy. If this war could have been won militarily, I'm convinced it would have been won by now.

This ambush you talked about must have been during the 1st of the 8th's battle of August 27th, which I wrote you about. It was in my brigade. I did a story on the 1st of the 9th, which took part in that fight. I didn't hear about the accident with artillery—the military tends to hush up bad news—but this kind of thing just happens when artillery is called in when there is close fighting.

The flying boxcar and the caribou, a smaller version of a boxcar, are workhorses for small bases like Song Be, along with the big Chinook helicopters. Fixed winged planes can land on a very small airstrip like ours and do it regularly.

I'm going to be careful about using marijuana over here. It's hot stuff. Yes, I have met up with the guardhouse lawyers. I just keep quiet and know I am not missing much by not taking their advice. Drugs are not a legitimate escape as far as I am concerned. Weed is everywhere but frankly, I find writing letters to you more worthwhile.

A Chinook is the large helicopter distinguished by its two large humps with two large rotors on each hump. They are relatively economical in comparison with the flying cranes, monstrous 3-million-dollar grasshoppers that I hear are being pulled out of Vietnam because of their high operating cost. I am told that the cost of the gas required for a crane to take a bulldozer out of the jungles is enough to pay for the bulldozer. There is a new C model Chinook that will take its place—it is a juiced up model of the old Chinook.

Military Police; Dump Accident; EOD Team

September 10, 1970

I tried some rice wine just now. Wheee! It had a kick like a mule—I hope it isn't fatal and I can still write.

I spent yesterday riding around with the military police (MPs). There were two things of interest that happened. First, an MP patrol found an 81mm mortar round that hadn't exploded. They called in the EOD (Explosive Ordnance Disposal) team. We also found smaller 79mm grenade rounds. All three live rounds were set off by a stick of C-4 explosive. No big deal. The other happening was tragic.

A woman, searching for usable material in our dump, was backed over by a 2½ ton truck. The MPs searched out the story that I couldn't write; I couldn't publicize such an army accident. The woman was taken to the 15th Medical Detachment and Medevaced out on a helicopter. She later died on her way near to Saigon. It's now under investigation.

The MPs had been defending their use of tear gas in the dump by saying that accidents could happen if they didn't keep the unauthorized people out of the dump. This afternoon, with the accident involving the woman, their case was strengthened. The frail Montagnard woman about 40 years old was still alive when I saw her, gasping for breath before the helicopter picked her up.

I got a chance to see the countryside on patrols of the towns of Song Be and Phuoc Binh, both off limits as of two months ago to army people. The country I watched was beautiful in its own unique fashion and when the camera comes, I plan to hop aboard a MP patrol and shoot up some film.

I had a look at the dump where this woman was critically wounded. The wastage is unbelievable. I found an unfired 79mm grenade, a number of M-16 magazines and various other war materials that anyone could scrounge and hand over to the VC.

I did a story on the EOD team, two men, today. They are fascinating. They have staggering high security clearances, which include work with nuclear weapons. They are brave men. They say that no two disposal jobs are quite the same. As they put it modestly, "We know we are some of the best in the business. Just ask around, see who would take our job. We're all volunteers."

They are talking about survival of the fittest. They have lived through many tense situations, especially the older E-7, a real character. His partner, a Spec 4, did a lot of talking. It was the old pro that really fascinated me. They are pretty free; no one can tell them their jobs. A colonel tried to one day, and they told him they could be told to do something but not how to do it. They would have blown up his headquarters, quite legally, if he hadn't backed down.

Becky, I found a dragonfly-like insect in my tent last night and had it mounted. Unfortunately, the mice got it. I'll try again. The insects here look like horses or large dogs. I'll catch a big one yet.

Tonight we're having lightning with clouds in between blunting the brilliance of the flashes. The light from the moon and lightning only adds to the flares we fire up every night.

Vietnamese Interpreter; B Company

September 11, 1970

I was playing ping-pong as a partner with Sergeant Nahn, a Vietnamese interpreter for the 15h Medical Detachment. We were winners, mostly because of his fine slam shot. It's the only ping-pong table on Buttons. The sergeant is one of the few Vietnamese I can communicate with. In a way, learning English was a lingering death for him. He sees his people through our eyes and doesn't like what he sees. I asked him what he would do when the Americans leave. "I love my country," he said, "and I will never leave it. If the Communists come in, then I'll probably be just a body." He still thinks he has hope. Also, as a member of the South Vietnamese Army in his old outfit he had no future. He and one other man were the only soldiers to survive in their platoon after a Communist attack. He was wounded in the slaughter but not badly enough to escape the clutches of his army.

I worked on a story about B Company, 1st Battalion of the 8th Cavalry. You remember me telling about the 1st of the 9ths August 27th air ground firefight? Well, Bravo Company on the ground had their own firefight. They were outnumbered 120 to 90 men and yet killed 18 NVA while losing only three of their own men.

Their secret was near total camouflage and an excellent commanding officer. If I had to be a grunt, I would want to be in his unit. He's an aggressive commander yet an understanding honest man who his men trust. They did have massive jet, helicopter and artillery support. They weren't outnumbered in terms of firepower.

Dad, the fishhook is southwest of Song Be. The Cambodian border near me is fairly straight.

When winter comes, you'll have to tell me about it. I'll be desperate for snow by next winter. I miss it.

THE BEST CO WE'VE EVER HAD

My dad dated this Cavalair *clip to October 7, 1970, and the dates he gave for this and the other clippings from that month suggest he somehow knew the issue the clipping came from.*

"He is the best damned CO we've ever had," insisted Sergeant Vinc G. Materne. "If we ever lose him, it will be bad for us." His commanding officer is Captain James L. Williams from Colorado Springs, Col., and the sergeant seems to echo the feelings of the rest of his unit, Bravo Company 1st Battalion of the 8th Cavalry.

"You have to have people who have confidence in themselves." Comments the captain, accounting for his success with his men. "If you hunt the enemy, then they don't have time to hunt you. We keep them off balance." His infantry unit has been very successful in doing its job.

Since June 1, they have killed 47 NVA while losing only four of their own men. In one battle on August 27 and 28, they killed 18 attackers, quite a feat considering they were surrounded and outnumbered.

"We were on a routine patrol outside FSB Betty," related Capt. Williams, "to see if the enemy was moving through the area."

One reason they hurt the enemy so badly was the NVA wasn't sure where the Americans were. They couldn't see them. Sgt. Materne, an Agana, Guam native, is certain Charlie didn't see him.

"I had camouflaged fatigues on," he explained. "I just sat, watching them move toward us. They weren't sure where I was even after I opened up on them. Camouflaged heavily, we are the only infantry unit I know who wears camouflage like we do. It really works." He killed an NVA officer and helped effectively blunt the NVA attack. He was awarded a Silver Star for Gallantry in Action plus a Purple Heart for shrapnel wounds received in the action.

Sergeant William B. Custer, a killer team recon leader from Cumberland, Md, is convinced of the importance of another specialty of Bravo Company: Its small patrols: "Sending out small patrols has worked out beautifully. The whole company goes on reconnaissance." Sgt. Custer already has a Silver Star. Fourteen people in the company have or will receive a Silver Star.

The company received a stand down for three days. Captain Williams, who is just as well liked off the battlefield, described the rest period in Bien Hoa as a time that "gave everybody a chance to blow off steam." He didn't exclude himself.

NVA Troops, Supplies Hit by Alpha Troop

Using warrant officers—helicopter pilots—as the primary source for stories was unusual. This was in the October 7, 1970, issue of Cavalair.

FSB BUTTONS—Another in a series of battles involving Alpha Troop, 1st Squadron, 9th Cav took place near the Cambodian border south of Song Be. As usual, the cast consisted of a Pink (Hunter-Killer) Team on one side and a host of well-armed NVA regulars on the other.

"Those were bad guys all right," said WO John C. Bartlett, a Cobra pilot. "These men were all carrying weapons." As in earlier engagements, Bartlett acted as a coordinator for artillery, air strikes, Blue Max, and the Alpha Troop choppers.

The other member of his Pink Team, a LOH piloted by WO Robert B. Long was involved in the thick of things. At one time, Bartlett watching from above, estimated that Long had five to eight men shooting at him with AK-47s.

While blowing up the enemy structures with grenades and rockets, the aviators observed secondary explosion and other indications of war supplies stored inside. At one point a small stream was set afire when an estimated 500 gallons of gasoline spilled out of an enemy storage bunker that had come under the Skytrooper's guns.

When it was over, helicopters had accounted for nine kills, seven of those being credited to Long and his LOH crew. Artillery and airstrikes were each credited with three kills.

A Bad Day

September 12, 1970

I saw my first civilian war correspondent today, Dick Swanson from *Life* magazine. What a pompous ass. He strutted into our hooch, blared out in his golden voice, "You PIO?" He expected us to drop everything and find him a ride to Saigon. I did some running around trying to find him a helicopter and then a second thought, a plane. He wouldn't talk with us, his mind on greater things I suppose. He didn't thank me when he left. He must be a lousy reporter—he showed no curiosity.

Have you every read "Lord of the Flies"? I never thought such heartless brats existed but I ran into some today. Children are innocent, right? All day we'd been cleaning our dilapidated jeep, which had been misused and its innards forgotten. We needed it to travel off the base and two of us managed to get it started. It's a roofless thing with bad brakes and a rickety transmission. We decided to take it to a water hole about five miles outside of FSB Buttons (also known as Song Be) to have it washed.

There is a group of kids we'd heard about that would wash a jeep for a fee. We reached the water hole, slowed down, and were mobbed, even attacked, by eight crude little hellions who demanded they be allowed to wash the jeep. The only English words they used were profanity.

We picked out some boys and drove it down to the water for the wash. While we waited we were threatened, poked, insulted and generally mistreated. One of the boys had horrible burn scars on his face—he seemed to especially dislike us. We hadn't brought our M16s with us so we couldn't threaten them properly with the rifle butts.

Finally they finished, drove the jeep out of the water themselves, across a dirt parking lot, then jumped off and let the jeep slide into about four feet of muddy water.

The final indignity was that we had to beg a Vietnamese Army truck driver to tow us out of the water. By this time the kids were giving us a wide berth. And these are the Vietnamese kids we're supposed to be fighting for. The only child who treated us well was a girl selling drugs. We managed to get the jeep started and drive home.

I walked into the brigade briefing in the command bunker this afternoon, still bedraggled from the jeep incident, and nearly didn't salute the brigade's colonel, the commanding officer. I was immediately set upon by a lieutenant colonel who got in my face and got warmed up. My hair was too long, my boots unpolished, my fatigues too dirty, my mustache too large, and didn't I know I should stand at attention while talking to a field grade officer? By this time I was terrified with visions of being summarily transferred to an infantry unit.

Then the colonel stepped in and I was prepared for the ax. He had mercy on me, was even kind. He said I shouldn't get too scared, that it wasn't that bad although he didn't like long hair. And my hair was only long by officer standards; I'm no hippie. I think they were playing good officer, bad officer to put me in my place. I'd been trying and didn't deserve to be mistreated.

Innocents

September 13, 1970

I found myself a good typewriter for a change in Phuoc Vinh. I flew down from Song Be this afternoon to bring down some stories and take a rest.

After I wrote you the letter about the jeep dunking and the run-in with the brass, another story appeared. It seems that Alpha Troop, 1st Squadron 9th Cavalry had a field day yesterday and I didn't know about it. The trapped

I later learned that I shouldn't take pictures in the tactical operations center, the command bunker—I might unwittingly reveal secrets. Fortunately, I got this picture of Major General George W. Putnam, Jr. (right), and his aide, Sergeant Brookhyser, before I knew better. The general would have objected but was genial, allowing me to take this shot.

100 lightly-armed Montagnard VC in the open and killed a number of them. They were thinking of calling in an air strike with 500 and 700-pound bombs but someone, thankfully, stopped that nonsense. It is very possible that these "VC" were innocents. There is no doubt that many women and children were involved. This has been an area where a lot of people have rallied to our side. Listening to the helicopter pilots involved was a nauseating experience. They are just a bunch of trained killers. I hear even our colonel was mad at them—good for him.

Alpha Troop Catches NVA Troops in Open

I never believed in measuring success via enemy body count—this is an extreme example of what happens when units pad their kills. It is not flattering to the Army if a reader is paying attention but was printed nonetheless in the September 19, 1970, Cavalair.

FSB SNUFFY—"A" Troop, 1st Squadron of the 9th Cavalry recorded 22 kills recently in a daylong engagement, reaching a climax when a large number of lightly-armed Montagnards were caught in the open northeast of the firebase. A number of the enemy carried AK-47s.

It was the same area from which a large number of Montagnards have rallied. And, it was an elderly woman who rallied to the Blues, "A" Troop's ground force, that tipped the copters off to the location of a large group of the enemy on the run.

The day started when Warrant Officer Robert B. Long from Selma, Calif., was scouting an area of garden plots in his LOH (light observation helicopter). He discovered five hooches under construction and was dropping smoke grenade on the hooch when two of the enemy ran out. He called in the other member of his pink team, the Cobra, who killed them with rockets.

Mr. Long flew back in with grenades and eight more individuals ran out. The M-60 machine gun in the LOH, which had jammed earlier, jammed again. Unarmed, Mr. Long's chopper was forced to leave the contact area.

As Mr. Long withdrew, Warrant Officer John C. Bartlett from Whitefish, Montana, rolled in again with his Cobra on another rocket run.

The Blues were called in from Song Be to start a ground search of the area.

On the ground, the Blues worked into the afternoon, moving through the area. An interpreter finished talking to the rallier about 2 o'clock and the aircraft started searching for a large group of the enemy moving to the west.

The helicopter found the group and a chase began. Warrant Officer Stanley C. McCaw, who recorded seven kills for the day, said he got there just when the Blues arrived: "We couldn't tell how many other kills we had," said the Hammond, Indiana native, summing up the later action, "it was getting too dark."

There were no American casualties.

Innocent Montagnards Killed

September 14, 1970

It's pretty much confirmed—those Montagnards killed or injured in that strafing of the 100 caught in the open out of FSB Snuffy were innocents controlled by two Viet Cong. We had a *Stars and Stripes* reporter here today, gathering information for a story on the kills. It appears that nothing will happen from all this.

I got a press card today. I had to comb my hair and take off my glasses, you know, my kooky granny glasses. These morons, they asked me if my ½ inch thick lenses were prescription. They're like our flag lovers at home—all for appearances and show—and couldn't care less whether you're a decent fellow or not. All I'd wanted to do was show another new guy how our briefings went. They must have been waiting for me. The colonel isn't known as a nice guy.

One guy in our office hasn't done anything for 1½ months except sell 17 books last week. He is a liability; we (us two new guys) want him out of here. We all like to mess around but not to the point of such sloth. All he can do is spell.

Things have deteriorated in the PIO office to the point where Dave Lewis and I, both from the 2nd Brigade, are the only writers working in the division. Our major, our commanding officer, has alienated the civilian press. Dave tells me that civilians are very independent anyway but the major may make communications impossible.

I'm getting jumpy. I want to cure these symptoms by going out on a large movement with the infantry. The field is where the stories are.

Bad Night at Phuoc Vinh

September 16, 1970

It's *very* early in the morning. I was stuck in Phuoc Vinh for the night. There should be a special place in hell for thoughtless people playing the stereo in the transient hooch at 12:30 in the morning. Some insensitive baboon has now further bigoted me again jazz pieces I already disliked. I wish I knew how many hours of carefree slumber—in college and here—were lost to such broken records. Maybe I can get some sleep once I return to the Song Be mud flats tomorrow.

Transient Hooch

September 17, 1970

I'm home in Song Be although I never got any sleep. The problem with the soul brothers in the transient hooch in Phuoc Vinh was that they were high on drugs, marijuana or worse. They turned the light on at 3 a.m.—they must have thought the moonlight was dawn. Dave Lewis and I decided we'd never get any sleep. We finally caught the Charlie-Charlie (Command and Control) bird, the Colonel's helicopter, up to Song Be.

I bought another crossbow, an old fashioned one. I have a larger bow on order so another package will be coming home soon. I was gaily blasting away at Song Be with the new film you sent me.

You remember that lieutenant colonel that chewed on me 4 or 5 days ago; he must have been put up to it. He was charming and not at all authoritarian tonight. How strange. I just heard that he was given his own battalion, maybe that's it. He's an old information officer. I was surprised when he jumped me that day because all in all he's treated our PIO shop well.

The lights just went out, a common occurrence, but at this late hour it's irritating. The power is always going out. I should consider myself lucky, having electricity to run a refrigerator, several fans and the lights. By grunt measurements I'm not roughing it. The lights just came on.

I found that the guy who prides himself on not doing anything for 2½ months is being punished. Supposedly, this is the assignment where all the bad boys are sent to reform. In fact, I can attest that it is one of the pleasantest assignments in the division, if you ignore the surface mud and dust. I suspect that I was sent up here because they think I look odd. They did me a favor anyway.

The base was invaded by swarms of bees today. Everyone is "popping smoke," using smoke grenades to discourage the aggressive bees. Some dud threw out a white phosphorous grenade instead. I didn't see it happen but was told that the area was burning lustily. I can imagine. That is the kind of mistake that can get you incinerated.

The fellow I am kind of replacing is leaving next week. He's one of those guys who knows how to scrounge and take advantage of the system. The room he built which I sleep in is wood paneled, dug into the ground and has a TV which works haltingly. He is a fine photographer but tends to be selfish—everyone expects him to clean out this tent of all the fans, the TV, the radio and whatever else he can call his own. We are wondering if he really bought all his things, like his fans, originally. He has enough bluff so that no one dares to ask him. I find him hard to believe—I thought his types were myths thought up by patriotic gentlemen from World War II.

Napalm Drop; Air Strike

September 18, 1970

There is a terrible fascination with watching someone try to kill someone else, especially when the would-be killers are jets. I was in a Chinook helicopter on a mission to drop drums of napalm on an enemy bunker complex. We were circling, waiting for some reason, and found ourselves with ringside seats to a workout presented by several small jets. They'd swoop down like acrobats, erratically twisting and turning in a dive towards their targets in the jungle.

They would release their ordinance and rise swiftly out of range. I don't know what they were dropping but there seemed to be secondary explosions after the explosive hit. It was serious business but pure poetry in motion. The enemy on the ground couldn't have been more remote. This certainly wasn't the more personal face-to-face war of the infantry.

We circled for an hour or so, then landed after setting the net of napalm drums on the ground. We refueled on Fire Support Base Snuffy, then again took to the air with the net of drums beneath the chopper. Without much more adieu, we dropped the napalm on the bunkers, igniting the substance with a grenade. We were near the Cambodian border at a 2000 foot altitude and I was surprised, I could see Fire Support Base Buttons in the distance.

Yesterday I got a pair of earplugs, which helped, but I still got a headache from the racket the Chinook made.

Run-in with Officer

September 18, 1970

Damned lifers. Captain Hagler from Intelligence (S-2) captured me walking into the briefing this afternoon. My mustache was too long, he would dock me a week's pay if this happened again and he didn't want any of those hippies around.

He destroyed the briefing for me. I shaved and was walking back to the Tactical Operations Center (TOC) when I noticed a gathering of starch-spined enlisted men, a major, and Hagler. "Hey you," Hagler yelled, "get over here!" He was grilling four grunts he'd captured. They were much sloppier than me. He finished them off and I was left over. He told me he wasn't a lifer, that he didn't have white sidewalls (shaved the side of his head) but he didn't like lax personnel. Finally, he released me after adjusting my beanie hat.

The three members of the PIO office have taken an oath to avoid the TOC and never go to briefings. The deciding factor was when Dave Lewis got humiliated for not saying "sir."

I had a look at the supply yard for our 2nd Brigade. They estimate that they move ½ million pounds of materials a day. They supply not only FSB Buttons but also all the other landing zone (LZs) in the area, which includes all the firebases in Phuoc Long province, the 2nd brigades area of operation (AO). I was impressed by the size of their operation but they were an unfriendly crew as a whole—all they cared about was the story.

Reassigned to Bien Hoa

September 20, 1970

You will be glad to hear that I'm being reassigned from the 2nd Brigade to the 1st Brigade, which means I'll be moving from Song Be to Bien Hoa. I'll probably be no safer however. I'll still go out to firebases for stories.

I came down to Phuoc Vinh this afternoon in a flight of six Hueys that bypassed a thunderhead from the monsoons. Hueys are great for seeing the countryside, which looks like a garden of crabgrass. We kicked out safe conduct passes between Buttons and Phuoc Vinh. They are small simple pieces of paper with pictures of Thieu and Vietnamese written in strange scrawls.

Living in Bien Hoa should be better: modern roads, little mud and dust, a big PX, and a modern movie theatre. And Long Bin and Saigon aren't far away. As disadvantages, saluting and lifer skytroopers are in.

Bien Hoa; Long Binh; Mission; Boa

September 22, 1970

I didn't write yesterday in part because a lot happened.

I flew to Bien Hoa from Phuoc Vinh. At Bien Hoa I took a 10-mile trip to Long Binh and looked at how the generals and general staff live. The have paved roads, flush toilets and to top it off, a group of buildings looking like a college campus and air-conditioned. It's the center of the Vietnam command. You ought to see the PIO shop there—we're bush league by comparison although they received our reject, our major.

I know who's really cleaning up from this war: the Coca Cola Company and the brewers. There are supply yards full of huge boxes of nothing but soda and beer. And I average 3 to 4 cokes a day.

Bien Hoa will be more comfortable than Song Be: better showers, less mud, hooch girls, two big PXs, movies, Long Bin, Saigon and my own little private cubicle.

I spent $21.00 or 2330 piastres on a large crossbow, a Montagnard knife, an old bell and a bracelet I'm wearing made of brass.

I've finally started meeting people who will leave 'Nam after me.

Alex Boutzil just fixed a cartridge tape player. He's in a good mood—

1. In Country: August 15, 1970, to September 30, 1970

he's leaving Song Be for the States tomorrow and he's got no one to talk to but me. He's the kind of guy some enjoy making fun of—it makes them feel "smart." They're the fools, not Alex. We're listening to the Lettermen.

I drove out to the Mission today, probably for the last time for a while. I've grown to like the sisters who live and work there. They're Christian women who are putting their lives on the line for what they believe. I can't honestly say I have their kind of faith but I respect them for what they think and do.

I left in a funny way. It was ready to rain and the head sister helped keep my new buys from getting wet. She was fussing over me like a mother hen. I told her not to worry—I realized I was taking my chances of getting wet. Trying to calm her, I said, "Since I can't do anything else, I'll pray." Then it dawned on me what I'd said. From her reaction, I couldn't have said anything better. She was delighted. "God bless you. Good luck," she exclaimed, smiling broadly and walked away. Her small fragile body disappeared into her handbuilt workshop. I had an indescribably pleasant ride back to FSB Buttons.

It's funny. I've grown used to hearing the firing of 155mm rounds. They can go a long ways and I can hear them trace a path through the sky after the guns fire.

I'm glad to leave FSB Buttons. The lifers are on the rampage. They never have anything constructive to say and there are so many of them here. I hear that Bien Hoa, although farther in the rear, has less harassment. Our hooch girl will do our dirty clothes and polish our boots in Bien Hoa—not bad. Prostitutes, by the way, are called boom boom girls here. There are thousands of them and some are very pretty.

I've been flying about like flying is going out of style: globemasters, caribous, Hueys, Chinooks—I've tried them all. And I've got my eye out for more exotic ones. The names of firebases will change from ones like Snuffy, Buttons and Sally to Gary Owens, Nancy, and Green.

Did I tell you about the 12-foot boa one unit have here on Buttons? It's a handsome snake with black and white greenish splotches and eats chickens. It is popular at feeding time—gobbling chickens is more interesting than eating mice or rats, I'm told. Don't envy them too much, Becky, they only have one snake. You make up for size with quantity, right? And your boa's size is only a thousand meals off.

Pardon the Buttons mud. There's enough of it on this paper.

Left Song Be

September 23, 1970

I'm out of Song Be for good. I dragged my baggage collection off to the plane and made it to Bien Hoa. It's hotter here but I can manage. We have a collection of dogs, cute loved little things. I don't live far from Bien Hoa's massive airstrip. It's a Christmas tree this time of night. It has jets, sophisticated ones, flying in and out constantly.

I'm writing a story on enemy "slaves" who have rallied to our side. It'll be my first journalistic challenge of Bien Hoa.

For $10 a month I can have a hooch mate polish my shoes, wash my clothes and clean up my room.

It's funny how things have changed. When I first arrived in country in Cam Rahn Bay, I came off the plane already crouching, waiting for the bullets to fly. Nothing's come my way since so I've long since stopped ducking. You get used to being in very little danger as soon as you discover the odds are in your favor. Now I fearlessly go about my business. I'm no longer as impressed by someone being in Vietnam, especially if they live in Long Bin or Bien Hoa, maybe even Song Be.

SCARED—COULDN'T FIGHT
THEY LEFT HIM TO DIE

I periodically wrote stories about poor civilians caught in the middle of the war zone. This story was used in the October 15, 1970, issue of Cavalair.

FSB Green—"I've been hungry for a year; no rice, no medicine, no clothes and we were forced to eat bamboo shoots and corn instead of rice. My feet were infected and I have a headache. I often had to give up the food I'd gathered to the VC, even when I was hungry. I was afraid I'd starve, so I became a Chieu Hoi."

These are the insecurities the small size VC farmer-producer faces. These are the woes of Tran Van Tit as told to SSgt. Dinh Van Tan, a veteran interpreter. Along with a friend, Nguyen Van Nong, Tit walked for three days to Chieu Hoi at this 1st Air Cav Div firebase.

He was recruited into the VC in January of 1965. "I had a VC friend in Bien Hoa," he recalled, "who wanted me to join the Viet Cong as part of the fighting team. So I went into the VC but discovered I couldn't fight—I was scared—so they put me into the supply team.

"Sometimes I worked with regular forces carrying ammunition. Other times my duty was to grow rice and potatoes and give what I grew to the fighting forces. I worked near Bien Hoa in 1965 and 1966. In 1967, they moved me to hamlet number ten, just west of what is now Landing Zone Green. They issued me a weapon."

After interrogation, Tit's friend Nong took a helicopter ride to see if he could spot where their village was located. While Tit waited, weaponless after rallying, he was given two APCs for his headache and waited for his friend to return.

His next stop will be the Chieu Hoi center in Song Be, where slavery will end and a new life, a life of freedom, will begin.

Kit Carson Scouts; FSB Green; Ralliers; Army Music Group; Tom Preece

September 25, 1970

I had to get to bed early so I didn't write last night. Yesterday I was compiling notes for a story about the Kit Carson Scouts who are trained near the First Team Academy (FTA) several blocks from where I'm now living. A couple of Americans helping the Vietnamese cadre run the school say the program is a good alternative to putting enemy soldiers behind bars. It's also successful in saving lives, American lives mostly. The South Vietnamese don't need them. Captain Robinson, in charge of much of the program, says it has several missions. They work in tactical operations as scouts, help locate enemy units, identify dead and wounded enemy soldiers and probably most importantly, act as interpreters. Their status is in question once the U.S. Army leaves the country.

I awoke at 6 a.m. and caught a Huey up to FSB Green. I took notes for two stories. One was on the ralliers at Green, two Chieu Hois. Their story was simple. Members of a small cell of VC farmers, they were driven from their fields into the jungle when Green was set up, August 11 of this year. Scattered in the jungle, they were hungry, poorly clothed and without medicine although they had been in bad shape even before the GIs moved in. There has been a steady trickle of ralliers giving up to the Army as they grow hungrier. It takes a brave VC to rally. Green incidentally is about 50 miles northwest of Bien Hoa.

The other story was impromptu. Special Services, in charge of entertainment for the Army, had a band at Green playing rock, soul and country western music. They sounded good. Running their amplifiers off the base's electric generators, they enthralled the motley crew of grunts, a captive audience.

A fellow named Ed Riley, lead and rhythm guitarist, was the group's outstanding member, I thought. A musician who'd played with country western great Buck Owens, he has a job lined up on the *Hee Haw* show once he gets out of the Army. He was a medic before joining the group. They go out to most of the firebases every month. They were well received by the audience.

Tom Preece, a shake and bake staff sergeant (he went to NCO school) and a radio telephone operator (RTO) for Echo Recon was the day's biggest find—no story of course. He's a tall thin soldier with a bachelor's degree in English working on his masters. I had what was probably the best bull session so far in 'Nam with him. He would like to get into the PIO office and I wish he could. Right now, he's what's called a stringer, an unofficial part of the PIO staff who turns in an occasional story. He acts as our eyes and ears. Tom is sophisticated and cultured, even in his filthy fatigues, living in a half culvert hooch 3 feet tall and 8 feet long on a firebase. He hasn't been shot at yet and doesn't look forward to the first time. He's a draftee, 23 years old and married. I'll put in a good word for him.

Fire Support Base Green is small by my standards, muddy and with red soil like Song Be. It's out in nowhere, also sunny and hot. I got a farmer's tan, a sunburn where my fatigues didn't protect me.

Spec 5 Plant, the photographer at the Bien Hoa's PIO office, went on an operation to see if one of the two ralliers could locate his old home. He had a strenuous cross-country march through the bamboo and several leeches got to him. I want to go on one of these operations. Plant's force didn't find a thing but he got pooped out.

Vietnam doesn't smell like the States. This constant dampness changes scents. We have a lot of exhaust fumes. There is also the smell of fuel oil mixed with human wastes. And it smells different still when I'm outside the base.

I was introduced today to the grease gun—you probably know another name for it from World War II, Dad. A short-range weapon, it fires 45-caliber ammunition. It's a slow-firing machine gun and, I'm told, perfect for the close-in fighting of the jungles although not consider sophisticated enough for modern warfare. Its round doesn't ricochet like the M-16's. It's lightweight, an advantage over the M-60 machine gun. And built simply, it's hard to jam. It cost something like 16 dollars to make—not expensive enough for the Army.

Vietnam has some small mountains—I saw them from our Huey as we came back from Green. The country near dawn and at dusk is some sight.

Scouts Assist Cav

I ran across many infantry units using Kit Carson Scouts. Their unique combat knowledge and perspective was valuable. The October 15, 1970, Cavalair used this piece.

BIEN HOA—They're like Indian scouts of the old American West, they know their own people. Many divisions in Vietnam have tried Kit Carson scouts with a good deal of success. It's a life saving concept. As an officer working with the 1st Cav's Kit Carson scout training program, 1st Lt. Paul T. Warren should know.

Chief Division Scout Nguyen Cong Giae, formerly a hamlet chief for the V.C. and now an American Silver Star winner, runs the training side of the division's scout program.

One of the Chief Scout's instructors, Thach Huong, a free Cambodian, recognizes that some of his students have common problems. "They have a hard time adjusting to Americans," explained Huong. "They are really bothered by the G.I.s the first time. Yet they realize the G.I.s are the ones who need them."

The month-long Kit Carson course stresses learning English, understanding American equipment, how to warn of booby traps, understanding camouflage and ambushes American style, and how to gain the confidence of villagers when asking for information about the enemy.

The scouts need little training in jungle warfare, however. Some NVA soldiers in the school have a better understanding of jungle tactics than many Americans.

Spec. 5 Edgar B. Lemn, who lives and works with the Kit Carson scout cadre and students, feels no fear for his safety. Lemn's relations are friendly with the former NVA, VC, Free Cambodians, Civilian Irregular Defense Group (CIDG) and Montagnard men he works with. "We train them in administrative tasks," he commented. "They probably know the field better than we do. Scouts have no formal rank, though on recommendation, they can become chief scouts."

Duong Cong Can, for three years a political affairs specialist for the VC, now teaches English in the school. "They have a hard time learning English," Can maintains, "but we have a few that already can speak English."

First Stories Printed

September 26, 1970

Yes, the kid got his first stories in the paper. Only my "Uses Lots of Oil" story is at all satisfying. I didn't write the headlines.

I talked to a guy from Los Angeles who had a police scholarship to go to college and worked for 9 months as a motorcycle cop, an elite group in a good police department, he said. What an engaging guy. He had me in stitches telling, about a policeman's side of a small riot-brawl. He took a horrible beating from a woman who he refused to hit. Another patrolman, a sergeant with no such qualms, opened a huge gash in the woman's head. By that time she'd nearly incapacitated my friend. He makes his style of policeman sound warm, understanding and ultra-human. And although it's not fashionable in my generation, I believed him. I like to think there are good men like him in police departments throughout our country. He says there is no shortage of new police recruits. He wants to go back and become an officer in the police. He thinks Army MP training would be silly for him. He went into electronics, then photography, in the Army with the LA police force's blessing.

I tried writing my new stories with mixed success today. I feel kind of stoned, as a dew user would put it.

We have a new CO although I don't know more than that he's a major. He has full authority to remove anyone he wants (Colonel's orders) and he's not like his predecessor. I will meet him soon.

Wild Man

September 27, 1970

I worked on a story on grunts going back to the world today. At random, I picked five guys. Ronald (D.J.) McMillian from New York City was by far the most interesting of them. He worked as a disc jockey for radio stations as well as being a musician. He's an outspoken, militant, friendly and very intelligent Black. The Army has misused him and yet he remains sane. He originally enlisted as a 71R20 MOS (radio-TV announcer), almost the same MOS as mine. He said he was screwed over by his Black Army recruiter, ended up 11Bush (infantry, a grunt). He was contemplating going to LBJ (Long Bin Jail) before returning to being a bush bunny for 35 days before he leaves Vietnam. What a wild man.

SHORTTIMERS PLAN AHEAD

I have to wonder why I would write a story about soldiers about to leave the country when I had so much time left—I suppose it gave me hope. The October 15, 1970, Cavalair *used this story.*

BIEN HOA—In a division of 20,000, there are usually as many interesting stories as there are men. Try it yourself. Just spend an afternoon at the DEROS and R&R center and you'll spot everything from gargoyle makers to professional bird watchers.

I talked to five short timers at random.

"When I was a little feller, I started riding bulls," Sgt. Steven Deisley told me.

"Oh, really?" I asked, not quite sure I'd heard right.

"Yeah, I rode bulls in high school and college. I plan to become a professional rider on the RCA (Rodeo Cowboy's Association) circuit when I get home. Money is the most rewarding part of the profession."

Encouraged by Deisley's unusual story, I turned to his friend across the table. "What do you plan on doing," I asked, "and by the way, what's your name?"

"I'm James Tucker, a sergeant, and I'm looking forward to my wife and motorcycle, not necessarily in that order. That's all. I'm just a simple hicktown boy from Dallas. Maybe I'll go to technical college."

He didn't have much to say so I looked around and discovered that Sgt. James Lodate was short too.

"I'm just looking forward to what everyone else is going back to: my home, my girl and my motorcycle." My theory was going bad; I was about ready to abandon ship when I spotted SSgt. Charles Stuart.

He greeted me with, "I plan to go to work for the CIA."

"What ever got you interested in doing that?" I asked expectantly.

"I used to be affiliated with Special Forces in the Army and got interested. I'll get to travel a lot and the money is good. I was eleven bush (infantryman) for six years, three in 'Nam." Now that was something I'd never run across before.

I walked into the EM (enlisted men's) club, ordered a coke and sat down next to a fellow with a nametag reading "BRO D.J." He turned out to be PFC Ronald McMillian, a soul brother from New York City. He was very talkative so I asked him what he was going to do back in the world.

"After I tour the world, I'm going back to being a disc jockey. I used to work on radio for WPXI and WTOY in Roanoke, Virginia. I'm also a musician, I play the drums, guitar and bass."

Their experiences are as diverse as a case of C rations. Their common bond is that they spent a year of their lives in Vietnam making the numerous sacrifices of an infantryman. While waiting for the "Freedom Bird," they look much the same but take the time to talk to them and you'll discover they're very special people.

Leica Camera

September 30, 1970

I just was given my own Army camera, a Leica with two additional lenses. It's a great outfit but I don't like the rangefinder for focusing or the discipline required to write down every picture I take. I haven't done much with it yet.

They kill bugs over here with DDT! I see them spraying it all over, on firebases and even in Bien Hoa.

I went out to firebase Green this morning but had a bad day. I couldn't get a flight from Green to a smaller firebase called Mystery. I finally gave up. Tomorrow I'm flying by Charlie Charlie bird to the other important firebase, Gary Owen.

It looks like I'll get my chance to be a real combat correspondent, going to firebases regularly and even on short operations in the jungles.

Enclosed is a chieu hoi leaflet to encourage enemy soldiers to give up. I did a story on the two chieu hois in the leaflet, Nong on the left, Tit on the right. They had chieu hoied the night before I went out to FSB Green for the first time. They seem to have been well treated—the Psyops people (Psychological Operations S-5) are decent fellows as a whole.

I've also included a 5-cent small bill of MPC—worthless in the States. There are different designs and sizes to the bills. I haven't seen a greenback since I hit 'Nam. The MPC is fun to look at but falls apart too easily.

Chapter 2

On Assignment: October 1, 1970, to December 31, 1970

During this period I was hospitalized for malaria-like fever, and also routinely flew to firebases and on infantry resupply missions gathering stories. At this time I obtained my own cameras and accompanied an infantry unit for a five-day monsoon jungle mission that found three caches. I started pumping out stories and pictures on a wild variety of subjects, including pet dogs. One odd assignment included accompanying Patches, a civilian correspondent, during Christmas when she was distributing presents.

FSB Gary Owen; Charlie Company 2/7th; Recovering Bodies; Chaplain

October 1, 1970

I went out to Fire Support Base Gary Owen today, the other major firebase in my new brigade besides Green. I liked the mud better, which had more sand in it. I had a chance to go out into the field and you won't believe the company I went out to: Charlie Company, 2nd of the 7th, *the* Charlie Company that Jack Lawrence immortalized in his CBS TV documentary.

They were having a good day today. For the first time in weeks they had a chance to sit in one place, resupply themselves, eat a warm meal, and talk to me. It's called a logging operation where a helicopter lands in an area that has been cleared in the jungle, in this case it was an old road through an area that had been defoliated. They were friendly on the whole.

They had just finished humping in a three-canopy swamp jungle looking for two bodies from two helicopters that had a mid-air collision. There were originally eight men on board but only six bodies in the wreckage. The missing bodies were pretty ripe when they found them.

There was a protestant chaplain there giving a mini-sermon on the downfall of King Saul. The chaplain was a nice friendly extremely informal guy. He didn't wear a shirt when giving the sermon, a no-no even for a protestant technically, but this is known as a battlefield expedient which saves a situation in a time of need.

Waterlogged Company

Retrieving American dead is an interesting subject but not an acceptable item for our division's paper. The reason for the unit's wet tramp mercifully wasn't included. This was printed in the October 21, 1970, Cavalair.

FSB GARRY OWEN—It was a picnic compared to what Charlie Company, 2nd Battalion, 7th Cavalry had recently been doing out in the jungle.

The day before the company was in a rain-soaked, triple-canopy jungle swamp. "We were in water all day," Sgt. Doug Braun recounted. "We slept in the water last night." Capt. Ray Martinez added, "At least we had our air mattress to keep us afloat. The ground just can't absorb all that water." Someone else added, "Yeah, and I don't know how to swim, either."

But today was log day and the relaxed atmosphere on the sunny LZ was as close to a "day off" as these skytroopers had seen in a long time.

My desk in the Bien Hoa PIO office was plush only by grunt standards. I spent many days collecting stories on firebases and returned to this relatively safe place in the rear to type them and write letters home. It was routinely hot—no air conditioning—and the manual typewriter was a dog but it did work.

2. On Assignment: October 1, 1970, to December 31, 1970

"Hey Joe, you want to share this box with me?" asked a grunt, sifting through C-rations. A slick trying to jockey in the remote clearing complained that a tree was in the way.

After a parley, someone decided to blow the tree with claymores. Bodies scurried to shelter, but when the smoke cleared the tree was still standing. A second round of claymores did the job.

The company was being resupplied from FSB Garry Owen. They dried off and worked on a suntan. Then they stocked their packs in spread out little groups, ate their C's, drank their soda and beer, and just plain relaxed.

The 1st Sgt., SFC Loyd "Pappy" Vaughn, a grey-whickered surprisingly old man in comparison to his young troops, was enjoying the luxury of log day. "We did this two and a half weeks ago but not in a landing zone as good as this," insisted Pappy. "Loggings like this are rare."

Chaplain (Maj.) Ralph C. Workman, surrounded by infantrymen, gave a sermon on the downfall of Saul. He'd flown in especially for the informal session and the men appreciated the gesture.

Even Knothead, a German shepherd, seemed to enjoy a break from the arduous job of scouting the jungle with his handler, PFC Richard Andrich.

After an hour, the helicopter returned to fly out what the grunts couldn't carry. The troops roused themselves after a not so typical day in the life of a grunt and prepared to head back into the bush.

Unloading Huey helicopters was a basic part of log missions and troops did it with gusto.

I puzzled over this picture until my friend Kevin Perrier clued me in. Soldiers on firebases didn't have access to stores like those of us in the rear. They also had little space for storage. The Army would periodically fly in a tiny mobile store, a Flying PX, with merchandise the soldiers wanted, largely consumable items. It must have been set up the day I went out for the logging mission.

My Combat Assault

October 2, 1970

Another wild day—gee, am I pooped. I got up at 5:45 a.m. for the fourth day in a row. I caught a bird at the Flying Circus (the local flying group) and flew up to Phuoc Vinh. They kicked me off that chopper—too many people—so I had to catch another bird. Like many reversals, it was a blessing in disguise. I got a ride on the 8th Engineers colonel's bird instead. I got to talk with the radioman on board—a fellow PFC. I can get a ride with him over the Cav's area of operations on a free day.

I got to Fire Support Base Gary Owen and it was moving day. They moved to FSB Pershing, an old deserted base.

I got to ride in the vanguard going in on a "Charlie Alpha" (combat assault) with the second platoon of A Company, 2nd Battalion, 7th Cavalry. We went in shooting both M60 machineguns on all six Huey helicopters blasting our ears deaf. This is standard procedure. As it was, there was no resistance.

We dismounted the helicopters and the grunts fanned out. I blasted away with my Leica—the operation was quite photogenic. This was about

9:15 a.m. In short order six 105mm howitzers were lifted in and five were ready to fire at 11 a.m.

I have to hand to the Army; it can be well organized sometimes. A flying crane lifted in a Case 450 bulldozer and the engineers got to work. By the time I left around 12:30 p.m., the backbone of a new firebase was set up. Then the backbreaking labor of filling sandbags was just beginning.

As I departed, all of Alpha Company and part of Echo Company, plus the artillery, were on a new working base out in a large clearing where the old FSB Pershing had stood. I got mighty tired of being hit by the windblown debris caused by the wind blast from Chinook and Fly Crane blades.

I flew back to FSB Gary Owen and from there to Phuoc Vinh, our base camp not far away. I went to visit the division PIO—my big bosses with the division darkroom, where I would get my army films developed. At some point I realized the film in the camera had jammed. Although a Leica camera has great optics, it's otherwise a clunky camera. I had made the mistake of loading it with a 36 frame roll of film, I usually used a shorter film, and the film jammed.

I figured all I had to do was unload the film in the darkroom and the pictures would still be good as long as the film had advanced. I told a darkroom technician my problem. He said, "I can take care of that." and opened the back of the camera, exposing the film to the light! The idiot! If I had my darkroom at home, dad, I'm sure I'd have had some great pictures. Now I've got nothing. I can write the story but it will be a shadow of what it could have been without the pictures.

I talked at length with Alpha Company 2nd of the 7th. They are one of the only companies in 'Nam that go everywhere with fixed bayonets. As one guy said, "It catches on vines but we've gotten used to it. It is hand if you want to cut vines." A staff sergeant said, "It's a morale factor. It's got a definite psychological effect on the enemy." 1st Lt. Tom Dasenbrock from Omaha, Neb. told me about an ambush. "We got a coatimundi (Vietnamese raccoon) in an ambush. There wasn't much left of him after the claymore mine went off."

ANOTHER FIRST TEAM FIREBASE

This is an early example of "ain't we just the greatest" journalism. It really was an amazing spectacle and made it into the October 28, 1970, Cavalair.

FSB PERSHING—The 1st Cav's airmobility did it again. In the first wave, Hueys swept into the abandoned firebase, their twelve M60 machine guns splitting the air with lead, nearly breaking the eardrums of their cargo of grunts with the clatter.

The combat assault was over almost before it hit the ground. At 9:15 a.m. 2nd Platoon of Alpha Company, 2nd Battalion, 7th Cavalry controlled the turf of FSB Pershing without suffering a casualty or seeing an enemy soldier. The skytroopers fanned out to provide base security as soon as the Hueys hit the ground.

The rest of Alpha Company streamed in. A Case 450 bulldozer appeared, the workhorse of HHC, 8th Engineer Battalion, hanging from a flying crane. The 105mm howitzers of Bravo Battery, 2nd Battalion of the 19th Artillery were flown in, one by one. Elements of Echo Company, 2nd Battalion, 7th Cavalry were added to the population.

The orderly stream of choppers, guided in by the Black Hats of the 11th Aviation Group, would hover only long enough to release their cargo and then disappear, like a migration of noisy birds, sailing out of view in a small cloud of flying debris. The base began to take shape.

By noon, what had been a quiet field strewn with the remains of an old fire support base was now an active new firebase with a population larger than some small stateside towns. The backbreaking labor of filling sand bags and digging bunkers began.

In another demonstration of lightning quickness and polished teamwork, the Cav's coordination looked as good as that of a winning football team.

Upcoming War Operation

October 4, 1970

Tomorrow I'm going off to a huge operation at the outer edge of War Zone D, my brigade's area of operations. It's west of Bien Hoa about 25 miles.

I had a few classic Vietnam pictures—this one is probably the best. Defoliation looked like this, probably from Agent Orange. It appeared in *Pacific Stars and Stripes* on October 20, 1970.

There will be an Arclight (B-52) mission, then the 1st Cav will move in on the area en mass. There should be some stories there. We had a brigadier general walk into the briefing at 6 p.m. today and dominate the scene for 50 minutes—the briefing was much longer than usual. So, watch that area.

I'd better take a shower and go off to bed. My head is aching but I'll be better tomorrow. P.S. I forgot. Our photographer came down with malaria. He was feeling bad yesterday and went to 15th Med but they couldn't find anything wrong with him. Today they must have found something.

Getting Sick; DINFOS Roommates

October 5, 1970

I had a bad day—I didn't sleep much last night. I found out that Song Be is to be phased out this month and that the big operation did go off today. I saw 14 choppers at one time carrying troops to Charlie Alphas (combat assaults).

I got a letter from my DINFOS roommate, Alan Carrell. It seems that I lucked out in my assignment. A fellow DINFOS graduate and roommate, Tom Mano, is stationed only 80 miles from the Demilitarized Zone in a not-too-secure area. I'm lucky. I will write Tom.

The arclight really rocked Phuoc Vinh last night, or should I say early this morning. The craters must be something. I've seen a lot of big holes. Certain parts of the country look like a meteor shower had hit.

Sick Call

October 6, 1970

I went on sick call today—what a disaster. They gave me some potent pills to kill the headache but it didn't really make me feel well. I didn't even get to see a doctor.

I took over Cecil Cotton's room—he left for the States—because it has a light fixture, something my room lacked. The PX system here is really sad—you can't buy light fixtures, just bulbs.

Today was cloudy in my mind. Very little happened—I was in Bien Hoa all day. I wrote two uninspired stories; one I was ready to tear up.

The big operation north of Phuoc Vinh has stirred up some resistance although it's still light. A chopper crashed and burned at Phuoc Vinh and two of the three crewmen were injured. Another chopper was hit by ground fire and forced to land to check damage. No one was injured and the LOH was taken out for repairs.

The incidence of malaria is still at zero on the charts of our brigade.

"Jo's Operation Telephone Home"

Calling home wasn't an option for me—letters were my gigs—but there were a few fortunates who took advantage of this new program, which expanded according to subsequent stories in our paper. The October 21, 1970, Cavalair used this piece.

BIEN HOA—You want to call home? "Jo's Operation Telephone Home" would like to make it a little easier by paying for the call. It's a program just swinging into action at the Bien Hoa MARS (Military Air Radio System) station, located at the 1st Cav's VIP Center.

This new program is the brainchild of Miss Josephine McDonnel, Owanso, Michigan, who felt obliged to do something for the soldier in Vietnam.

"She's raising money from various people in the States," explained Spec. 4 George Belanger, a VIP Center clerk. "It's a public donation fund. We have received over $500.00 this month and expect more later on. We pick ten people per unit. Three dollars are sent in a letter and the money is used to pay for stateside costs of the MARS call."

Capt. Maxwell Jouanicot, in charge of dispersing the money, said, "The unit commanders decide who gets the money. Those chosen must be below the rank of E-6, must have five months in country, and must have distinguished themselves by superior performance. Their financial condition is also considered.

The program started the night of Sept. 29, and we've had eight calls so far. It's not always easy to get calls through by microwave. Eventually, we plan to put through a hundred calls a month.

Admittedly, it's not the money so much as the thought that's important. That someone back in the world, by this act of appreciation, is showing that they haven't forgotten—that's what counts.

Currency Exchange Day

October 7, 1970

Today was "C" day, currency exchange day. A lot of black marketeers were hurt but it was painful for the GIs because everybody had to turn in their old MPC (Military Payment Certificates), funny money that we're forced to use instead of greenbacks in Vietnam. I waited in line for five hours; I picked the wrong place to convert money. It was worse because I continue to feel tired and listless. The only good part was that I was surrounded by first sergeants, lieutenants and captains, all as fed up with the wait as me.

All the old currency becomes worthless in two days. I heard that enraged Saigon citizens were trying to stone GIs. Also, the exchange rate, MPCs to piastres, has changed with more piastres to the MPC dollar. So, in one strike, a currency battle has been fought.

Admitted to Medical Ward

October 10, 1970

Yesterday, they finally admitted something was wrong with me. I returned to the dispensary. I insisted they take my temperature, which they didn't do the first time I was in. "You sure do have a fever," said the medic. "It's 104 degrees." He took it again with the same results. They admitted me to the medical ward at Bien Hoa. My fever's been stubborn today, hovering around 101 degrees, but I'm feeling better. They say I might have malaria; they haven't said for sure. I took 14 pills yesterday.

I was lucky to be out of the office. A colonel ordered Lt. O'Daly to send a reporter out into the bush for a certain story. Because I'm gone, that only leaves Al Brown, the other reporter. That leaves O'Daly without any writers when Al sallies forth. The guy two beds down from me has stomach problems and is being fed intravenously. Boy, he looks sick.

In Medical Ward

October 11, 1970

The thermometer keeper tapped me on the shoulder at 3 a.m. this morning. He was too late. Two hours earlier I had started my nightly sweat-in-bed routine—I was hot. By the time he arrived I was cooler, not an impressive showing on my temperature chart. I tried to get back to sleep in my water habitat with little success.

Dracula, the man with the big needle, appeared with ghoulish delight around 7 a.m. That needle was in too long—gag—although I'm getting used to it. That's at least the 4th time they've drawn blood out of my arms. I'm feeling like a junkie with all the holes in my arms. They're not sure I have malaria but I've got the symptoms.

I'm not alone. At least five guys in my immediate section that I've talked with have most of my symptoms too. A fellow across the aisle from me is throwing up and just finished a bought of chills. A female nurse just gave him a shot. I haven't had anything like that—he says he has been diagnosed with malaria.

I have been taking my malaria pills faithfully but their limitations now show. Even when I recover, I'm told I'm subject to relapses and probably won't work for several weeks. Note: I weigh 140 pounds. Fighting weight!

Hospitalized

October 12, 1970

93rd Evacuation Hospital, that's where I'm at. Yes, they think I have malaria so they jeeped me over to Long Bin, not far. I'm in Ward 5 with dozens of fellow sufferers. It's air conditioned and well kept up. It's a very large complex and well equipped. There must be hundreds of patients here. Now what happens? I hear horrible things about malaria. Can I really have it?

I have a new uniform: white slippers, baggy (although not as much as fatigues) blue pants and a same-colored loose-fitting shirt. It's practical.

Mekong Delta

October 13, 1970

There's not much to add from yesterday. I'm still hospitalized with a fever but am completely mobile and do walk around.

I've been talking with a guy from a unit working the Mekong Delta. The war there isn't like the Cav's. They have more booby traps and mines. It's wetter, swampier, and the firing up of sampans is a bigger undertaking than in Cav country. He's short (his tour is almost done), has ulcers and an incurable skin disease. He's a pretty gloomy GI though talkative.

My condition is the same as yesterday. I was leeched this morning and get a blood smear in a few minutes. They still won't say I have the malaria bug but the doctor seems to think it's self-evident.

Don't Have Malaria

October 14, 1970

Now they don't think I had malaria but only some tropical virus. I recovered too quickly it seems. Now I just enjoy the air conditioning, play cards and trade war stories.

One guy was telling of his unit's policy of not taking prisoners. They sounded like it did little more than any VC unit. I've come across few American units with POWs.

I may get out of the hospital tomorrow. I'm curious about the PIO office's response to my illness. Will they accept me back without a reprimand? I've never been sick before.

I will hope to make my exit. Until then, I will think about home and your cold weather.

2. On Assignment: October 1, 1970, to December 31, 1970

Out of Hospital

October 15, 1970

They let me out! I'm back in Bien Hoa looking for things to do. The doctor never did figure out what was wrong with me; it's still possible I have malaria because it is a strangely unpredictable hard-to-diagnose disease.

Enclosed are three stories in the last *Cavalair*. "Shorttimers" is my favorite, the one I told you I was writing. They used it as I wrote it in the first person, which surprises me.

Everyone tells me I look pale and sickly plus look like I've lost weight. I probably have lost weight. I have some pills for the anemia.

I returned to three of your letters. The mail is coming better now. I should have some film to send home for you, Dad, to develop.

After the air conditioning at 93rd Evac, the hospital, the heat really is bothering me. I'm not sure in a climate like this if air conditioning is a good idea because you can never go outside if you live in cool air all day. It's better if I get used to being hot.

I was talking to my doctor, Major David, a draftee who says the doctor's life in 'Nam isn't much different from home except for the diseases and the surgery problems. Cambodia was a zoo, he said, but now that things have slowed it's an easy life for the doctor. The female nurses don't have it bad. Besides being some of the most admired and watched women in 'Nam, they work in air-conditioned buildings and are well protected from most of the war. It's a good experience for civilian nursing plus the pay as a lieutenant is good. If you have a specialty the Army wants, they can make it a profitable experience without the hassle of the straight Army.

The ride from the hospital on the road through Bien Hoa City, the Vietnamese section, is like traveling through another world. There are miles of little shops and thousands of people line the roads. The jeep weaves through traffic of Lambretta three-wheel passenger-carrying golf carts. The wayside is filthy, little kids relieving themselves into the debris. Motorcycles are numerous. It's foreign to my upbringing.

First Team Books; Jungle Diseases; Echo Recon 1/12th; PIO Reunion

October 16, 1970

What is it the 1st Cav has that no one else has or wants? The answer: 18,000 First Team History Books, the ones the PIO staff is supposed to sell. And you ought to see the size of an ordering blunder of this magnitude—takes up a whole building. We have sold 7000 and the remainder are scattered about in little caches.

I overdid it a little today. I went out to the bush and picked up three stories. The first two were on a firebase, medics and the dental operations in the field. The third was about a reconnaissance company.

I came across cases of jungle rot, boils and ring worm being treated in the little dispensary on FSB Mars, a new firebase of the 1st Battalion, 12th Cavalry. I couldn't take pictures because the guys, mostly grunts, were standing around naked with what I thought were horrible skin diseases. There was a guy with jungle rot all over his legs and butt—I thought he looked very bad. A medic assured me that they had seen much worse, that this trooper would recover fairly quickly. Another of the ten medics (including a doctor) was working on a ghastly big red boil on a fellow's fanny. This kind of infection is common especially this time of year during the seasonal rains. I saw ringworm patients too. As a whole they looked very ugly and painful though I'm told that in the infantry these things are common. Things have improved since the new brigade commander started stressing good health instead of troop strength like his predecessor. The new backing for health has improved morale.

The dental team that came out to the firebase is not a bad idea either. They take care of all minor emergencies that crop up in the field before they become serious enough to be taken out of the field. Basically, they do temporary fillings and extractions, what they can do with the least equipment. The grunts are suspicious because it cuts down on their "sham" time in the rear.

In the afternoon I flew out to another logging for Echo Recon, 1st Battalion, 12th Cavalry to see what they had found. They put on an 82mm mortar just after I got off the slick. Then, in the cramped little log pad, they took off and didn't come back for nearly 4 hours, far too long for me in all that heat. They were barely 500 meters from a bunker complex they'd been looking over—they didn't show it to me. They have been working the "Seven Hills of Rome": as the mission was called to look over, as their small fast-moving outfit can, the bunkers and other fortifications in the area.

This unit has not lost a man in a year—have they been lucky? They are a little gung ho which might account for their low fatality rate. They have excellent point men who can read the forest like a book. One Cambodian Kit Carson scout who walks point discovered an automatic ambush of claymore mines yesterday that would have hurt the grunts badly had he missed it. He was just doing his job to hear him tell it. A Sioux Indian from Ft. Thompson, S.D., Sgt. Alvin Long Crow, discovered the 82mm mortar while stringing his claymore for the night. He was walking over a little mound that shouldn't have been there, an accident he took advantage of. He walks point too, during the days. I had fun listening to them but it was nearly 6 p.m. before the chopper came back to pick all the remains of the logging plus 6 passengers. The

2. On Assignment: October 1, 1970, to December 31, 1970

trees were mighty close, it seemed to me, as we winged it out off into the sunset.

I made it back just in time for a small PIO reunion. The whole staff from Song Be was there for numerous diverse reasons. We also had two roving reports from USARV (U.S. Army Vietnam, a support command) Steve and Roger. I sat over in our little club nearby drinking beer and talking about our observation on the war. Roger was right down my alley. He too thinks this is a political war, fashionable but true. He has the same contempt for the establishment back in the States. He may have to sleep on an air mattress on the floor because of the crowd in our small hooch. Steve, who's already selling out to the establishment—he's a lawyer—didn't talk much. A fine one I am to talk anti-establishment; I haven't done much to hassle it.

For a fellow in frail health, I overdid it today by general agreement. But there's no action in Bien Hoa and even the field is slow unless you work at it. I'm not going down to Saigon like so many of my compatriots. Boom boom girls don't interest me. I find journalism more addictive plus the time flies right along. So I flew all around.

VIET K-9 TURNS INFORMER

This pooch is a hybrid of pet and scout dog, unique in my experience. Vietnam dog pets were everywhere but none of our dogs in the rear had this sort of utility. This story was in the October 28, 1970, issue of Cavalair.

FSB PERSHING—As everybody knows, American GIs jealously love their plentiful collection of dogs. But, it is a rare case when a dog can give a lifesaving tip in return.

The mascot and early warning system of Alpha Company, 2nd Battalion, 7th Cavalry is such a hound. His name is Frag. He's the company's dog. They adopted the Vietnamese pooch as a pup and he's been loyal to them ever since.

"He acts like a scout dog except that he's smaller," the barrage from the proud grunts started, each adding something. "When he smells the enemy, he crouches down and looks extremely miserable. He's saved us several times. He goes everywhere with us."

He's not much to look at. A small yellow-brown hound, friendly at the first meeting, he looks helpless and harmless. But in the bush, where large size often is a disadvantage, Frag's keen senses and agility have gained him the company's respect.

"We got him from the Vietnamese," explained 1st Sgt. Fernando M. Quintes. "I doubt they would have let us have him had they known what a good VC smeller he'd become."

As a member of the team, Frag is pampered and given lifts. He makes an odd sight, wolfing down C-rations or perched on the pack on the First Sergeant's back.

He was in one of the first waves in their remote firebase, taking the jungle clearing with the rest of the troops. He didn't find a VC, but then neither did anyone else. Some days, Frag just has to play the meek dog routine. But give him a chance and he's a wolf.

Boom Boom Girls; American Flag

October 17, 1970

Lt. O'Daly is a good dude and I would like to become a good writer just as much as he'd like me to be one. But it takes work and a healthy body and mind. My appetite is improving—a good sign—so my return to health should be brisk.

One of the guys showed me a picture of his boom-boom girl, quite an expensive dish for about 3000 piatres (20 dollars). The rate should go up now that the exchange rate has changed. Her name is Cuc, he tells me. "She approached me in the lobby," he says. Sounds romantic. He says your parents are going to think you're working with a real pervert, he says. I'm always giving him a bad time about it but he is clean living compared to many guys who fall so low as to bed with hooch mates. Hooch mates are supposed to be honest girls and it's bad to take advantage of them. The Saigon prostitutes don't claim to be honest or poor working girls.

This guy is one of the few non–pot-smokers in the area. He doesn't like pot for the same reasons I don't. It doesn't add anything to our existence and we don't need a refuge from lifers because we aren't surrounded by lifers. O'Daly is no lifer and he's our only boss.

I wrote a story about a SSG Trueblood who discovered to his horror that his outfit didn't have a decent American flag. So he sent home to his American Legion post in Bloomington, Indiana, and had them scout around for a "special flag." The congressman from the 7th District in Indiana, John Myers, was contacted and asked for a flag that had flown over the U.S. Capitol building. He came up with the flag for August 12th. Representative Myers wrote, "We are very grateful for the job you and all our boys are doing for us and we hope you will be returning home to your family very soon. Meanwhile, warm good wishes."

Trueblood is really excited about getting this flag—it's like waving a flag before the bull. This is dandy but what good is it doing? How does this help the grunts dodge bullets? The flag is a symbol for our country, not the country. Of course I'm a patriot American but I don't see how waving the flag helps us much.

Special Flag for Quan Loi

American flags were and are a powerful symbol. This article appeared in the November 3, 1970, Cavalair.

BIEN HOA—One day several months ago, Staff Sergeant Ronald K. Trueblood noticed that his unit's American flag was getting worn and tattered. Noting the sad state of the banner and looking for a worthy replacement, he decided to write the American Legion Post in his hometown of Bloomington, Indiana, to see what his friends there could do.

They decided to come up with a special flag, not one that could be easily purchased in a store downtown. Someone got in touch with John T. Myers, Indiana's 7th District representative to the U.S. House of Representatives. Congressman Myers agreed that the replacement for the tattered flag, which had flown over Quan Loi during many extremely bitter hours of fighting, should be something special.

In a letter to Trueblood, a member of the 322nd Aviation detachment, now air traffic controller for Bien Hoa Army Base after moving from Quan Loi, Myers wrote. "We will make arrangements today to have a flag flown over the U.S. Capitol Building. We are proud to be able to represent you with this flag. We want you to know we are very grateful for the job you and all our boys are doing for us and we hope you will be returning home to your family very soon. Meanwhile, warm good wishes, John Myers."

The flag now flies proudly over the detachment's compound. The new flag was originally flown over the Capitol Building on August 12, a year to the day since a savage enemy ground attack on Quan Loi was beaten off.

PX Hopping in Long Binh; Brigade Activities

October 19, 1970

I finished three stories yesterday so suddenly I'm in good shape. Tomorrow I'm going out to FSB Pershing and see what's up there.

I just finished PX hopping (shopping) around Long Binh. What an immense place it is. It's a city, not a base. It has everything although I doubt anyone told them the war is anything but an ongoing struggle with conniving hooch mates and corrupt garbage collectors or a disagreement with their local insecticide sprayer about who and what should not be sprayed. It must be like a zoo.

The war is more apparent for the Cav. I went to a long briefing last night. Four aggressive determined gooks shot down one of our Huey choppers. It blew up in mid air; something vital must have been hit. No one survived.

One of our battalions is moving its firebase after having a base, FSB

Mars, for only about a week. They are going into an enemy infested area in War Zone D. It should be fun to watch and full of stories.

The 1st Brigade area, mine, is hopping with cache finds, strange trail markings and even firefights. Our brigade has had most of the activity of the division. I may go out for three days with a grunt unit—this should be illuminating but not that dangerous. The NVA and VC just aren't killing many GIs or attacking in any force. Like you, I wonder if they can't or merely won't.

The 2nd Brigade PIO crew has been getting their name in *Stars and Stripes* like they're doing something right. We in the 1st Brigade want to see if we can do as well. Going out on a grunt expedition might just do the trick.

Photo Lab

October 20, 1970

I called up the photo lab at Phuoc Vinh this afternoon to find out what they'd done with my pictures of the Charlie Co 2/7th Cav logging mission. They said they had no record of it. Then *Stars and Stripes* came out this afternoon with a picture from that roll on page 6 [*the photo my dad's friend spotted*]. Not bad although 2nd Brigade is still way ahead. The photo lab's records aren't to be trusted—they obvious developed the roll and printed the pictures.

You ever have one of those days you just couldn't get off the ground? That was my sad story today. I could not get a ride on a chopper today because the PIO just doesn't rate in the Army priorities. I had to write off today as a waste and goof off.

I don't know if I'll every get my films home to you. Quite frankly, I'm not sure I want any pictures to remember Vietnam by. I want to avoid at all costs getting sentimental about this war.

It's still wet—the monsoons are still here—although I'm told that the dry season will make me wish I were back here in the mud. It's green now. The weeds grow splendidly—every once in a while we have to hack the tops off them. The greenery eats away at the sand bags, bringing sand and dirt spilling out of them. I hear sand bags cost the Army a lot. I'd like to find something that doesn't cost the Army a lot. I wonder what Bien Hoa Army Base cost to run? A billion?

I'm off to war on the chess board with a friendly Lieutenant Talbott who is short, 2 days left in 'Nam. Don't I wish?

I considered softening my blunt, guileless and at times unfair letter but it is an accurate reflection of my thinking then. I was a reasonably typical hardworking long-suffering often disgruntled enlisted man frequently hassled by officers, which all shows. I don't want to edit the life out of my letters. And to be fair, the Lt. Colonel Vesser I refer to, at times somewhat disparagingly, had a distinguished career, ending up a lieutenant general. And now that I've amassed my work from that day, I realize he contributed to a staggeringly productive day.

Touring with a Battalion Commander

October 22, 1970

What a long perplexing day. I'm not sure I want to figure it out. I caught my bird out to FSB Pershing and all hell broke loose. I met Lieutenant Colonel Vesser, a Rhodes scholar and now the commanding officer of the 2nd Battalion of the 7th Cavalry. He was a strange man with his patrician air about him that I don't want to judge although he wanted a good deal more out of me than I'm capable of giving him. He wanted me to go out humping with Bravo Company 2/7th and go where the action is. He wanted me to do it tomorrow and I can't comply because I'm not ready logistically or done with the stories I have now. He gave me the royal runaround today and I wish he didn't know my name.

Artillery, specifically 2/20th Artillery, is planning to fire its 600,000th round of the Vietnam War. They have been firing like mad the last week. They were firing for troops in contact and blocking missions, around targets to prevent enemy troops from finding downed helicopters full of dead men. This is a battery of 105mm howitzers, the same outfit I watched fly into Pershing during the firebases's rebirth.

I watched Charlie Company 2/7th climb up and down a hundred-foot ladder hanging from a Chinook flying overhead. The blast of the rotor blades was blowing things, like grass and people, all over the place. It took several hours for the whole company to go all the way up and all the way down the ladder. All this to keep the skytrooper name untarnished although they probably could care less. One grunt asked me if I had the whole thing staged so that I could take pictures. I told him that such a thought was preposterous— I thought it was just as stupid as he did.

Then I took pictures of the dental team that comes out to all the firebases. I have a good deal of respect for them. I like their view of modern dentistry and they really are doing the GIs a favor by flying out. It is surprising what can be done with a little electricity and 80 pounds of dental gear. It's not that much worse than a dental office. He had a drill, that's certainly a good start.

Then I found the vaccinator and royal keeper of the dogs in the majority of the 1st Cav. As you probably know, the dog in Vietnam is a loved little beastie. And nothing looks more forlorn than a little pup getting a big shot. This vet guy, partly civilian trained and the rest in the Army, runs out to all the firebases checking dogs. Artillery medevaced their mascot mongrel pup for a broken leg—that's how important a dog is. The vet says, "Dogs usually don't have a bad reaction to the shots. There have been a few cases of rabies in the Phuoc Vinh area. A shot program for dogs is just good preventive medicine." He really didn't sound that gung ho but I livened up his prose to the level it should have been. It should make a good story.

I tried to get hold of the doctor at the firebase for a story about "combat surgeons." It seems this is the right guy but he was in the rear checking the profiles on men, whether they had recovered enough to return to the field, losing their profiles. I will see him tomorrow.

I flew out with the lieutenant colonel to Echo Recon, 2/7th. They had a boat operation earlier this month and shot one enemy soldier dead. The grunts don't like boat operations because they feel like sitting ducks in the middle of the river. They had outboard motors on their ten-man rubber boats but refused to use the motors because they made too much noise. Their story just points up the weakness of the boat mission and the survival value of being distrustful of the boats.

Two guys were up on watch while the rest of them sat in the boats in the river for some reason. One of the guards found a NVA bunker and called for help, "Lieutenant!" Thankfully the lieutenant knew what he was doing. He climbed the riverbank to see what his new man was up to. They spotted a couple of men. "Are those our guys?" asked the newbie. The lieutenant's comment was "hell no!" and opened up on the NVA. He killed one and recovered the body after a chase. Meanwhile, the majority of the grunts in the patrol—scared to death in the boats—tried to deboat with limited success. No one drowned although they were lucky. This is the kind of action, verging on the disastrous, that Americans have a knack for pulling off for no logical reason.

I had twenty minutes to collect all my notes about the boat fiasco. Then we flew out in a roar, winging it over the tips of the treetops. I thought we were going straight back to Pershing but I was sadly mistaken. A group of rangers, only put in a short time earlier, spotted NVA only 40 years away. The rangers are an elite group I'm not very familiar with. Anyway, they called in a pink team—a light observation helicopter (LOH) and a Cobra gunship that work together. The theory is that the LOH tries to draw fire and the Cobra swoops in and blows the daylights out of the firer.

By now I was overhead in the Lt. Colonel's command and control chopper. I've never watched a LOH work out before from the air. Twisting and swerving right at the treetops, it was hard to believe it could defy fate like that. Anyway, some sad gook fired at the LOH, missing of course. Then the fun started. The Cobras moved in. There was one to start with and two were added when it was clear that something down there was returning fire. The Cobras were pretty savage about using the minigun, rockets and flachet rounds.

2. On Assignment: October 1, 1970, to December 31, 1970 55

It reminded me a great deal of the jet strike I saw about a month ago in that napalm strike. The Cobras were probably especially venomous because the NVA had shot down three choppers in the last week. It was very fun watching except that the colonel was in the way. He was running the operation from his command post, wearing his headset-helmet, and playing with the frequency controls in the bird's radio. I couldn't hear much except the explosions when the Cobras moved down within range. I was a bit overwhelmed by it all. We finally quit and flew back to Pershing, then stayed on the command and control chopper (we call them chuck chuck birds) to its and my home in Bien Hoa.

Also, I discovered what made those big holes I've been looking at from the air. There are tens of thousands of big holes throughout the jungle. The holes of various ages are from old air strikes—this War Zone D area is on the road to Saigon and has been fought over for years. The colonel pointed out some craters, a series of them, from a B52 strike a month ago. Very educational.

As you can see, it was a wild day. I still don't trust this Lieutenant Colonel, any lifer as young as him (38) I'm distrustful of.

I'm going out again tomorrow. Until then, my tired body and mind have to have a rest. So be of good cheer.

Problems Won't Stop Cannoneer's Shooting

You'd expect firing on a firebase, generally from the resident howitzers. I had a good time chronicling the tasks and firing of these crews. This was printed in an October 1970 Cavalair *issue.*

FSB PERSHING—"The mud's been giving us a bad time. One afternoon, five guns were put out of action. We were firing a gap for the troops; one gun jumped out of the ground, the other four sank in. We've put timbers in place to mount the guns on and that has solved the problem."

Captain Randall L. Rigby has had peculiar situations cropping up as his 105mm howitzer unit, Bravo Battery, 2nd Battalion, 19th Field Artillery, has become one of the most active batteries in Vietnam.

"We've been firing quite a bit," Spec. 4 Jerry "Smiley" Gates, howitzer crewmember, commented. "We've been firing a lot of blocking fire due to the heavy ground-to-air fire that our choppers have been taken recently."

"Contact missions, especially in support of Bravo Company, 2nd of the 7th, have also been responsible for eating up large quantities of ammo. We fired 1200 rounds in three days," recalled Rigby.

The battery expects to fire its 600,000th round very soon. Preparing for the occasion, the unit painted a shell bright red with 600,000 scrawled on it side; it's ready for immediate delivery when the time comes.

For the artillery, there is no break time. "We have action day and night, it's not like an eight-to-five job," 1st Lieutenant Allen Norris explained without looking like it was so bad. "These guys went 48 hours, two nights, without sleep. Yet morale is higher than it's ever been. They like to shoot."

So far, the battery has sustained only one casualty during the increased tempo of firing. Beehive, the unit's pup mascot, had a run-in with a block of ice. The six-week-old puppy got a foot caught under an ice block and broke a leg. "We had to MEDEVAC our dog yesterday," someone groaned mournfully.

Despite the hardship losing the battery dog causes, the artillery keeps constant vigil, ready for any situation, like the other night when the enemy tried to cross a bridge toward an American company. Artillery was firing 100

Echo Recon, 1st Bn., 12th Cav is enjoying their log mission. They got a chance to get resupplied, receive mail, eat a hot meal, and relax.

to 150 yards from friendly positions at 1:30 in the morning and making it look routine, as the cannoneers yawned.

COMBAT INITIATION IS TOUGHEST; INFANTRY FRATERNITY IS EXCLUSIVE

I didn't write the headline for this article—it's too long although I agree with the sentiments. I would have stuck to either the first half or the second half. Again, this is from a Cavalair *issue, probably in October 1970.*

Initiations, as any member of a club or fraternity will tell you, can be a pretty jolting experience. Being initiated into the ranks of the battle veterans is perhaps the most traumatic of all initiations.

Sgt. Don Leopard, a new man in Echo Reconnaissance, 2nd Battalion,

We all had to deal with the buffeting wind from helicopter blades. This photograph was published in *Cavalair,* our division's newspaper, in the November 3, 1970, issue.

7th Cavalry, received his initiation after spotting a bunker while pulling guard on the riverbanks overlooking a rubber raft operation.

Along with his CO, 1st Lieutenant Dennis Pieck, the sergeant helped avert disaster for Echo Recon.

"I found a bunker and called for help from the lieutenant. I showed him the bunker and when some figures came into view near the bunker I asked him if they were our guys. His only words were 'Hell no' and we both opened up on them."

Sgt. Thomas Kennedy, the third man on the bank, managed to get in on the tail end of the fighting with the small band of NVA. "They tried to drag the dead one away that the lieutenant had shot but we low crawled up to their position and captured the body. We had to take that hill or they would have used it against us. Thankfully, we were the ones that took them by surprise."

If Leopard and company hadn't been able to neutralize the enemy, the entire platoon might have been placed in mortal jeopardy. Most of the platoon was still crossing the river in ten-man rubber rafts.

"I was trying to get out of my boat," PFC John Tavasci said. "There were only three men on shore, the lieutenant and the two fellows pulling guard. We began hearing noises as we were getting out of the boats; they were making contact right over our heads. We had a hard time making it up the steep banks. We were lucky the lieutenant knew what he was doing."

"We found river crossing sites and rocket launching platforms on the way down the river," explained Kennedy. "We also came across a night defensive position where 20 NVA had

John Tavasci uses a radio telephone, which is how units kept in touch with their commanders. He was the new guy referred to in the infantry fraternity story. Radio telephones were big and clunky; primitive compared to modern cell phones.

camped recently. It was obvious that we were about to run into something. Fortunately we found them first."

VET NEEDLES PUPS

Like many GIs, I found our dogs' adaptability and charms endlessly fascinating. This was printed in an October 1970 Cavalair.

FSB PERSHING—The protective and paternal instincts of GIs are brought indignantly to the surface when someone starts messing with their dogs. GIs don't like anyone with their bedraggled collection of hounds, there is someone who does nothing else.

He's the friendly Army veterinarian, Sp4 Harry Penland from the 495th Veterinary Detachment in Bien Hoa, who spent a day recently at FSB Pershing scouting the dog population and needling all the dogs he could find.

"I've been in 'Nam 16 months," Penland recounted. "I started working with sentry and scout dogs when I first hit country. I received civilian training in veterinary medicine while in college and the rest I received in the Army. I've been working with pets on and off ever since I was a kid."

Penland has seen a lot of dogs in his time in Vietnam: "I've vaccinated between 500 and 1000 dogs against rabies while I've been here. I just got into the 1st Cav about two months ago and I'm not the first one to treat the dogs."

Penland vaccinated a typical patient, Wolfgang, the TOC pup. Held down by a sympathetic sergeant, Wolfgang let out a yelp when Penland jabbed him in the rump with the needle. It was all over in no time and Wolfgang scampered away as soon as he was released.

In a hardened yet friendly voice, Penland explained the philosophy and facts behind the dog vaccination: "There have been a few cases of rabies near Phuoc Vinh so a dog vaccination program is essential to the health of GIs. It's just good preventative medicine.

"DIDN'T EVEN FEEL IT"

I managed to swallow my fear of dentists and publicize how they roughed it for the troops. This was in the November 3, 1970, Cavalair—*from this point on I sent full* Cavalair *issues home so they can be reliably dated.*

FSB MARS—"Aw, I didn't even feel the drill or the needle," exclaimed Specialist 4 Robert Delaney. The Skytrooper was impressed by the job the dentist had done filling an aching tooth. Delaney walked out of the dingy bunker and stepped into the gray mud of FSB Mars.

The dentist, Captain William Kennedy, was out to the firebase for the

Spec 4 Penland gives Wolfgang his vaccination.

day. "We do stuff that can be done with the least amount of equipment," he said. "We do temporary fillings, extractions and other basic but necessary jobs. As long as we have electricity, it's all right. Our drill and light don't need much power."

Kennedy examined Delaney before he put in the filling. "There just isn't enough space for his teeth in his mouth," explained the dentist. He exposed his anesthetic for the small operation that followed, a huge needle. In short order he'd numbed Delaney's mouth and drilled at the offending tooth. In a few minutes he had the tooth filled.

Specialist 4 Dick Morrison, dental technician, handed the dentist the tools of his trade and talked: "We come out to take care of emergencies and business has been brisk."

As part of Alpha Company, 15th Medical Battalion, the dentist and his

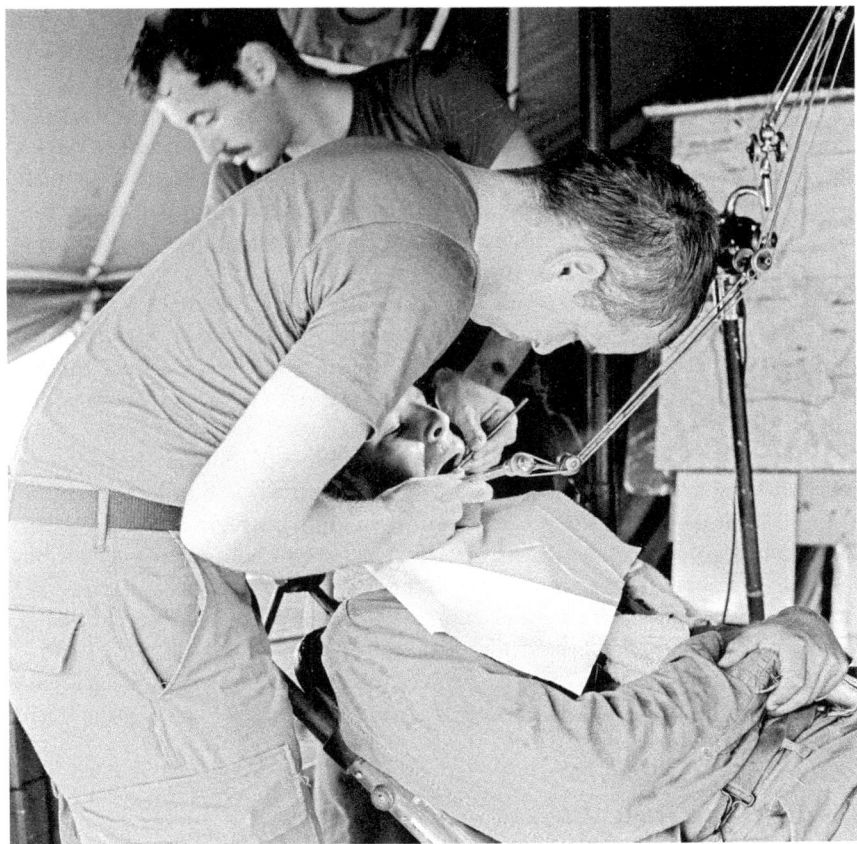

Firebase dentistry was spartan but the equipment was similar to what would be found in any stateside dentist's office.

assistant support the 1st Brigade of the 1st Air Cav Division. "We go out once a week and remain there as long as we're needed," Kennedy said.

RECON: THE PROFESSIONAL'S JOB

I'm surprised at the variety of stories I collected that day—this is a real war story. It appeared in the November 3, 1970, Cavalair.

FSB MARS—"You're always looking for the same things. Cut trees, hillsides, water or a lot of cover. That's where you look for bunkers." Specialist 4 Gerald Siegel describes his role in Echo Reconnaissance, 1st Battalion, 12th Cavalry. For eight months a point man with an ace of spades on his boonie hat, Siegel is an important man in his all-volunteer outfit.

Echo Recon's job recently was to scout "the seven hills of Rome," a region near FSB Mars. As a small, fast-moving and experienced outfit, they were able to find a large bunker complex without any trouble.

"I was running a claymore out for the night and walked over a small mound that shouldn't have been there. So I called someone else and we started digging, cautiously. We came up with an 82mm mortar." Sergeant Alvin R. Long Crow related. Long Crow, a Sioux Indian, made the most important find of the large bunker complex his group was searching. He is a point man when the recon unit is on the move.

"I like working with a small recon unit like this better than a line company. We're quieter and most of the men in the platoon are E-5s with experience; it makes working together easier. By the way, there's a little bunker complex over there and the NVA cut that tree, not us," Long Crow added with a gesture in the appropriate direction.

The Echo Recon group has been together, most of them anyhow, for ten months. This setup has led to well-coordinated teamwork, but the individual, as in all infantry units, still sticks out in the clutch performances.

First Lieutenant John C. Austin, the Recon CO, told what his unit has found in the area after reconning the first five of the seven hills of Rome. "We came across a brand new bunker complex that the NVA had been building. We found 3 mess halls, 1 classroom and 16 bunkers."

As an outfit of bush professionals, Austin feels his men have one achievement in which they have taken immense pride: "We haven't had anyone killed in this outfit in over a year."

Wildlife; Weather

October 23, 1970

Yesterday I saw a large gathering of oriental monarch-like butterflies on a dirty sweaty OD green T-shirt. I got a good look at them while I was rattling off questions to one of the guys. I also saw three gorgeous swallowtail butterflies fathered on some meat on the ground. The place was alive with insect life.

I've been seeing more birds as I fly in choppers. The whirlybird scares the birds yet it moves fast enough so they can't fly very far. There are large black and white crane-like birds but most birds don't get close enough to describe but they look radically different. I've seen sparrow-like birds close to the English sparrow. But all the others look hunch-backed and deformed by my temperate-zone criteria.

Lt. O'Daly has embarrassed me, much to my delight, by trying to get me promoted. I didn't think I had enough time in grade but he pointed out that I was wrong. He has gone to bat for me and none too soon. I go before a

I found a unit outside a firebase practicing climbing a ladder into a helicopter, something my infantry friends assured me they actually did in the field. The picture had the following caption when it appeared November 18, 1970, in *Cavalair*: "STEEP STAIRWAY—Skytroopers from Charlie, 2nd Battalion, 7th Cavalry made a short, steep journey up a 100 foot ladder to a hovering Chinook over FSB Pershing."

promotion board tomorrow and now I'm highly recommended. I can hope. I have to put on the very best good boy image. Appearance is everything. For the $60-plus, I don't mind pulling a little of the lifer routine on them.

The most prominent thing today was the weather. It rained for 8 hours this morning starting around 2 a.m. It started up again about two hours ago at 6:15 p.m. The rain is steady and I got soaked walking and running the half-mile back from the briefing.

Not much happened today because of the weather.

Some enemy hack has been making broadcasts to men within the American Army. Today it was in Spanish to the Mexican Americans, trying to woo them to the right side of the war. Everyone laughed but I wonder if it was fair to be contemptuous. There is a definite problem for Mexican-Americans, like the Blacks and American Indians, being discriminated against, although the Army is not as bad as many institutions. I don't think the problem is so bad that there will be ralliers to the NVA side.

I couldn't go to the firebases today because of the weather. Tomorrow I won't do much because of the promotion board. No humping in the boonies for a while for this kid. I'm just not ready.

I hear wild things about changing tours to ten months instead of the current twelve months with drops coming in waves. I have to see it to believe it. I have to be the one "skying up" (leaving) Vietnam before I have faith in anything the Army, officially or unofficially, tells me.

Mail Service; Promotion Board; Driver's License

October 24, 1970

Six or seven days without a letter from me? I've been writing more than that! Crummy mail service.

I went before the Specialist 4 board. They insisted on asking me a lot of lifer questions I thought were unimportant. My partner, Al Brown, in the afternoon, didn't have my problem. They asked him about his job and he talked away. I must have done something wrong by their standards to rate such poor treatment but the results aren't in yet—they may still score me well.

I got my driver's license the other day and today, my first day as a driver. I drove our new Major and Lt. O'Daly around seeing as how I had nothing else to do. I gave them a few thrills and jolted them a few good holes in the road (there are many holes to hit) but started learning how to drive. I got lost once over on the Air Force base although I found them in time at the officers' club. It's a Mickey Mouse license: they have me down to drive not only ¼ tons trucks (jeeps) but also ¾ ton and 2½ ton trucks. I've had enough troubles with the jeep.

FSB Ares Construction; Dog Characters

October 25, 1970

I flew out to FSB Ares, a new base, today. They were still in the construction stage. The base hummed with activity. Soldiers were digging bunkers; filling sand bags; dragging, rolling and carrying logs; or just playing sand bag supervisors. The mud brings back fond memories of Song Be—it's a striking red color. I couldn't find anything to write about so I was content to take pictures.

The weather is odd. We got out of Bien Hoa this morning very late because of fog. When we sailed upwards, it appeared the fog went up only a few feet. We flew at barely 2000 feet yet were above the clouds like a jet liner at 20,000 feet. It was indescribable, our little chuck-chuck bird putt-putting along at 90 miles an hour at the most. The clouds were fluffy and we could barely see through the holes between the white mists to the ground. I was cold above too. I could have used a coat to stay warm.

Tomorrow I'm preparing for my little jaunt into the jungles with the grunts. Curiosity and the wrong kind of magazine assignment brought me back to the good earth. No flying around in birds for three days but I should give you a lively ongoing description of where it's at and what the grunts sees and maybe a little of what he feels. It has great story potential. For three days I won't be able to write though.

I should mention our dog characters; I've never said much about our hooch pooches. There's Blanche and Tuck; Blanche is the mom and Tuck her pup. Next door there's Coco and his mom, who is unpopular and whose name I don't know. George, a dirty black mutt, lives across the street. Every hooch has its contingency of the little Vietnamese beggars. They are cute and well fed from scraps, often the whole meals from our mess hall.

A Chinook cracked up at FSB Ares yesterday. Everybody thought a major catastrophe was about to take place; a Chinook is a lot of metal to become a swirling mass of wreckage. Fortunately for the U.S. taxpayer, it wasn't that bad. The bird must have just blown an engine and made a passable landing. A new engine was flown in and the Chinook finally took off. I couldn't see any signs of a wreck this morning—it must have cleaned up well.

A wise grunt once told me that I'd never know what jungle combat was like if I didn't go out there myself. Many of us supported the troops in indirect ways. It bothered me that I was able to lounge around on firebases talking to the soldiers and not be directly involved in the war. I volunteered to go out with a patrol to get that authentic feel of what it was like. If I'd had more sense, I would have refused to do this but I was curious.

Monsoon Mission with Echo Recon

November 2, 1970

I haven't written for nearly five days—I'm sorry about the time lapse but I think I have a decent excuse. I went out with the grunts and became a real life war correspondent! It was an invaluable experience and, at the same time, a not-too-subtle horrible experience. Oh, I didn't get shot at even once, you understand, but the life of a grunt is dehumanizing in my estimate.

I couldn't get out to FSB Pershing so I settled for FSB Green. The only outfit I could go out with it happened was the tiny Echo Recon, 1st Battalion of the 7th Cavalry. I knew several of the guys. As it happened, because some of them stayed behind at an ambush, there were only sixteen in the platoon, not including me. I could hardly guess that I would be where the action was. I really lucked out.

I got out there just after the platoon had combat assaulted into the area southwest of FSB Connell. I felt out of place besides the dirty grunts, me in my clean fatigues and unblemished rucksack. We humped slowly about 150 yards into the bush and set up for the night. It was then that I noticed the horrible rotting smell that permeates the jungle and, as I got wet which was most of the time, I noticed my own smell. We set up our tents. I was paired off with a guy who was just about to leave the unit for a rear job. We fixed up an ingenious poncho tent with air mattresses underneath—mine leaked—and started eating a supper of C rations and LRRPs (Long Range Reconnaissance Patrol) dried food packets.

I got to talking with my best friend in the unit, SSG Tom Preece (Yireka, CA) and his friend Sgt. Bruce Gottsche (Arnolds Park, Iowa). The jungle is a very noisy alive place; it has such things as obscene "fuck you" lizards who repeat their ultimate obscenity seven or eight times. "That's not too bad, that's about average," commented Bruce on the lizard we sat listening to. He told me that there was a re-up frog in Cambodia and the lizard and the lizard and the frog would get into very relevant though repetitious dialogue on the subject of a soldier reenlisting in the army.

Tom told me, "As far as we're concerned, Bien Hoa *is* the world. You will probably get more sleep out here than on an LZ or in the rear." I slept poorly the whole time I was out but I did get to sleep early, had I been able to sleep. "Guard duty," Tom promised accurately, "usually does not last more than two hours."

The rotting forest floor glows at night from foxfire-like fungus we have back in the States. Fireflies are active. June bugs act like C-130s, crashing into ponchos or mosquito netting at night. The cicadas over here are loud, sounding more like sirens than bug calls. A leech got me on the temple and arm and really bled me although I didn't feel a thing. The jungle remains wet so the leeches hunted us up in the bushes' leaves. The leeches fell off when I sprayed them with insect repellent.

I went to bed around 7 p.m. when it got good and dark, no electrical generators here. Next morning after packing up and eating we started humping for what I thought would be all day. We headed for hooches that the battalion commander had spotted from the air. Fortunately, someone had made a mistake and put us in 800 meters west of where we were supposed to go in. After barging slowly down 200 yards of wait-a-minute vines and other things grabbing the body, we stopped and sent out a squad to find a stream. It was a seven-man patrol if you can imagine. I found two small leeches.

2. On Assignment: October 1, 1970, to December 31, 1970

Everyone was sitting around reading paperbacks, writing letters, reading a pocket New Testament Bible or just lying around and smoking, waiting for the patrol's return. At 10:45 a.m. the patrol returned. They had found an undistinguished-looking bunker built into the ground with a tin roof. It was only a short distance from where we were so we quickly went over to look.

After looking for booby traps—there weren't any—they removed the roof and killed the spider defenders. We peeled back the tin, started shoveling dirt, and uncovered what turned out to be a large cache. It contained 11 Thompson sub-machineguns, 14 45 caliber grease guns, parts for 60 caliber machine guns, an M-79 U.S. grenade launcher, 3 60mm mortar tubes, Springfield rifle parts, mausers, SGSs, CDCs, M-1 carbines, a 75mm recoilless rifle and finally, right at the back, *two* 75mm American-made howitzers. When the battalion commander was told about the howitzers, he was taken completely by surprise. "I'm speechless," he gasped. A bystander said he nearly swallowed his cigar.

The best part of the find for the grunts was that they had a chance to get hold of a weapon to take home, just as long as it wasn't American made or automatic. I got an old beat up CKC sniper rifle, a Chinese-made weapon

Soldiers from Echo Recon dig around in the bottom of the first cache. Rifle barrels and other contents of the cache lay behind them. Similar pictures from this day were published in the December 16, 1970, issue of *Cavalair*.

which shoots a 7.62 caliber round. It was packed in grease. Everyone was telling me how unusual this kind of find was. The battalion lieutenant colonel promised the platoon ice cream.

I got my first taste of guard duty and completely soaked in the deal. I had no idea how guard duty worked in the jungle but there is a sleeper that had never occurred to me. No one can move through the jungle, day or night, quietly. It just can't be done. Consequently, the force in the fixed position has the advantage; they can hear the opposition coming. The night disguises almost any position. So guard duty is keeping things quiet and staying in contact with the squads and division by radio. I had a brief course out there in call signs and radio jargon. I had a good time on the hour and fifty-minute guard except for the first night. I got wet and slept wet all night. It took me two days to dry out.

The next day we were preparing to send some of the cache contents to the rear and getting a logging, a kick out from a Huey helicopter of hot chow, C rations and LRRPs. At the last moment I decided to go out with Tom's squad on a hunt for hooches down the stream nearby. It was raining and miserable although we were only traveling with a weapon and ammo, not backpacks. I found a giant land snail shell I'll try to send home.

We got kind of lost and were floundering around. I even walked point for 10 feet up a hill. We got up the hill and looked around in the thick shrubbery. I stuck close to Tom and was the second man behind Tom when we spotted the second cache in two days. It was a rerun of the earlier cache except for a different kind of contents. Again we took off the roof, taking care to avoid a booby trap at one end of the cache. Again it had a false floor and we dug it up again. This was held 309 82mm mortar rounds, 108 120mm mortar rounds, 2,635 51 caliber rounds, 21,600 30 caliber machinegun rounds and 2 87mm boxes filled with anti-personnel mousetrap-type mines. It was all arranged very neatly but being good GIs, we ripped it up.

We moved our camp to the second cache for the night and this time it didn't rain. I had a good guard though I got this paranoid feeling like something was going to happen but of course, nothing did.

Next morning, October 30th, the squad that had found the first cache found a third. This was—I was told—a more typical cache without the false floor. I forgot to mention there is a good chance that an American unit came through this area before and may even have found cache number one but were fooled by the false floor. Anyway, cache number 3 contained 1000 electrical blasting caps, 35 boxes of 82mm mortar rounds (3 rounds to a box), 2 cases of 7.62 ammunition, 3 cases of 30 caliber, 1100 Chicom grenades, 13 75mm howitzer rounds, 51 boxes of C-4 explosives (75 pounds a box), 3 boxes of C-4, 40 pound boxes and one 25 pound box of TNT.

A platoon from Bravo Company, 1/7, the six guys from the stay behind ambush, and an EOD (explosive ordinance disposal) team came in to us the same way we had come. One of the EOD men said that there were was roughly two tons of C-4 explosives in cache number three, the most he had ever come across.

They started getting the nets together and managed to lift out the howitzers and the recoilless rifle. The Chinook had a rough time tugging the net out of the jungle; the load had real substance. I forgot this was the next day, the lift out I mean. Next day was just so slow they managed to waste most of the day. We started preparing areas to lift out the contents of the caches, the parts we wanted to keep. We finally got the ice cream they had promised us. They were generous, a half gallon for each two of us. We prepared to explode cache number three only to find that we had to take out part of the cache contents before the explosion. We were told that we would be pulled out and the search left to Bravo Company for more caches the next day.

The next day was hectic. The biggest thing was the blowing of the 108 120mm mortar rounds and what a bang. It blew debris hundreds of feet in the air and the EOD man assured me that this was nothing compared to what cache number three could do. They still hadn't gotten a chance to blow the cache when we left at 3 p.m. We had cleaned out cache number one, the biggest find.

We flew out as another platoon of Bravo Company came in. When we got back to FSB Green, they had already cordoned off the area around the newly assembled 75mm howitzers that looked strangely ornate and outdated beside the 105mm and 155mm howitzers we now use. The lifers have taken the big guns to heart.

I'll write another angle tomorrow but I'm growing pooped now. This five day jaunt ending yesterday tuckered me out so badly that I couldn't have written a letter last night even if I'd wanted to, which I did.

My Memory of Monsoon Outing

I got caught up in writing this story and never addressed many major things I still remember. I was amazed at how miserable it was working the jungles during the monsoon season. I can testify to how uncomfortable I was being constantly wet. Besides the leeches, I had diarrhea, prickly heat and surprisingly, was cold at night. And taking pictures was a fright—pulling my camera out of a plastic bag that kept it dry. The light meter for my camera was dissolved by the bug repellent I used on the leeches and ruined.

Our information office was going to send out a photographer to take pictures and I had the satisfaction of telling them I was already there and needed more film. Considering how little light there was, the pictures came out remarkably well. I had an awful time showing the guys with their packs because the jungle was so dense.

Steve Blough, Tom Preece and Bruce Gottsche are in their packs moving through the underbrush. Tom claims a copy of this picture helped him get a job with the Veteran's Administration. This and several companion photographs appeared in *Cavalair* on December 30, 1970.

Cache Newspaper Article

My primary goal in my jungle expedition was to gather information for a magazine story about an infantry unit mission in the jungle, inelegantly referred to by soldiers as humping. Because we unexpectedly found the cache, an article was put in our newspaper first, bragging about our success. I don't remember writing it and, based on the comment I scrawled on it for my parents, I didn't think much of it. I'm including it in part because I never obtained the negatives to these pictures.

Cache Magazine Article

I thought the magazine editor chose pictures well and knocked himself out laying out the story. I remember him telling me that the article was too good. By this I think he meant that, by the time this magazine came out, our division was leaving Vietnam and downplaying the active war. This also explains why one of my pictures didn't make it onto the front page of the magazine. It would have helped my Army career if this article had been printed when it was written but the magazine wasn't out until almost five months later, around March 24, 1971!

2. On Assignment: October 1, 1970, to December 31, 1970   71

Finds Biggest Cache Since Cambodia

SOUTHWEST OF FSB CONNEL – "And last we found two 75 vintage 1941 U.S. howitzers, complete, in excellent condition," radioed the Echo Recon, 1st Battalion, 7th Cavalry Skytroopers as they concluded their day's report of cache finding to the battalion CO.

"I'm speechless," the colonel replied.

SSG David A. (Smitty) Smith and his 16 man platoon had started off the day combat assaulting into an area reportedly occupied by several hootches. Two hours later, the squad led by SSG Ken Voskuil located a bunker with a false floor. The platoon removed the roof and discovered 11 Thompson submachineguns.

The also found 14, 15 caliber greaseguns, parts for M-60 machine guns, three 60mm mortar tubes, numerous rifle barrels, a 75mm round and the two howitzers. The area started off very inconspicious but would end up looking something like an out of the way junkyard.

The next day, SSG Thomas Preece, feeling left out in not being in on the first find, found another cache. Much the same sort of setup was encountered, including another false-floored bunker. This cache yielded 309 82mm mortar rounds, 108 120mm mortar rounds, 2,635 51 caliber rounds, 21,600 30 caliber machinegun rounds, and two 82mm boxes filled with anti-personnel mouse trap type mines.

Voskuil and his squad also found another cache, making it three for the day. It was different from the other two, there was no false floor. It contained two tons NVA C-4 explosive, 105 82mm mortar rounds, 1,100 Chicom grenades and miscellaneous odds and ends. The EOD team flown in to blow up whatever couldn't be airlifted out said "This is the most C-4 we've ever come across in one cache."

A GOOD DAYS WORK – SSG David A. "Smitty" Smith (Altanta, Mich.), left, the platoon leader of Echo Recon, 1st of the 7th, SSG Ken Voskuil (Merced, Cal.), the leader of the 3rd squad which found the cache, and Sgt. Stephen K. Blough (Bristol, Ind.), the platoon sergeant try to keep track of the cache's contents.

DIGGING PAYS OFF – Sgt. Jesse Reed (Grandview, Tenn.), top, Sgt Stephen Blough, SSG David Smith and SSG Ken Voskuil dig into the greasy barrels, bolts and magazines for a variety of different rifles.

U.S. Army Photo's And Story
by PFC Conrad Leighton

LOOK OUT FOR THE FROG! – SSG David A. Smith and Sgt. Stephen K. Blough watch the removal operation from one of the bunkers in the 1st of the 7th cache find. The cache's frog and spider defenders made a last stand against Echo Recon. The remains of the camouflaged roof can be seen near the top of the picture.

OPEN CAREFULLY – Sgt. Stephen K. Blough takes a look at a box of ammunition just as Echo Recon, 1st Battalion, 7th Cavalry was surveying the false floor in the cache.

CACHE

Story and Photos by PFC Conrad Leighton

It was just another area in the bush that the men of Echo Recon had to check out but there was gold in the bush this time. A neatly camouflaged cache covered by sheets of tin was worth numerous items. As the men checked the area for booby traps, little did they know American-made howitzers were hidden beneath the flase jungle floor. (Above) The men of Echo try to determine just how big the cache really was as they looked for another entrance to the hideaway.

2. On Assignment: October 1, 1970, to December 31, 1970

With thumbs up and peace signs flashing, the 16 grunts waved good-bye to their Huey taxis. Unfortunately the platoon was approximately 800 meters west of their hoped-for insertion. Grunts are not noted for their good luck.

But the men were in early and Staff Sergeant David "Smitty" Smith, platoon leader, had his men set up for the night. Somewhere southwest of Fire Support Base Connell, poncho-liner tents went up and Smitty took names for a guard duty roster. Nobody knew where they were but the leeches had found them. By 7:30 everyone was trying to catch some sleep in anticipation of the next day's humping—it never happened.

Echo Recon, 1st Battalion, 7th Cavalry was to have one of those rare days when they could do no wrong—a field day.

The misplaced Charlie Alpha put the crack unit right in the middle of three caches that produced hundreds of items, including two ancient 75mm howitzers—American made.

On that day of destiny, Echo Recon awoke to a gray, damp morning dew which clung to everything. Gathering their gear amid the usual grumbles, the platoon set out for an area where the battalion commander had spotted several hootches. After hacking away the vegetation and ramming their bodies through the wait-a-minute vines and other clinging tendrils, Smitty decided to send out a seven-man squad without packs.

The chosen ventured off, while the others waited. About 11 a.m. the patrol returned.

Staff Sergeant Ken Voskuil and his third squad didn't find their objective—a stream—but did find an old abandoned bunker with a tin roof and a booby trap at one end. Smitty moved the platoon into position for a look.

The bunker was a disappointing sight and there was no hope for any find. The bunker was dug 15 feet into the ground with the roof at ground level. But the scattered debris gave the secret away. The rusty mortar rounds and 75mm howitzer rounds weren't booby-trapped afterall. Neither were the rifle stocks. A thorough search was in order.

Smitty, Voskuil and Spec 4 Calvin Snow crawled into the bunker and poked around. They discovered a false floor. "I can see weapons all the way to the back wall," Voskuil yelled. The word spread, but how much was down there? As it turned out, there was something for everybody.

Everybody pitched in. The roof was quickly stripped off. Shovels were put to work. The tin buried beneath the soil was rolled back slowly, exposing the cache. Inside, it looked like an American cache instead of Vietnamese.

Eleven Thompson sub-machineguns, 14 .45 caliber grease guns, a M-79 grenade launcher and a M-60 machinegun were pulled out.

(Left) The men of Echo dig out the last pieces of one howitzer. Sgt. Ken Voskuil (center) has his hands full as he tries to decide what to do with the gun parts. Behind Voskuil (left) platoon leader SSgt. David Smith tries to pry loose yet another piece of the ancient gun. (Right) The Skytroopers take a break as the job nears completion.

As the digging moved towards the back wall, big hunks of metal, their use unknown, materialized. Then things all fell into place. The numerous 75mm shells dictated a logical conclusion--a recoilless rifle. The huge chunks of metal, a casing for the weapon, finally gave the secret away. There was one 75mm recoilless rifle but the prize read: 75mm M-1 J. C. Brill Co. 1941--not one but two American-made howitzers.

Everyone gathered around the radio as Smitty called Lt. Col. Anthony Labrozzi, battalion commander. Smitty saved the howitzers for last. The colonel was speechless but he did manage to say the platoon would get an ice cream drop for the find.

Visions of sticky fingers danced in the men's minds as they set up for the night. Smitty planned the next day's strategy--more patrols, the platoon was lucky hot.

Rain greeted the men as they awoke to the misery that often befalls the grunt. But Staff Sergeant Thomas Preece led his five-man patrol into the bush, without packs, looking for more buried treasure. The patrol worked its way down a stream, hitting a wall of shrubbery. Preece climbed the small hills that formed a miniature valley. He floundered around looking for clues, not unlike a big, thin hound on the scent. Suddenly he reversed his direction and 40 yards later his smile betrayed his find--a second cache.

The second cache was almost identical to the first, false floor and all. Several booby traps were spotted and along with the mines at one end, put out of commission. By late afternoon the readout was ready: 309 82mm mortar rounds; 108 120mm mortar rounds, 2,653 .51 caliber rounds, 21,600 .30 caliber machinegun rounds and two boxes of anti-personnel mousetrap-type mines.

That compared favorably with the first cache which contained two tons of NVA C-4 explosive, 1,100 Chicom grenades, 414 82mm mortar rounds, 108 120mm mortar rounds, 21,600 .30 caliber rounds, three 60mm mortar tubes and one recoilless rifle plus the howitzers.

The following day it was Voskuil and his squad that played Sherlock Holmes. Their discovery, the third in as many days, was a neatly stacked cache under a peaked roof. The count read 1,000 electrical blasting caps, 105 82mm mortar rounds, two cases of 7.62 ammunition, three cases of .30 cal ammunition, 1,100 Chicom grenades, two 75mm recoilless rifle rounds, 11 75mm howitzer rounds, 3,945 pounds of NVA C-4 and one 25-pound box of TNT.

After that find, there was a meeting of the clan. The 4th platoon of Bravo Company, 1st of the 7th, along with an EOD team slashed their way to the last cache site. Six disgruntled members of Echo Recon, left behind in an ambush position to

(Above) Sp 4 Tim Payne, Echo's RTO, pauses to think about the day's work. (Above Right) The digging was often bogged down by the mud and the logs used to support the cache. (Right) There was a lot to uncover and count. (Opposite Page) PFC Bill Blank, the platoon medic, relaxes with a good book as the day's work is done.

2. On Assignment: October 1, 1970, to December 31, 1970 75

protect their foraging buddies, also joined the group.

The EOD team contemplated the expected explosion of cache No. 3. "I've never come across this much C-4 in one cache," Staff Sergeant Ramond Merrell said. His booming dream never came true as the Bravo Company platoon did the honors.

On the fourth day, the howitzers and recoilless rifles were lifted out by Chinook. And the promised ice cream--vanilla and strawberry--was dropped in. It had been months since the men had enjoyed such a treat and the race was on to beat the sun. The pleasure was doubled when the men learned Echo Recon would be lifted out the next day. Suddenly the filthy fatigues with layers of dried mud, memories of constant monsoon soakings and the steady pounding of the sun became lighter.

The traditional bull session was free and lively that night as the discussion ranged from re-up frogs--an obscene lizard--to the miseries of field duty.

Smitty recounted the events of the past days.

"They spotted hootches northeast of where we were inserted and we never found them. But that small trail Ken (Voskuil) found led to that cache, not the hootches. The day we found the first cache was the day we were supposed to have found the hootches. With this find I'm not sure I'll ever get out of the bush early. There wasn't supposed to be any caches in this area."

On the day of extraction for Echo Recon, the EOD team blew cache No. 2 containing the 120mm mortar rounds. The platoon hid in the hole left by cleaning out cache No. 1. The explosion, only 200 yards away, shook the ground and smoke rose 200 feet in the air. Bits of burnt wood and leaves came down like monsoon rains for several minutes. Then the platoon crawled out--intact.

The men stacked the last 82mm mortar rounds for back-logging. The EOD team headed back to Phuoc Vinh and Echo Recon, late in the afternoon, humped overland to the LZ where several Hueys disgorged another platoon from Bravo Company and consumed the men of Echo.

Within minutes, the platoon was at FSB Green, inhaling C-rations and wondering about an after-dinner encore. After all, they had hurt the enemy without firing a shot.

Taking Own Pictures

November 4, 1970

I've been working hard to take my own pictures so I don't have to go out to the firebases with our obnoxious brigade photographer. Lately I may have outdone myself. As a writer I've been getting more photos in papers than he has. Part of his problem is that he plays poor inside politics: he's antagonized the photo lab, which he needs worse than I do. So the photo lab people keep losing his stuff and pumping out mine. I've been friendly with them—we seem to get along well. I'm doing okay as a writer too, although I'm rewriting more than I ought to be. I still need work.

I didn't get promoted this month but I'm not sure I care. I know I'm doing the job of at least a specialist four.

FSB Durall; Chieu Hois

November 5, 1970

I went out to FSB Durall today instead of FSB Ares because I thought there was more going on. There wasn't much more going on, in fact there was only one story to be had: A Vietnamese family who had been working for the VC Chieu Hoied to one of our helicopters. They were waving flags to attract the attention of the bird and in sad shape, suffering from malnutrition and malaria. The only man in the group had an advanced form of a disease like polio, probably polio itself. They were taking a chance but looking at them today, they were in such bad shape that death might have been a blessing. Their problem was they didn't know how to rally to the American (allied) side. The VC had told them they'd be killed if they gave up but they heard a radio broadcast from Saigon telling them to rally to the government who would take care of them. When told they would be sent to live in Chieu Hoi village, they were much relieved.

We gave up on the Flying Circus pad this morning after getting bumped off another helicopter. We decided to try Sandy Pad, which handles cargo-carrying Chinooks and had a bird we could catch. We shouldn't have the bump problem with Chinooks because they carry 30 to 35 people, not the 5 or six of a Huey. They are something to watch with a load. There is a trap door in the bottom of the Chinook with a curved metal bar with a load adjuster which rolls up and down the bar. The load hangs below and swings over the jungle, which goes flying by like a fast-panning movie camera.

You've seen one firebase—you've seen them all. I've tried to see the differences between them but there just aren't very many. They all have artillery, a TOC, they're all round, and function the same with operations coming out of them. For the men living on them, it's a dull way of life with a variety of

2. On Assignment: October 1, 1970, to December 31, 1970

miseries to choose from, like militant lifers or rambunctious mud that gets into everything.

The weather changed dramatically after a typhoon hit Da Nang a week ago. The monsoons are supposed to end soon and the dry season start. The dry season must have started because it hasn't rained for two days. The light readings are better for photography but it's growing hotter. I'm glad my body has grown somewhat accustomed to the heat and moisture.

I finally came across a whole group of troops who are to be longer in country than me. I'm approaching three months in country. I have 280 days left. The grunts don't feel so bad about the war—it hasn't been a very hot war lately. An old man on his second tour told me that it used to be that in War Zone D you never went out in groups less than company size. No platoon operations are common. Everything seems to say that the enemy has either pulled back or his forces have been destroyed. From a military standpoint, I don't see how they can win now. They seem to be relying on our pullout, a smart play.

Photographer Wants to Write

November 6, 1970

Today I bought a can of Dutch Masters cigars and relaxed. Everyone was telling me that somehow the cigar just doesn't fit my image; they're just too big for my small body. It never rained today; what a welcome change.

I just heard that Echo Recon, 1/7th Cav shot several enemy troopers today. They didn't stop findings things even after I left. It's a little frightening. One of the fellows in the shop named Cormandy was telling me that maybe the reason I was sleeping better last night was because I wasn't as nervous as I had been after leaving the bush several days ago. He's almost surely right. I wasn't able to sleep the whole time I was in the bush and awhile afterwards. I will think twice before doing anything like that again.

I forgot to mention that I saw Ton Son Nhut Air Port yesterday while returning from Phuoc Vinh. We landed there to pick up some officers before landing at Bien Hoa. It's big like Bien Hoa Air Port and not far away. But if you've seen one sprawling military complex, you've seen them all.

I mailed off a package full of film, a shell, and an NVA P-38 (can opener) that I found in a 120mm mortar box at the caches. The P-38 was used to open a tin can with fuses (an impressive war trophy, huh?). Let me know if the film turns out.

I'm going out to the firebases tomorrow. I don't know which one for sure. Our average morning recently has been being bumped off the bird we want. We make reservations on the bird only to discover to our eternal frustration the next morning at 6:00 that we've been bumped by a dog team or a chaplain. I forgot to tell you that if I hadn't done the grunt (turned out cache) story, I would have had to do a chaplain story. Admittedly, Al Brown didn't want the bush but are chaplains better? Probably actually, even for a stubborn agnostic.

Our photographer is trying to beat me at my own game. He decided today to write a story. "If Leighton can take pictures and get them in the paper, why can't I write a story?" Poor guy, he may be a specialist five making 150 dollars more a month than me but still doesn't have the sense to concentrate on photography. He should concentrate on his MOS and learn it before he tackles mine. He must not have been listening when I told him about all my experience as a photographer. He must think I just pick up a camera and presto!

Battalion Surgeon; Medics; Grunt Trading

November 7, 1970

I blew it; I lost all my notes for the Chieu Hoi story. I'll have to go out and collect the notes again.

I got two stories today, one about the battalion surgeon of the 2nd Battalion, 7th Cavalry. His story should be a good one. He is not having his time used effectively, he feels, in being assigned on a firebase. Besides, he thinks his 91 Charlie MOS medic (a head medic acting the role of a doctor) would effectively take away what work the surgeon does. He feels that with the medevac concept of evacuating the badly wounded bypasses him and his kind of doctor. Consequently, the rear is the place for him—he thinks—where he would have all the sophisticated diagnostic equipment he's used to.

We sat down and had a great talk, me scribbling away. He offered me a cold root beer, a luxury on a firebase. His 91C medic is a very bright guy who ought to go to medical school after he gets out. The doctor, Capt. Michael P. Coyle, Jr. (Hackensack, N.J.), has been trying to talk to this fellow, who surprisingly is a tall mild-mannered black, into going back to what he'd planned to do before entering the service, medical school. Coyle said Sp5 Harold D. Jones (Houston, Tex.), the medic, has learned an amazing amount about diagnosing diseases.

I talked to Jones. He says his responsibilities are extended to such things as sanitation, garbage control, and keeping up food standards besides being in charge of the medics. The medics under his command do most of the work—the doctor doesn't do much. He's is also in charge when large scale epidemics break out. Several weeks ago, 50 or 60 guys came down with immersion foot, a foot disease, and all of them could have gotten profiles where they wouldn't have been allowed to work. To avoid this, Jones called in for a shipment of foot powder and socks. "We decided to face up to the problem instead of medevacing everyone. We had them out sunning to dry up the problem." Jones and Coyle work well together. They take turns going out to companies in the field on log days, usually taking one or two men out of the field every time they go out. They feel it's a morale booster.

The other story was about packages from home and their effects on the grunts in the field. PFC Donald Crow, an outgoing guy from Lynn, Mass. told me: "Packages from home are kind of like a super market, you order things. When they get here we start trading. It's a sight watching everyone cooking spaghetti in canteen cups or something similarly outlandish. We can be shrewd traders like I traded a can of Nestle's Quick for a can of tuna. What I didn't tell the guy was he needed milk to make the stuff with.

Trading gets sophisticated; we even have credit. Canned goods are easy to trade. There was a pleasant comforting feeling about getting stuff from home, they said, despite some of the impractical stuff gotten. Just as long as it was food, there was no problem. As one healthy chubby-looking GI put it, "Yeah, if they can send it, I can eat it." Another thing that you'd never expect without some thought was the packages for holidays: Halloween pumpkins, Christmas packages and Easter eggs. One guy had his R&R clothes sent to him too early and had to hump them because they couldn't be eaten. As some trooper put it, "If I get a package out here, to pass it around is considered only fair. I take what I want and pass the rest around. Everyone shares the stuff anyway, and it's usually understood that everybody gets something. There are no hoarders because you have to hump what you keep." One skytrooper, Sp4 Joseph Calvitti (Paterson, N.J.) summed it up when he said, "The real unfortunates in this company are the ones that don't get packages. It's an attractive nuisance we'd be sorry to be without."

I had to take a Chinook again today but did well for hitting the firebase so late, around noon. It was fun except I added on to my sunburn. It's growing hotter and didn't rain again today.

Troubles Gathering Stories

My memory doesn't fully jive with my letter from home and the story itself—I think I sugar coated both my letter and the story. I still think my memory is right.

Collecting material didn't always go well and I had troubles this day. It was hot and dusty on the firebase, my time was running out, and I hadn't found much. I talked to units lounging around temporarily on firebases before returning to the jungle, hoping to find something. Usually infantry soldiers were happy to talk but these guys were morose and answered in short unhelpful sentences, miserable even as grunts go. I collected what I could and flew back to Bien Hoa Army Base to my manual typewriter under a hot tin roof. I sat down dejectedly and this story came out, heaven knows from where. It's a good story even if it required some creative writing and stretching the truth, the upbeat tone most prominently.

Skytroopers Say Packages Create Pleasant Problems

This story was in the November 25, 1970, Cavalair *and also was picked up by* Pacific Stars and Stripes *for the December 9, 1970, issue.*

NEAR FSB PERSHING—How important is a package from home? And what can you do in the bush when Mom decides to send you a ten-pound birthday cake or an inedible Christmas present?

The answers are: either you eat it, share it, hump it or throw it away. A whole trading culture has sprung up to handle any problem that might arise, like having more than you can eat or the wrong goodies.

Several members of Alpha Company, 2nd Battalion, 7th Cavalry of the 1st Air Cavalry Division opened their company's system to view. PFC Donald Crow gave a running description: "It's kinda like a market place. We order it and get it from home. Then we start trading. There are even the sharp traders, like me. I traded a can of Nestle's for a can of tuna fish. What I didn't tell the guy was that he needed milk. It gets sophisticated; we even have trading on credit. Ever seen anyone cooking spaghetti in a canteen cup or downing anchovies in the field? That's what can happen."

Spec. 4 Joseph Calvitti told about the mystery packages that come only at certain times of the year, the holiday packages: "We had a Halloween pumpkin on one of the firebases that somebody had discovered in a package. Christmas packages are another source of the unexpected. And Thanksgiving should be swinging."

Every once in a while someone will get something he can't use and can't throw away, like R&R clothing, but packages are usually put to good use. As one big, healthy-looking skytrooper put it: "If they can send it, I can eat it." Capt. Kenneth Berquist, the new CO of Alpha Company, approaches the problem from an uncomplicated angle: "I don't get any packages but then I get the surplus from the other guys."

It's generally agreed that the contents of food packages are a welcome addition to C rations and LRRPs. As one grunt summed it up, "It's an attractive nuisance we'd be sorry to live without."

Economizing; GIs Leaving; Fight

November 8, 1970

Four letters from you, what a haul! You're still in that period when I wasn't writing.

Over From Silver

MARS Calls Popular

BREAK IN THE ACTION — PFC Pablo Garza pauses beside a battle-scarred tree near Firebase Pershing for a letter home. Garza is with Company D, 2nd Battalion, 7th Cavalry. (US Army Photo by Spec 5 Rodney Plant)

Enemy NCO Tells Story

PHUOC VINH — The recon mission that Delta Company, 5th Battalion, 7th Cavalry was on started out to be a quite normal one. But the mission turned out very unusual; not only did it result in a prisoner being captured, but the interrogation that followed proved quite fruitful.

Checking out a suspected enemy location, the Bravo Company Skytroopers spotted two individuals wearing green fatigues. After a quick, one-sided firefight, they captured one wounded NVA soldier and two AK-47's.

As they waited for a MEDEVAC chopper for the wounded man, an initial interrogation was carried out.

The wounded prisoner said that there were two other persons with him, one male and one female. He thought the male was dead and the female, a squad medic, had escaped.

Further questioning revealed that the prisoner had been an NVA for three years; in that time he had become a squad leader for a common liaison squad, based in the Song Be region.

He said that he and the rest of the squad moved into South Vietnam across the Cambodian border and had moved to their present location to set up a communication network. Their mission had been to gather food for the NVA and establish a secure liaison route into South Vietnam.

by Spec 4 Tom Higginbotham
and Spec 4 David Moore

FSB SILVER — Spec 4 Felix Hernandez called his wife in Louisville, Kentucky. Sgt. George Williams of Ninety-Six, South Carolina called his parents. And PFC Dale Morin called Muskegon, Michigan to talk with his girl friend.

On a recent evening at Fire Support Base Silver, each of these men placed a call to someone back in the United States through the Military Affiliated Radio System (MARS).

During the past several years, MARS stations have been set up at U.S. installations in all parts of Vietnam. And recently, a MARS station went into operations at Firebase Silver where it will serve Skytroopers of the 2nd Battalion, 8th Cavalry, 1st Air Cavalry Division.

Men who had spent many months in Vietnam living and working in the jungles as infantrymen were often getting their first opportunity to talk to people back home.

"It really makes you feel better," said Specialist Hernandez of Bravo Company, 2nd of the 8th who spoke with his wife via MARS, "almost like you were home."

Besides the people who maintain and operate the MARS stations here in Vietnam, the system also relies on Ham radio operators in the United States who voluntarily receive and relay the messages from Vietnam. To complete the call, the Stateside radio operators establish a long-distance telephone connection with the person being called.

Since the MARS radio cannot receive and transmit simultaneously, the conversation usually begins with an ironic-sounding greeting like: "Hello, Honey—OVER." (the "OVER" is necessary to the system's smooth operation) Parties on both ends of the line, however, seem to readily get into the spirit of the call.

Skytroopers Say Packages Create Pleasant Problems

by PFC Conrad Leighton

NEAR FSB PERSHING — How important is a package from home? And what can you do in the bush when Mom decides to send you a ten-pound birthday cake or an inedible Christmas present?

The answers are: either you eat it, share it, hump it or throw it away. A whole trading culture has sprung up to handle any problem that might arise, like having more than you can eat or the wrong goodies.

Several members of Alpha Company, 2nd Battalion, 7th Cavalry of the 1st Air Cavalry Division opened their company's system to view. PFC Donald Crow gave a running description: "It's kinda like a market place. We order it and get it from home. Then we start trading. There are even the sharp traders, like me. I traded a can of Nestle's for a can of tuna fish. What I didn't tell the guy was that he needed milk. It gets sophisticated, we even have trading on credit. Ever seen anyone cooking spaghetti in a canteen cup or downing anchovies in the field? That's what can happen."

Spec. 4 Joseph Calvitti told about the mystery packages that come only at certain times of the year, the holiday packages. "We had a Halloween pumpkin on one of the firebases that somebody had discovered in a package. Christmas packages are another source of the unexpected. And Thanksgiving should be swinging."

Every once in a while someone will get something he can't use and can't throw away, like R&R clothing, but packages are usually put to good use. As one big, healthy-looking Skytrooper put it: "If they can send it, I can eat it."

Capt. Kenneth Berquist, the new CO of Alpha Company, approaches the problem from an uncomplicated angle. "I don't get any packages but then I get the surplus from the other guys."

It's generally agreed that the contents of food packages are a welcomed addition to C rations and LRRPs. As one grunt summed it up, "It's an attractive nuisance we'd be sorry to live without."

CLC Graduates Praise Course

BIEN HOA — The men stood at attention in the large classroom, while the instructor read the names of the top six honor graduates.

It was a proud moment for these men for they had more than successfully completed a 10-day series of tests and oral presentations which demonstrated their leadership ability.

The 1st Air Cav's Combat Leadership Course, given to selected men who show outstanding leadership potential, is conducted here at the First Team Academy.

"It's not really that tough of a course," said Spec 4 James Gavin of Delta Company, 2nd Battalion, 8th Cavalry. Gavin had graduated first in his class with a total of 964 points out of a possible 1000.

"Most of our time was spent in class taking written and verbal tests. Each of us had to give a 15 minute presentation on some light infantry weapon without using notes. This measured our ability to express ourselves coherently, which is important if you're going to be a leader out in the bush," he concluded.

"Overall it was an outstanding graduating class for no man scored under 800 points,"

indicated 1st Lt. Ben Garcia, the course's chief instructor.

PFC Michael Kenny, one of the top graduates remarked, "The cadre is really on the ball here and presented us with an excellent course of instruction."

'Sniffer . . .'

(Cont'd from Page 1)

Officer of the 1st Brigade, and Spec. 4 Ben Semien received numerous readings several days in a row in an area in War Zone "D" that later produced one of the largest cache finds since Cambodia.

NVA Nosed Out

"Near Firebase Myron in Cambodia, one of our Sniffers was flying a mission when they spotted an NVA sitting under a tree. The chopper pilot wheeled the bird around, circled, got clearance to fire and opened up," said Smith. As a result of this, the doorgunners killed two NVA, the sniffer operator, Spec 4 James Gray, killed two more and then an accompanying Cobra rolled in to finish the fight, killing 10 more NVA.

Capt. William Pennington and Spec. 4 Terry Seymour conduct the 3rd Brigade Sniffer operations, Spec. 4 is Lawry Arnold and John Cannon provide support for DIVARTY in AO Chief, and Spec. 4 William Wiegand is currently the sniffer operator for the 2nd Brigade.

Recruiters Needed Now

WASHINGTON (ANF) — Soldiers interested in recruiting or career counseling duty are advised that now is the time to request such assignments.

More recruiters and career counselors are needed in light of the Army's efforts to move to a modern volunteer force.

Openings for recruiters in grades E5 and above exist in most major Continental United States areas. Requirements and application procedures are spelled out in AR 601-275.

Interested soldiers in overseas areas should apply at least six

months before their eligible date for return from overseas.

Vacancies for career counselors in grades E-5 and above are at battalion and higher levels at many locations worldwide. AR 601-280 has full information.

Volunteers selected for either of these assignments will be programmed for attendance at the five-week Army Recruiting and Career Counseling Course at the Adjutant General School, Fort Benjamin Harrison, Indiana.

Unit career counselors and personnel officers may be contacted for additional information.

8 The CAVALAIR
Nov 25, 1970

SNIFFER CREW — Spec. 4 Lawry Arnold (left) and Spec. 4 John Cannon check out the meter readings on their Sniffer machine. A positive reading on the dials indicates that something out of the ordinary is happening on the ground below. (Photo by Spec. 4 Jerry Poindexter)

They're trying to cut down on the war costs. They've cut the amount of flying time for Huey helicopters drastically and LOHs to a lesser extent. This means that the 1st Cav, which prides itself on its air mobility, is going to sacrifice part of it for the sake of economy, a painful but necessary step.

Walking to the briefing, I saw the aftermath of a jeep accident. The jeep went out of control and rolled over on the highway. It ended up with wheels straight up like a dead cow. The two riders escaped with only minor injuries—they were lucky. The jeep wasn't badly hurt; from my cowboy experience with the jeep dunking in Song Be, I know that jeeps can take a beating and recover in no time.

90th Replacement has around 2000 GIs stranded in its barracks and outside, waiting for their freedom birds. With all the drops that have come down, someone wasn't planning for the increased number of soldiers leaving 'Nam and so this pileup. Because of this, we had the unfortunate privilege of receiving our much-detested captain back for a final visit. Cussing out the 90th Replacement people, he was going to Saigon to party it up. He was drunk to the max, Lt. O'Daly told me after he'd staggered out. It seems that besides the fellow being hardened hopeless lifer, he can't hold his drink. He's just like a little kid and just received a bronze star—what a laugh.

When I was out humping last week, I was bothered by a heat rash that I'm told most guys get out in the boonies. I thought it would wash right off with the dirt but it's back giving me a hard time. I feel like someone is constantly sticking little pins into my skin. It was worse in the bush when I was carrying a pack. I'm going to take several showers a day until it clears up.

I saw a fight yesterday, the first I've seen in this country. This big Hawaiian dude was pounding this short six-foot fellow without doing much damage but my imagination was stimulated. I could just see me try to defend myself against a big heavy-set fellow like that who could get that mad that fast. He was throwing the other guy—who was strictly on the defensive—around by the hair. I knew that aggressor was a bully from the day before but didn't expect to see this.

Our Poor Jeep

November 9, 1970

There is going to be some news team doing a story on what a new trooper does going through the FTA (First Team Academy), the place I came through just after I joined the 1st Cav, so keep an eye out for that. Another, a man from CBS, is interviewing a fellow on FSB Ares, a grunt from Charlie, 1/12 Cavalry. You can feel a little superior to the news on TV about Vietnam in my area because, in my humble opinion, I can cover a story in more depth. They can't say anything more profound than the war is a screwed up mess and most of the GIs are restless. I hope to send you pictures of my grunt expedition so you won't lack tangible proof that I did go out. I finally know the photos came out well and I'll con them into giving me a set to send you.

Everybody seems to be leaving—nine freedom birds came in last night, about 1800 people's worth. Drops are really coming down though none for me, no 9-month drops yet. Eric Whorley, an ex-grunt sergeant who lives in the office, is so short that he's been delegated to doing nothing the remainder of his time here, about a week.

Our jeep is giving us a bad time again: some dud on guard duty last night, using the jeep, put diesel fuel in the gas tank instead of gasoline. We had to take the choking jeep to the maintenance yard to have the tank drained. Some zealot in his zeal brought the jeep down in front of another place and forgot he'd left it there. We thought someone had skied up with our jeep although we couldn't understand how anyone could be so stupid as to pick *our* jeep with its shady reliability record (in for repairs every two days, etc.). Sadly our hopeful disbelief was well founded—the junker was found and our dreams of a new jeep shattered.

I'm flying out to FSB Durall tomorrow where I was about three days ago. I hope to see my old grunt buddies from Echo Recon and see how the warriors are doing. For such a small force, they've been doing their share of killing this last week. This is unusual for them. I'll be curious to learn how all this action has changed them—I'm a little apprehensive. I've come across men before who know they've killed someone—often in a direct confrontation—and they have a bit haunted or hunted look to them.

It's an unstable world here that I can't really adjust to. I've seen enough now so I wouldn't miss the place if I left. I haven't felt this way up until now. There are moments of great excitement and high adventure but it feels false, scary and pointless.

I've got to take a shower to drown this heat rash and go to bed for the early awakening.

Stay Behind Ambush; Football; Kent State

November 10, 1970

We just had a meeting of the two writers and two photographers in Bien Hoa along with our boss, dictator O'Daly. It appears that we aren't meeting our quotas. It isn't that we aren't writing more than any other brigade; it's just that we aren't writing up to his expectations. It's not bad, now that my bush story is finished. I can relax and do five stories a week. Relax? That's not the right word because stories are getting hard to scratch up.

Today I went out to FSB Durall and got the story of Echo Recon's stay behind ambush on old played-out FSB Green. I talked to a sniper, Sgt. Steve Harbeck (Ithaca, N.Y.), who put holes in two NVA scroungers that tried to police up the left behind goodies on the abandoned base. The run-ins took place on November 5th, 6th, and 7th. No Americans were hurt. The Americans counted three NVA bodies and one blood trail they said had to be that of a dead man. These are some of the quotes I got out of Steve who I knew before today. He's an ex-law student and a very bright guy. "We assaulted our own firebase twice," Steve explained with an air of excitement about him. "There were all the NVA in the world out there just two hours after the last cannon had left. That's the first time I've seen a live one. My platoon leader was ready to give me an article 15 for making too much noise, my knees were shaking so much. I've never been so scared in my life. Then after the fight we made a tactical combat assault a DI (drill instructor, drill sergeant) would have been proud of. We did everything by the book and damned if it didn't work. The only non–American equipment the three bodies had on them were their belts and their sandals. Everything else was GI from head to toe, except their AK-47s of course. This has got to be the most unbelievable thing I've ever done."

Smitty, the platoon leader, was right out there with the rest of them. He got caught cleaning his weapon one time. He borrowed Tom Preece's weapon and went to it. Tom was on the radio and everyone said he was scared. This was the first contact he'd been in. This happened just after I left them for the rear. Maybe I should have stayed five days more for this story? These guys are not my idea of a pack of trained killers although when put in a situation like this, they can do little else.

I never get away from football, even here. We have TV and radio replays of games all the time. I hear some yoyo wasting his time now on a game. I'd have to sacrifice my letter writing home to accommodate the sports and have no intentions of doing that. Even the firebases are no refuge and even in the bush they may have transistors tuned in too.

I suffered through one of those disgusting Ohio natives (who thought it self evident that because a grand jury from Ohio blamed the students for the Kent State murders, that the federal government's investigation just didn't exist. He said if he'd been a guardsman, he would have killed them like the dogs they were). [*I went to Ohio Wesleyan University prior to the Army—I could have been one of those students.*] I was furious but couldn't change such a committed fascist. We have our share of primitives over here. He said we should have won this war long ago. I asked him how we could have won it. This stopped him, especially when I added that we had nothing to fight for. "Why can't those kids back in the States keep their mouths shut like the GIs coming back from Vietnam?" he asked. I just gave up; he's a traitor to his own generation, he's sold out.

Now it isn't the mud on firebases, it's the chopper blown dust that makes life miserable. And with the sun beating down, it begins to feel like a sand storm in the Sahara. The red mud of FSB Durall makes me look like I have tanned arms but I know it will wash off.

I took a joy ride in a chopper again tonight about 6:15 p.m. with a lighthearted pilot who loves to fly low. We were coming back on the Charlie Charlie bird from firebase and went low over the land as a very red sun was setting—it was beautiful. I take it you wish for a little warmth in Nebraska these days. We've got what you want here in the tropics. Vietnam has its fragrant breathtaking irresistible scenes, even if the bomb holes do show.

Echo Recon Stories

Multiple stories came from Echo Recon, the unit I went out with in the jungle, because I got to know them and they thought of me when something happened. Small teams of Americans would set up ambushes on firebases that had just been closed, resulting frequently in fights with enemy scavengers. This is an especially good view of the gritty, bloody, violent world of the grunts, concerned with kills and personal survival.

First Mission Hot for Sergeant

This Echo Recon article was in the December 2, 1970, issue of Cavalair.

FSB GREEN—His platoon, Echo Recon, 1st Battalion, 7th Cavalry, found themselves watching as the NVA calmly conducted police call on newly abandoned FSB Green. Echo Recon decided to upset the enemy's salvage operations and Sgt. Steve Harbeck found himself caught up in the action.

"There were all the NVA in the world out there less than two hours after the last cannon left. That's the first time I've seen a live one." So began Harbeck's tale of his first contact with the enemy. It lasted for three days.

The afternoon of the first day the machine gunner and the grenadier combined for a kill as they hit a squad of NVA nosing around inside the still intact berm. After the first enemy soldier died, the platoon charged in as the NVA were scampering over the other side of the berm. "We made a tactical combat assault which would have made a DI (drill instructor) proud," Harbeck maintained with a grin.

"The next day was a rerun," commented Harbeck. "I had a field of fire this time and triggered an ambush. That was when all hell broke loose. We assaulted our own firebase a second time. I brought down two NVA this time though I didn't kill both of them. One man crawled out to the wood line and escaped but he left the blood trail of a soon-to-be-dead man."

When asked what he thought about actually being in contact, Harbeck replied, "My platoon leader was ready to give me an Article 15 for noise, my knees were shaking so much. I've never been so scared in my life."

Charlie appeared again on the following day and a classic firefight erupted when both sides saw each other at the same moment. Not much came out of the exchange but the damage had already been done. Without suffering any casualties themselves, the men of the 7th Cav had killed four NVA in three days and put the scavengers to their heels.

At one point, the Americans could have hit the NVA but thought they were GIs. "The only non–American equipment they had on them were their belts and their sandals, everything else was GI from head to toe. Oh, except for their AK-47s of course."

Treating Ralliers; Amateur Forward Observer

November 11, 1970

I winged it from Sandy Pad out to FSB Ares today and found two good stories.

In the first, the medics and battalion surgeon on Ares had to face an invasion of civilian patients, 35 Chieu Hois suffering from malnutrition, malaria and tropical skin diseases. The doctor decided that the people, predominantly kids with no young men or women not surprisingly, needed baths. So they were all marched to a shower outside and given a going over. The kids didn't mind the water but weren't willing to scrub hard enough so the doctor, head scrubber, and the medics plus helpful grunts pitched in for a kid scrubbing which I would love to have watched. The kids enjoyed the water. When the people first appeared, an old dehydrated woman was the only person in danger of giving up the ghost. They gave her liquids rapidly by feeding her intravenously, which she didn't mind, taking it stoically. The doctor said that a good diet with more meat would have done more good than all the medicines he could give them.

Then by nosing around like a good reporter I found a story in artillery. They had an amateur FO (forward observer, the guys who direct artillery in the field) who for one of the first times was calling in artillery. And he wasn't calling in on battery but four and managed to stay cool and pull it off. He simultaneously was handling artillery from three different firebases, a monumental job when you consider he was a platoon member in the middle of a firefight where his platoon had been ambushed and three of his good friends hurt. They thought he ought to get a medal on the firebase for he'd succeeded without much formal FO training. His old platoon leader said he always caught on quickly and was always cool plus a natural-born leader. The guy's name is Sp5 Lannie Swanson from Minot, N.D., and he must be a near genius to do all this over a radio.

2. On Assignment: October 1, 1970, to December 31, 1970

CBS news was on the firebase yesterday and probably has live pictures of the Chieu Hois. How lucky can they get? They had a request in to shoot a typical firebase and what do they fall into? Discouraging. That's the firebase I was going to when I accidentally ended up on FSB Durall instead but I would have missed my sniper's story so I guess I can't win.

Do you remember the story I wrote on the diseases the medics were treating during the monsoon season and how gory but honest my wording was? Well, it never got printed. This is the kind of stuff the Army doesn't want publicized. I've never seen anything back in the States on it. Unfortunately, I didn't get a story on the medics in and they felt a little hurt.

Some grunts have questioned whether their lives are being put in jeopardy to save some Army money. There are fewer loggings done now than there used to be. They've come up with a new rig that doesn't require a big landing zone. They throw a ladder out the back of a Chinook and the troops slowly climb in, sitting ducks for any gooks around. If they're going to cut corners, I wish it wouldn't be in our support for the grunts. Given the kind of tactics we're using, lack of support for what is already a precarious existence could be fatal.

I'm going to start reading even more books on firebases. I waste more time sitting and waiting than anything else, including rooting around for stories. This is probably a situation the civilian press doesn't face. Communications are bad out here so stories have to be gathered personally. The only way is to hitch rides on birds that have no obligation to take me or leave when I want. It breeds wasted time and jumpy nerves unless I find an outlet and reading is it.

P.S. Since my birthday is fast approaching, I might as well tell you what I want. I want *FOOD*! Grunts tire of C rations and LRRPs but rear people like me tire of potatoes and ham. Send me something with great variety.

HE'S A CLUTCH PERFORMER

It's unseemly to gush over what a soldier did but what this man accomplished under fire was amazing. I found this in the December 2, 1970, Cavalair.

FSB ARES—Spec. 5 Lannie Swanson is one of those clutch performers that every grunt is proud to have in his outfit.

Remaining calm under a barrage of rocket and small arms, even after three of his friends have been hit, Swanson called in artillery fire from four different batteries located at FSB Durall, Connell and Ares. He managed to pull it off without making a mistake and without a great deal of formal FO (forward observer) training.

His former platoon leader describes him as an "easy going guy who really catches on fast. Nothing excites him. He has had only three days of formal FO training but he took the initiative and learned the rest himself."

"It's a hassle for someone to adjust even two batteries at once. The artillery liaison officer was stunned that anyone could do what he did. He called in the fire within 100 meters of his position. Very few trained FOs would dare to do that."

Another officer, an artillery coordinator, was also impressed. "It's really gratifying to see someone like that. He really utilized his fire support."

What is surprising is that he had to do everything over one field radio while in contact with everyone simultaneously.

Civilian Correspondents; Cache Thoughts

November 12, 1970

I went out to FSB Durall today and couldn't find a single printable story—pretty sad. But I got a chance to talk to several members of the civilian press from CBS news. Not surprisingly, the only unit they could go out with was Echo Recon 1/7th, my pals.

Do you remembering me bragging about my knowing at least as much about Vietnam as the civilian correspondents? Well, I got a good indication today of the somewhat superficial approach of the civilian press to the war, at least the TV people. I stayed out with Echo Recon and developed a decent story, I thought, in five days. They will spend one day, never pull guard, never do any work, or encounter any of the misery associated with gruntdom. They were friendly, though, and might find something.

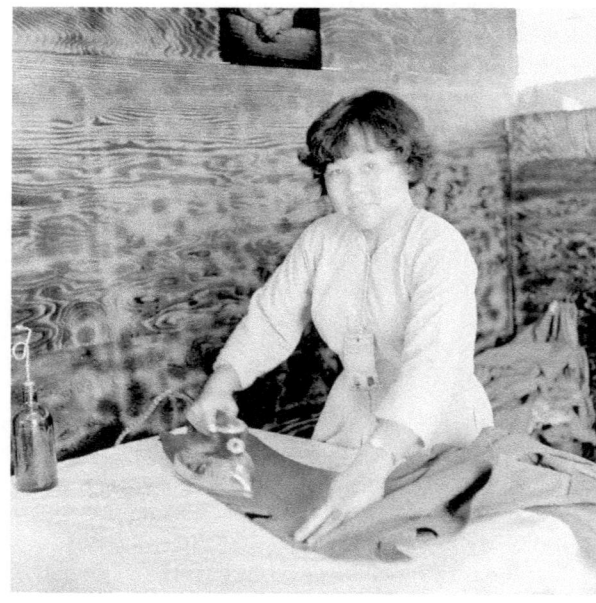

In the rear, we were expected to make ourselves presentable with clean, pressed fatigues. We had hooch mates, Vietnamese women we would hire to do our laundry and press our clothes. I think this woman was my hooch mate at this time.

2. On Assignment: October 1, 1970, to December 31, 1970

This correspondent, the announcer, knew Dick Swanson of *Life* magazine well enough to say that he doesn't talk much to anyone. This fellow was different, talking and prying into things like the press should. And I guess my main objection is that they get all their information from the higher ups, not the enlisted men. Being an enlisted man, I feel I have an advantage. Their approach to dew (marijuana) for instance struck me as naive; they actually had doubts about its presence. I know better. They were treated like visiting dignitaries, which of course they were. They have influence the likes of which our poor division paper can only dream.

Tomorrow I'm returning to 93rd Evac and see what stories I can pick up. We have a number of injured men in the wards there. I'll probably have to hitchhike.

Your letter came, Dad, so you finally know I'm out of the bush. The 75mm howitzers from the first cache were old and perhaps came from the aid you helped deliver to the Chinese during World War II. The CKC is a regular rifle I got from the cache. It is a little longer than an M-16 and a good deal heavier. I hope to get a stock for it although I'm not sure I want to keep it.

The caches were lightly booby-trapped but the NVA had taken few efforts to do anyone in. The caches were put up quickly it seems and we're not sure they wanted many booby traps. There are few booby traps around in fixed positions these days. The stylish thing is Alpha Alphas (automatic ambushes), set up by us every night and set up by the enemy when they know someone is in the area. We have few casualties from enemy booby traps. Our worst problems are with careless Americans who throw the wrong stuff around and create booby traps for themselves by accident.

Radios are very important—it's how units communicate. The colonel as an example was told by radio what's in the cache and responded by radio what he wanted taken out and what he wanted blown in place. Our paper is a weekly by the way with a circulation around 15,000 copies.

The American strategy seems to be to keep the enemy under control while keeping casualties down and slowly work to get out of Vietnam. At one time, everyone traveled in company size elements because the enemy was running in groups equally as large. Now the vogue is platoon-sized elements of 20 or so men covering a large area. Finding any sizeable force is rare but it's happened a few times this week, although not bigger than platoon-sized. It's kind of a non-war. In briefings, on a typical day there will be one KBH (killed by helicopter). The briefer would sound like this: "Sighted, one individual in black pajamas evading to the east. Result: one NVA KBH." Not a battle by any means. Echo Recon came up with one of the biggest tallies of the week: 4 kills. I'm not sure what an aggressive combat division is doing playing patsy this close to Saigon—maybe they'll pull us out?

I appreciate good old Nebraska's winter because it's not here and getting hotter. I've reached the point where 80 degrees feels like 70 degrees but that's the limit of my adaptability. After that I'm the usual, hot and miserable.

Buying Liquor; Bitten Foot; Confused Patient; Not Shoot First

November 13, 1970

The Army is finally getting really enlightened. Now you can buy bottles of hard liquor, like the E-6s and above used to, for beans. I went and bought a 40 oz. bottle of Jim Beam for $2.25, not bad. So I'm sitting here sipping bourbon out of a topless Fanta root beer can and smoking a cigar. This is the life.

I went down to the 93rd Evac Hospital and it was a roaring success. First I talked to PFC Steven Lankhorst (Fremont, Mich.) from Charlie, 2/7th Cav based at FSB Andre. His story: "It was after 9 p.m. and already dark. The moon was shining; it had just stopped raining. My boots were off and I didn't want to take them off to relieve myself so I was walking barefooted. I stepped on something that felt like a broken stick that jabbed me. I stopped. I had a funny feeling it wasn't a stick so I kicked "it" off. At first I thought a lizard had bit me, but the bite was the wound of a snake. I couldn't see what it was—the night was too dark. My whole body was rigid when the guys were carrying me.

We reached the landing zone about 9:40 p.m. after we'd awakened the whole camp. They went all out for me. You know what it's like for one man to walk through the jungle during the day. Well, you can imagine what it was like at night with two guys carrying me. Suddenly, I looked up and it was 11:35 p.m. I don't know what happened to those two hours. My metabolism was going wild. They kept telling me to relax but my whole body was tense. I felt relaxed but I couldn't talk; I couldn't tell them I was relaxed. I recovered quickly. If I see a snake, I'm the type of guy that turns and runs. I'm lucky it was dark or I would have screamed. It's funny now but it wasn't funny then." Definitely my kind of horror story—I'm afraid of snakes too. He's recovered rapidly and should be released tomorrow.

Lankhorst had made a friend in the hospital, PFC Steven J. Wheeler (Eldorado, O.). He has a strange story to tell but isn't a member of the 1st Cav so I can't write about him. He said: "I thought I had gone to sleep in one of my beds in the hospital—I wasn't supposed to go to sleep in a patient's bed. I had worked in the Good Samaritan Hospital in Dayton, Ohio—a nursing home. I started asking to go home when I saw someone and they told me I was in Vietnam. We had a few rounds about *that*. It didn't take long to notice their uniforms were wrong. Only then did I realize I was in the Army and in

Vietnam. I started asking questions. Who was I? Who are my parents? I know I have a girlfriend because of a letter she sent me. I still don't know if I have any brothers and sisters." This guy definitely sounds lost. He is partially numb on one side of his body and still having trouble talking. They don't know what's wrong with him. It could have been a disease or a shock? He still has bad dreams. He seems like a smart guy but has the cast of a man much older than his 21 years. It's now primarily his time in the Army that he has trouble remembering.

The third story, which I will write up, is about Corporal Frank Perez (Brownsville, Tex.) who was wounded in an ambush sprung on his platoon. He's a member of Echo Recon, 1/12th, the same platoon that the celebrated forward observer was from. He was shot through the arm and had a bone hit. He's in traction at the 93rd Evac although healthy other than the arm. He said: "We gave them the benefit of the doubt and they didn't return the favor. We could have cut them down but thought they might be innocents like some 40 Chieu Hois that we had just gotten from another company in the last day. We had the element of surprise as far as we were concerned. We saw them first. On an ordinary mission, we would have shot them up but we were on a search and rescue mission, not a straight combat mission. The lieutenant made the decision not to fire and I still think it was right—we had no way of knowing. We sighted two men without weapons, we thought. We expected to find only four people. But the way they retaliated, we thought there were ti-ti (a little bit) more of them. They were firing rockets and small arms at us. We, Sharky and I, were pulled out using the jungle penetrater seat. The other guy was pulled out in a litter because his whole side was laid open. Luckily, no one died." Despite being in traction, he was friendly and talkative. He seemed lonely so I talked with him for about an hour. "It's a hassle eating on your back but what can I say?" he proclaimed as he gobbled down some fish (it's Friday). "What's the horse pill for?" he asked a nurse jokingly who had handed him a cup full of pills. I find his story encouraging. There still are people, even in the bush, who do things on principle.

I'm trying the hospital war story approach. I hear that even Lt. Col. Vesser is in this hospital from injuries he suffered somehow. I'll find out what happened but won't talk to him. Ours is an enlisted man paper with enlisted man news; even the officers actively support this. We have a relatively good paper considering.

BARE FEET GET BITTEN RANGER SAYS

Combat was a dangerous place, not just thanks to the NVA but also jungle denizens. This was the first in a string of stories about unpleasant jungle creature encounters, making it into the December 9, 1970, Cavalair.

NEAR FSB ANDRE—PFC Stephen Lankhorst, a new member of Charlie Company, 2nd Bn 7th Cav has a personal horror story to tell. Having just finished ranger training at Phuoc Vinh, he was getting settled into Charlie Company. He told his story calmly with a trace of humor in his voice.

"It was a little after 2100 and already dark. The moon was shining, and it had just stopped raining. I didn't want to put my boots back on just to go out so I went barefoot, without the sandals a veteran grunt would have worn. I was walking out to relieve myself when I felt something like a stick jab me. I stopped, with a funny feeling it wasn't a stick so I kicked 'it' off.

"At first I thought it was a lizard. The wound, however, was from the fangs of a snake.

"My whole body went rigid while some guys were trying to hold me up. They went all out for me. You know what it's like for one man to walk through the jungle during the day. Well, you can imagine what it was like for two guys carrying me to a logging site at night.

"We had to wake up the whole camp, it all happened so quickly. It started hitting me after I got on the medevac bird.

"Suddenly I look up and it was 2335; I don't know where the time went. My heartbeat was going wild. They kept telling me to relax but my whole body was tense. My mind was at ease but I couldn't talk."

"I recovered quickly so I guess these people know what they're doing. 'We haven't lost anybody from a snake bite yet,' somebody insisted to me. I've pretty much recovered now; it's kind of funny now but it wasn't funny then."

CBS's FSB Ares Pot Party; Operation Scrub

November 14, 1970

You probably saw the CBS footage of the pot party last night on FSB Ares, a big scandal because some lieutenant was supposed to be watching the CBS team and blew it. So, they got pictures of a whole group of guys down at the water point all screwed up on dew. The Army's so mad that they want to kick the civilian press out of the 1st Cav for good. It should be fun to watch. It's an Army cover up being exploded again. Everyone readily admits there's a marijuana problem over here but no one's honest to the civilian press so the press is forced to go under the table a little. It's funny though, the press has really been out in force around here recently.

I looked into the possibilities for another story but don't see how I can make it work. There's a division-wide economy drive to bring in all unusable or unnecessary equipment. There's everything from armored ducks to crystal sets, millions of dollars of gear but nothing really important, I feel. Economy has been forced down the generals' throats and compliance grudging at best. Why should they trot this out at a radical new concept when it's common

2. On Assignment: October 1, 1970, to December 31, 1970

practice in private industry? And all kinds of people want credit for this program called "Scrub."

Tomorrow is payday and three months in country for me. It's going faster as time goes along. I learned that our least-favorite junior lifer photographer has less than four weeks left in 'Nam and the PIO—he got a thirty-day drop. We can come up with better photographers to replace him. Eric Whorley left today for the world.

I'm going up to Phuoc Vinh tomorrow to write captions for the color slides from my jungle mission and collect my salary. I'll get to see the gang, minus our recently departed unlamented captain. A lot of guys have derosed too so we have many new people.

We have a nightly curfew now for 10 p.m.—everyone is to be in bed then. There have been too many knifings (where I don't know) and the lifers want it stopped.

You remember me telling you about the guy from our PIO office that had a temporary assignment at *Stars and Stripes*? He was the most unpopular enlisted man in our PIO office. Well I finally got to meet him and what a dud! He's a coward who thinks putting himself out on a firebase is putting his dear little ass in jeopardy. Poor baby. I'm routinely on firebases, big deal. He's taking a turkey out to a firebase for a Thanksgiving picture for *Stars and Stripes*, big deal. There may be some sour grapes here—he's the guy who apparently poisoned the well for a current 1st Cav journalist, like me, getting a similar plum temporary assignment with *Stars and Stripes*.

I found out what happened to Lt. Col. Vesser—he was playing John Wayne. He had his chopper flown into the middle of an active firefight and got shot in his rib cage, not a serious injury. I would expect more caution and common sense from a Rhodes scholar although I'll admit I don't know what happened.

I didn't tell my parents that the following Scrub story was mine but I'm sure that at a minimum the opening sentence and parts of the body were my work. Below is the page with this article on the top.

Cache Pictures; Story

November 16, 1970

I went up to Phuoc Vinh and stayed the night. I tried to get the cache pictures to send you but will have to settle for the story in the paper—they lost the negatives. I took a look at the color slides I took in the bush for the magazine. They were excellent, developed in our own lab and my exposures were right on. I have a good shot at making the cover of the magazine, in fact several of mine are in the competition. PFC Turner, the editor, for this magazine issue, should stay off my back now. I've done my two bits worth.

Operation Scrub Eliminates Excess

PHUOC VINH — Remember the dusty old .50 caliber machine gun or zeon searchlight the supply sergeant had to climb over to fetch a Skytrooper a new pair of LLW jungle boots? Or the amphibious duck acquired during some long-forgotten campaign down south in the Mekong Delta?

During the past two months a combined program of command emphasis and typical 1st Cav ingenuity has reduced both the piles of unnecessary gear and the paperwork that once made getting rid of it a formidable task.

Dubbed "Operation Scrub," the project has turned into an all-out and highly effective effort to trim down excess equipment which once was an asset but has now become excess baggage for the Cav's combat and support units. As a result, money is being saved, and much of the equipment is being redistributed to units that need that type of equipment.

Discard the Unneeded

"Scrub is an effort to get equipment on hand and not needed out of the way,"

explained Maj. David A. Rarig, Division project officer. "Operation Scrub," he said, "is lightening the load. Our units have accumulated equipment for which they once had a need, but no longer use."

"To get rid of it," Rarig said, "we had to eliminate the paperwork involved in equipment turnovers." Under Operation Scrub," he added, "the paperwork is done by the DISCOM (Division Support Command) people at Bien Hoa who are the experts in the field."

According to Rarig, anything not in a unit's property books can be turned in with no questions asked and no paperwork required. The result has been a collection of unneeded equipment at Bien Hoa which includes everything from trucks to fire extinguishers. As of November 16, 199 vehicles had been turned in along with 2591 generators, 3983 weapons and thousands of smaller items such as steel pots and helmet liners. According to Rarig, almost $2 million worth of equipment had been brought in by November 16.

Rarig explained the origins of Operation Scrub as an "effort to make do with what we have" on the part of the Department of the Army. "The priorities of the country are going in a different direction," he stated.

But, the major added, the original project, conceived Vietnam-wide as "Project Scrub" by USARV, called only for the elimination of excess equipment not on the units' property books. But the 1st Cav has expanded the project into its own "Operation Scrub" with several unique adaptations, aimed not only at trimming the excess but making it possible to apply practicality as a criteria for discarding equipment.

POTS AND PANS "SCRUBBED" — Mess utensils no longer needed to feed the Cav make up part of the mountain of equipment in Bien Hoa. (US Army Photo by Pfc. Daniel Ramlow)

Operation Scrub, he said, extends the original idea to include TO&E equipment as well as surplus.

This means that Cav units desiring to make a free turn-in of excess gear can turn it in at one of six major collection points at Song Be, Mace, Phou Loi, Bearcat, Phuoc Vinh or Bien Hoa. Most of the unneeded gear is then trucked to a central collection yard at Bien Hoa where DISCOM personnel take over. Also, there are three turn-in points at each brigade and a DISCOM officer to coordinate the project at brigade level.

Mountain of Savings

A project officer was appointed for each Cav company when Scrub kicked off on October 1. The result has been an impressive mountain of equipment at Bien Hoa, and dollarwise, an impressive savings.

"This program wouldn't have been successful if we didn't have command emphasis and people going around to the units to make certain Operation Scrub was fully understood,"

explained Capt. Gordon Lee, the DISCOM project officer in charge of Operation Scrub in Bien Hoa. Lee heads a staff which moves the incoming material back into supply channels where it can be claimed by units which need the discarded gear.

At Bien Hoa, a team of civilian experts working with DISCOM determines whether equipment can be channeled back into supply, sidetracked for repairs or is unusable except for salvage.

WO McDonald Smith is in charge of the mountain of equipment he fondly refers to as his "Pandora's Box." But, along with seven other men under him, Smith has brought a semblance of order to the tons of Army gear which have accumulated at his Bien Hoa turn-in yard in the last few weeks.

Commenting on the success of the operation, Lee added, "There are enough people who realize that this is an ideal method of returning excess equipment so that we've been able to run a successful operation."

OUT OF THE WAY — Hundreds of steel pots and helmet liners made their way out of the stockrooms and into the Bien Hoa collection yard where they will either be assigned to salvage or will re-enter the supply channels. (US Army Photo by Pfc. Daniel Ramlow)

Saved From VC...

(Cont'd from Page 1)

continue. I slid down and crawled into the brush. I found a depression in the ground and rolled myself into a ball," he said.

"I thought I was going to get captured. I had no weapon, no survival radio. The Cobra went down before I could radio its location, but . . . I knew the Blues and Alpha Troop were out there looking for us."

Faces Anthill

Bartlett lay on the ground listening to the enemy movement around him. Suddenly he heard bamboo break and saw seven VC walking toward his position.

"I put my face down on an ant hill," said the Skytrooper. "The ants were driving me crazy but I didn't make a sound."

They moved closer until one was only 15 feet away; Bartlett could see him standing with his weapon, looking for the craft his comrades shot down but were unable to locate in the heavy jungle terrain.

Suddenly the sound of aircraft broke the air and the VC moved past him deeper into the forest. He turned on his back and looked up through the jungle canopy and saw a cobra circling above.

"I wanted to get up, yell and wave my arms, but I knew better," said Bartlett. Meanwhile, the men of Alpha Troop spotted the fallen Cobra and the Blues rappelled to the bird. It was a Huey that discovered Dulin in a nearby field.

Half - Dazed

The co-pilot, Dulin, found himself walking aimlessly through the jungle when he regained consciousness. He was only 50 meters from the bird and was returning toward it when he heard enemy movement on the other side of the Cobra. He ran down the ridgeline and into an open field. Still dazed from his experience, he hid himself in the tall grass until he saw a LOH and a Huey pass overhead. Dulin jumped up and waved his arms frantically. The Huey came down and pulled the young pilot to safety.

Bartlett was hiding, listening to the sounds of the aircraft but "when I heard the Hueys, I knew that they were inserting the Blues, but the VC were between them and me."

He started crawling in the direction of the Hueys, ignoring the enemy around him. When he came within 30 meters of the Blues, everything became still. For a moment he thought that they had left, but he suddenly saw them in a clearing near the bird.

Gathering his courage, Bartlett yelled out: "Blues, I need help!" Then, "Blues, this is Bloody Bart (his nickname). I've got VC on both sides of me. I'm going to run to you, just don't shoot me."

Giving an Apache yell, the loudest of his life, Bartlett broke through the jungle cover into the clearing and into the arms of 6 foot 3 Sgt. John Coble pointman for the Blues.

"If he wasn't so tall, I'd have kissed him on the cheek," the rescued Skytrooper said.

A Huey came in and Bartlett was soon returned to FSB Buttons and a reunion with his co-pilot. The two men had been down for almost two hours.

Days later, the two pilots were again flying, undaunted by their experience. "I'll fly until the day I leave," said Bartlett.

Enemy Deaths...

(Cont'd from Page 1)

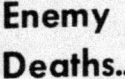

another kill was registered. On a third occasion the enemy thought it would bring down a chopper but the end result was another NVA killed by helicopter. In the last instance Alpha Troop called for some help after more ground-to-air fire. Aid came in the form of aerial field artillery and an air strike. From the turmoil, three more NVA were killed by helicopter, one NVA killed by AFA and two by air strike.

Alpha Co., 1st Bn., 7th Cav. uncovered a small cache in Long Khanh Province Nov. 20, while carrying out a ground recon mission. Inside the structure were a small amount of CHICOM grenades, B-40 rocket rounds and mortar rounds. On the next day, exploiting the initial cache, Alpha Co. captured 102 CHICOM grenades, 67 82mm mortar rounds, 16 B-40 rounds and an assortment of fuses and rifle parts. Also captured were one 9mm pistol, one CKC rifle and one French submachine gun.

In Binh Tuy Province southeast of FSB Silver, 27 people rallied to the South Vietnamese Government.

EASY GOES IT — Sgt. Clay (Cowboy) Mays of Echo Company, 2nd Battalion, 5th Cavalry cautiously works his way down a grassy sloped hillside near FSB Cheyenne. Mays is a native of Fort Worth, Texas. (US Army Photo by Pfc. Ron Russo)

I've been trying out different kinds of cigars and poisoning myself in the process but it's something to do. I have six different brands and haven't settled on one yet. I may just quit. This place drives me a bit loonie and I need my security symbol, a big fat smelly cigar.

My Echo Recon cache story finally came out but the paper was filled with errors in fact, one for each story. If I can get a copy to send you I'll document it. It's obvious that I'm going to have to pin my hopes for greatness on the magazine story and the pictures, which tell Echo Recon's story more thoroughly anyway.

This week's newspaper was much more pictures than story. Next week's I hope will be the other way around. I'm a writer, not a photographer. I'm still mad at the photographers down here in Bien Hoa, they're just not trying very hard. So on I go, blasting away and gaining the distrust of the photographers by invading their domain.

Army vs. Drugs

November 17, 1970

The new sniff-them-out missions are over here looking for drug users. With that stateside exposure of the pot smokers on FSB Ares, the officers are out in force, too late of course. I'm not sure this problem isn't as big as the Army. Lt. Col Fry, at the end of the 1st Brigade briefing tonight, said he'd been conducting his own investigation and found a user in the course of his sleuthings. He said this was despite the excellent ongoing program on Ares. He said that if it was this bad forward, what was it like in the rear? Precisely.

Mom, I know how you feel about Dad's typing fast. I take a long time to type my stories on the job, although I'm faster than just about everyone in the office. But I agonize, go slower, over the letters home, even when I'm tired. I'm the only one who writes so much to one source. I enjoy being different and writing home keeps me out of trouble and all this practice has helped—I've sped up.

Air Force Rocketed; Cigars; Scout Dogs

November 18, 1970

Bien Hoa took incoming last night on the Air Force side. Three men died. They missed the POL (Petroleum, Oil and Lubricants) point by about 15 feet with one round. Another hit a hooch. That takes care of Bien Hoa's somehow being holy—it isn't. I heard the sirens but not the explosions clearly. We always envy the Air Force their facilities but they paid for their luxury last night by being a more attractive target.

I'm quitting cigar smoking. I have a can full of cigars with a sign reading

"I'VE QUIT, TAKE ONE, Conrad." I'm not sure I've had any takers. I was only on that cigar kick for a week but I'm having a time quitting now that I've started. I'll do it if I have to make a bonfire of all those cigars so I can't keep my fingers on them. It takes fortitude.

They're talking about moving part of the 1st Brigade somewhere in the near future if the enemy makes a move, according to Lt. Gen. Davidson. I could be where the action is. It's possible the move could start the day after tomorrow. I don't know what position this places the 1st Brigade PIO though I'll play it safe.

I did a story on scout dogs today. They have come up with a dog that is trained differently from the old types. He isn't on a leash and goes as far as 50 meters in front of a platoon, giving advanced warning of any NVA with evil intent. This requires a better-trained dog. Such a dog is King, a large 80 pound German Shepherd who's being given a new handler after his old one got a rear job as a truck driver. Supposedly he is "inquisitive, aggressive and raring to go" according to a lieutenant. I haven't heard much about the success of dog teams in the bush although they've been here since 1966. Our imported dogs has disease problems. The local Vietnamese dogs are immune or at least hardier than the imports.

Sp4 Marvin Butteris is from Mt. Vernon, Iowa [*where I spent several years in high school*] is the dog's handler. He knows many of the guys I knew in high school but was standoffish so we didn't talk long. His old dog caught a blood disease and is out of action for several weeks at least, so he got King. I remember his old dog Smokey because he nearly started a dogfight in a helicopter on a ride from Bien Hoa to FSB Green about a month ago.

I cleaned up my M-16 today, wiping and rubbing off the mud and rust. I'm going to try it out tomorrow. I haven't fired it since I hit country. It has the old style flash suppressor but it fires the same bullet at the same speed and is in no way inferior except that it has a bad habit of snagging vines as you trip through the jungle. It also tends to collect a wad of mud at the end of the barrel because the suppressor is like a stick with three prongs.

GI's Child; Water Point

November 19, 1970

I didn't write yesterday because I was recovering from a sunburn. I also was trapped up at Phuoc Vinh when I arrived from FSB Andre too late. I can't recall ever being in such hot sun without a way to escape. It must have been a hundred with high humidity out in the open on the firebase. It's getting really hot, probably like you experienced, Dad, in India.

I ran across a fellow whose wife gave birth two days before, a 6 pound 11 ounce girl. He didn't find out about it until two days later and was worried.

2. On Assignment: October 1, 1970, to December 31, 1970   97

This is the kind of spot young marrieds get into when forcefully separated by duty. Since he couldn't get his hands on cigars, we gave him one of mine and got a picture. He found out after the Red Cross in Phuoc Vinh gave a message to the Echo Company rear, which sent a courier on his regular morning run with the message. He's a radar operator, detailed digging postholes when his CO called him into his tent with the message. The guy was so relieved.

The other story is hardly a story. They have a water point at FSB Andre where they draw and filter water for base and grunt consumption. It's a little stream that they widened with C-4 explosives and every afternoon from two to four they have swimming time. It's about 300 yards down a road from where the firebase sits so they had part of Echo Recon pulling security. A couple of grunts were swimming in their birthday suits when we walked up to the swimming hole. They were supposed to be pulling security but didn't seem to be taking it very seriously; they paddled around, washing like they rarely could in the boonies. Big Dan Ramlow and I decided to take a dip. We each wanted a picture of the event to send home with us on an actual live firebase, swimming. The water was almost too shallow to keep him decent; I didn't want him to make a nudie magazine cover. With my vast height, it was no problem for me. The water was nice; this was the first time I had a chance to soak in water, before this it's been all showers. It was a refreshing break from the heat and sun. Even wars have their good times.

Let me read your letter and drink some Cutty Sark ($3.40 a bottle). As for your criticism of my writing, I think it's well founded. I do tend to overwrite. I've been trying all sorts of approaches to stories—I'll keep trying to improve. Some of my stories are rewritten so sometimes you're seeing only the remains of a story. They aren't very good at cutting back stories, often killing them in the attempt to fill a small space with a bigger story.

I spent today flying back to Bien Hoa and getting hot, not much else. This heat takes it out of me. Everyone else is in the same shape. Firebases are getting old—people are getting tired of our faces. The hot season is approaching. Your talks of winter setting in are so hard to envision when our hottest months, I'm told, are January and February. Doesn't sound right, does it?

Becomes Proud Papa

GIs worked to keep their attachments to home. Keeping close to the other side of the world and learning about big events presented major challenges. The December 9, 1970, Cavalair *used this story.*

FSB Andre—Many a nail has been bitten to the quick and many hurried letters of nervous encouragement have been sent by an American GI to a pregnant wife back home. There's a feeling of helplessness that can't be avoided, as the two are on opposite sides of the world. But more often than not, the outcome is a happy one.

So it was for PFC J.B. Runkle not long ago here. His wife, Martha, had told him the child should be born sometime in mid-November. The tension had been building up as the time fast approached.

The day of the news found Runkle on detail, digging holes for a fence around the TOC. He had just started to shovel when some told him the CO wanted to see him and the secret was out.

"A six pound, 11 ounce girl! Congratulate me! Wow, what a relief," yelled Runkle to a buddy. The Red Cross from Phuoc Vinh had sent a message to Echo Company rear, who sent the word out with a courier.

Like most GIs, he won't quite believe he's a father until he sees his child. "I can't wait to get a picture of her, see her when I go on R&R in February. Now I really have something to look forward to."

A Top Dog

We not only had dogs that were pets but working dogs that were valued combat companions. I located this article in the December 16, 1970, Cavalair.

BIEN HOA—Spec 4 Marvin Butteris, a dog handler in the 25th (Inf.) Scout Dog Platoon, lost his dog Smokey to a blood disease common to imported canines. At the same time, King, one of the sharpest dogs in the platoon, lost his handler, Spec. 4 Larry Patterson, when Patterson became a truck driver. So Butteris and King were paired up and a close new relationship has sprung.

"He was the honor dog in our class in the States," explained Butteris, "so I knew King even before I arrived in Vietnam. He's probably one of the best dogs in the platoon."

King is a large German Shepherd weighing about 80 lbs. 1st Lt. Arthur Bills, in charge of the 25th Scout Dog Pn., had nothing but praise for King. "He's definitely one of the best dogs we've got; he's aggressive, inquisitive and raring to go."

King is an off-the leash dog. "King will go 50 meters out in front of me," said Butteris, "as long as he can see me, depending on the terrain. He gives a warning earlier than Smokey, who worked only on a leash. He makes my job safer."

Butteris expects great things from King once they begin working together. "He's the kind of dog that works all the time, not just on a leash. And he's got a good record. His company never walked into anything. They got hit once from the rear, but that wasn't King's fault since the wind was wrong."

2. On Assignment: October 1, 1970, to December 31, 1970

Thoughts on Writing Home

My parents were both fine writers and commented on my efforts. Although I have every reason to believe they enjoyed what I mailed them immensely, I bet they were puzzled frequently. They told me my atrocious spelling provided them hours of amusement. Now that I'm editing my letters, I see what they put up with. I've softened my bluntness, tightened up my writing, and limit what is included. I had many moments however when I wrote well. I remain proud of how inquisitive I was.

93rd Evac; Medic; Rocket Casualties

November 20, 1970

I visited 93rd Evac Hospital again and picked up only one story. On the side, I picked up a release form from Perez for the story I did following my last visit; I didn't know I needed it when I first wrote the story. He's going to Japan in a week so he'll be in good hands. I needed his signature so that if he dies, they wouldn't be in danger because of the inappropriateness of a story about a dead man. It's not likely he'll die—he's healthy if I ever saw anybody who's healthy. A new PIO First Sergeant wanted this release policy backed up.

I found a story after talking to a medic in for an infected finger. He didn't mind the bush, said he got a certain pleasure from doing things for the grunts. He usually considers himself just another grunt. He was in a firefight recently. He's attached to Delta Company, 1st of the 7th Cav, and was in the thick of it. He admitted that in this firefight, because he had no big wounds to attend to, he fired about 35 magazines of ammunition from his M-16, about 600 rounds, although I won't mention that in my article. He says he usually has only 8 magazines on him but he was using other guys' ammo. Usually he doesn't fire. They had one Kit Carson scout killed outright.

The medic, in this man's eyes, is in a platoon to provide for treatment of skin diseases and keep morale up when they get into trouble. He says he enjoys the bush when there aren't firefights. He told me his point man really had his stuff together, in fact had probably saved his platoon. So I talked to the point man.

What a disappointment. I've never come across anybody in 'Nam I considered as screwed up as this fellow. The hospital's Cav representative told me earlier that this guy was a big mouth who I wouldn't want to talk to. Not realizing this was the same guy, I waded in. I asked him about the engagement and he gave me one half-ass quote before becoming hopeless. He admitted that his platoon had been outnumbered but that's all I got. He was totally inconsistent. He claimed to have been a demonstrator in the SDS and then said all those radicals ought to be locked up. He said he'd learned a lot in 'Nam he could use when he got back to the world. It's hard to get across what a disagreeable conversation this was. Most grunts, believe it or not, are gentlemen. This guy was the worst type of opinioned slob. I wished I'd paid attention to our representative and avoided him.

I tried to interview another GI and was embarrassed. He too had been walking point when his unit was hit. I knew I wasn't going to get much out of him when I saw the tube into his nose and the plastic and tape all over his stomach. He could barely talk. I just mumbled some inappropriate remarks and left.

I got some distressing news about the "light" casualties that the Air Force suffered from that attack, now they say by 107mm rockets. *Stars and Stripes* said the Post Commander described the casualties as light. It's true four men were killed but 18 men were injured. Four of the injured came to 93rd Evac. They were amputees and gut wounds, not minor things. These wounded were maimed for life, not "just" injured. I find it disgusting the military holds back information of what really happened to our men, to us.

I'm flying out tomorrow to Dacus, a new firebase, to look at some 8-inch guns they've driven in by road.

Medic's Job Includes Being "Just a Grunt"

A medic in battle had it—if it's possible—even worse than a regular grunt as they aided the wounded. In this case, being a regular grunt took precedence. This story was used in the December 16, 1970, Cavalair.

FSB DURALL—The medic has one of the most dangerous and demanding jobs in the bush. As the first link in an elaborate medical chain, he is expected to be in the thick of every dangerous situation. PFC Harvey Stringer recently had a chance to show how it is done.

As a member of Delta Co., 1st Bn. 7th Cav., Stringer found himself in the middle of a hot firefight. "Most of the wounded had shrapnel wounds. I was running back and forth patching up the guys as best I could while I dodged bullets," said Stringer.

Medics are usually thought of as non-combatants but Stringer backed away from this somewhat. "Medics usually don't shoot, but in this last firefight I shot up several magazines. All the men were patched up and I was in the thick of it so I fired back."

Stringer's attitude toward the other GIs in his company explains somewhat why he fired back. "When I'm not playing medic, I'm just another grunt."

In battle, his job is primarily one of determining who is hurt the worst and trying to give them first aid. The worst injury in the firefight was obvious in this case and there was nothing Stringer could do about it. "Our Kit Carson Scout was dead just after the encounter started. He was the only serious case; the other injuries were minor."

Are medics fearless? "Not really," indicated Stringer, "just sensible. I wasn't scared badly at first, but we all got worried when Charlie started hitting us from three sides. The third platoon came in on the enemy from another direction and the contact broke, but I was scared."

Stringer said he didn't mind the bush too much. "I like the bush, there's no hassle there. I kind of like it—when I'm not in a firefight, that is."

Volleyball; 8-Inch Guns

November 21, 1970

I just finished a game of volleyball and my stinking body is cooling. It's the national sport of Vietnam, you know, and the Americans have picked it up with relish. We have a few "refinements." You can stick a hand, body or foot over or through the net at any time. They're known as bush league rules or jungle rules. Injuries, suffered in these battles, are the inevitable result. It's fun and relaxing plus the body doesn't fatten up so fast.

We had a party up the road with a trailer full of beers and sodas on ice. Steaks were cooked over charcoal as the artillery mess hall was celebrating something, like being alive. They had an American band, which turned me off because they played jazz with no rhyme or reason to its beat. It was a good idea despite the band.

I got a look at some 8-inch guns and other miscellaneous equipment out at FSB Dacus. About $120,000 a gun, they aren't expensive by air machine standards. It's the most accurate weapon within its artillery class in Vietnam. The 175mm gun shoots farther with a longer barrel but isn't so accurate. These large guns are used to break open bunkers and provide smashing support for ground troops. There are two of these huge self-propelled guns out there. The other half of the battery—both 175mm guns—are in Phuoc Vinh. Each round weighs about 200 pounds. They have several men out there who can carry a round alone. The gun loads itself once the rounds and powder are put into the feed pan. It's quite an instrument although I still can't understand why they set them up way up in nowhere—the Army must be up to something.

To drive in the big guns, which can only come by ground, several squads from the engineers were brought in to clear an old grown-over French-built road. Something large was needed to knock down the trees in the way. For this purpose the engineers have the D-9, the biggest dozer in Vietnam; there are only four of them in the whole country. The D-9 belongs to a road-clearing battalion and can flatten any tree in the jungle. It reminds me more of a tank than a dozer. It weighs 56 tons.

They had a wild time making it down the road. It took five hours to take the convoy down the road with the D-9 clearing a path despite the engineers spending five days before messing with the road. They'd swept the road for mines and Delta, 2nd of the 7th Cav pulled security on the road. At one spot, the road hit water so they brought in a chassis of a Sherman tank and the parts to a portable armor vehicle launching bridge (AVLB). It folded off the tank and uncoupled. Armor has always fascinated me. Two dusters, light fast tanks, were posted at each end of the firebase when I got there. I've never come across a forward base like this one.

A firebase volleyball game shows how jungle rules are applied.

This week's paper is out. It was a slow week for me, only one story in it. I'm sending the whole issue. Our brigade has a lot of pictures but Brown got only one story in and no byline. I don't think the photos this week were all that great. I like the cartoons inside. This issue as a whole wastes considerable space: not the dinner menu (page one), Christmas cards (page two) and all of page seven. Maybe I'll have to pick up the camera again so I can get more in the paper. Photography is so much easier than writing because we only take the pictures and someone else does the lab work. I haven't been sluffing off; my lack of exposure is just bad luck.

2. On Assignment: October 1, 1970, to December 31, 1970

Americans can be such disgusting bigots—American soldiers often treat the local Vietnamese shabbily. Part of the problem is that the South Vietnamese aren't trusted any more than the North Vietnamese. To the typical hooch mates or bar girls at the clubs around here, the only words they must recognize are insults, the four letter words and worse. The most typical remark from a GI is a contemptuous, "Ah, shut up, gook!" After one particularly repulsive encounter between a loud mouthed GI and a bar girl, I gave a pained look at the fellow standing next to me and he seemed to understand. "We've only made things worse by being over here," he said sadly.

It's growing hard for me to work—everyone seems to be trying to sap what little initiative I've got. And the weather doesn't help. Time is galloping along when I stay active so I'm going to cultivate one of my stronger traits, my perseverance. I may not be the smartest guy here but I'm determined and relentless. I've been reading about picking up jobs in the States and chances of getting a job doesn't look so hot. Maybe the Army is the best place for me right now. Tomorrow I'm going to write and relax.

ALPHA CO. BULLDOZES HEAVY GUNS THROUGH JUNGLE ROAD

Giant machines have always fascinated me, all the way back to my wanting to be a "choo-choo train" engineer as a boy. Because we primarily worked with comparatively small helicopters, I enjoyed getting my teeth into really big contraptions for the December 16, 1970, Cavalair.

FSB DACUS—As a pioneer in moving men and supplies by helicopter, the 1st Cav take air mobility somewhat for granted. Problems arise, however, when something like a giant artillery piece, uncarryable by any present day chopper, is needed deep in the jungle.

Alpha Co., 8th Engineer Bn., with a collection of huge specialized machines demonstrated recently how it done by opening a French road to FSB Dacus, so that two 8-inch guns could be moved to the remote outpost.

The D-9, a 56-ton bulldozer, was the backbone of the operation. Recently introduced in Vietnam, it has the power to fell any tree in the jungle. Its operator, Spec. 5 Fremont "Rocky" Staples, said of his machine, "The cab is heavily reinforced or I would spend all my time dodging trees."

Another unusual contraption was an Armor Vehicle Launched Bridge (AVLB) mounted on the body of a Sheridan tank. At one critical point, the road was washed out. The AVLB was driven up, the bridge released, and another problem was solved.

With two dusters providing security, the convoy of three deuce-and-a-halves, a D-7 bulldozer, a portable command post, a recovery vehicle, two 8-inch guns and the D-9 pushed down the overgrown jungle road.

"There were a lot of soft spots and mud holes in the road," recalled SSgt. Steven Reynolds. "We were nervous because there were many spots perfect for placing mines."

Part of the game of jungle warfare is surprise and certainly nothing could be more surprising to the enemy than the bellow of the big guns delivering their payloads to an ill-fated customer. Now, thanks to the engineers, infantrymen in the 1st Cav's area of operation will have extremely accurate pieces of heavy artillery on call.

Example of Our Newspaper

The issue of our division newspaper, the Cavalair, *I referred to follows. It's dated after the letter but otherwise fits well. This layout is pretty typical, other than the spread of our cartoonist's work, which was present only periodically. We had a provocative picture of a pretty girl in each issue, to remind us of what we were missing. When I sent magazines home, I would scrawl comments to my parents critiquing the issue.*

Smoking Pot

November 23, 1970

The pot party was the story that CBS news team picked up at FSB Ares; the Chieu Hois were just a smoke screen, unplanned but effective. I haven't seen fellows on firebases floating in a cloud of marijuana smoke but then, I've only started visiting water points. I know it's bad in the rear. It's funny, while the U.S. tries to impose its laws on the GIs, the Vietnamese peddle all kinds of hard drugs freely and legally.

Addicted; Dog in Heat

November 24, 1970

Several of us were talking about this guy in our office who is a drug freak of some kind. He's not big, shaggy and imposing but small and slouched with an aimless stare. He loves smoking dew but we think he's hooked on stronger stuff. He has said he'd quit shooting heroin when he got back to the States. He reportedly said, "Do you know how much it costs over there? Hundreds of times more." We think he'll have a hell of a time quitting.

Our hooch pooch Blanche is in heat. She had a litter of pups a month before I came and is at it again. All the males in the neighborhood are after her body. She's enjoying the attention but is always fighting, keeping most of the males at a distance. We have no idea what we will do with her new puppies.

NVA Rice Cache Falls To Cav

Cache was the magic word in the 1st Air Cav's area of operations during the week ending Nov. 8, with rice in the spotlight.

A seven and one-half ton rice cache find–the largest uncovered since the Cambodian operation–was found by Skytroopers from Bravo Company, 5th Battalion, 7th Cavalry, 18 miles northeast of Song Be, on Nov. 8.

While conducting ground reconnaissance along a suspected enemy infiltration route, the unit spotted two huts under the triple canopied jungle overhead.

Concealed within each structure were 30 100-pound bags of rice, totaling 6000 pounds. The rice find was well preserved in burlap bags under the protection of the buildings.

A steady stream of ralliers continued to pour into First Team firebases throughout Cav Country, as 81 individuals quit the enemy–rallying to the GVN.

Regional Forces units, operating with the 1st Air Cav south of FSB Cheyenne, received a large group of 52 ralliers at the village of Va Dat. The individuals indicated that they were from the village of Te Le and that the village was under the control of a small number of VC soldiers.

Delta Company, 5th Battalion of the 7th Cavalry received 29 ralliers while operating near FSB Snuffy. The area surrounding Snuffy has produced hundreds of ralliers during the past several weeks. All of the ralliers were moved to Song Be following initial processing. They will be provided land and homes in one of the several "New Life Hamlets" located near Song Be.

In other significant action during the week, Echo Recon, 1st Battalion 7th Cavalry–on two consecutive days–staged two successful stay-behind ambushes on the site of the newly closed FSB Green.

In the first contact of the morning of the 4th, Echo Recon spotted five individuals. They engaged the enemy with small arms and called in aerial artillery. Following the brief encounter, a sweep of the area disclosed one VC KIA.

Again the following morning, the recon element observed five enemy soldiers approaching the now deserted fire base. The ensuing engagement resulted in two NVA KIA's.

Continuing to sweep the contact area, the men of the 7th Cav located a heavy blood trail. A Combat Tracker team was inserted and followed the trail through dense jungle. Although failing to track down the wounded enemy soldier, the team captured an NVA demolitions bag.

In the final action of the reporting period, an element of Bravo Company, 5th Battalion of the 7th Cavalry, detained one NVA wounded in an earlier encounter, near fire base Snuffy. The detainee was evacuated to Song Be for further interrogation.

CAUTIOUS ADVANCE – PFC Steven Durham, armed with an M-60 machinegun, checks out the main bunker of a complex as Spec. 4 Arnold Pereya and Danh-Tu, the unit's Kit Carson Scout, provide security. The complex was uncovered by 1st Air Cav Skytroopers nine kilometers east of FSB Pershing. (US Army Photo by PFC Daniel Ramlow)

Vol 4 No 46   1st Air Cavalry Division, Republic of Vietnam   November 25, 1970

'People Sniffer' Picks Up People Smells, Not People

"One of the things the Airborne Personnel Detector (People Sniffer) absolutely cannot do is smell people," according to Lt. Col. James L. Templeton, division chemical officer of the 1st Air Cavalry Division.

And although the sniffer is still relatively new, it is still not a cure-all, said Col. Templeton, but it is valuable in conjunction with other instruments in obtaining intelligence information, and it is used extensively throughout the 1st Air Cav.

Other things the Sniffer cannot do is count people, and differentiate between man and animal.

Capt. Fred Smith, assistant division chemical officer, explained the workings of the Sniffer as "picking up things associated with man–gasoline exhaust from engines, cooking fires, personnel smoking and personnel engaged in the acts of working or moving." He noted that carbon particles, emitted when something is being burned, are one of the best indicators. He added that carbon traces emitted when the 1st Cav blew up enemy munitions captured at the massive Rock Island East Cache area in Cambodia, were picked up five days later.

"But usually the Sniffer operation produces more indirect evidence of the enemy's presence," Smith said. "Continuous Sniffer readings in an area have normally been backed up by other intelligence sources.

Col. Templeton explained the Sniffer as "a rather compicated detection device designed to collect and analyze air samples for the presence of particles which are normally associated with human activity."

Detects The Unusual

As air enters the Sniffer machine through a flexible hose attached to the bottom of a Huey Slick helicopter, it is analyzed immediately for the presence of matter which shouldn't be there unless something interesting is happening under the greenery.

The 1st Air Cav now has six Sniffer units, operated by the 184th Chemical Platoon under the command of Capt. Robert Parker. A machine is assigned to each of the Cav's three brigades while one is used out of the Cav's Phuoc Vinh Division headquarters by Division Artillery. Two other machines are kept as back-ups and maintenance floats. Each machine in operation is assigned to a chemical contact team which flies with it and analyzes the data it feeds out.

The machines can be installed in a slick in about five minutes and removed in the same length of time, allowing the Sniffer teams to conduct about 350 missions per month in the dry season, and about half that number during the rainy season.

Sniffer readings have resulted in numerous contacts with the enemy. 1st Lt. Kenneth W. Carr, assistant Brigade Chemical

(Cont'd on Back Page)

Thaksgiving Dinner Menu

This year's Thanksgiving dinner in Cav Country will feature all of the traditional goodies including roast turkey, dressing, mashed and sweet potatoes along with the ever popular mincemeat and pumpkin pies.

While the menu may vary slightly from place to place, here's what the gourmet's table should look like tomorrow:

Shrimp Cocktail	Hot Rolls
Crackers	Butter
Roast Turkey	Fruitcake
Cornbread Dressing	Mincemeat Pie
Turkey Gravy	Pumpkin Pie
Cranberry Sauce	Assorted Nuts
Mashed Potatoes	Assorted Candy
Glazed Sweet Potatoes	Assorted Fresh Fruit
Buttered Mixed Vegetables	Iced Tea with Lemon
Assorted Crisp Relishes	Milk

WAITING GAME – PFC Billy Pash of 2nd Platoon, Company B, 2nd Battalion, 7th Cavalry looks for movement in a tunnel leading to a bunker in the complex found nine kilometers east of FSB Pershing. (US Army Photo by PFC Daniel Ramlow)

War Stories

CAV CHRISTMAS CARDS FOR SALE – AND PLEASE MAIL YOUR CARDS AND PACKAGES EARLY! The First Team Gift Shop is selling beautifully colored Christmaas cards–pictured above–at $.50 for a box of ten.

Also available at a new adjusted price of $3.00 is the 1st Cav's Yearbook. By the way the 1970 CONUS Christmas mailing deadlines for APO located in RVN are listed below.

Items must be mailed prior to dates indicated in order to insure delivery prior to Christmas Day for Non-CONUS addresses. It is highly advisable for Skytroopers to mail early to avoid the tremendous last-minute rush.

SAM Parcels (Space Available Air) . . . . Dec 4
PAL (parcel Airlift) . . . . Dec 7
SAM letters (Space Available) . . . . Dec 10
Airmail . . . . Dec 12

General Forsythe Heads Volunteer Army Project

WASHINGTON (ANF) – Lt. Gen. George L. Forsythe, former commanding general of the 1st Air Cavalry in Vietnam from February 1969 to May 1969, has been assigned as special assistant for the modern volunteer Army, Secretary of Defense Melvin Laird made the announcement recently.

In his new position, Gen. Forsythe is responsible for raising "to the maximum extent possible the number of enlistments and reenlistments in both the Active Army and Reserve Components." He reports directly to Secretary of the Army Stanley R. Resor and Gen. W.C. Westmoreland, Army chief of staff.

Appointing Gen. Forsythe to this position is one of the first steps taken by the Army to reach the target of zero draft calls by the end of fiscal year 1973.

Gen. Forsythe served as commanding general, U.S. Army Combat Developments Command before assuming his new duties. He is succeeded by Lt. Gen. John Norton, who had been serving as deputy director, Project MASSTER, Ft. Hood, Tex.

Thanksgiving Message

Almost 350 years have passed since the Pilgrims paused to commemorate the bounty of the autumn harvest on the first Thanksgiving Day. In the same spirit of brother hood and humility, let us offer thanks for the freedom which we have preserved in the Republic of Vietnam during this past year. As Americans, we too often take for granted our own nation's peace and liberty – these are the same blessings which have been denied the people of Vietnam for so many years.

W. J. McCAFFREY
Lieutenant General, US Army
Deputy Commanding General

For God... And Country

by Chaplain (LTC) John C. Borley

In quietness and in thrust shall be your strength...Isaiah 30:15

Frequently men in the barracks who have problems will say, "I've tried everything I can think of and nothing seems to help. What should I do? Much to their surprise, the best answer is not to do anything in a hurry.

The first step in overcoming the destructive emotions of worry, fear, tension, and anxiety is to "be still." God has given each one of us a tremendous reservoir of inner strength and wisdom, and all we have to do is use it.

The psalmists said, "Be still and know." In other words, be still and believe–believe that God has put within you a hidden power that can be summoned to your aid whenever you find yourself struggling to overcome a personal difficulty.

A few years ago, a friend told me that he didn't have any tensions because he had learned to sit loose. At the time I thought his statement was rather humorous, but now, I believe that it is good to sit loose before acting.

If we learn to master this simple lesson, we will not make the error of magnifying everyday problems until they are all out of proportion. If we say to ourselves, "Easy does it!" then we will be able to collect our thoughts in order to act rationally in every situation.

Point Man Catches Enemy Round In Grenade, Walks Away From It

by SSgt Lee Graham

FSB MACE – The old expression "...a funny thing happened to me on the way to..." now has a deadly serious meaning for PFC Daniel Sileo.

The 3d platoon of Delta Company, 2nd Battalion, 5th Cavalry, 1st Air Cav was on its way to link up with the company's 2d platoon which had encountered heavy contact in a bunker complex some three kilometers away. Upon moving toward the 2D platoon, Sgt William Lent, a squad leader, warned the platoon–"We'll probably get contact on the way to the second platoon."

Sure enough, 500 meters later the platoon was fired upon by an enemy soldier with an M-16 rifle.

Sileo was walking point and a round hit a fragmentation grenade he was carrying on his pistol belt.

He and his slack man, Spec. 4 Ronald Waerzeggers, immediately hit the ground and before they could return fire, the enemy had fled after firing on them.

Sileo said, "I was really scared when I discovered that the round lodged in a frag. To think it came that close to me and the frag didn't go off gives one the feeling that was the closest I've ever come to getting hit."

Sileo has been in the field since September and said that he's not ready for any more "close calls."

CAV ASSOC RICHER – CSM James W. Maddox, middle 1st Battalion, 5th Cavalry presents a $500.80 check to the First Team's scholarships Business Manager, 1LT Allan Epstein. Lt.Col. Bill Burkhardt, commanding officer of the 1st of the 5th, looking on from the side, initiated the drive to raise the money in memory of two deceased members of the unit.

2. On Assignment: October 1, 1970, to December 31, 1970

Tahn Linh Chieu-Hois Tell Of Success Of PSYOPS

by PFC Alan Saralecos

VO DAT — As the deuce-and-a-half pulled up to the Chieu-Hoi Center, the ralliers began unloading with looks of unsureness in their eyes and faces sunburnt and crusty with sweat-hardened dirt.

On the evening of November 3, the 57 Montagnards rallied to an RF (Regional Force-company on operations north of Tanh Linh. They were brought to Vo Dat and three days later were joined by seven additional ralliers who also rallied to the RFs in the same area.

As the ralliers began to adjust to their new surroundings, and the initial shock of being among the steel-helmeted, armed soldiers began to subside, the ralliers began to tell their story in bits and pieces.

Most were residents of Tanh Linh hamlet, they said. Many

"From information we have received from the ralliers, the broadcasts were understood by all the people in the area."

"Other operations in the area have shown leaflet drops played a large roll," Cooper said. "Fifteen 'Chieu Hoi' leaflets were found in a bunker complex in the area."

Bring Belonging

The ralliers brought most of their worldly possessions with them; they included a few crude, homemade tools, some well-worn and torn clothes and pots that showed years of use trying to prepare rice, roots and vegetables to provide some nutrition to their growling bellies.

The livestock also came along. Four pigs which were crated for the journey by using bamboo which was woven around them, and a chicken whose crating was the same as if someone was crating a prized dog for shipment.

After interrogation, the ralliers were sent to the Chieu Hoi center in Ham Tam where they would be sent out to re-settlement camps to begin a new life. This life will include shelter, land to grow food and medical help to cure the disease and malnutrition acquired through years of running and hiding beneath the jungle canopy

were in need of medical care, including a large number of women with babies and the aged ones who seemed to mirror the war-torn history of their homeland in their sun-grooved faces.

Throw In Towel

They were tired of being laborers for the Viet Cong and growing rice and vegetables to support communist operations while their own families often went hungry. They were tired of fighting, tired of sleepless nights, tired of trying to rake a life out of soil that knew only failure and hardship. They were people who had "thrown in the towel."

PSYOPS activity played a major role in their decision to rally, according to 1st Lt. John M. Cooper S-5 officer for the 1st Air Cavalry Division's 3rd Brigade. Cooper said, "Generally speaking, the morale of the village was low, due to improper diet and lack of medical supplies."

As part of their round-the-clock PSYOPS program, the 1st Cav's 3rd Brigade flew missions over the area of the ralliers' former homes every day. "PSYOPS broadcasts and leaflet drops played a significant part in leading the people of the hamlet to rally," said Cooper.

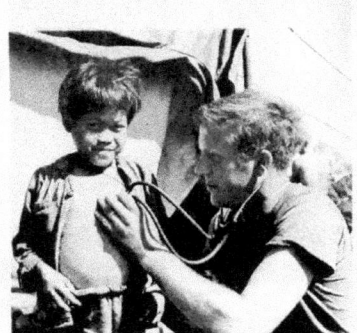

IT TICKLES — Youngster who came in with ralliers at FSB Durall gets a checkup from Capt. Peter E. Dixon. (US Army Photo by Spec. 5 Rodney Plant)

Former Medic Says

Drugs Are Fun...For Awhile

(Editor's note--This is the first of two articles on drugs, both written for the CAVALAIR by a former combat medic. In this first article he discusses various drugs and the second takes a look at the amnesty program.)

by Spec. 4 Stef Gubar

"Yeah, but we know all that ju___ — too often the answer when many of us are confronted with another newspaper article on marijuana is called dew, grass, pot, Cambodian red and a variety of other terms. But the facts about the weed, whose botanical name is Cannabis Sativa, are not so well known. And it is probably the form of dope most GIs will first come in contact with during their Vietnam tours.

Most GIs have heard that marijuana is not physically addicting. This is true, although the user may develop a psychological dependence out it. This means that the marijuana smoker would much rather be high all the time than refrain from marijuana. When he does stop smoking he becomes depressed and immediately lights another "J."

Everyone has heard that the use of grass leads to the use of hard drugs. This is not necessarily true. But it is true that the majority of hard drug users began using grass. Not everyone will graduate to hard drugs; the question is who will not be one of those who do?

Regardless, marijuana remains illegal. This is probably the biggest argument for not using cannabis weed. Federal law states that the use of possession of marijuana is a crime, punishable by 10 years imprisonment and a $20,000 fine. Under military law, the offender faces court-martial, up to five years in prison and a dishonorable discharge.

The law also frowns on the use of lysergic acid diethylamide, commonly known as acid and LSD. How this drug works on the brain is not known. Experiments were being made using acid as a cure for asthma and organic diseases. The experiments stopped when the results of the use of acid were revealed. With just one trip the

user can destroy enough chromosomes in his body to cause his offspring to be born deformed.

Some acid users have not returned from their trips.

Speed kills--and not just on the highway. Speed is an amphetamine in many forms. It speeds up the heart beat and all other body functions. The user is pepped up and cannot sleep or ___ ___ ___ is that it destroys a tremendous amount of brain cells, which cannot be repaired.

The opposite of speed is found in the barbiturate drugs. They're downers. They slow down your body. These drugs, when used with alcohol, are the most dangerous. The biggest problem with barbs is coming down. This withdrawal is more dangerous and painful that that caused by any other drug. Barbs

include nembutal, seconal and many others commonly known as reds, yellows or blue heavens.

The last group of narcotics include the opiates, heroin, cocaine, opium and others. The opiates cause the degeneration of all cells. Even if it is only smoked, the opiate is addictive because it causes a drop in the blood sugar level as well as other effects. The average life span of ___ ___ ___ ___ ___ from ___ ___ will die of an overdose or be killed trying to get money to support his habit.

These drugs are the most common in use in Vietnam. All these drugs are capable of providing the user with a euphoric feeling, of a way of getting away from it all, but the offsetting debate to this is: Is it worth it, considering what one might have to pay for it later?

U.S. Dog, RVN Chicken

Lead Troops To Rice Find

FSB CHEYENNE — An American dog and a Vietnamese chicken teamed up to lead a platoon of 1st Air Cavalry Division Skytroopers to a large enemy rice cache near here recently.

A squad-sized element of Bravo Company, 2nd Battalion, 5th Cavalry, on patrol near this fire support base of the 1st Cav's

3rd Brigade, discovered signs of recent enemy activity as close as 100 meters from the base perimeter. Several spider holes and hootches were found with pots, pans and miscellaneous items in them.

The following day, a dog team was brought in and Bravo Company's 3rd platoon further searched the area. The platoon leader, 1st Lt. John D. McLaughlin, Jr., said that the dog, Caesar, alerted a chicken. The chicken flew off into the jungle brush, and when the dog and the Skytroopers gave chase, they came upon the rice storehouse.

According to PFC Bruce Congo, the storehouse was well-camouflaged and even had a padlocked door which the Skytroopers pried open. Congo said that part of the roof was also lifted to get to the rice.

Capt. Charles E. Wells, commanding officer of Bravo Company, assigned a squad-size ambush to cover the cache overnight in case the enemy returned to the area, but no activity took place.

The following day, the rice was loaded into 44 bags, and trees were cut back so that a Chinook helicopter could extract the rice from the jungle.

Lt. Col Leonard P. Wishart III, 2nd of the 5th's commander, explained that the ricywas donated to refugees at the Vo Dat Chieu Hoi Center.

SSgt. Gene Grimm, platoon sergeant of the 3rd platoon, added that this was the biggest rice cache found by his company since the Cav entered Cambodia.

WELCOME VISITOR — Sgt. Ted Yoshimura guided log bird in as it arrives to resupply 1st Cav Skytroopers of Company D, 2nd Battalion, 7th Cavalry at the FSB Pershing. (US Army Photo by Spec. 5 Rodney Plant)

The CAVALAIR 3
Nov 25, 1970

FSB Jupiter; Vietnamese Tour; Heroin Addict

November 25, 1970

I flew out to firebase Ares today because I couldn't reach a small firebase near Ares called FSB Jupiter. I got lucky, they were sending troops from Ares to Jupiter, so I got there at 2 p.m.—late.

There was a group of 8 Vietnamese officers, headed by a Lt. Colonel, who were visiting the 1st Brigade. Escorted by an American Lt. Colonel, they were given a two day introduction to airmobile operations. They watched from the air as troops Charlie Alphaed into Jupiter. At the start there was only a "command vault" as they called it "constructed" by an air strike. By the time I arrived the visitors were at Jupiter itself surveying the place. They probably won't have a chance to use this knowledge because they are being trained to be battalion commanders of armored cavalry groups—tanks. I talked to one of the Vietnamese who spoke passable English. He was impressed by what a huge amount of territory that just one brigade could cover. I had a sense they were telling me what they think I want to hear, not what they think.

I got to talk to the engineers who open up firebases, maintain firebases and destroy them at the end. There were only four of them out there today blowing trees. They had their work cut out for them. They had C-4 sitting all over, wrapped around trees and they had a forest of trees to blow. The

2. On Assignment: October 1, 1970, to December 31, 1970

ROTOR WASH

SKYKING-Fast Service

PHUOC VINH -- "Are you working, sir, are you working?...SKYKING 5, sir...SCORPION? ...Ringing, sir...Did you reach SCORPION? ...Roger that, sir..."

Sound familiar? This jocular jive belongs to Buckeye PFC Ronald Dawkins, one of the 20 operators who manipulate SKYKING switchboard, the bustling First Team manual telephone office.

Working in eight-hour shifts, three operators supervised by a team chief are on duty at all times. They route more than 3500 calls daily.

"Keeping up with the heavy volume of traffic is a daily challenge," maintains Switchboard Foreman Spec. 6 Robert Heinritz, "but we pride ourselves in processing most normal drops within five seconds and priority drops, which light up green on the board, in less than three. Rarely must a subscriber wait more than ten seconds for service."

SKYKING switch can provide service to any major U.S. command in Vietnam. Most calls, however, are placed to First Team subordinate units via either multipair cable in Camp Gorvad or by VHF radio shots to distant firebases.

"One of the most satisfying services we perform is patching the grunts to a MARS station," discloses 1st Lt. Thomas Gerken. "From a remote basecamp, a GI, using an ordinary field phone connected to the SKYKING system, can chat for five minutes with his family or friends back in the world."

As of September 1, SKYKING switch has re-directed more than a million calls over a one year span, a conspicuous achievement for a division system.

"We may not be Bell Telephone just yet," acknowledges operator Spec. 4 Francis Murphy, "but we're trying."

CPO Monitors All LNs

PHUOC VINH -- Monitoring the nearly 1000 civilian hired personnel is a task that makes life a little easier for those who both work on the installation.

All local nationals on the installation except those who work for PA&E, the PX, and the 31st Engr Bn are monitored by the office.

According to Lt. W.L. Jenkins, the office is also responsible for the paying of all direct hire personnel, supervising the coming and going of all civilians through the south gate, and keeping records of all permanent hires.

There are approximately 110 direct hire personnel working on the installation that are paid by the office. Included in this group are KP's, secretaries, nurses, dental assistants and female searchers. All the other workers that include between 350 and 400 housemaids and some 490 daily hires are paid by the units that they work for.

To help combat smuggling and unauthorized personnel from entering the compound, all civilian workers enter and leave the area through the south gate where they are searched and their ID's are checked.

According to PFC Laddie Hula, there is very little trouble with smugglers. When a smuggler is apprehended he is turned over to the Provost Office for legal action and barred from the post.

An access and barred record is kept on all permanent hire personnel.

Lt. Jenkins stressed that his office is not responsible for the hiring and firing of the workers. This is done by the individual units.

Free Holiday Greetings

PHUOC VINH -- 1st Cav soldiers will be able to get a bit nearer home for Christmas this year. Instead of the usual letter or snapshot, they can now send voice recordings of film clips to their home town radio and TV stations.

These personal messages can be recorded at the Radio-TV section of the Phuoc Vinh Information Office, located in Building 7785 in the Headquarters and Headquarters Company Area. Anyone wishing to utilize the service may drop by from 8:30 to 11:30 a.m.

The service is free and there is a 30 second limit on tapes and film clips. Opportunity to send these personal messages is provided by the U.S. Army Home Town News Center, Kansas City, Mo. through its annual "Holiday Greeting Program."

Last year the center distributed more than 4,500 Christmas releases to local radio and TV stations requesting its "hometowner" service.

6 The CAVALAIR
Nov 25, 1970

Skytrooperess Of Week

BOXED IN -- Our lovely lass this week appears to be a girl who enjoys that "boxed in" feeling. She is miss Susanne Benton, starring in "Cover Me Babe." (Photo courtesy of 20th Century Fox Studios.)

Cav's High Wire Act 'Digs In'

By Spec. 4 Dave Moore

FSB MACE – "We had a man fall today. He dropped about 15 feet, but he caught himself before he hit the ground, and he wasn't hurt."

According to SSgt. James Moors, the job of the wireman has its dangers. "Just about anybody who climbs poles sooner or later gets lax and has a fall." He says, "there's one thing you have to keep in mind; you have to be sure to dig in–especially when you are going up." Moors refers to the use of steel spurs which the lineman wears against the inside of each foot. The man keeps his grip on the poles by digging the spurs in as he climbs.

During the past few weeks, however, the linemen of the wire section, commo platoon, Headquarters and Headquarters Co., 3rd Brigade, 1st Air Cav Div, have also been 'digging in' in another sense. These men are presently digging in on the job of providing a new communications network for all of FSB Mace.

"It's going to be a complete rewiring," says Moors who works as wire section chief. The newly functional system that was put up in a hurry when the 1st Cav's 3rd Brigade moved out to Mace is being replaced. "What we are installing now," says Moors, "is a more permanent operational cable system."

To facilitate the new system, the men of the wire section are working long hours laying multi-line communication cable, erecting new utility poles and stringing commo wire. According to Moors, the entire rewiring should take about three weeks. "The whole section's been working hard," Moors states and he tells how the wire section worked daily to maintain communication lines despite the wind and rain of a tropical typhoon which recently swept through the area.

When the communications system is complete, the wire section will be maintaining more than 100 telephone lines besides hook-ups to long range VHF systems and the MARS network.

In addition to their responsibility for the brigade's communications network, the wire section also strings most of the lines which carry electrical power from the centrally-located generators to other points within the firebases perimeter.

U.S. Army Photos by PFC Ron Russo

landing zone was the poorest I've seen in some time and the trees big. They kept moving from firebase to firebase building berms. It's hard work but their time must move quickly. They don't like choppers around until they can get the woods pushed back far enough so the flying debris doesn't bite the skin. One said he'd been on thirty firebases a month during the dry season.

Our heroin addict was at it last night. I went out at 2 a.m. to relieve myself and there he was, kneeling with his needle. He asked me if I was surprised. I told him I wasn't. He kept turning the light on after asking me for a lighter, which I lent him to get him off my back. I went back to bed and ten minutes later heard him throw up. I talked to Ed Howard, our Black ex–Chicago cop. I asked him if he thought our guy is an addict. "Yea, I've seen too many of them in Chicago." This guy is hiding down here from the officers in Phuoc Vinh—he awaits his court martial for leaving guard duty. He's a total loss to the Army and probably will be not better when he gets out. He ingratiated us with FSSE (Forward Support Service Element), a group of really fine drinking buddies of mine in the hooch next door, by stealing one of their mattresses. He never seems to go to bed and is constantly asking for things in the middle of the night. We will rid the hooch of him tomorrow if he doesn't leave peacefully. He's not the violent type thankfully.

I'm beginning to think that Vietnam is an invaluable experience for me—I'm getting the chance to meet everyone from princes to bums. No one from now on can accuse me of being a shallow inexperienced small town boy and get away with it. I haven't quit either cigar smoking (totally anyway) or volleyball. I'm a smelly mess from both habits.

Black Hats; Dangerous Drunk; Sandy Pad

November 26, 1970

I talked to some black hats (flight controllers) at Jupiter yesterday who had been at Ares when the CBS pot party broke and after. They even knew the guys in the show. One of them watched the whole thing and thought it was a gas. They thought grass smoking was okay—it isn't the cardinal sin some oldsters think. It's not nearly as dangerous as an aggressive drunk, I'm convinced, after an episode at FSSE last night.

Yesterday evening I talked to a new guy at the FSSE hooch who comes from southern Missouri. He seemed a nice enough guy, telling me how he missed his trap line and his Missouri hunting grounds. He was a proud new father—his wife had just had a baby boy. He was proud of how unfaithful he'd been with his wife and what a great fighter he was. I had enough sense not to test him on anything controversial. We were drinking away. He was working on a bottle of bourbon. One of the virtues of FSSE drinking sessions is that, even if the boys get drunk and get to arguing, everything remains peaceful. The Missouri guy blew it.

Mike Blackwell, a fellow from Maine, was up and the Missouri guy polluted out of his gourd. Mike was helping him back to the hooch when the other fellow pulled out a knife and started playing with it. Mike was shocked and called a couple of the other guys. The drunk kept them back with the switchblade, said he was mad because he was just a jeep driver. SFC Stalder, the NCOIC (non-commissioned officer in charge), tried to reason with the guy. The drunk ran out the door and threw his knife against the building. They finally got the guy back to a room where he crashed in bed. Next morning, well guarded, he was led off to a more secure area where someone can keep him more on a leash but not in the stockade.

I've had no trouble from pot smokers, even heroin addicts, at least not to the point of them threatening to attack me. I can't believe that marijuana is any more dangerous than alcohol. This is not to say that drugs like heroin can't render people pretty worthless.

I couldn't get out to FSB Jupiter today so I wrote a story about FSSE and the red hats and what their ground workers do. They control the hook (Chinook) pad where I'm always getting rides. They support the 1st Brigade. I took a lot of pictures.

I had a GREAT Thanksgiving meal, the best I've had in Vietnam. I was

Hovering Chinooks with crews hooking loads were a common sight on helicopter pads.

Top: Cargo and GIs are loading into the back of a Chinook. Several mules are lined up—they may have been going on the flight too. *Bottom:* The 1st Cav's band is coming out of a Chinook.

so stuffed I didn't eat supper. Our volleyball game was the usual knockdown drag-out dog fight that we all love. I was returning balls with my head. I've caught on now—you've got to be merciless and aggressive, fearing neither net nor opponent. Great fun. I'm thinking of what it must be like back in the cold although today was a good day, not too hot.

Pad Serves 1st Brigade

Moving troops and supplies by air was a complex undertaking. A key element was a staging area—a helicopter pad. According to the comment I scrawled across the newspaper, this article was heavily rewritten—shortened probably. It was in the December 16, 1970, Cavalair.

BIEN HOA—The gigantic rotor blades of the Chinook churn the air as the helicopter struggles to lift off the supply pad with its load of artillery pieces or soda pallets dangling beneath its belly. In a few moments, the bird is airborne and heading with its cargo toward a distant firebase.

This is a common enough sight in the 1st Air Cav., but what about the day-to-day activities at the supply pads where the big air machines come to pick up their cargoes? Sandy Pad is one of those places. Amidst a sprawling complex of supply yards, Sandy Pad handles everything from fuel bladders to grunts heading out to the bush.

"As one of the groups supporting the 1st Brigade, we see most of the supplies going out to the firebases," explained Spec. 4 Mike Blackwell, an RTO air traffic handler of the 1st Forward Service and Support Element (FSSE).

On a typical day, Spec 4 Alan Richmond orchestrates the activities of the incoming birds with the red hats, the supply handlers and hookup specialist. Log representatives check the nets to make sure that everything is going out that was called for.

The 1st Air Cav. Band, flown out earlier in the day, comes in by Chinook. From the control tower, the musicians look like small animated dolls as they walk off the bird.

Another hook comes in with a load of mules, the four wheeled variety. The mules are driven out of the Chinook amid the fumes of its jet engines, and within minutes, passengers scramble aboard and the big bird is gone.

As a part of the vast American supply network, Sandy Pad is helping keep the 1st Brigade's lifeline open.

New Lieutenant

November 29, 1970

My chances of promotion appear to be zero. There are three times as many Spec 4s as PFCs—they don't need any more Spec 4s. As allocations get fewer and more names added to the list, I get pushed farther to the rear. You said you'd take me home despite being a PFC because it looks like that's what I'm going to be.

Our hooch got cut in half: the PIO on one end and the 1st of the 30th Artillery on the other. There are a group of soul brothers on that side who play their music loudly at all hours of the night, especially during pot parties. I wouldn't dare ask them to turn down their damned tape decks but someone else did the job for me last night, about 12:15 a.m. The first sergeant of the 1st of the 30th had a drug raid and caught a couple of fellows with the goods, as far as I could hear and see. The music went off to my relief.

We got Lt. O'Daly's replacement as O'Daly gets ready to leave 'Nam. O'Daly is training this new Lieutenant White. The early signs of my new boss are not auspicious—he has shown little curiosity about our office.

I went to the PX to buy new razor blades and found they've run out so I'm chopping at my face with an old blade.

Cameras

November 30, 1970

I mailed the Mamiyaflex home this morning. I've decided to use only 35mm film, which I can get easily and rapidly here. To do this I'm buying a relatively cheap but effective 35mm camera for the remainder of my tour, a Nikonos II with a 35mm lens. It is water and dust proof, a smaller and lighter camera I won't worry as much about.

FSB Green; Artillery; Office Squabbles

December 1, 1970

I went out to FSB Green, which has been occupied since three days ago. I did a story on Bravo Battery, 1st Battalion, 21st Artillery which was firing for troops in contact about 2 miles northwest of Green. They were firing thousands of shells for Charlie Company, 1st of the 7th Cavalry, which for three straight days has had contact. Today was not Charlie Company's best day. They had 1 line one, 4 line twos (that's euphemistic Army jargon for 1 killed, 4 wounded). The CO (commanding officer) of the company was shot through the leg and his lieutenant killed. It appears that the NVA were protecting something. Every big whig in the brigade was out there, the Colonel himself and about half his staff. I got some shots of the 105mm howitzers being fired and the piles of litter from boxes the shells were crated in. I had my earplugs in after the first few eruptions of the guns. For just three cannons, they made an awful thundering. I'd hate to try to sleep with that kind of action going on.

Our Second Lieutenant White made more indication of his dudhood today; he got in a disagreement with our 1st Cavalry Association clerk, Ed Howard. Ed had a hangover from the night before and the lieutenant expected him to get to work, so Ed did though he was dragging himself around. Ed, I should mention right now, is a good diligent worker and I consider him to be a good friend. Anyway, for some reason, the Lt. got teed off at Ed and locked Ed's heels. Ed, being an old Chicago cop, would have none of this and told the Lt. this. The Lt. started grilling Ed, a Black, using the condescending term "boy," which made Ed's blood boil. Ed told him that they definitely weren't going to get along and the Lt. called up Phuoc Vinh asking for a replacement for Ed. Ed, who has been getting bored by the Bien Hoa scene anyway, said that was fine. He'd like to go to USARV as a clerk anyway. Lt. Epstein, another lieutenant who Ed also works for, was egging on Lt. White. I will love to see Lt. O'Daly's reaction when he gets back from a trip he's taken up to another one of the divisions. I'm wondering if Lt. White is going to survive long—I could do better than he's done so far.

Unless White goes, I will be all too willing to return to Song Be. They've been getting more stuff in *Stars and Stripes* to their undying glory than the 1st Brigade (my brigade) has. Plus, I can pick up more crossbows and talk at more length to the sisters at the mission. It might not be too bad. Bien Hoa is getting to be a bit of a grind; maybe I need some excitement.

I also did a short feature story on reading on the LZs and the trivia competitions that go on. Did you know that the record for raw egg eating is 24 in 9.4 seconds? Questions on food, sports, disasters and so on are big when the guys have nothing to do. Also good books are read, the main problems being availability, finding good quality books is not always easy. But after the initial two weeks of setting up a firebase, these guys (mortars, Echo Company) have a lot of time to sit around and vegetate or build their minds. They said that beyond letters from home and class 6 goods (beers, sodas), reading was the most important thing they've got out there. After you get used to a firebase, there is very little unusual business to be had on a firebase—it's an extremely boring way of life.

1st of the 21st Arty
Provides Booming Support
Cannon Crew's Teamwork Essential
to Fire Mission

Artillery played an important and often unsung role in supporting combat units. There was a page spread with story and pictures in the December 30, 1970, Cavalair, *to accompany the never-ending headline.*

2. On Assignment: October 1, 1970, to December 31, 1970

FBS GREEN—The battery was momentarily invisible behind its own cloud of gun smoke as projectiles screamed over the jungle canopy. The crews threw themselves into feverish activity as piles of brass and discarded packing materials collected outside the artillery pits.

Three guns of Bravo Battery, 1st Bn. 21st Artillery were lending support to Charlie Co., 1st Bn., 7th Cav for the third straight day of heavy contact firing. Every once in a while, when adjustments were made, someone would yell, "Be careful! These will be coming in close!"

The crews had a chance to show some finesse. As the shells were slapped into the breech and the brass pulled like a tooth from the gun's mouth, the teamwork of a crack cannon crew became obvious.

The concussion from the three guns made eardrums ring even after the firing was over. Sgt. Kelly Clark, in charge of one of the guns, said the crews have to worry about more immediate things than their ears: "You can't fool around with earplugs when your buddies are getting shot at."

The firing stopped, though no one knew for how long. The guns, running dangerously short of ammunition, were resupplied and a start was made at cleaning up the growing dump outside the pit berms.

The crews watched as the big boys worked out. Blue Max was making run after run. Air Force Dragonflies went into seemingly reckless dives, dropping their ordnance and climbing into the safety of the blue sky.

Then, late in the afternoon, it was arty's turn again. The firebase was again dominated by the screech of warheads reaching escape velocity, leaving waves of smoke in their wake.

The artillery crews were in their element.

LZs Contain Trivia Pros

War could be awfully tedious, especially on firebases, and GIs came up with hair-brained activities to fill their time. This was in the December 23, 1970, Cavalair *and the December 20, 1970,* Pacific Stars and Stripes.

FSB GREEN—The most insidious enemy of the GI on LZs is boredom. After a firebase is established, there just isn't much variety in the life of a mud-and-dust-eating LZ inhabitant. But creativity isn't dead among the populace.

Worried that minds might crack under the tropical heat, the troopers have come up with numerous activities for keeping minds intact. For instance, they read everything they can lay their hands on.

Two of the most popular books are the *Guinness Book of World Records* and the *New York Times Encyclopedic Almanac 1970*. With these two authoritative gems, the "mosts" of the world appear like magic before the eyes of LZdom. "Do you know who ate the most hamburgers at one sitting?" asked

Top: A 105mm howitzer crew is in the midst of a fire mission, a loud and smoky business. *Bottom:* There was considerable work required before firing; a howitzer crew is busy with preparations.

PFC Joe Duffy. He answered his own rhetorical question with, "Phillip Yazdick, Chicago, 77 hamburgers."

These two books have done for trivia development what weights do for musclemen. According to noted trivia authority Sgt. Charles Wall, "Those books are good for hours of learning trivia. One of my favorites is the 100 yard dash record for raw egg gobbling, 24 eggs in 9.4 seconds."

3rd Field Hospital; Wounded Talk

December 2, 1970

Al [*my fellow brigade writer*] and I are going down to the 3rd Field Hospital in Long Bin where some woman correspondent is working on a Christmas project, bringing presents to the 1st Cav. I'm going to play photographer for a day because Al refuses go down with the only photogapher we have working now.

I got down to Long Bin and proceeded to get lost, though not hopelessly. It's a huge place, going on and on. If I hadn't known about Highway 1 it would have been almost hopeless. It's about ten miles from Bien Hoa Army Base to Long Bin and none of the roads really qualify as straight. I got an awful lot of bad advice about where I was and where I wanted to go. It's a strange countryside with Vietnamese villages surrounded by Army bases.

I did find the four wounded though only two of them could talk. The captain of Charlie Company, 1st of the 7th, was one that couldn't talk. He was shot through one leg and the other was broken or something. His men said he was a gung ho type of guy that just loved to kill gooks and his method of finding them was walking down trails. This is how he got into trouble. He and four other men went down the trail and spotted something ahead. They knew there was something in the area and were moving cautiously when an ambush was sprung on them. All five were hit in some way.

The point man, in one of the intensive care wards, was hit hard and the lieutenant right behind him, Lt. Roger Anderson from Minnesota somewhere, was killed. Behind him must have been the captain who was hit in the legs. The RTO and the squad leader were hit with shrapnel and claymore balls though not seriously. The captain paid dearly for his enthusiasm and recklessness. He was in pain when I tried to talk to him and said he'd have to be interviewed some days later. When I went over to interview one of the lesser wounded, the captain let out a howl when the nurses tried to move his left leg. It's doubtful he'll ever go out in the field again in this tour in 'Nam.

I settled for a talk with Sp4 John Gaudet (Gardner, Mass.), the RTO. "I wasn't badly wounded," he said, "but I couldn't have walked on my foot with the shrapnel in it. It was scary. They (the FO [*forward observers*] and RTOs) were calling the stuff in close. Artillery and Cobras were coming in 500 meters away, pretty close. We ran into a bunker complex and they defended it. This is the hottest place we've ever been other than Cambodia. This is where we got another man, also from second squad like our lieutenant, killed."

Sgt. Dale Morrison, a squad leader from Cucamonga, Cal., was hit in the knee with something, they're not sure what. He said, "We ran into an old gook latrine. I don't know what we were hit with. We found shrapnel from a B-40 rocket but it looked like a claymore pellet in my leg so they may have fired both. It was an old bunker complex they'd just moved back into that we were scouting. We'd killed eight gooks before they started taking a toll on us. My platoon hasn't received small arms fire for two months; the last time we were up in this same area, our sergeant was killed." I would say that the second platoon ought to stay out of that area.

Gaudet, who worked closely with Lt. Anderson, said the lieutenant wasn't like the captain, he didn't look for fights. He was a real tragedy as far as Gaudet was concerned. "It really gets to haunting you," he said. The lieutenant had only been in country a month. He already had the respect of the troops. Gaudet thought the lieutenant was going to make it. Some medic had told him that they got the lieutenant out just in time but he heard later, when he asked, that the lieutenant was dead. None of these guys, except for the captain, were in favor of the war.

All these war stories are too much for me. I like a nice peaceful war where no one is killed or injured. I'm glad I missed Cambodia [*the Cambodian incursion; our division was heavily involved just before I arrived*]. I don't have much interest in making a hero of myself in the bush if this is the end of the story—in agony in a hospital bed.

The lifers came in to visit the wounded to pick up their spirits. It's funny. No one cares for a grunt until he's wounded or killed. Then somehow he's gained a kind of immortality.

3rd Field Hospital; Patches Musgrove; Saigon; Unit Funeral

December 4, 1970

I got my first look at the road to Saigon and the outer limits of Saigon in the area near Tan Son Nhut and MACV headquarters. Al Brown and I were hitching to the 3rd Field Hospital to see a woman war correspondent named Helen "Patches" Musgrove, the mastermind and general vitality of Operation Santa Claus. She won the American Legion's Unsung Hero Award last year for her efforts to bring in thousands of Christmas presents to lonely GIs. I found it an upsetting experience in the final analysis.

Patches nicknamed herself for the hundreds of patches sown on her fatigues from the units she's gone out with. She's been in Vietnam for 9 years

2. On Assignment: October 1, 1970, to December 31, 1970

and has three purple hearts. She had her teeth knocked out one time. She's humped with her boys and seen more things than I ever want to see. She is also a registered nurse. She is proud of having had boys die in her arms. And yet I think she has missed the whole point of the war.

It never seems to have occurred to her that maybe we shouldn't have ever come to Vietnam. It never occurred to her that there could be any other sides to a question than hers. She had no respect for the "fools" who hold views contrary to hers. I never opened myself up, knowing what I'd be in for. And she never for an instant stopped talking. Even during lunch she would sit there, always dominating the conversation. I don't see how she could eat. At 53 years old and a widow, I'm amazed to find her here. She is the kind of person that showed proudly a wooden carving of F. William Fulbright graphically showing him with his head up his ass. That kept me quiet if nothing else did.

She is a different kind of war correspondent. Most correspondents seem to want to work themselves out of a job by exposing the war in all its absurdity. Not Patches. She insists on making the news, making a big show out of helping her boys in Vietnam, letting the folks back home show their appreciation and, I feel, soothe their consciences by sending gifts.

She had mailbags full of packages that had already been sorted. She told me that the Navy had a ship on the way with gifts that we, Al and I, shouldn't mention because "those people back there in the U.S. trying to cut the money to the war might raise a howl." She has done this Operation Santa Claus two years prior to this one. This is the first time she's done it in the 1st Cav. She is a pleasant enough person as long as you don't talk too much but her rhetoric gets boring and repetitious after a few seconds.

She was very hard to take pictures of, going at a run and often for no reason as far as I could tell. She is the lifer's kind of correspondent. She brings gifts for the All-American Gis. I'm a GI but repulsed by the whole business. She'd probably remember our names but I doubt if she really knows anything about me or cared. She certainly didn't listen to me. I don't want to have grunts being killed and someone grandstanding, sending packages from home, when they should put pressure to get us out of here instead.

Saigon was a trip in itself. I've never seen that many motorcycles in such small streets or that many people packed into a small area. Americans tend to build everything bigger and a crowded street to us isn't like this. Crowds will disappear in America but crowding never does in Vietnam.

I saw the aftermath of an accident on Route 1 before I hit Saigon. A big semi-trailer truck collided with a Vietnamese motorcyclist with predictable results. I got only a momentary view of the body of a man face down in the road, his face and feet a mess of blood. I'm sure he was dead. I'm told that happens every day. Life is cheap here.

Saigon seems to be thriving with all the American money and stolen goods. I would like to know how they acquired all the wares they were selling. I noticed a few months ago a shortage of poncho liners. I saw all kinds of Vietnamese clothes made out of liners. I've heard a lot of stories about corruption and I'm beginning to believe some of them, even most of them.

Back to yesterday, the reason I couldn't write was that I was talking to Jim "Rapper John" Borovey (Miami Beach, Fla.) who had a funeral for his old unit. I caught wind of this when he gave me a ride from the Air Force side of Bien Hoa complex. I asked him one of my routine questions, what he did? He said he was a dentist. I told him I was a writer for the information office and the fun started. He said his unit had just died and they had held a funeral. He had pictures and wanted to do a story but didn't know how to release it so it could get in the papers. I told him that our office probably could handle this. He talked to Lt. O'Daly and promised to come back when the story was completed. This was about two weeks ago. About two days ago he admitted defeat and returned, asking me to write his story. I've never been impressed by such funerals and am not above parodying one. O'Daly liked the story, said it was good and entertaining in a very odd vein. [*I haven't found the story.*]

Lt. White may pull through yet. He has been talking more, acting like a human being, and findings that we aren't a pack of wolves in the information office. I may have gone off half-cocked in judging him—I hope I was wrong. He loosened up enough when I blew into the office, still trying to recover from Patches. I told him about Patches' Fulbright bust and he said he'd never be able to get along with her. Good comment; he can't be all bad. As I was saying, there may be hope for him.

Jeep Driver; Thor the Dog

December 5, 1970 [*my 22nd birthday*]

Driving a jeep was about all I did today. Our only remaining photographer, Ramlow, was out in the field today so I had to play rear photographer and menial driver. It got kind of exciting trying to keep too many balls in the air. I managed finally to pick up the wrong man at the 10 a.m. bird. I really felt bad about that until I learned that he hadn't brought down our mail—then I took a "screw him" attitude. It was Al who finally went up and captured the mail intact.

I ended up throwing out the story about Charlie 1/7th because it was too gory; who wants to read the grim truth about what war actually means to someone who get the raw end of the deal? I threw out the copy and relieved the lieutenant. He said he could send it up to Phuoc Vinh but I said I'd rather not—they wouldn't use it anyway.

I did a story on the dog next door, Thor by name, whose owner wants to take him home. Al Brown accused me of writing "another one of those dog stories," to which I retorted that DINFOS said children and dogs were sure things for well-read stories if they were handled right. If he can do a story on a tarantula that was found crawling on a guy's arm one morning and made a pet, I can talk about dogs.

Blasted typewriter keeps skipping spaces and I can't type as fast on this one. Al is using the good one. And forgive my spaces as you would have me forgive yours.

I almost had a story today but it died on me, literally. I've noted a large number of pregnant Vietnamese women working in the kitchens of our mess hall. I've always wondered if they worked when they were pregnant out of choice or necessity. I suspect the later. Anyway, this afternoon, two fellows came in and asked me if I wanted a story. They said a Vietnamese woman had a baby while working in the mess hall. They had learned about this when someone came into the dining hall asking if there was a medic in the house. I went up to make a story out of it. Sadly, the woman had a miscarriage.

I got the mail for a change and, as I suspected, the letters have been flooding in from home and stockpiled in Phuoc Vinh. Letter #65 to 67 [*we numbered letters to keep them straight*] were downed with gusto.

On the firebases I've seen some exotic butterflies but my five days in the bush were the best for everything. The secret to studying jungle life, it seems to me, is staying in one place and watching things crawl. Moving as fast and often as a grunt does, you miss a lot.

How Dog Story Began

The way I remember the Thor dog story's genesis, I was walking down a road near our hooch and a soldier had his dog on a leash. Big Al and I were grumbling about how hard it was to make our quota of stories and I said, "I'll bet I can write a story about that dog." My reference to this story in the letter above may be the result of my boast. This is one of my favorites—I like dog stories.

GI's 4-Legged War Trophy
to Swap Sunshine for Snow

I remember this yarn making it into the Cavalair—*I am missing pages from the paper I suspect it was in—but* Pacific Stars and Stripes *used it in their December 20, 1970, issue.*

BIEN HOA—During a year's tour in Vietnam, GIs develop a startling knack for accumulating some outlandish collections of war trophies. They are understandably reluctant to allow those prized possessions to fall by the wayside.

Sgt. George Dexter is especially proud of his prize possession, his dog Thor. So proud, in fact, that he's taking Thor home with him. Dexter is quick to defend his pooch from the assaults of prudish pedigree specialists. "I've become attached to him. He's different from other dogs. He doesn't act like a dog," Dexter says loyally.

Thor isn't any breed of hound in particular. He's a small, thin, black and white splotched, easy-going Vietnamese dog with a winning yawn. Thor is known in his neighborhood for his ability to celebrate every noteworthy occasion by sleeping soundly through it.

Thor cost 500 piasters as a pup in Saigon. The trooper who bought him gave the little mongrel to Dexter.

Thor is, like his master, a unit mail clerk with his own DOD 285 card. Dexter acquired the card for Thor in response to a sergeant trying to get technical on Thor and throw him out of his own doghouse, the post office. It's hard to believe that Thor, an affable canine, would have chewed on the offender without Dexter's help.

Thor also is blessed with a cast iron stomach. "He eats whatever I eat," claims Dexter. "Spinach, pickles, olives, celery, carrots—and he loves sardines."

Like any prospective GI trying to get into the Army, Thor has to take a physical before he can go back to Dexter's world. He made an odd sight in the land of the unleashed dogs strutting down the road on a leash. He and Dexter hitchhiked to Long Binh for a dog checkup. They'll have to go to Saigon for an export license. Later he will become the first Vietnamese dog in Green Bay, Wisconsin.

Reconstruction from Memory

I promised to avoid telling stories strictly from memory—I don't want to be one of those old war horses whose stories get more heroic every time they're retold. Now I've been accused of being a goodie-goodie who must follow the rules, and with some justification. My respect for honesty and fair play naturally led to my fascination with the actions of the wicked. Thus I was a sucker for an improbable story told by an old (forty-year-old maybe), pudgy, nondescript senior sergeant living in a nearby hooch, FSSE most likely. In the evenings we'd all get together to talk and trade stories. I have forgotten every tale I heard there except this one. I have no written record of this in my letters home—no surprise there—but I remember enough of it to reconstitute the sergeant's confessional.

Wicked Soldiers

You will find this hard to believe but before I reformed, I was a very different person from what I am now. I was more than happy to do bad things.

I was stationed in London years ago and had a buddy who was the strongest man I've ever known. I don't know if you're familiar with London telephone booths but they have many little panes of glass in frames. When he was bored, he'd push the glass out of the frames with his finger, which required great strength. And he was a rough and ready companion in the periodic bar fights we'd get into.

London was a lively place with many attractions for servicemen. We were short of money—the army certainly didn't pay us much. My friend and I hit on a scheme to make money: we rolled queers in Hyde Park.

The poor homos really weren't very good at spotting each other. I would pretend to be queer—I know you find this to be hard to believe but I was slim and good-looking then. I'd lure my victim to a secluded park bench and hold his attention while my buddy snuck up on him and cold-cocked him with a single punch. My friend had a devastating punch that never failed him. We then took their money.

We got flush on our new scam. We never got reported or caught. We made real nuisances of ourselves in the pubs, flush with our earnings.

One day I attracted another customer, a beefy big-boned bloke who I wouldn't have picked for a queer. The process was working perfectly. I lured him to a secluded bench, kept his attention, and my pal laid his usual mighty blow on the fellow's jaw.

We were both caught flat-footed when our mark shook his head, looked both of us in the eye, smiled, and said, "If there's anything I like more than loving, it's fighting." Then he beat the tar out of both of us. Our side business was finished.

I bounced the above story off of a gay friend, also a Vietnam veteran. He wanted to know what the lure did on the bench and assured me that gay men can spot each other. He thought, as I do, that the story is preposterous.

Firebase Christmas; Dump; Drug Raid; Race Issue

December 7, 1970

Pearl Harbor Day. I managed to catch a Chinook bright and early today (9:30 a.m.) and made it to FSB Green. I have a running directive to pick up Christmas stories early for our Christmas issue, which we start to put together next week.

So, I looked into the condition of Christmas on a firebase. There were a few elusive Christmas trees but they didn't last long. One fellow got his tree on Thanksgiving Day out in the bush. He didn't want to hump it for a couple of weeks so he had it backlogged to the firebase. When they got back to the firebase to pull base defense for a few days, they got the tree back. He and his platoon got around it for a picture.

But the joys of a Christmas tree on a LZ, unless you can protect it, are short lived. This guy, PFC Robert Schroeder (Milwaukee, Wis.), said he had to throw it away this morning—the idol desecrated when it rained last night and a hook [*a huge skycrane helicopter*] came in too close and knocked it into the mud.

So, the joy of Christmas lies with the packages—food packages. As Schroeder said proudly, "We don't even go to the mess hall when we can eat food from back in the world." It's not only the food but the thought and the link with the States that counts, as I see it. The grunts (Schroeder's a grunt with D 1/7th) may not celebrate Christmas on Christmas Day but they celebrate it when they are given the chance. As Schroeder said, "We've been celebrating Christmas for three straight days and we're going out again to the bush tomorrow." It does soften the life a little as maybe you can see.

Most writers aren't willing to lower themselves to look at some things on the firebases such as the garbage dump. Feeling a bit superior in this respect, I discovered that the dump was an interesting and important part of a firebase. As SFC Aubrey Walker (Eastman, Georgia) put it, "It's just a garbage dump. There isn't a fancy Army terminology for it." The VC are known to virtually mine the riches of old dumps on abandoned firebases. In fact this is why stay-behind ambushes have been so effective.

"The enemy can still use this stuff," said Walker, "if we don't destroy it first. Because we always have people on our firebases, we were given the detail of tending the dump (He's a member of Echo Company Mortars 1/7th). We make sure that everything is burned, save good items that shouldn't be destroyed and keep the sanitation level high."

I talked with him at some length about the Army waste and he noted that sadly the Army was wasteful on a massive scale. He agreed with me when I said that I thought we could come up with a more economical Army without losing firepower and the like. The dump is just a big trench dug by one of the earthmoving machines where everything is dumped in and burned; the popping of old M-16 rounds and unopened C ration cans in the fire are common. The guys in Echo Mortars ended up with the detail about once a month. I was told that KP [*kitchen patrol*] is worse—a guard on the trash trench just ends up sitting around listening to the radio.

I was pleased to find about half the guys I humped with from Echo Recon, 1/7th on the firebase—many of them for good—they often pull the men out of the field after a certain amount of time. Tom Preece is out of the field with an infected knee. Steve Harbeck was on the firebase joking away. David "Smitty" Smith, the old platoon leader, has malaria and is in Cam Rahn Bay. And that is only the beginning. It made me feel quite a bit better—it isn't as easy for them to be killed now.

There was a drug raid next door among the Black population of the

2. On Assignment: October 1, 1970, to December 31, 1970

2nd of the 19th Artillery. The soul brothers were having a noisy pot party around midnight. The Captain and some of his men charged in and routed the party, marching them outside. They had a thorough search where they must have found what they were looking for. Anyway, the Blacks in toto were taken away to the stockade or some other guarded area and we were left in peace.

I find myself in a bind in Vietnam about the race problem. The Blacks tend to be thoughtless for the feelings of the whites over here. They have a clannish noisy handshaking-handclapping ceremony that they do between one another called giving a little dap. It's like a fraternity sign, showing their solidarity with the cause. They are the perfect targets for drug raids because they so blatantly flaunt the drug laws. Last night you would have had to be deaf not to know there was a party. And you would have to only walk past to know they were smoking dew. The worst part for the rest of us nearby was that they were noisy! Despite this, I still feel that many of the Blacks' gripes are horrifyingly legitimate.

Regarding the war, we keep finding a large number of old hooches and bunkers and abandoned base camps but very few of the enemy. Few men have been killed although the charts in our brigade are deceptive. The atmosphere is generally getting to be more like there isn't a war at all. There are rumors that the 1st Cav is the next division to leave for home. They keep saying that we have been getting a large number of in-country transfers, which indicates that we are the next division to leave. I have to see it.

Your packages arrived up at Phuoc Vinh so I plan to fly up there tomorrow.

Somebody said they saw a couple of B-52s on the runways [*of the Bien Hoa Air Force Base next door*] the other day. Bien Hoa is big enough for them. There are even rumors we've had U-2s here at times. I don't doubt it. The military is artlessly cloak and dagger sometimes. Some of the guys have pictures of them.

Truck from Phuoc Vinh

December 8, 1970

The only thing I did today was go to Phuoc Vinh for the mail. I got my usual lousy service at the 8th Aerial Port but the fixed-winged flight arrived in time for me to get to Phuoc Vinh, pick up the mail, and catch a ride by a ¾ ton truck by road through the countryside from Phuoc Vinh back to Bien Hoa with Dave Lewis and Don Fry, who are coming down here to work. It was quite a ride.

At one point we found ourselves unable to pass an immense recovery vehicle, a giant tank used to recover other tanks. With several heavy machineguns aboard, it would be no wimp in a fight. It was moving down the road too slowly. From the air I've noticed tracks of what I thought had to be tanks. I finally saw what made the tracks: a wagon train of tanks forming a little mobile firebase of their own as they prepared for nightfall. It's a very different warfare concept from air mobility [*the concept on which the 1st Cav is based*]. I would want to mess with a tank even less than a Cobra gunship.

This was the longest ride I've taken on the ground in 'Nam. We must have gone 50 miles although by chopper it probably is only 25 miles. We had to take a 25-mile detour to avoid a large river.

The scenery just wasn't like Nebraska [*where my family lived at this time*]. I always have a feeling of being cramped by Vietnamese landscapes. Rice paddies are small, not the large expanses of fields that Nebraska and America in general is famous for. The feeling is much the same as cramped Saigon. It's not that the country is dead—if anything it's too alive and too cramped. I was amazed to find such a fine asphalt road in Vietnam.

It looks like I may be staying at Bien Hoa for some time—they have more bodies than they know what to do with for the meantime. Replacements are coming from other divisions, most of them longer in country than me. I may always be—relatively—a newbee in 'Nam.

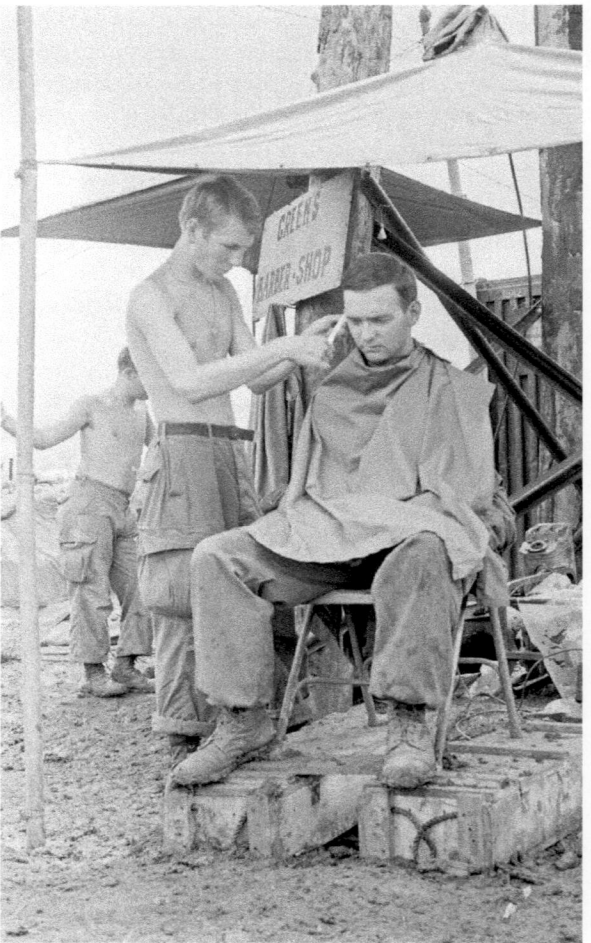

This soldier is getting a haircut at FSB Green—the sign says so. Despite the dust and mud, GIs on firebases were expected to be presentable.

2. On Assignment: October 1, 1970, to December 31, 1970

Firebase work and housing were pretty condensed—privacy was at a premium.

It was a wet walk over to the office, where the letters are. The monsoons haven't completely stopped.

Becky [*my younger sister*], I tried to catch a giant cricket but couldn't manage to kill him. Why don't you send me some bug killer; I could send you better specimens and more of them. I've got the jars. We just don't have good drug stores (any drug stores) here. You'd be fascinated by our lizards. They move fast and are hard to catch.

I've been getting letters from people and they seem to think I'm up against the wall, have it tough in Vietnam. I bet Jimmy Leighton [*my cousin*] that he's having it harder in college than I was having it here. It's my theory that it's not so hard if you don't have a choice.

Stripes Article; Tripping Specialist; Two Week Leaves

December 9, 1970

Someone said I had a picture in *Stripes* so I took a look and sure enough. I was initially disgusted because I wanted a story in it—not just a photo. When I looked more carefully, I noticed I had a story right underneath the picture. They'd shortened it, taken out a little. In my version there was a fourth possibility—you could hump goodies on your back. [*This was the article "Skytroopers Say Packages Create Pleasant Problems" in our division's*

11/25/70 *newspaper which included the fourth possibility. It was common for us to submit articles we'd previously used to* Stars and Stripes.]

I flew out to FSB Jupiter today, the realm of the 1st Brigade of the 12th Cavalry. Very interesting. There were several fellows from other divisions who had recently come into the Cav. They see the same early signs of a brigade and division being pulled out. Blade time on choppers has already been cut but there is something new one guy told me that was strange—I'd never heard it before. He and several other GIs were cleaning off old M-60 and M-16 ammunition—it seems the supplies on ammunition are being cut back. Also, all of our replacements are in-country transfers from divisions that are leaving. About February Nixon should announce a huge new troop pullout but by virtue of all these men derosing [*leaving country*]. If the Cav goes home I don't know where that leaves me.

I did a little story on a grunt tripping specialist—kind of the company clown. "It just happens. I don't plan it that way," said Sp4 Rey Perez (Los Angeles, Cal.) a bit forlornly. He is one of the clumsiest guys in his company and along with his heavy pack, has a consistency about his tripping unrivaled in her sphere of influence. But it isn't necessarily bad.

"It may have saved my life in my first tour. I tripped and fell one time just as the enemy opened fire on my position, hitting the man behind me. The bullet was meant for me. But most of the time in my first tour in 'Nam I didn't have any trouble in tripping mostly because I was walking through rice paddies instead of jungles." But this didn't last.

Sgt. John Anglin (New Concord, Cal.) explains what happens when his buddy falls. "You have to see it when he topples, he starts swearing. He gets mad and calls everybody FNGs (newbies [*actually fucking new guys*]). It's funny. He is a morale booster after you've really sweated it up a steep hill and watch Rey go up the hill behind you."

Capt. Jim Hackett (Hollister, Missouri) says Perez has his falling down to an art form. "He even manages to trip up hill—he falls quite a bit." He is a good dude, Perez is, and I'm going to try to make it a funny article.

The 1st of the 12th is by and large the hardest battalion to dig up stories on. And I feel I've finally traced things to the source—the battalion commander. He is unpopular with his troops. He insists on clean-living, shaved and hair-trimmed grunts in the bush—what nonsense. The spirit in the battalion is sadly lagging behind battalions like the 2/7th although they still have one of the biggest body counts in the division, a lovely statistic. They are good soldiers but not especially happy.

Colonel Stevenson, the brigade commander, went up in my eyes today. You undoubtedly remember the 2 week leave back to the States that is supposedly open to GIs in 'Nam. Well, the Colonel pointed out today that he is upset with an arrangement that leaves the grunt, as usual, out in the bush.

2. On Assignment: October 1, 1970, to December 31, 1970

All the rear people (mostly officers) have been the first to sign up. Stevenson feels that a new arrangement, a quota system, should be worked out so that the rear people are, if anything, at a disadvantage. This makes abundant sense and is good politics besides.

FSB Jupiter is very pretty. You can see the foothills of the Central Highlands from the hill on which Jupiter is located. The land has a roll to it that is pleasant—you can see over the jungles instead of into their depths. I'm taking my camera out next time and blast away at it. It's in a better strategic position than most—the enemy has to climb up a hill to attack.

The monsoons were supposed to stop before the beginning of this month and haven't. I was dampened again on the way to the briefing—I would have been soaked if I hadn't been in a jeep. I expect to be in Bien Hoa for some more time—it looks like they don't need me at Song Be. Hope so.

HE'S A TUMBLER

Combat was full of men with unique traits—this guy's specialty was slapstick. This was in our Morale Booster section of the January 20, 1971, Cavalair.

FSB JUPITER—The skytrooper knew it was going to happen yet there was nothing he could do about it. Then, as he walked down the trail with other members of the 2nd Plt., Co. B, 1st Bn., 12th Cav., it did happen. With all the grace and style of a dying gazelle, he toppled face down on the trail.

The 1st of the 12th's own Fred Astaire, Spec. 4 Rey "Recondo" Perez, whose fancy footwork has turned into something of a bush comedy routine, remarked: "It just happens. I don't plan it that way."

Perez, however, believes one of his tumbles may have saved him. "I tripped once, and at the same moment we received fire," he exclaimed. "They hit the guy behind me but I know the bullet was meant for me."

Sgt. John Anlin gets a big kick out of Perez's antics. "Everybody falls now and then, but no one falls like Recondo," he remarked. "He does have the heaviest pack but when the guy falls you know he must be the platoon character," Anlin commented.

The platoon members all rib Perez about the finesse with which he executes his moves. "After you've struggled up a steep hill and you're all pooped out, it's good comedy relief to watch Recondo struggling up the hill behind you," explained Anlin. "You have to see it. He falls, starts swearing; you laugh, he gets angry." Anlin added, "Surprisingly enough, he's a real morale booster."

Even Capt. Jim Hacket wasn't above making a snide comment about Perez: "He even managed to trip uphill." Perez immediately retorted: "I've even seen the CO tumble fanny-over-tea-kettle."

To remain sane, one cannot always take the bush seriously. Taking all the ribbing into consideration, Recondo Perez still hasn't lost his sense of humor. He still manages to joke about his stumbling shortcomings. So if you see a GI take a nasty spill along the trail, and if he gets up and repeats his performance within 60 seconds—don't be alarmed. It's just Recondo Perez showing off again.

Defenseless Children; Killing Snake; Underweight GI; 1st Sergeant Trouble

December 10, 1970

I went to FSB Green this morning with Dave Lewis to introduce him to our firebases. I let Dave have the story I thought was probably the best.

It seems that American soldiers found two defenseless children after barely averting fragging them in a bunker. Charlie Company, 1/7th again found some bunkers. To make sure that no one came after them, they were methodically throwing grenades into the bunkers. On this particular bunker the soldier, a newbie, was hesitant to throw in the grenade so he listened for a moment. He heard a child crying. Since they had the bunker surrounded, someone investigated and found two little kids. One that could talk fairly well was five, the other we think about two. They were happy healthy-looking kids and surrounded by food. Their parents were nowhere to be seen, a real tragedy. The kids will be sent up to Song Be and God only knows what happens afterwards. The grunts had some trouble with the little one who kept making noise. They tried to bribe him into silence and keep the parents from coming to his rescue.

My story was on a five-foot 9 inch 95 pound GI who manages to hump nearly his own weight in pack and ammunition. He says it is the long humps, like the seven clicks yesterday, that really exhaust him. On the other hand, he has one of the lowest profiles in the platoon, great for hitting it [*dropping to the ground*] in a firefight. He is Sp4 Marcos Arquello, a friendly Mexican-American from Vaughn, N.M. His secret for staying slim is not eating much, just fruits and LRRPs, which is an advantage because he doesn't have to carry as much food. He had to take three physicals to get into the Army. "I was thin but I'm healthy," he said. He's never had clothes in the Army that fit. He is a good soldier despite being forced to slow up on long marches.

Bravo Company 1/7th—Arquello's unit—also had a run in with a 14 foot boa. It was late in the day and everyone was tired and grouchy. One man stepped over this beautiful black, green, and white boa and got the scare of his life. It was coiled up in the middle of their path. So they "blew it away" with their M-16s which I don't think was very bright and made the poor snake into a mass of pulp. They didn't want to cut a trail around the snake. I told them my sister would have been outraged—she would have tried to catch it and take it home. [*My sister Becky kept two snakes, one a boa.*] He said you, Becky, might have thought twice if you'd seen the snake yourself. A more common snake to kill is the bamboo viper, something I have no pity for. It's referred to as the "three-step snake"—the number of steps you take before dying after being bit although I suspect that's an exaggeration.

We had some trouble with the first sergeant out at Green. Now we need boarding passes to get into and out of the firebase, working through the 1st sergeant. It's funny, the first time I looked at him I had a feeling I was going to have trouble with him—he gave me a hostile look. I had to run down Dave to get a pass for him too. The sergeant gave me a bad time about not being very official with him, calling him first sergeant. He stopped me in the line and instead of telling me to bring a gun along the next time I came to a firebase, he told me he hoped the next time I was in a chopper I would crash and be without a weapon. I was furious and couldn't understand it—the last time I'd seen him he was friendly enough. Then I realized that I was wearing my wire-rimmed "granny glasses" instead of my straight ones and that must have been it, because from the moment he looked me in the eye he was looking for a fight. I didn't oblige him, of course, but it all goes to show you where the sentiment lies among lifers—it's all appearances.

I've been told that I'm picked to go with Lt. White, who likes me, and cover the travels of Patches Musgrove, taking photos and writing stories with abandon. It's a challenge—I'll admit—but I could get my name up in lights. But then, I don't dig conservative journalists. We'll see.

John Hlavacek

I had forgotten John Hlavacek. He is described as a globetrotting reporter/foreign correspondent. He interviewed me because my parents lived in Nebraska. He worked for KMTV, a television station in Omaha not far from Fremont. What I probably didn't know then was that he was a student of Carleton College in the same period that my parents were. They undoubtedly knew him and were, in all likelihood, friends.

December 15, 1970

Mr. John Hlavacek came today and did a tape, me being one of the people in it. I felt kind of flea-bitten in Army fatigues, like a model showing off a ghastly dress. And I was, of course, nervous like T.V. men always seem to make you feel and act. I was a jeep driver today and this is how he pictured my job—I hope he doesn't play that up too big. His equipment isn't elaborate, just a 16mm Bolex camera and a small cartridge tape recorder. I had a hard time talking to him, although I didn't expect him to ask controversial questions by the very nature of his mission.

He made one little impromptu speech, telling why he kept coming back. He said these interviews, the thousands he's done in 'Nam over the years, have made him more popular in Omaha than Bob Hope, which is probably true. I'm sure it makes the folks at home feel better to see their lost George, the finance clerk fighting the war in Bien Hoa, wave and walk like a stick man. They can see George is more afraid of Hlavacek than the V.C. and they know that things can't be too bad. Tell me what you see. This kind of shot my day to go out to the firebases and, with the Patches ordeal coming up, I don't know where my monthly quota of stories will come from. I'm sure I won't lose my job.

The candy the Riegels [*my relatives in Colorado Springs*] sent me never adjusted to the weather. They've begun to melt in the wrappers and not in the mouth. The air is so moist that it creates a delightful sticky substance reminiscent of lollypops half sucked by kids. The goo is all over my shelf as I slowly eat them. This would never happen in Nebraska.

I mailed off the color slides today—hope you receive them in good shape. I am very proud of them; they are without a doubt the best color slides I've ever taken and were the ones that weren't used.

Air Force Rocketed

December 16, 1970

I wasn't going to write but we just had incoming five minutes ago, there was no doubt about it. There were big explosions, the sound of debris falling just after the blast, and the sirens warning everybody after it was too late. I knew what it was after the first blast but I was in a good position. I happened to be down on the floor looking over my assignment for a by-mail oceanography class. It was like the Fourth of July, flares hanging from parachutes everywhere. I didn't go out until the rockets stopped coming.

Usually I envy the Air Force their flush toilets and jungle fatigues but not on nights like this. After the attack last month, the Air Force dudes take any explosion dead seriously. They don't do the clowning around that killed those airmen last time. The army side makes a lousy target, especially the Cav rear. We're all spread out. I just lay there, hoping that my luck was good and computing the odds in my favor.

The dogs were all out barking—they didn't know what was coming off. I can't say I'm very impressed by the security of the bastion of Bien Hoa when rockets arrive. It reminded me of the artillery I heard impacting the first night I was out in the bush although these were a hell of a lot louder and less friendly.

I can hear the artillery working out. The guerrilla can hit anything if he's willing to take the chance. I don't know how to read this new round of rockets, whether they are aggressively attacking Bien Hoa or this goes under the heading of "dying gasps."

I flew up to Phuoc Vinh today using these air force runways. The Air Force here has been putting out jet strikes like they're going out of style. The traffic is heavy with birds on all manners of combat and supply business. It's by far the biggest target in this area. I hear the artillery again but it's way off—I don't even know where it is on post. It almost makes me feel like I'm at war.

I heard five or six rounds hit and the air force is only a mile away, the runway half that distance. I haven't heard any planes or jets take off since the attack. I wonder if they hit the runway? I'll find out.

I mailed off the money orders for the Nikonos. I went up and returned from Phuoc Vinh and generally lounged around today. I'm going to see the movie *Woodstock*. That will get me out of 'Nam for an hour or two.

Dexter, the mail clerk from next door, just told me the rounds hit at the VIP Center. This may involve the Army. I'm going to go over and check it out.

A little later ...

Like all late night rumors, rocketings should be taken with a grain of salt. Several rounds landed about a quarter mile from the VIP Center on or near the Air Force's runway, which stretches a long ways. No planes or jets have been allowed to land. I watched a couple coming in for an approach and suddenly veer off, probably toward Tan Son Nhut airfield near Saigon. One round landed about 400 meters from the snack bar and movie theatre where I'm always going. The rounds came in at 8:20 p.m.

It's getting late. It really wasn't exciting for very long. Well, don't get mortared or anything. I'll sleep well tonight despite all this.

Watching "Woodstock"; Patches; Jeep; Snatch

December 17, 1970

It doesn't seem that anyone was killed last night or, as far as word has gotten around, even hurt. The jets are coming in. I can hear a freedom bird landing at this moment. All in all, the VC missed, though they proved that the whole complex is vulnerable.

I went to the movie "Woodstock" this afternoon. Very interesting though I'm not sure what the message was, the interpretations were up to question. It's very much a modern movie with the use of split screens, short sequences and rapid switches; an eye wrenching spectacle. The line into it was the longest I've seen since I hit country. The movie seems to hit on everything including the war. There was one sequence that could have been taken in 'Nam and kind of haunted me—it was out of place. It seems the Army donated the time and crew of a Huey chopper to medevac sick youth from the rock festival. They had good pictures reminiscent of what we watch every day. There were some delightful nude scenes that reminded us of one part of the present day youth movement we lack—beautiful girls.

I realize I've never commented on the cultural hollowness of an army base. I've heard many complaints that if we're going to invade a country, why don't we have the right to understand the people, to promote understanding and all. I've heard grunts in particular become bitter about not even seeing the country they are fighting for. They can say they've seen 'Nam, but what really have they seen? Nothing but the worst. In the rear, we have some chances but it's still pretty grim. TV and radio are the biggest attractions. Movies are everywhere. I can read but can't go anywhere to sightsee.

And around 8 p.m., I find myself without things to do. I can't get a date and escapism is rampant. Alcohol, mostly because it's legal, is the most popular painkiller. Dew [*marijuana*] runs a close second. I spend my time writing letters mostly but I'm an exception.

This Patches thing doesn't sound so bad. She doesn't have enough packages for the whole division, just one brigade. It sounds like her campaign was a bit of a failure. I have all kinds of film and cleaned the Leica's lens so I'm ready to go. Maybe she won't travel over all three brigades now with her lack of packages. But I'll have to endure the incessant babble of Patches, a lingering death.

We had a new distributor put into the jeep and the points and spark plugs replaced and checked. It's like brand new. The transformation was striking. Before the repairs, it was the worst I've ever seen it. It was choking and gasping like a dying old man. This afternoon when I started it, it purred happily like it had a heart transplant without any complications. The jeep is an important and much-coveted part of every office. Hitchhiking, though completely legal to the point of a jeep having to pick you up, is still a bit demeaning. I've gotten used to hitching rides to Long Bin although Saigon is forbidden as far as I'm concerned. I am basically not that daring, don't like to take chances unless the opportunity of escape is readily available, and a jeep's nice.

Our little dog, Snatch, nearly got run over just a minute ago. She let out heartrending screams after suffering a glancing blow off a slow-moving passing jeep. The jeep stopped and everyone ran to aid the dog. About five or six of us were surrounding Snatch, trying to determine with flashlights what was wrong. As it turned out, the attention probably saved impressionable Snatch from going into shock. She finally got up and limped away to the Post Office hooch to recover. Her most appealing characteristic is her small size and the odd loud yelps that emanate from her small furry body. She's one of our resident characters; we'd hate to lose her.

Patches Plays Santa; Hate Leica

December 18, 1970

Patches, a little muffled by her Santa Claus outfit, paraded down the street in front of the 3rd Field Hospital, starting off Operation Santa Claus. There were at least four generals present for the occasion. Patches is going to have enough gifts to pass around to the entire division but the Navy ship with the packages hasn't made it yet. All this showmanship is repulsive. The whole idea should be to give unselfishly and I feel quietly, where I'm convinced Patches is doing this for herself. She produced a ludicrous Santa Claus, with patches. The Vietnamese passing by couldn't understand the outfit's significance but did laugh. One GI, rolling past the street in a truck yelled, "Damned long-haired hippy!" She was as repulsive to me as any hippy.

I hate the Leica camera I'm using—it failed me again. The film got stuck again and I was fortunate to salvage any of the film. A much less expensive Pentax I borrowed from a friendly captain was beautiful by comparison. I hate the loading system and the viewfinder too. The lens is nice but that's all—the body is simply atrocious. I know it's an expensive camera but the rich snobs are welcome to it.

Patches' Santa Suit; Cav Leaving?

December 19, 1970

Ho! Ho! Ho! Patches didn't make it today as Santa because she lost more than ten pounds in her Santa suit yesterday and was hospitalized because of the loss of water. I have to admire her toughness although it serves her right. No one should walk around in a flak jacket padded with pillows covered by a stifling Santa Claus suite. A big helper playing the role today said he'd never do it again. Today the crowd was less highbrow, just a couple of colonels and Brigadier General Burton walking through 93rd Evac and 24th Evac. I took a sample of gifts: a pocket New Testament Bible ("But I'm an atheist," complained the recipient.), a small face cloth ("Why it's OD green, they know what we need," hooted the GI) and finally a deck of cards which no one complained about.

I'm disgusted because I was more photographer and jeep driver than writer today. Brown and Lewis [*the other two writers*], without the drag of my Patches task, are getting their quota of stories. I can't find the time. I'm losing touch with the firebases although material is getting harder to come by now that we have three writers down here.

Patches' gifts aren't going to make it for Christmas so I'm getting a breather tomorrow. We start handing out presents again December 27. It's tedious work taking photos of dignitaries inside dimly lit hospital wards.

None of these will be great photographs. Lt. White is always there to assure we get the pictures he wants although I don't blame him. I have a major looking over my shoulder too and drive the jeep, although he's a nice enough guy. In fact, the reason I got stuck with this chore is because my lieutenant trusts me. So, between playing with the wheezing Leica and driving the jeep, I get tuckered out.

We are approaching a turning point in the war; I'm convinced that the Cav will be almost gone if not completely gone by the time I leave Vietnam. I'm also convinced that the signs of a Cav stand down will come in no more than two months. We're still finding caches and a few enemy soldiers but by and large the division is doing practically nothing. We're in a good position to leave.

I've learned that Bien Hoa Air Force Base is slowly being turned over to the ARVNs. Those hot jets I thought were phantom jets are actually F-5 Freedom fighters, piloted exclusively by the Vietnamese Air Force. Once the ARVNs receive all this American equipment, maybe they'll decide they have something to fight for. I hope so. It would make leaving simpler.

I've given up on a White Christmas but still hope to come home in June.

Touring with Patches; Davy Crocket

December 20, 1970

This was one of the wildest days of my short confusing career as a PIO man. Provided with transportation along with Patches, we did a whirlwind tour of all the 1st Brigade firebases.

First we stopped at FSB Green where Patches had a gift throwing session and I blasted away with the camera. With our own Huey helicopters (my favorite form of transportation), we had the time to lounge around the firebase. I talked to several of my friends from Echo Recon and actually dug up a story, proving I could still do it.

For a week Echo Recon was led down a long trail by a Chieu Hoi, who they only knew as Davy Crocket because they didn't know his name. He'd been down the trail only twice and yet managed to go down the entire network with only one major blunder where they were lost for a day. Davy expected to be shot by the lieutenant of Echo Recon because he failed them and in tears, Davy asked to be shot. The lieutenant was flabbergasted. Davy's problem was that he was trying too hard. He'd been with the NVA for something like 5 years and risen to the rank of sergeant major but had never been paid. He'd grown tired and Chieu Hoied to the ARVNs. Echo Recon, a sensitive lot as a whole, trusted their Davy Crocket and he was faithful to them. As Sp4 Garry Walker (Beloit, Wis.) explained, "He told us where everything was. Once he told us where an ambush was; he knew they knew we were coming because a chopper had given our position away. We trusted him to the max and if he told us something, he was invariably right."

Davy wanted to be Echo Recon's Kit Carson scout and the whole platoon was in favor of the idea. Unfortunately, he is out of action for the next couple of months.

Like many war stories, this one doesn't have a particularly happy ending. Echo Recon had to leave the area to get some rest. Davy was turned over to Charlie Company, 1st Bn., 7th Cav who didn't set up a good relationship with him. They didn't trust him and what's more, they didn't protect him. Charlie Company can be screw-ups; they were the company that just a few weeks ago had five men ambushed. While Davy was talking to the CO of Charlie Company, the other Charlie (the enemy) moved into position and picked Davy out of all the troops, shooting him through the mouth. He lost 6 teeth but won't die. The NVA were obviously after Davy; they could have hurt the whole company had they wanted to. Charlie Company's failure was punished—their CO was removed—but the damage had been done. The fellows from Echo Recon were upset and yet helpless. For without being able to talk with Davy Crocket except through an interpreter, they had formed a strong bond with their new man.

Feeling better after talking with Echo Recon, I was off again with Patches to FSB Dacus, the realm of the 2/7th. Here I worked up another story on being a Santa Claus. "It was hot!" commented one of Patches' reindeer that played Santa for a day. "It was worth it however," he added. "I'd rather do it in a hospital. Some of the guys there were all screwed up and they were glad to see Santa." Sgt. Larry Stone (Waukee, Iowa) was a little more eloquent. "There's a personal satisfaction," he said, "in doing something for someone else." Then he commented on his outfit. "I'd make it a knit instead of from fur if I were in 'Nam. This'd be great back in Iowa. The beard isn't bad but the flight jacket used for padding is no help. Yet it wouldn't be worth it to gain weight so I could discard the flight jacket because then I'd never lose the weight. I'd rather be padded with discardables."

These soldiers were stand ins for Patches because of her experience the first day of Operation Santa Claus. Patches was talkative as usual: "I was heartbroken that I couldn't be Santa Claus this year. It's never bothered me like this in years past. I lost 14 pounds and had to be hospitalized. It's always been important to me to bring the Christmas spirit to Vietnam. I guess those 2 pillows and flak jacket are finally too much for me. I've always kind of prayed my way across Vietnam. If anybody had told me I'd be in Vietnam nine years ago I would have laughed at them. But I believe God had me here for a reason. This will be my last year in Vietnam; when I can't be Santa I can't go out with the troops. Christmas is one of America's great traditions." Her talking can be touching at times. I don't know how I'm going to write the story.

Patches is a strange person. Her reception on the firebases was basically good because the foundation of her little operation is basically sound—the troops *do* want to see Santa on Christmas and be reminded of home. They appreciated the effort but I know most wouldn't have appreciated her politics.

From Dacus we went to FSB Andres, also in 2/7th. Next we flew to 1/12 at FSB Jupiter where her reception was probably the best. A crowd of nearly a hundred GIs crowded around her as she hurtled present into the mob. Then she took some time to relax.

She talked with Lt. Col Malloy, the CO of the 1/12th. It was incredible. She admitted she was anti-McNamara, anti-Johnson and especially anti-Fulbright. She said she's been asked to run for the senate. About this time the Colonel asked her what she *was* for, a fine question. She said she was for those people supporting the military during a military war. Even Malloy seemed taken aback by her rhetoric. She seems a nice old woman until she starts talking politics and morals.

After Jupiter we flew to a small firebase called Nancy, which I'd heard of but never managed to get to before. I'd heard they had a rat problem because the base had belonged to the ARVNs for a while. We flew in and I was amazed—it was a beautiful setting, probably the prettiest setting I've so far encountered in 'Nam. Up on a hill, it overlooks a large village built in and around huge boulders, several boulders rising a hundred feet or more above the village. The land was open and, in the late afternoon, didn't look like Vietnam. This is known as the Woodcutters' Area because of the large woodcutting industry that I'm told is important to the Vietnamese economy. Consequently, the war isn't allowed to infringe that much on this area. Unlike most of War Zone D, it isn't a free fire zone—a camp has to be attacked before we can open fire. Nancy, in American hands after a long absence, was being cleaned up, killing all the rats. We didn't stay long—it was lovely flying out of FSB Nancy.

We headed for Saigon to take Patches and her helpers home to the 3rd Field Hospital. There was a good deal to see. We spotted an armored cavalry camp unlike anything we have in the 1st Cav. The supply yards around Saigon look so big from the air. We looked at the city of Saigon itself and noticed that many houses didn't have even token front yards, so unlike our yards back in the States. We could see thousands of bodies of tiny people scrambling for a living below us. And we could see the filth and pollution. The lieutenant and I agreed; we prefer to fly over Saigon instead of drive through it. The chopper headed back to Bien Hoa, passing farther south from the route we'd taken in, and could see the American bases seemed to surround Saigon.

I got back to the office, arranged the film I'd taken, talked to the guys and got a surprise. I got two stories in *Pacific Stars & Stripes* today! Dexter, the guy next door, came in with it must have been twenty copies of the paper. The story about his dog was one of the stories. He shook my hand and laughed.

If this letter seems wordy and a touch irrational, please pardon me, I started it too late.

OLD FOES BECOME FRIENDS

This is perhaps the saddest and most poignant story I collected, especially if you consider the additional facts from my letter above. It was in the January 20, 1971, Cavalair *and the February 1, 1971,* Army Reporter *with the headline "Davy Crocket Is Still American Hero."*

NEAR FSB GREEN—Bonds of amazing strength are built overnight in the bush. The grunt, far from being aloof to the new man, is probably one of the most sensitive and understanding individuals to be found anywhere. Maybe it is because of the importance of having a reliable friend in a tense situation.

So it was with Davy Crockett. Nobody knew his real name, he was just given a name that seemed to fit. For a week, Davy, a rallier, led Echo Recon, 1st Bn., 7th Cav. down a long elaborate trail system.

As an NVA sergeant major, Davy had seen nothing but a bleak future with the communist forces, so he rallied to the ARVN. Because he knew the location of a long trail studded with caches and NVA outposts, he was introduced to the recon platoon and a close working relationship was established.

According to Spec 4 Timothy Payne, an RTO for Echo Recon, "He'd been on the trails only twice before, yet he was almost invariably correct in the paths he chose and the trail signs he read, with one exception. He goofed up, lost a trail and we took a day to get back to the right path. He took it very seriously, since he mistakenly thought the lieutenant was going to have him shot. In tears, he asked the lieutenant not to shoot him. He was just trying too hard."

Although the caches had been cleaned out before their arrival, the long trek down the trail was a success. "He did lead us to an NVA regimental headquarters, which we've never been able to find before, plus a Bangalore torpedo factory," Payne added.

Walker noticed a difference between Davy Crockett's senses and a typical American soldier's. "His sense of time and distance are different," noted Walker. "He could hump farther in the jungle than we could. What took us a week to walk didn't take him nearly as long."

Despite all the obstacles, Davy came across as a warm human being with his own bag of tricks and surprises. "He was a lifesaver," confided Payne. "He pulled out a gigantic plastic bag full of cigarettes when we had run out."

Tim Payne, referred to in the story "Old Foes Become Friends," was talking on the radio during my first tramp with Echo Recon 1/7th. I've always thought Tim had an expressive face. He shows it here with the classic look of a long-suffering grunt.

After leaving Davy in the care of another American unit, Echo Recon came into FSB Green for a breather. However, word soon came that their new ally had been wounded and MEDEVACED. Now the men of Echo Recon say they want him back as soon as the former sergeant major recovers.

Drunken Major; Supply Realities; Ice Plant

December 21, 1970

Last night was strange; the officers were having a booze-in at the artillery mess hall across the street from my hooch. One drunken major was in one of the big drainage ditches near the mess—he thought there was incoming. There wasn't incoming other than a flying beer can or something; he was just paranoid. While the major was making an ass of himself, I was across the street talking to the head sergeant of FSSE. What he said was fascinating so I took notes.

The sergeant's specialty is supply and although I've noticed the supply network's complexity and the unbelievable wastefulness, I've never had the problems explained to me so well.

The 1st Cav has been spoiled for a long time, he explained. We use something such as radio headsets until they are so dirty that they won't work. Then we leave the dirty sets in a corner and get a new headset from supply when all we'd have to do is clean the old headsets. A piece of equipment will sit out in the elements and rust because one unit doesn't need it. Another unit desperately needs that very piece of equipment but is forced to order the piece from the States instead. Consequently, scrounging becomes the rule and as long as supplies keep flooding in, there is no problem, just a great deal of inefficiency. But the Sarg says what is about to happen is that supplies are going to dry up and people who have been relying on scrounging will pay dearly. For as supplies are stockpiled and traded in Vietnam, units with oversupplies aren't reordering new stock because they have too much. They end up supplying the rest of the units in the area with their surplus and scrounging units don't reorder the items either.

He assured me that after a certain amount of time, if an item isn't reordered, it's taken off the supply list as unnecessary baggage. Then everybody finds themselves screaming for the same item which nobody, suddenly, possesses. He said that a certain crucial part to an electrical generator was about to create big trouble for this reason. You might not hear this is a conventional economics course but it's one of the facts of Army supply which you, Dad, may have faced when you were a supply officer.

Operation Scrub is another case of the Army not recognizing economic realities. This campaign scrubs all Cav units of their excess equipment, of everything they aren't using. It's a sound idea but falls down because of its execution. The plan is to put the goods back into supply channels except that units with excess equipment aren't asked what units need these goods. Supplies pile up at Scrub yards yet nobody comes for equipment. Tools are left to rust and jeeps sitting while other units vainly try to order the items, not knowing the equipment is close at hand. Also, because the equipment has to be in top-notch shape, used goods—though still useable—are often thrown away because they aren't new.

Given the system, supply men are driven to practically become robbers. The Sarg says he's actually stolen unused equipment to make sure his men are kept in lights and mosquito netting.

I visited the Bien Hoa Ice Plant today. By using an antifreeze-like brine solution circulating around huge rectangular steel water containers, 300-pound blocks of ice can be produced in about 48 hours. Blocks are made 180 at a time. The brine solution is 12 to 15 degrees. A civilian contractor, PA & E (Pacific Architects and Engineers), runs the plant. It provides ice for many of the mess halls and medical centers as well as other units in Bien Hoa. Ice, behind only letters and packages from home, is one of the most sought-after commodities on firebases. I'm doing a story on it.

I hope you have a Merry Christmas and all that. It's funny; I don't miss a Christmas tree, just the snow.

Olathe Leaves; Congressional Inquiries

December 22, 1970

Olathe, Kansas's citizens banded together and collected money to bring some of their boys home for the Christmas holidays and three 1st Cav fellows were recipients, very happy ones. The story I wrote is an outgrowth of the new two-week-leave policy just started for GIs. This idea tickles my fancy much more than Patches' Christmas operation.

All three of these guys were in the bush or on a forward firebase; I'm not sure the towns' people understand what a great idea they've come up with. It's especially good for grunts. A grunt's life may depend on how much sham time he gets—mine really doesn't. As one fellow said, "It really makes you feel good that someone wants to get you home. We couldn't have done this otherwise; we never would have been able to afford it. We hope that other people can get as good a break as we got." There is some indication that the idea is spreading and with their all-consuming hang-up a lot of fellows here have with going home, this is a delightful, if long-shot, possibility. Two of the three are married and one has a two-week-old son. They say their worst problem will be that they won't know what to say.

In collecting the story, I discovered another Vietnam position I never dreamed existed. There is a guy who handles nothing but congressional inquiries. The townspeople inquired about their three soldiers to two senators and got something done. In this case, the inquiry specialist helped the three guys arrange to fly home, a complex undertaking given the system. But he explained to me that often congressional inquiries in response to letters from constituents are not always much help.

He says he's seen everything. He's had cases where a GI writes home that he's sitting in mud when writing the letter and his folks go into shock—the Army is mistreating their boy. His job is to tell the folks that their boy isn't really in much danger as long as the bullets aren't flying—the mud is part of a grunt's life. Also there is the GI who lied to his parents, said he lost his orders for a Silver Star he was awarded in Vietnam. He had to tell the parents the hard facts of life—their boy's a bum.

He is a troubleshooter and public relations man. He says he enjoys the job although he's getting worked to death. He said that sometimes he does well; sometimes he has to take "the party line." He is a nice guy, a diligent worker, and I'm sure he gets things done.

Burn Accident; Ice; Bush and Firebase Cooking

December 23, 1970

Even before I flew out to FSB Green this morning, I had a chance to play reporter and quench my curiosity. Two GIs came up to the tower at Sandy Pad and said a man had been shot and to call an ambulance. Knowing we hadn't been attacked, I was pretty sure it was an accident. I checked it out. Apparently a guy, while spraying fuel oil on a fire burning weeds outside the berm, fell into his own fire and had his back covered with second, maybe even third degree burns. Men around him ripped off his clothes and put out the fire. The worst problem was that the guy was going into shock. They calmed him down and were waiting for the ambulance to come charging up.

At ten minutes after I got there, they decided the ambulance would never come and left with him. As it turned out, they were about right. Another ten minutes later an ambulance leisurely drove up and asked if anybody had been shot, not very concerned. They drove over slowly to check out the choppers. I finally had to walk over and explain to them that a guy had been burned and was going into shock and was long gone. Seeming unconcerned, they drove off. Not an impressive emergency response, not at all.

I developed my ice story. The grunts said the artillerymen get ice all the time—they always have a cold can in their hand. The main thing is that something is cold. One guy said, "I don't drink beer but if it's cold, I'll take it. We had Fresca—which no one likes—but we went wild about it anyway." Another explained, "We never get enough ice to cool everything. One of our basic problems is that ice melts. But on the other hand, nobody likes to drink hot water and that's about what we get in the bush." With any kind of an opening, I should have fun with this story.

On the culinary front, you can't always be a discriminating eater out in the bush but there is a group that believes in doctoring up their LRRPs and C rations. Some of the added ingredients include dried coffee, cream, hot sauce, dried onions, and black peppers. "It's an individual act," a lieutenant explained to me, "you eat your own cooking." One man found he likes spaghetti now that he has stuff to mix it with. One guy insisted, "Despite our mixes, we don't gain much weight." Standing up, he showed his thin bones.

I visited the mess hall on FSB Green, the only hot chow producer in 1/7th. It will be a good story but one of the cooks made it hard. He was griping—must have thought I was from the IG (Inspector General). He said they ought to do a story on promotions—he thought he deserved one, in fact he knew it. When I told him I was having the same trouble but couldn't print it in the paper, he asked why did I have my job if I didn't print "the truth." I tried to tell him that there are many different views of what the truth is but he wouldn't listen, he just kept getting madder. Since he was a big Black outweighing me by at least 60 pounds, I held my peace. Another cook came to my defense. I was collecting a good story, which was favorable to the cooks because they are well known for their food. I'm still going to write it.

But it really gravels me when a Spec 5 chews out a PFC because he, the Spec 5, hasn't been promoted. It's unfair and to me, it seems that his promotion board was right—he's too insensitive and stupid—he couldn't handle the responsibility of a staff sergeant. I didn't take it as seriously as I might have because the rest of the guys understood my position, and I don't control what is printed in the paper. This attitude, unfortunately rampant among many of the Blacks, is that soul and feeling transcend logic, which I say isn't so. They should be as honest as the rest of us—they can't make us honest by being dishonest themselves. I was proud I didn't lose my cool when he got irrational but I assure you, it's a soul-wrenching experience to hold back.

Dad, I have been making the most out of the Patches experience—I have to admit that it was fun in many ways. Now that life's returning to normal and I'm back out on the firebases, I'm enjoying that too. Time runs swiftly. Fragging means to be "hand grenaded," to be injured by a thrown grenade. It's a rough business and relatively rare. When the troops' tempers get hot, the shrapnel occasionally flies and I want to be far far away.

GIS PREFER THEIRS "ON THE ROCKS"

When it was hot, cooling off was every soldier's obsession. This was the first in a string of ice stories, making it into the January 20, 1971, Cavalair.

FSB GREEN—Air conditioning is the GI's dream in the stifling tropical heat, but what can be done when there's none? Firebases may have the answer.

The GIs on LZs profit from one of the coolest field expedients created by man, a body conditioner of sorts, a beer or soda cooled on ice.

The grunt is especially receptive to the idea of cooling off after an iceless period in the bush. "Hot water is about all we drink out in the bush," explained Spec 4 Ron Moore, a member of Co. A, 1st Bn., 7th Cav.

Consequently, upon leaping off the birds that have carried them from the steaming jungles, there is a stampede of thirsty infantrymen to the coolers. "It's the first thing we head for on a firebase," explained PFC Larry Bailey. "It's one of the longest lines you'll find on an LZ."

The bush warriors' worst problem in the cooling business is one of the hard facts of life. "One of the basic problems, " said Moore, "is that ice melts. We never get enough ice to cool everything we want to cool."

A hardy skytrooper, in his enthusiasm over a refreshment being cold, is often willing to overlook little things, like whether it's alcoholic or not. "I don't drink beer," claimed PFC John Trueblood, "but if it's cold I'll drink it anyway."

There is sociability and sophistication about sitting with a can, sipping slowly on its cool contents that may even pass up an air conditioner. A GI might grow tired of an air conditioner, but he'll never outlive his appreciation for a cold soda.

Victim of His Own Chow

I generally wasn't a fan of Army food but I don't think I was showing much sensitivity to a cook's plight. The army cooks had to deal with dreadful conditions—preparing food on a firebase in particular was awful. The Cavalair *used this piece in the January 20, 1971, issue.*

FSB GREEN—"We end up feeding everybody in the battalion, even the dogs," said SSgt. Norbert Steinwandel, mess steward of HHC, 1st Bn., 7th Cav. Admittedly, the dogs are fed out of the garbage cans, but the statement is basically true.

"Our biggest problem is keeping things clean," explained Steinwandel as he talked about the challenges peculiar to a forward-area mess. "Sometimes we get stuff so dirty that we have to send it to the rear, but usually we can maintain the kitchen ourselves."

The weather has a maddening effect on cooking. "Mud is one of our worst enemies," commented PFC James Harris. "You not only have to live in the mud but cook standing in it. When it's dry it's not much better because then we have problems with the dust."

Despite all obstacles, the food keeps cooking and the GIs stay satiated. "We're the only hot chow producers in the battalion," maintains Spec 5 Barney Osborne. "We fly meals out to the bush and also feed the troops at FSB Green."

There has been only one recorded victim of the 1st of the 7th's chow. Steinwandel said he came to Vietnam thin but didn't stay that way long. "I weighed 143 pounds when I came in," he insisted stubbornly, "and I'm hitting 228 now."

Christmas Eve

December 24, 1970

I caught a butterfly for you, Becky. It doesn't seem to be too different from the ones I sent you. I tried to nab a colorful hornet but he nearly stung me and got away. Late afternoons here remind me of a similar time on a hot day back home, a gorgeous red sunset that tints everything. I can hardly wait to get the Nikonos I've ordered and send film home.

I wrote up yesterday's three stories and now have a headache. Since soldiers are famous drunkards and tonight is the holiday night of all nights (except New Year's night), I think I'll try to get drunk for the first time here.

The discipline required to write a letter to you every night has helped my Army writing immensely—I find I can write faster. You are right. I write more feature stories instead of hard news—hard news is so grim, uninteresting and repetitious. On the other hand, I grow more and more fascinated by the men fighting the war. My education here is more in human relations and human values. I have many weak moments and am not sure my true feelings—whatever they are—come across.

Bob Hope will be in Long Bin. I don't feel very interested in seeing this living legend. I like his humor but I don't care for what he's selling—he supports the military too much. He is from the World War II generation and maybe that's where he gets his politics. But this isn't World War II and I fear he makes us staying in Vietnam too comfortable. A rousing Bob Hope is no help even if he seems a nice man.

I've got to close this letter in a hurry. The steaks at FSSE are getting cold.

Fireworks; Bob Hope; Personnel Action Office

December 26, 1970

I just got a new ribbon for the typewriter, isn't it swanky? I didn't write yesterday—I played too much volleyball and overheated.

I was up until midnight on Christmas Eve and watched the fireworks. It went up with a yell of, "There go my last year's taxes!!" Christmas Day started with light, artificial military type. They put up about a hundred aerial

2. On Assignment: October 1, 1970, to December 31, 1970   149

flares within a few seconds—what a spectacle. Someone on the Air Force side was firing tracers, an added toast to Santa.

Late Christmas day, around 6:30 p.m., while playing volleyball furiously, I spotted funny lights on the horizon. Choppers? If so, there must have been a real flock of them, I thought, and sure enough. Sixteen Hueys, more than I've seen flying in formation, winged right over us with red and green smoke going out of their passenger compartments. It was beautiful and expensive but, big deal, the cost of wear and tear plus the gas is just a drop in the bucket.

Bob Hope held his audience in Long Bin, not exactly a war zone, but he did really well. I'm glad I didn't go—I would have gotten a first rate sunburn. And I still could see it. They're replaying the show right now on the tube—I can hear the applause and howling. Only a certain number from each unit were allowed to go. I stayed at the office, where it was quiet, and started work on my oceanography course. It's a rough course—it's more geology than anything right now.

I interviewed Capt. Harry Porthouse (Toledo, Oh.), the head of the Personnel Action Office of the 1st Cav. I wrote a story on Congressional Inquiries from this office—I told a little bit about it in the Olathe story. The captain feels that congressional inquires, that are the forwarding of letters from congressmen who have received letter from an irate American, are overused. He has three writers and two typists doing nothing but looking into inquiries. He said that just because a letter comes from a congressman doesn't mean that more can be done. In fact, he says that usually if the people would come directly to his office, he wouldn't have nearly as much trouble; the job would be done sooner. Only in rare instances can a letter to a congressman actually help.

His office handles special leaves, 212 discharges, and compassionate reassignments and many others, 30 in all. He doesn't mind the congressional inquires because he has a fetish about being honest and getting to the bottom of a problem. He often works as a source of information when someone doesn't understand the regulations. He showed me a list of the inquiries he was looking over. One was from a PFC who had been in grade for 5 months and said he wasn't getting promoted fast enough—what a laugh! I was impressed by the office; they appeared to be honest and really trying. I wouldn't mind working in an office like that although I enjoy the PIO much more.

Porthouse handles implementation of the two-week leave back to the States. The whole leave picture was a mess when tickets were put directly onto the market for sale. All the officers and clerks got there first. Also, tickets cost too much for everyone but the rich. They have changed the ticket sales system to an allotment by unit and assigned troop strength. The captain assured me that the Cav would get a much fairer shake and that men out in the field—in the bush—would have a better chance to escape for a while. It now costs $369 to fly to Oakland, $442 to Chicago, and $479 to New York. That's almost reasonable considering the distance of the flights. That's by charter jet with Pan Am and World Airways; Northwest Orient costs more because it's a scheduled flight, costing more than a chartered flight. "Like any new program," Porthouse commented. "It has its bugs. But I have no doubt it will be a fine program." I agree except that I'm not sure anyone is going to be in Vietnam long enough to enjoy it.

You ought to hear the rumors about the Cav leaving; they're beginning to make sense. The SFC from FSSE said that all equipment would start coming in at the beginning of January. Capt. Porthouse as much as said that we were about to leave when I asked him if he had any contingency plans for a pullout. And the battalions in the bush just aren't going after fights like they used to—firebases have stopped moving like they do in an active war. It all adds up. Everyone is now convinced we are the next unit going home but this would mean the end of the war because American forces are down to the very backbones now.

No one was on their toes—it was lucky that Brown and I were both in the office. First we got a call from a civilian correspondent, a Britisher, asking if we could get him to Saigon and, when I said that it probably wasn't possible, he asked where we could put him up. I didn't know the answer so I told him I'd call back. I walked over to Lt. White's hooch and asked him what we should do. Passing the buck, he said to call back and find out if he already had a room or if he should come down and sleep on the cot in the lieutenant's room. So I walked back to the office.

In the meantime, somebody had said to call Phuoc Vinh, that a civilian correspondent was coming down at Castle Pad and to get transportation for him by calling up one of the units. Ignoring those orders, I called the correspondent and told him that since our jeep was put away for the night, I'd walk up the short way to the R&R-DEROS Center and lead him back to our office. I went up, picked through the route and stepped in a waterhole walking back with him. We got back to the office and Al told me the first sergeant from HHC Rear had called and said they had no place to put up the correspondent.

Knowing perfectly well that the FSG didn't know what he was doing and, a little annoyed by all the conflicting orders, I walked with the press man over to the lieutenant's hooch and, sure enough, he had room. I don't mind all this late-night action as long as I don't act like a mindless PFC. Following orders would have screwed the whole thing up.

The Britisher, a young man with long hair in Army fatigues, had been out to the third brigade (FSB Mace) covering a rice denial program. The villagers down there are harvesting their rice and the NVA are used to taking part of the crop as taxes. The Americans have tried to stop this funny business with some success, to hear this chap talk. Tomorrow I get to drive him down to Long Bin, which I've finally figured out a little. Also we get to pick up this week's *Cavalairs*.

Personnel Action Can Solve Your Problems

The office described in this piece did work similar to what I did in my long career as a government bureaucrat. I may have had more of an affinity for this odd form of personal service than I generally admit. This was used in the January 13, 1971, Cavalair.

BIEN HOA—Rumor has it that a heated congressional inquiry, triggered by a letter from an irate serviceman, is the quickest way to save a situation for a GI. But is this really so?

Capt. Harry Porthouse, head of the Personnel Action Branch of the Adjutant General's Office, said he had been having heavy use of the congressional inquiry setup. But in most cases, he explains, the same result would be achieved anyway.

"It usually takes about 30 days for me to receive a letter back from a congressman," estimated Porthouse, "yet if a man takes a complaint up the chain of command to us instead, it can probably be handled faster."

Three writers and two typists work on nothing but inquiries. "Medical and assignment inquiries are the two biggest items we handle," commented Porthouse. "If a man has a problem we can't solve, we send it to the IG but this happens rarely. I'm not saying that you shouldn't write your congressman. It is a right every soldier knows he has and many use."

"Our office handles 30 different functions in all. Congressional inquiries, 212 discharges and leaves have the heaviest traffic but the other more specialized functions are important to certain GIs too. We try to protect both sides: the Army and the individual."

"But we have this problem with GIs writing their congressman before they see us," said Porthouse. "Early outs, for instance, should come to us first to give us a chance to solve their problems early. A congressman can't do anything more than send us the GI's letter anyway."

Personnel Action will be happy to handle your congressional inquiries but they would like to keep their other clerks at work too.

The Word "Skytrooper"

I had a thing about the word "skytrooper." It's a highfalutin' glamorous term for the good, honest word "grunt." My parents had inculcated in me an intolerance for clichés and word abuse. I marked up an issue of our magazine about this time with all the times skytrooper was used—an impressive number really. It bugged me that we were prettying up a grunt's usually miserable existence.

Killed Stories

December 28, 1970

 I went up to Phuoc Vinh today and picked up mail—three letters from you. I'm going to start planning for R&R in about my 7th or 8th month—where I don't know. It could get expensive if I go to Hong Kong and buy fancy cameras.

 Don't get too shook by that rocket attack—they weren't aiming for me and would have to have been mighty poor shots to blow me away.

 When I went up to Phuoc Vinh, I talked to or, more accurately, argued with the editor. He has been doing a poor job recently, I think, so I gave him a bad time, getting specific about the shortcomings of recent papers. He was touchy—I think someone else might have gone over the same ground earlier.

 I discovered that several of my stories had never been given a chance but killed on the spot: most prominently my "Christmas Tree Story" and my "95 Pound Grunt" story. What really was infuriating was he couldn't tell me why. This lieutenant, the editor, wants to be cautious, sacrificing vitality—I feel—for safety. I'm relatively new to the PIO game but I know good writing when I see it and he doesn't. I'll send you copies of the stories that didn't make it and let you judge.

 I made a pointed attack on the front-page article that was used, pretty thoroughly destroying it, I thought. I said the article was all pro-war at a time when we were about to withdraw in possible defeat. I liked DINFOS, my AIT (advanced individual training), because they taught us to be as honest and make things as interesting as possible, things my editor doesn't appreciate. I can't continue to turn out stories that aren't used and a paper produced of no value. I was polite enough so I won't lose my job, although the lieutenant may hold a grudge against me.

 Part of the problem is the short-timers' disease where people don't care because they're leaving soon. Since virtually everyone is short, no one wants to send stuff in from the brigades. And also because the Cav is about to enter standing down procedures, still more will think they won't be here long.

FSSE Friends

December 30, 1970

 One of my favorite 105mm howitzer shots got in *Stars and Stripes*—again they made a good choice of what they used.

2. On Assignment: October 1, 1970, to December 31, 1970   153

Lt. O'Daly came back from Hong Kong—had a great time buying inexpensive suits and shirts, stereo equipment and great buys. He spent well over a thousand dollars but seemed to get his money's worth. I'm thinking about the place myself. He said the place was a good fit for a variety-starved GI like me. But it would be expensive for me, too, and I'm cheap.

I'm glad the lieutenant is back. He has common sense and is fairly cool. He still holds out hope for the Stripes job and appreciates my problem with an overstaffed underproductive office. He said he'd have a talk about the killing of my stories with the major and maybe the editor, the culprit. I'll be sorry to see O'Daly go.

I wrote up a story on horseshoes yesterday, tying it in irreverently with the Cav's cavalry tradition. I've enclosed a copy for you to see. I had fun with it, doing it for my FSSE friends I'm always jabbering with. SFC Wilson is the supply specialist I wrote about in an earlier letter. He's been in the Army 16 years and is a good egg. He's been in Vietnam less than a month but keeps proclaiming how war is hell as he sips on his cold beer—they have the biggest freezer in the area. I was worried that he would destroy the beautiful arrangement at FSSE but he's taken to it like a duck to water. And he loves to play a lazy game of shoes.

I got a ride from an air force major who often gives the briefings at the 1st Brigade. I asked him where all these air strikes were going. He said that it was all secret but with a smile. We, Dave Lewis and I, said that it was belaboring the obvious to point out all the fully loaded jets taking off and bombing something. He just grinned.

EXPLAINING ART OF HORSESHOES

I showed my playful side when writing this, making fun of competitive sports. Being the pitiful athlete that I am, I've always had it in for gifted jocks. It was used in the February 17, 1971, Cavalair.

BIEN HOA—If seamen are good swimmers and airmen good parachutists, what are cavalrymen traditionally good at? Horseshoe pitching, of course. In the modern 1st Cavalry Division, about all that remains of the mounted cavalry's past is the horse's head on the division's patch and horseshoes in the division's horseshoe pits.

Hardly reminiscent of a cavalry charge, horseshoes is a friendly sedate game. In the Vietnam sports world, it lies somewhere between a fierce jungle volleyball game and a chess match. And like all sports, it has its amateurs and its pros.

SFC James D. Wilson (Columbia, S.C.), a veteran with 8 ringers in a row on his record, is the resident pro of the Forward Services and Support Element

(FSSE). A horseshoe traditionalist contemptuous of barnyard rules, he rides roughshod over the native FSSE competition.

There are a few dangers peculiar to FSSE. "We've come close to having ringers on our dogs when they sniff around in the pit," explains Wilson. "Also, the sun keeps setting too early so we keep throwing in the dark."

Wilson commented on the strenuous aspect of the game. "Sometimes you get tired, after bending over picking up horseshoes a couple of hours." It requires endurance to overcome the pitfalls of horseshoes.

One of the present victims of Wilson's aggressive shoe game is Spec 4 Billy M. Knapp (Platteville, Colo.). "I've been throwing only about three weeks now," explains Knapp. "I've only beat the Sarge twice, once when he was throwing left handed. I'm catching on, though. I'm going to stay with it until I beat him thoroughly."

Part of Knapp's problem with the Sarge is the foxy old pro's daring us of psychological warfare. "You've got to have a lot of confidence to stand up to his ribbing," insisted Knapp, a bit helplessly.

Wilson and Knapp, like all true sportsmen, love competition. If football has its all-pro games and swimming its invitationals, why can't FSSE have its All-Bien Hoa Invitational Horseshoe Tournament and sustain the old cavalry spirit? Their only problem is that they'd have to expand across the street; they only have enough room for one pair of horseshoe pits in their front yard.

Hornets; HOH Crash; Sniper Rifle

December 31, 1970

I flew out to FSB Green and returned early, about 2 p.m. I came across a new kind of ambush in which two men were medevaced. The pointman, hacking through the undergrowth, didn't spot the trap until it was too late. He cut into a strange, large egg-shaped thing and they were promptly chased all over the jungle. The first three men in the column took the brunt of the attack although ten men in all were stung—by enraged hornets, thousands of them.

"You could call it a panic but you'd be in a panic too if you had 200 bees flying around your head," recalled SSgt. Delbert Hladik (Lincoln, Neb.), a relatively old (about 40) grunt. "We must have sounded like a regiment trampling through the forest as we did. I was number three." I talked to him on the firebase, out of the field because of troubles with swelling and itching after the numerous stings, 25, he estimates. "They chased us about 400 to 500 meters," he explained. "They just wouldn't leave. You'd be surprised what a GI can get through when he's at a dead run." From what he said, they were big hornets. I've seen some of them, Becky, in fact I tried to catch one but he was just too mean. As you know, stings can act just like a poisonous snakebite.

2. On Assignment: October 1, 1970, to December 31, 1970

As you remember with Nader [*an Iranian foreign student who lived with our family for a year*], reactions to bee stings can be scary.

At the briefing last night, we were told that a LOH had crashed with three line ones and a very serious line two. This means 3 dead, one near death. I don't understand the value of using euphemisms for death. I suppose that euphemisms take some of the sting out of the bad news but everyone knew the code. There were still gasps in the room when the briefer said three line ones.

I decided to give the Chinese sniper rifle from the cache to Lt. O'Daly. I just don't want to worry about it for the rest of the tour. It's all beat up and needs immediate care. I would rather make sure he gets it than lose it anyway if I register it this early in my tour, which I'm told often happens. It is really the last thing I want to bring home—they might think I killed somebody for it. I can't imagine the bloody thing hanging over my mantle. I'm much prouder of the crossbows.

We've got a Vietnamese band playing American music across the street. They manage pretty well considering that their music, which I've listened to, sounds very different from ours. They aren't used to our approach to harmony or being in key. The drummer isn't bad and the go-go girls are pretty.

First Stinging Defeat

Attacks on grunts came in many forms—GIs had to be alert for unexpected challenges. This story was in the January 20, 1971, Cavalair *and the May 1971* Garry Owen *orientation issue.*

NEAR FSB JUPITER—Skytroopers of the 1st Plt., Co. C, 1st Bn., 12th Cav. were handed their first stinging defeat recently. Fortunately, it was at the hands of a nest of hornets.

The lopsided fight began when the platoon's pointman inadvertently sliced into a pineapple-shaped hornet hooch, releasing waves of large enraged hornets on the helpless men. Their weapons useless, the infantrymen broke into a somewhat disorganized tactical retreat.

"You could call it a panic," admitted SSgt. Delbert Hladik, "but you'd be in a panic too if you had two hundred hornets flying around your head."

Hladik had been a borderline case. Although he was stung, no MEDEVAC was necessary for him. "My right eye puffed up and closed last night. I was stung about 25 times."

"The hornets chased us about 400 meters," the sergeant insisted, chuckling. "You'd be surprised what a GI can get through at a dead run. We think they'd been chasing water buffalo before us and had some practice. We must have sounded like a regiment during the retreat."

After the platoon had retreated to a safe area and secured a landing zone, a perimeter was set up and two of the more seriously stung soldiers were MEDEVACED.

After the incident, Hladik, obviously no insect collector, couldn't identify the attackers accurately. "They were big hornets though I'm not sure they were striped. I was in such a hurry."

CHAPTER 3

Into the Jungle: January 1, 1971, to February 27, 1971

I continued to write stories, many collected on firebases. I also accompanied the same infantry unit in the jungle again, which discovered a large enemy hooch complex. The division got into the process of leaving Vietnam.

New Year's Celebration; Brawl

January 1, 1971

I just finished opening that beautiful care package from you—much to munch on and think about. I'm sitting here gagging on the pipe you sent me and wondering if I can afford to smoke a pipe and stain my teeth. It is a good way to waste time.

You should have watched our new year come in; I felt some luck was involved surviving the experience. About two minutes before midnight (their watches were fast), the base was lit up by a barrage of flairs and fireworks. The tracers from all the M-60 machine guns on base lit the sky. We wondered where the bullets—five to one straight lead) were coming down. The 229th Assault Helicopter Battalion was going wild, although they have a nice open field next to them. They were all around the perimeter and a few shot from within. We were a little upset when they started lowering the bullet streams and we jumped down from the connex we were standing on. It was spectacular. I had a swig of some white wine and headed off for bed but missed the later festivities.

Some of the guys from 2/19th Artillery were all boozed up and feeling mean. About fifteen of them got into a big brawl right out in the middle of the street. It reminded me of the early morning dogfights we sometimes have, one of our major forms of entertainment. The dogs have more to fight about though—a fair maiden pooch in heat. But I guess the artillery crew had a good time duking it out.

The 2/19th and HHC Rear have teamed up to try to kick us out of our hooch into a less luxurious dwelling. Lt. O'Daly almost got into a fistfight with a captain because the captain—a REMF dud—was being obnoxious as only an unimaginative officer can be. O'Daly is a violence-spawned Irishman and big enough—the captain was a fool to hassle him. But this may explain our housing being imperiled. I hear the HHC fellows, the officers anyway, are rejects from the field. We might be safer in the field.

I'm sending you a picture so you can see what a hardened trooper your kid has become. Could you send me pictures of yourselves, especially pictures of Becky with the Bertram snake? Everyone thinks my sister must be nuts to like snakes; I tell them that my sister is smarter than little girls that play with dolls and it does keep her off the streets. They say, "But I can't imagine a boy wanting to go out on a date with Becky and her snake." I retort that she doesn't take her snake everywhere with her, including on dates.

The damned pipe keeps dying on me and Al is bugging me. He says that *Stars and Stripes* had an article about pipe smokers having lower than average IQs—that sounds fraudulent to me. I just ran out of matches; now I can stop burning my tongue.

Don't tell people I'm too bad off—I'm kind of enjoying this experience—although something is missing in my social life. I'll appreciate pretty girls more after this, that's for certain.

Sports; Airfield; Air Support

January 2, 1971

So Ohio State and Texas both lost and Nebraska's still in it. The Big Red [*Nebraska*] will be hard to live with for the next couple of months. You've said, dad, that you've never seen such football fans in your life as Nebraska's but you've never been in Vietnam. We have TV rebroadcasts of all the games and get pretty enthusiastic but we always know beforehand who's going to win.

The only deaths we've had recently have been from accidents, although occasionally the NVA kill one of our men. I was fortunate to have missed the Cambodian incursion. You can disagree on whether it was right or wrong (I'm not sure myself) but it was one of the bloodiest things the 1st Cav and a few other units have been in. I seem to be spending my time mostly writing feature articles, my best ones oddly enough on dogs, and from talking with infantrymen.

Damned noisy jets, they are bombing something this morning. They keep thundering off the airstrip about a half mile from where I'm typing. It's

3. Into the Jungle: January 1, 1971, to February 27, 1971   159

a fairly new airfield with everything from caribou freight flights to sophisticated jets touching down. It looks like a Christmas tree at night but thankfully is quieter then. We have Freedom birds coming in every once in a while. You can see some of the saddest and happiest GIs at the airport; the sad men are the newbies and the happy ones the veterans going home.

I continue to do a great deal of flying in choppers all over our brigade among the firebases. I grow tired of sitting, trying to be patient, waiting for a ride. I'm just a helicopter hitchhiker by profession and a writer second. But hitching is not only legal but the only way. I get the feeling the 1st Cav is overextended when I have to fly 40 miles in the air to a firebase. Virtually everything is flown in by air and protected by air, whether it be by the artillery flown in, Cobra gunships (armed helicopters) on station, or Air Force jets, which can arrive from Bien Hoa in a few minutes. You have to see it to grasp what a difference it makes in warfare. A much greater area can be covered. And although Vietnam is a small country, it doesn't seem small after traveling even a short ways through the jungle.

Cameras; Collecting; Poker

January 3, 1971

I went up to Phuoc Vinh for the mail and didn't find a camera to take out for a belated Patches photo session. Our photographer Fry is going out instead and I get to have two days in peace. My Nikonos hasn't come yet but it's okay; I want to work on this month's stories.

Talking of Becky trying to collect dead turtles, I tried collecting a large cockroach with similar results. The cockroach stunk so much that day after I killed it that I had to throw it out and wash my hands. Smaller insects I collected in the past weren't this juicy. I wonder how Becky's chameleons would compete with the ones here. We have one living on the wall separating my room and Al Brown's. He makes funny little noises like he's a Tarzan who's just swallowed a big bug.

Lt. O'Daly says he knows the date when the Cav is going home or, at least, the day by which the first of the brigades is gone. He, of course, won't say when or which brigade. The 1st Brigade, my brigade, is popularly thought to be the first to go into standdown. We'll see.

FSSE is being corrupted by poker with all that betting, losing, and carrying on. They don't drink much anymore—disgusting. They have a good time losing their money to each other. It's a disease that weakens the mind and the pocket book.

Lt. O'Daly is taking home that Leica I was using, as if it was his. It isn't registered on the property books of the IO office and someone was bound to pick up this free camera. The lieutenant said he'd trade it in for a Nikon setup or something. He asked me what I thought he should do with it. I told him I didn't need it—he should take it home. So I've kept my mouth shut so O'Daly won't be caught. It comes down to your definition of dishonesty. If it were up to the Army, the camera like the World War II Graflexes, would be burned. [*One of the last things Dad did as a supply officer in India at the end of World War II was overseeing the destruction of tons of supplies, including new Graflex cameras, which were burned. Dad said he wished he'd picked up one of those cameras and taken it home.*]

Grunts vs. Insects

January 4, 1971

I flew out to FSB Jupiter and on the way saw FSB Connell, which was opened up again. Connell is just a small base with three 105mm howitzers as defense. Jupiter was discouraging because nothing very exciting was going on.

I talked to the 1st Platoon, Delta Co., 1st Bn., 12th Cav. and they clammed up, most of them. So I did a desperation story on insects, more than just the bees of B 1/12th. They ran across spiders, scorpions, leeches (not strictly speaking an insect), ants, termites, centipedes and, of course, bees. Helmets were one of the spots most often hit by insects. One guy had a big bug in his helmet he couldn't dislodge and another grunt found his helmet inhabited by termites another morning. The medic out there insisted that insect bites were far from rare. It's a bug collector's dream and a grunt's horror. There are many wars in the bush.

December 24th, the platoon tried to get 4 or 5 of their men to a log pad so they could be sent out to the Bob Hope Show. They humped about 10 clicks (kilometers) and were really pooped out. Their commander, from the air, led them on a merry chase first one direction, then another. Right as they were heading into the final stretch, they were ambushed although no one was hurt. They were almost too worn out to fight. Charlie has a knack for hitting the GIs when the GIs least want to fight.

I was amazed at the number of new men in Delta Company; I've been out in the bush more than they've been. They'd just hit the firebase ten days ago. It was funny, me asking them what it was like when they hadn't been out there yet.

We've got a big thing going on comic books. Our favorites as (1) the Hulk, (2) Superman, and (3)X-Men, not Donald Duck or Mickey Mouse, which are too juvenile. I like simpletons and Hulk fits the type. He comes up with such classics as "Time to SMASH!" and "Hulk heard enough talk, time to fight." He'd definitely fit in the Army. Comics incorporating Vietnam may degrade them in my estimation by trying to make them relevant. They're subverting the true worth of comics, clichés and escape.

3. Into the Jungle: January 1, 1971, to February 27, 1971   161

I had quite a reaction to that pipe the first night I smoked it—I threw up. I was all ready to quit but have discovered that maybe it was the tobacco—I like Half and Half better than that Dutch stuff. The Half and Half reminds me of Mr. Larson—I can tell the tobacco by the smoke's smell. There's a certain nostalgia about it. It's good for appearances and tends to calm me down with all the fiddling. I don't inhale it. I refuse to smoke cigarettes.

Fleas and ticks are really hard on our dogs, especially Blanche, our hooch's pooch. So we gave her a bath today and, like most dogs, she didn't like the water. We use flea shampoo and let her loose afterwards to dry off. She rolled in the mud like a true dog but moved into the final weeks of her pregnancy a little cleaner.

As you remember, I gave Lt. O'Daly my beat up CKC sniper rifle. He just told me that it may be good enough to bribe a sergeant into letting the lieutenant home three days early. Just like the Army, a little gift under the table can speed things up. War trophy weapons are big status symbols, like fraternity pins, over here. They are as good as money if you know someone. Although O'Daly admitted that he's having troubles cleaning up the rifle, he thinks it may be good enough to do the trick. I'm glad the CKC was some use to someone because I didn't think it worth messing with.

Bug Wars

You'd think the poor grunts were always under insect attack but based on my admittedly limited field experience, attacks weren't constant, only frequent. I found this story in the February 3, 1971, Cavalair *with the headline "Grunts Dislike Entomology." There must be another paper I haven't located that used the "Bug Wars" headline.*

FSB JUPITER—The Vietnam jungles are an entomologist's dream and a grunt's madhouse as far as collecting insects goes. The insects are endless in variety, voracious in appetite, amazingly large, and staggering in numbers. For this reason, an entomologist could devote a lifetime to collecting insects. The grunt, on the other hand, spends his tour working up bug evasion ploys because he has to live with insects.

"It's constant insect harassment," commented Spec 4 Louis Thomas, a medic with D Co., 1st Bn., 12th Cav.

Similar to warriors of mighty armies, the insects show impressive ranks: scorpions, spiders, ants, termites, centipedes, bees and even leeches, not technically an insect, are all aggressive and numerous.

GIs use repellants and insect bombs with limited success, trying to protect themselves. But the insects strike mercilessly and at all hours. "Sometimes the termites start chewing on one of us in the middle of the night," explains Thomas, "and the victim leaps around doing a hopping Indian-type dance. Waking up in the morning with a spider or scorpion companion isn't rare."

Some bugs shake up the GI with their ugliness. PFC Jerry Levesque (New Britain, Conn.) was shook up by a multi-legged, clawed bug that refused to leave his helmet as the platoon was taking off for its morning walk. "I was balancing the pack on my back and picking up my helmet when I glanced inside. There sat this 'thing.' He kept clinging to the webbing, glaring at me, refusing to leave gracefully."

The worst part of the insect threat is that there are actually American casualties. Another unit medevaced two men when set upon by hornets. Delta Co. had encountered the same problem according to Thomas: "I'd never been stung by bees until I hit the bush and I hadn't missed a thing."

Speaking as a medic, Thomas sees his place as an anti-pest warrior. "It's pretty commonplace treating insect bites."

The insects have their own amplifiers, like stereo nuts, and irritate the GIs with everything from repetitious chirping to shrill buzzing. There is one particularly offensive bug. "We have this siren cicada," said Thomas, "it's so loud it can drive you nuts."

There is agreement between grunts that collecting insect bodies would be a success in the bush. In Thomas' words, "I see a new bug every day, unfortunately."

Butterfly Capture; Lieutenant's Footlocker

January 5, 1971

I just caught a butterfly for you, Becky, a good sized one. As a plus, Al Brown put on a nice show. "There's a huge moth in my room!" he howled much like a woman, frightened by a mouse. I found something to catch it in as Al yelled frantically, "It might be poisonous!" It was enjoyable. Enclosed is the butterfly—sorry it's so tattered.

I was jeep driver for Lt. O'Daly all day; we were mostly driving around Long Bin as he prepared to leave country. He had a footlocker for hold baggage. We finally found the building and he got in line. What an operation—the junk is rated right on the spot. Everything was also checked. One E-7 got caught. He had an Army suitcase, a poncho liner tucked in a suit and other no nos. He was just plain dishonest—it was fun to watch as he got in deeper.

My project for the next few days will be helping work up the brochure we give out when the 1st Cav stands down. That is the ultimate indicator that we're leaving.

3. Into the Jungle: January 1, 1971, to February 27, 1971

Hooch Move; Pilot Helmets

January 7, 1971

All I did yesterday was type stencils for the brochure to be handed out to the press when the 1st Cav leaves Vietnam. I worked on stuff like telephone numbers, flight schedules, and the names of the division's brass.

We were told that we'd have to move today. To start out we swore we'd tear down the room dividers in our hooch and take the wood but we finally had mercy on the 2/19 Artillery folk and left it standing. In an hour and a half we had all our household goods at the other hooch about two blocks away and started leaning up and room arranging. We still have separate rooms but it's just not as friendly a place with military intelligence on one side and the CID (Central Investigation Department or something like that) on the other. My room is livable but FSSE isn't next door and the volleyball net isn't in our front yard.

I've heard there's all kinds of mail up at Phuoc Vinh so I'm going up tomorrow to pick it up. The lieutenants always forget to bring the mail down for us so the task is handed over to an enlisted man who is forced to waste a day and capture the mailbag.

I went to the briefing last night and it's getting shorter. Nothing's happening in the field and no one seems very interested in what's going on out there. They are all getting ready to leave, going on "search and avoid" missions, which make firebases the place grunts don't want to go. Nobody seems to want to find the enemy anymore.

The helmets of chopper pilots are entertainment in themselves. One guy had American flag stripes on his helmet and peace signs are popular. But I saw my favorite a few days ago. As you may know, the 7th Cavalry—the 1/7th and 2/7th (both in my brigade)—are known as Custer's Own. Well, this pilot read "Custer Had It Coming" and I broke up on the Chinook, giggling to myself. It would be a great arm patch for a militant Indian.

Mail Run; ROK Soldiers; "Hair"

January 8, 1971

I flew up by fixed wing to Phuoc Vinh today to pick up the mail with little success. They only had today's offering. The rest of the week's mail is between Phuoc Vinh and Bien Hoa. I have a new address you should use that will come directly to me in Bien Hoa; I no longer will have to waste the time going into the jaws of the PIO serpent (Phuoc Vinh) to collect it.

I got a look at my first ROK (Republic of Korea) Army soldiers in the Bien Hoa Air Force Terminal. They were a handsome, healthy-looking crew and very orderly as they came in, almost as if they were being herded. They looked as unARVN as an American, once it occurred to me that they weren't Vietnamese. They've made a name for themselves over here as fearsome killers although not as brainy as American grunts. The adage, "He's hard as an ROK," has become their own.

More wild rumors are going around. In one the Cav is going to be pulled out of 'Nam in toto with everyone going back on ships. Another rumor has the PIO office moving from Phuoc Vinh to Bien Hoa when the ARVNs are handed Phuoc Vinh after receiving Song Be. The second is more believable, from more reliable sources.

I have wall-to-wall nudes in my new room from the collection of the elusive Daniel Ramlow. I never had trouble remembering what girls looked like until I got over here—it makes for a friendly room I must say. Boy, I've got everything now, even an ice cooler for sodas. Which reminds me, the weather has been beautiful: hot during the days but cool, even cold, at night. I'm told that February and March are much worse.

The statement about refugees from the American system going to Canada intrigues me. It's a good point that men aren't avoiding just the draft although I'd think it's the primary reason. How about young women—are they leaving too? I'm not giving up on the American system yet but if the Army is considered part of the system, I am at times sorely tried. I don't have it that bad: I don't have formations, have my own room, and don't have set hours to get up and go to bed. But I see many other miserable people around me.

My latest kick is the album "Hair." I'm not saying I like everything on the album but it puts life where it's at and I like the music. Dad, if you want to understand how it feels to be in my age group, "Hair" is the record for you. It is profane but gets into the ludicrous insides of patriotism, racism, nudity, and the basic irrational basis of human life. And the Army hasn't hurt its popularity—I hear it all over.

Morale; Year's First Kill; Entertainer

January 9, 1971

I just finished reading the lead story in the 1/11/71 *Newsweek* issue on the morale of the troops in Vietnam and I must say, they've hit it on the head. Drugs are rampant. Units are going on search and avoid missions. Lifers are on the run in many places with troops talking about fragging their leaders. It says more clearly what I've been getting at.

I went out to FSB Green today and had a good time talking with my friends in Echo Recon who are still actively engaged in hunting the enemy and running him to ground. They are considered one of the best recon units

3. Into the Jungle: January 1, 1971, to February 27, 1971

in the Cav since their jaunt with me. They've been finding all kinds of things. On December 31st they were chasing NVA around and managed to get a whiff of the CS gas they were trying to incapacitate the enemy with. They also got the Division's first kill of 1971 at 9:30 in the morning. A small patrol found a hooch and was poking through it and the brick kiln nearby.

One of the newbies was out nearby searching when someone opened up with their AK-47. He hit it (dropped to the ground) and couldn't figure out how they had missed. He is 6 feet 7, a very large target. They think he was not the target, that the NVA thought they might hit the Americans in the hooch area. Anyway, this new soldier, PFC Shannon Gibson (San Diego, Cal.) threw a hand grenade about 15 meters, a very short lob. He seriously injured one of the enemy and they all took off with the rest of Echo Recon in hot pursuit. They got a second shot at the wounded man and one of the sergeants is certain he was hit again but the fellow managed to escape again. This sergeant said this enemy soldier's getting up is the kind of thing that haunts you in the bush. The powers of an NVA soldier to keep from getting captured are legendary.

My second story is lighter, thank god.

Echo Recon 1/7th has a number of new men and for a while were afraid they'd have problems breaking them in. But it seems their new men have a good deal of talent and brains. PFC Michael Vasquez (Simi Valley, Cal.) is the prize example. He is an imitation and impressions artist. As Sgt. Jesse Reed (Spring City, Tenn.) described Vasquez's talent, "He can do a freedom bird, a chopper winding up and does a great radar tuning. He can even look like a radar." I couldn't believe it so I asked for a demonstration. He has a weird metallic electronic like whistle, which does sound like a radar. His impression of a mechanical man is priceless and this isn't the end of his talents. He is said to be an even better singer than he is with his impersonations and dramatic renditions of Greek gods and English lawyers. Vasquez said, "I try to show them my theatrical talents and they laugh at me." He is a Mexican-American who reminds me of one of my old buddies in basic training. He is good for hours of laughs and, as every good grunt will tell you, a grunt has to keep his sense of humor.

This week's *Cavalair* newspaper came out and was almost as bad as last week's. This issue has only one story and one lead of mine—that's it. I found out that another person besides our lieutenant editor has been killing my stories. We've just gotten a new chief of staff, a colonel, who has been killing stories right and left for no particular reason. This may be why I haven't gotten a single feature article in the paper in nearly a month. Until now, we've had some freedom but now there's very little. I'll write for myself I guess and send you a copy of everything I do from now on. I refuse to quit but I need an R&R.

Bush League Entertainer

Soldiers prized hilarious fellows like this newbie. And guys this talented were rare. The piece was printed in the February 3, 1971, Cavalair.

FSB GREEN—PFC Michael Vasquez is strictly a bush league entertainer but his fellow grunts don't seem to mind. He never ceased to tickle them with one of his impressions or dramatic renditions.

"He can do a freedom bird, a chopper winding up, and does a great radar tuning in," insisted Sgt. Jesse Reed of Echo Recon, 1st Bn., 7th Cav. and Vasquez's NCO. "He can look like a radar, too."

Listening to Vasquez "live," it became clear how he does on part of his act. "I actually whistle," explained Vasquez. "I have trouble with the Freedom Bird, though, since I'm always running out of air." The whistle itself is strangely metallic and electronic, seeming to come from nowhere.

He also does his mechanical-man routine and, in a live demonstration on the firebase, managed to surprise a GI enough to get him on the run before he realized that the mechanical man wasn't.

But Vasquez's talent doesn't end with his impressions. He also does dramatic scenes and expects his audience to be dutifully sober and critical. Fortunately, humorless grunts are in short supply in the unit. "I try to show them my theatrical talents and they laugh at me," admitted Vasquez. He does his dramatic interpretations of Greek gods and English lawyers with all the fervor of a Shakespearean death scene.

A lively sense of humor is as essential in the bush as having a good night's sleep. Many units have their clowns and their wits, but it must be better to have your own platoon Freedom Bird and English lawyer.

Dog Miscarriage; The Dap

January 10, 1971

The sad news of the day is that Blanche had a miscarriage—we just found one of the pups where she dropped it. It's all very sad to lose the pups—we'd watched the pregnancy from the beginning. We think someone gave her something because suddenly she looked ill. We were afraid this would happen.

We've decided to let three cooks live in our hooch because we have more rooms than bodies. They can feed us better and will bring a bar in with them. It shouldn't be quite so lonely although I don't see any great glow of intellectual curiosity about them so the socializing will probably be limited.

Nobody seems to be doing anything in the rear; it's just a long vigil for a dying war that no one knows how to end. The weather has been downright

3. Into the Jungle: January 1, 1971, to February 27, 1971

Michael Vasquez—the entertainer—talks with fellow grunt John Alfred Martin in early February 1971.

pleasant. I've spent my time writing stories, drinking sodas, and talking to Ed Howard about his life on the Chicago police force and before. He likes to talk and I enjoy listening to him; his upbringing and his "home block" hold little resemblance to mine. But that doesn't mean I can't understand what he's talking about.

He is an independent cuss who won't necessarily give another brother the dap if there are too many brothers around. When an offended Black asks him what's gotten into him, he explains that he thinks the dap has a tendency to become nonsense. Later on he slides in that he's still a cop from Chicago and enjoys the response he gets from his fellow Blacks. I think Ed objects to the same thing in the dap that I do. I liken it to putting American flags on everything you own—it has no real substance other than filling time or annoying whites. I don't think it helps Blacks get ahead—it's like the clubishness and fraternity bullshit I put up with in college.

I can hear someone playing "I'm an Okie from Muskogee," the direct opposite to the album "Hair." We've got everything over here from the radicals to the reactionaries. The Army has never been able to even out problems it acquires from its civilian soldiers. They are making a valiant effort to control the drug problem; the house for addicts over at Bearcat and the amnesty program are good ideas. From what *Newsweek* said, the drug problem gets worse the farther north you go but it's bad enough here. The Army is tackling problems that civilians haven't solved, things like drugs, race and educational opportunities. If the Army is to become all-volunteer, I would think it has to offer something the Army does better, hopefully away from its authoritarian approach to leading men.

Office Politics; Water Point; Cav's Leaving

January 12, 1971

Yesterday we had an office meeting. Lt. White stubbornly insisted Al and I turn in five stories while still being jeep drivers. It was an unhappy session, especially for Al, who kept being needled by White for being a shammer. Al, with his cynical attitude toward it all, was shook up by White's windy harangue. White won't accept that jeep driving takes time and that flying out to firebases is hard, often unproductive work. He also won't accept that no one else in the division is turning out the volume of stories that we are.

Ed Howard shows how a GI in the rear should dress—pressed fatigues and polished boots. I don't think we normally had the "Power to the People" poster in the PIO—I'm sure it was Ed's.

Don Fry also got mixed in. Being understaffed in the office, the jeep driving has to be done by the four enlisted men in the office. White, who doesn't mind driving jeeps, insists on us driving him for the status of it. Fry failed him yesterday morning when he was unable to get out of bed until 11:20 a.m. Don is one of those strange drinkers who goes to sleep after a bender and wakes up 16 hours later—it's incredible. And White was furious with Fry when he failed to get up. I was probably in the best position and kept my peace through most of it. I finally talked the lieutenant into four stories a week but I don't know if I can keep him there.

3. Into the Jungle: January 1, 1971, to February 27, 1971   169

I flew out to FSB Jupiter and saw the new firebase Darby on the way, also a 1/12th firebase. The only notable thing about the base is that nothing has been happening. With trouble finding anything, I looked into the water point situation. It's expensive to fly water into a firebase. So many of the bigger bases have their own water pumping and filter system near the firebase. Using ferric chloride and limestone to settle out the crud in the water and chlorine to disinfect it, they produce 2400 to 3600 gallons of pure "potable" water a day for Jupiter's use.

As a sidelight, the two guys that run the water point, both members of 8th Engineers, were at FSB Ares' water point earlier. One of them was watching as CBS filmed the pot smokers smoking through their shotgun and talking anti–Army. I asked the guy if he'd seen this happen before. Both guys said it had happened every morning—this wasn't just put on for CBS' entertainment. That's about what I expected.

The cooks moved in the day before yesterday and moved out yesterday—it turns out they weren't in their company area. They should have checked first—it's much quieter at least.

Enclosed is a clipping from *Stripes* confirming what I was expecting: the Cav is going home—at least most of it—before May. I still don't know where this leaves me although I'm convinced that Bien Hoa is the best place to be. It will be here the longest.

Al Brown on February 4th is going home for two weeks, taking advantage of the two-week-leave program. He says he'll be relieved to leave and buy some peace back home. He claims he can adapt to the cold in no time—I'm not so sure about that.

Your letter came and, as I was afraid, you did get caught in that blizzard. I'm sorry I missed it—a good big crisp blizzard doesn't whistle into town every winter. It was unwelcome for you—you must have made it home by now. Our weather by comparison has been perfection itself. It's dry, not very humid and cool by Vietnam standards.—90s during the day, the mid 70s at night. But I still have a hankering for a little winter weather.

NATIVE SOURCE

Water isn't something I would have thought was important in a war but when I found out about the water filtration system on a firebase, I asked questions and learned differently. This story was printed in the February 3, 1971, Cavalair.

FSB JUPITER—Carrying water in clouds would be much easier and cheaper than having it slung out under Chinooks. Flying water in firebases has become so expensive, in fact, that a different approach to water collection has been devised here. The engineers' answer is a portable water system, using native springs, streams and rivers as the source for their water supply.

Spec 4 Ronald Cooper and PFC Ronald Harvey run the water point here. Both are members of HHC, 8th Engineer Bn., and along with another group of engineers, they recently spent four days building a road to a small stream which, when widened with explosives, became the main water supplier.

With regard to the water purification process, Cooper explained that they use ferric chloride and limestone to settle out sediments and chlorine to disinfect the water. "We filter the water by utilizing a pump to push the water through," he added.

A water point with an abundant supply of water sometimes becomes the local shower and swimming hole, but this firebase's waters are not that plentiful. "We have a 1200 gallon water truck we fill two or three times a day," stated Harvey.

"Springs are the best source for drawing water," commented Cooper.

Open Mess System; Babysitters' Letter

January 13, 1971

I'm glad to hear you made it home and kept the car right side up. I missed the blizzard but not the hassle you went through driving through it.

I checked out the Officer and NCO-EM Open Mess System. I thought it involved the mess halls but actually it's a series of clubs in the 1st Cav like the one across the street that has a Vietnamese band playing. The clubs can make tremendous profits because of their unbelievable sales volume. They sold $210,000 worth of stuff last month. The clubs are in the four large bases: Bearcat and Phu Loi—where we have a few Cav men—and Bien Hoa and Phuoc Vinh. They spent $64,791.05 buying beers and sodas. There are two branches of the system—officers and non-commissioned officers/enlisted men.

They are constantly having their books inspected—it is a touchy area as you've probably heard following the Germany mess scandals. Christmas was a big period: $16,000 worth of bands, about $5000 more than a usual month. They gave away $3000 to $4000 in free beers and sodas to NCO/EM clubs during the holidays. For half a year their prices were up to make up for deficits from a previous man running the office. They made $48,000 in April as they were catching up but have lowered prices as they reached the point where they could pay all their bills. Beer—not surprisingly—is their biggest seller and produces the most revenues.

That greeting card from Tina and Stella fascinated me because they are very hard to remember. [*They were my babysitters in the mid–1950s. Old spin-*

ster sisters, Stella had changed more because she was a high school graduate. This was when my family lived in Winona, Minnesota.] The last time I saw them was ten years ago. The back of their letter—the outside—was more informative than the inside. They wrote: "Two of your greatest fans." That's quite a come-on for a letter, and being curious, I'm going to write them a good page and see how they answer back. They don't know I'm in Vietnam, I take it.

My typing is deteriorating too, Dad—I go too fast for my fingers. As it is, most of the guys in the office don't compose stories on the typewriter. Like you, I find it easier on a typewriter and it's faster and easier to read than my handwriting, but I'm still slow.

Ed Howard's little 7-year-old brother back in Chicago is in bad shape. He has a tumor on his bladder and is bleeding badly. The last news was six days ago and Ed is furious that his mother didn't call him instead of write him a letter. Ed can get a leave home but he rues the idea of going home less than 30 days to go in his Vietnam tour. He could get a compassionate leave for thirty days but it isn't a good thing to come home to. And the thing is that Ed's brother's fate is probably already decided—Ed would probably be too late no matter what. Ed's family is close-knit and he feels strongly that he should be there to defend his little brother from the pitfalls that Chicago is famous for. He's helpless now and wouldn't be able to do much if he was home.

P.S. It's amazing what a Vietnamese band can do considering they don't speak English and have a different concept of music. Lieutenant Epstein stole my shirt to play enlisted man—that's a switch. He wants to see the band in the enlisted man's club.

NCO-EM Club System
Provides Fun, Refreshments

The club system in Bien Hoa was a much appreciated and much used perk of living in the rear. I certainly hung out in them. They made an often-boring existence more tolerable. This article was in the February 3, 1971, Cavalair *and* The Army Times' *February 17, 1971, issue.*

BIEN HOA—Who buys $64,791.05 worth of beers and sodas a month? Who gave away between $3,000 and $4,000 worth of beers and sodas for the Christmas holidays? And who sold $2,000,000 worth of fun and refreshments last year? The NCO-EM Open Mess system of the 1st Cav, of course, better known as the Clubs System.

With 19 NCO-EM clubs in Bearcat, Phuoc Loi, Phuoc Vinh and Bien Hoa, the system provides food, drinks and live entertainment for the socially inclined skytroopers. Along with the 11 Officers' clubs, the entire system sold $210,000 worth in December, which gives some idea of the clubs' success.

According to Capt. Paul McKnight, the assistant G-1 in charge of the Club System, "My job is overseeing the custodians, the two of them, in charge of the NCO-EM and Officer mess systems. The custodians are what you could call the executive influence on the clubs, handling the day-to-day operations."

One of the tasks of the system's headquarters is finding entertainment. "We spent $16,000 on live bands in December, $5,000 more than usual because of the Christmas season," commented Spec. 4 John Blackmore. Entertainment, whether it be Vietnamese, Philippine, Korean, Australian or American, comes through an agency in Saigon.

The clubs have a great money-making potential because of their great volume and their "captive audience." The role of the club's system, however, is to provide entertainment rather than show a profit. "We're trying to make little or no money," explains Blackmore. "We're on a break-even basis."

Spec. 5 David Campbell, in charge of keeping the NCO-EM club's books, explained one of the ways of holding down profits. "We've increased entertainment at the expense of showing a profit. Consequently, some clubs, like the one at the VIP center, operate at a loss though the other clubs carry them. We've kept down prices which also cuts into the profits."

As might be guessed, "Beer's our biggest seller and produces most of our revenue," said Blackmore.

Helicopter Maintenance; 3rd Brigade PIO

January 14, 1971

My story for the day was on helicopter maintenance and repairs, which is vital to combat operations. C. Co., 229th Assault Helicopter Battalion (AHB) was the unit I looked into.

The maintenance men said that until they actually got to work on choppers, they didn't really know what they were doing and even then, it took six months or so to pick up on what they were doing. They have the TI teams (Technical Inspection experts) who are constantly looking over the crew's work because they, the TI men, have to answer for anything working with the bird later. They have 19 Huey choppers in their company to keep in working condition.

The pilots, they say, are the ones that make the maintenance crew's job easy or difficult. They have choppers built in 1966. They have other birds with as many as 170 bullet holes in them although they are still good choppers. Worn bearings and bolts plus lubrication are the main worries. There are 13 men in all working over the birds. They try to get 3 birds at a time although the flying required often forces as many as 6 at a time on them. The choppers are brought in every hundred hours of flying time.

All my fingers are jammed from playing volleyball. I'm more in my league now that I'm playing with 27th Maintenance instead of 2/19th Artillery but we still play jungle rules and I get all banged up.

Tomorrow is payday and for me, five months in country. I'm going up to Phuoc Vinh to pick up my earnings.

PFC Russo, the 3rd Brigade photographer, is sitting here talking to us. They have everything down there—the 11th Armored Cav (not 1st Cav) has a place in the brigade. There are fishing villages on the sea. They have much rougher living conditions and much wilder more irrational lifers. They have GIs constantly asking if the PIO is working. Russo thinks that they enjoy the PIO because taking photos and writing stories is what everyone else does in their spare time. Their PIO office isn't famous for overworking themselves but Russo is about the only actual combat photographer we have left in the division. Their lifers are far more venomous than ours it seems, mostly because we're more isolated from the 1st Brigade commanders and other authorities. As long as we turn out enough copy and photos, we're all right.

After five month, I finally got a hold of pants that fit me so now I'm the epitome of the spiffy trooper.

It looks like we're getting our old dog Tuck back because he's been catching a cold out at FSB Mace (a 3rd Brigade base). It now appears that Blanche has some pups left and we have the glowing possibilities of wall-to-wall hounds. This is just what we need—mindless friendly companionship we can throw bones to.

Nikonos Arrives; Elephants

January 15, 1971

It's a good day. My Nikonos II came so I'll start blasting away and send rolls home. And I got paid so I can pay the mamasan. Despite the acrobatic assaults of a playful monkey at the pay line, I made it back to Bien Hoa from Phuoc Vinh. The monkey was small and cute but he nearly bent my glasses. He stole my M&M candy from my pocket, the sly little imp. But he was as close to human as an animal can get. He had a mind of his own—I don't know whose he is.

The camera was the prize of the day. It's a solid little camera with interesting features like its stark simplicity and an underwater viewfinder. I can just see it on one of our canoeing trips back home or a firebase here. I will do a study of our VIP Center's swimming pool from underwater once I know what I'm doing with the camera.

In the briefing tonight it was reported that two captains from one battalion were injured in one day, which has to be a record in this slow period in the war. I've been surprised recently by the number of company commanding officers that have been hurt like this, many of them in foolish accidents.

A herd of more than fifty elephants were spotted in the northeast corner of the 1st Brigade's area of operations. The Air Force had spotted the herd several days before. The brigade's CO, Colonel Stevenson, made it clear that those elephants weren't to be fired up. We have talk of supplies being moved by elephants so many have been shot but no one is happy when action this drastic is taken. Apparently elephants, although on the run from the war, still are a surviving species in Southeast Asia.

Super Saber jets have been coming in to the airbase recently, especially yesterday, trailing a parachute as they land. They are far larger than the F-5 Freedom fighter. Bien Hoa is a very active noisy airport; some yoyo kept me up last night by trying out his propellers, which sounded good to me, and deafening. I saw a DC-4 today for the first time although it's not the oldest plane I've seen. This would be an antique aviation collector's dream.

Photographing Saigon

January 16, 1971

I drove down to Saigon with Ed, blasting away with the Nikonos, figuring it out. Saigon is a human jungle. With garbage and air pollution everywhere, I don't find it a desirable place to live but it's interesting. We drove to the Chinese section of town where Ed's girlfriend lives and looked around. Ed has a good attitude toward the Vietnamese. He doesn't allow them to take him for everything he's worth yet he treats them honestly and with respect. He says that he discovered some very fine people this way. He is anti the Vietnam mess but doesn't think it any call to mistreat the natives. Right on!

Saigon has some pretty sections and as the saying goes, you can get anything you want there. We were having fits with the locals' driving; they were out to kill themselves and maybe us in the bargain. You think American drivers are bad? American drivers are downright decent drivers by comparison. Americans signal, have their cars in decent shape, and don't demand the right of way in scooters like the Vietnamese. And Americans have some pollution laws for trucks. But I shouldn't condemn the place—I may be only looking at their slums. The place is thriving and no one seems to be starving but there are too many people.

All I got out of Saigon other than a roll of photos was a headache from the heat and truck fumes. Our reason for driving to Saigon was to pick up the *Cavalair* for this week. Until now the new staff of the paper has been killing my stories or refusing to use them. This issue was a surprise reversal—five good stories in one paper! I'm a staff member again. They rewrote several of them and added the word Skytrooper a time or two but generally it was what I wrote.

Lt. White flew up to Phuoc Vinh for a meeting of the leaders. He got all the dope on what's going to happen to the 1st Cav; the lieutenant told us about some of it. I can't tell all—I promised—but the gist of it is I'll be in Bien Hoa for a while. My bush beating days seem to be over—it's all REMF (rear echelon mother ——er) stories from now on by command. I'm looking forward to trying the camera underwater tomorrow.

The other night I saw a plane going overhead taking photos in the middle of the night. It had its own flashgun, a kind of explosive flash dropped behind the ship to light up the landscape. This was at 9:30 p.m.

Division Pool; Dog Story; Treating Addicts

January 18, 1971

I went swimming yesterday in the division's only pool and gave the Nikonos a try. It's a good underwater camera but focusing by guessing will take some getting used to. I got some strange looks when I took it swimming.

Unlike my friend Al, I can't see coming home for two weeks. It would be too expensive and only to return for months more. Seven months more at a maximum isn't *that* long.

Enclosed is one of my latest masterpieces, another dog story. When I discovered this dog story at 15th Med I also came across another I can hold for later. They treat a number of OD (heroin overdose) patients and other drug disasters. They are active participants in the amnesty program. They were working with a man today who had taken one too many LSD trips. He was a spastic ghost, looking kind of dead. They had a drug casualty in their own outfit. Someone gave their prized little pup an overdose of heroin and they couldn't save the pooch—he died. The medics were talking about the morbid sense of humor the drug freaks have. They'd love to get their hands on the sadist that poisoned their dog. The psychiatrist in charge of the drug program was on R&R; I'll interview him next week.

COLONEL RADCLIFF

We tend to imprint human characteristics onto dogs, in this case those of a mighty warrior. In the land of non-neutered leashless pooches, dogfights probably were inevitable. The GIs' and my interpretation of this poor dog's struggles were comic but it was inhumane. I transcribed this from my typed version of the story I sent my parents. It made it into the February 17, 1971, Cavalair *under the headline "Med Colonel Regarded as the Top Dog."*

BIEN HOA—Who was the most battle-scarred veteran that A Co, 15th Medical Battalion ever treated? There is general agreement that the reckless hero with the most purple hearts would have to be Colonel Radcliff, "top dog" of the company.

After a particularly savage pitched battle with Wooly Bully, the 229th AHB's dog, the Colonel was put under to repair the damage. "He took more ether than a normal person and was still fighting it," explained Spec 4 Gary Huntley (Daytona Beach, Fla.). A ripped ear was sewed up. Radcliff, affectionately known as Cliff, has a long history of rhubarbs.

He had so many battlefield injuries that he was given a medical record to keep track. His history reads like a battle report. For instance:

"7 Sept 70, Cliff was rolled today by a 5 ton dump truck while fighting with another dog in the middle of the road. This time he wasn't chasing the vehicle. Ol' Cliff was doing the dog a job until the 5 ton did him one." Or.

"16 Oct 70, patient received wound to left front shoulder while single handedly defending our club the Morgue, from a forward attack by a 229th AHB sapper dog. The raging battle ended with arty (water) and air strikes (chairs) when company personnel put the sapper into retreat. Cliff was medevaced. Patient received two sutures and was returned to duty."

Wooly Bully, who chewed up Cliff in the last affair of honor, is the blackguard of the area. "Wooly Bully is definitely a neurotic," insisted Huntley, psychoanalyzing Cliff's competition. "He's always starting fights."

Cliff has had at least one too many girlfriends. According to Spec 5 Bill Sischo (Ternary, Mich.), "He had a CC smear with positive results. In other words, he caught the clap."

He started out as a second lieutenant and has fought his way up to full bird now. "He's promotable after every scrap," commented Sischo, "if he wins."

Colonel Radcliff is fortunate he's a 15th Med pooch. "He's lucky to be alive," maintains Huntley, "I don't know what he'd do without us."

Dental Clinic; Hooch Invasion

January 20, 1971

I was thinking of going to Australia for R&R but it may be a last ditch affair—it is the most popular spot and straight time-in-country that counts.

Mom, the whole idea of "Hair" is not its nudity. If the nudity is offensive, just listen to the lyrics. It is obscene in many places but very funny and awfully true. I think of it as escape because, although it's making fun of everything, it nevertheless is all in fun. The show live might be shocking but the record is great.

Mike Paine's battalion [*he was the son of my parents' friends*] is coming down to my brigade so maybe I'll have a chance to get my hands on him. I know from reliable sources that his battalion is one of those that is part of the last brigade to leave Vietnam. I still doubt that he'll have a full tour in the 1st Cav.

A FO (forward observer) called artillery in on his own men the day before yesterday, killing four and wounding about a dozen men up in the 2nd Brigade. I don't know many of the facts. Thank God it wasn't in our brigade with anyone I know involved.

Today I went to the dental clinic down the road, working on a story about what they do for incoming replacements and grunts coming out of the bush. The dentist I talked with said he saw the whole panorama of teeth, from the worst to the finest. He says that one of the worst problems in Vietnam for the dentist is soldiers' lack of motivation. Many grunts let their teeth slide; others maintain clean mouths and good sets. This unit, the 40th Dental Detachment, has more work than the average dental group in Vietnam because they are the ones that run through all the newbies coming to the 1st Cav, as many as 42 in one day, for major work on their teeth. They also get all the grunts so their schedules are crowded and chaotic.

Our hooch has been invaded by a mob from Phuoc Vinh, several DEROSing and others back and forth from the whores in Saigon. I wish they'd leave but that's wishful thinking. I doubt if it'll ever be quiet again. I can close the door. Our local speed freak in DEROSing in a few days—good riddance.

Echo Recon Leader

January 22, 1971

I spent a long time talking to Lieutenant Lynch of Echo Recon 1/7th, my favorite unit's new commander. He's very impressive though you have to know his record before you'd guess how successful he has been. He's been in the Army five years and went through Tet in 1968. He told me in the battle for the Long Binh area, he knows there were 1200 enemy dead because he helped count the bodies. Jets were coming off the landing strip at Bien Hoa and dropped their bombs barely after taking off, then circling and coming back in.

He became a lieutenant when his own lieutenant was killed in an ambush. His men in Echo Recon think he is the best. He was trying to talk me into going out with them again. Ever since my first outing, they have been finding stuff. They found 114 Chieu Hois, all Montagnards, about two weeks ago. You've read the stories I've written about them and they had more material when I saw them next.

The lieutenant thinks we have won the war. He cites the obvious prosperity in the country as an indication of our winning, and he almost convinced me. I find myself in the position where I don't really care any more. I'm not sure we did wrong in Vietnam although I still believe the price was too high for questionable gains.

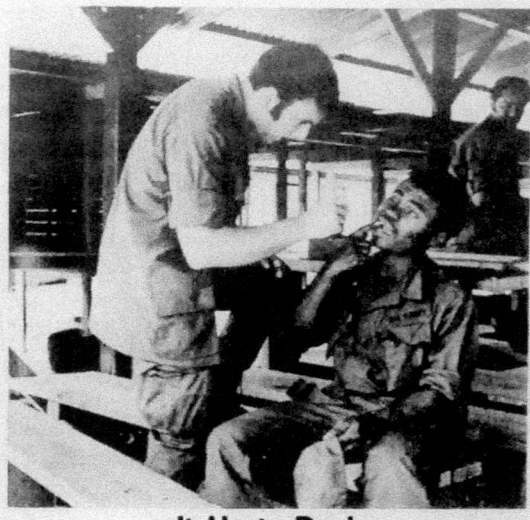

Newbies get checkup

Cav no place for toothache

by Pfc. Conrad Leighton

BIEN HOA – Horror! Horror! In the days of yesteryear, as we watched big bad Mr. Tooth Decay chase that cute little sparkling white tooth across the 'boob tube' each Saturday morning, we had our mothers to make sure we brushed our teeth regularly, had that semi-annual checkup, and stayed away from those (Ye Gads!) mouth corroding soda pops and candy.

Now that the "big green" has delivered us to the "Big Rock Candy Mountain", immeasurable amounts of candy and soda are consumed daily and only the 1st Cav dentists are left as replacements for mother's watchful eyes.

"I've seen the whole panorama of teeth from the very good sets to the extremely bad," summarized Capt. Sandy Termotto, a dentist in the 40th Dental Detachment, as he checked over the newbies coming into the First Team Academy.

Army dentists don't so much feel they have to drum up work as make sure the work is done. "We try to encourage the guys to get all the dental care they can out of the Army," explained Termotto.

"We don't work by fixed appointments because we are constantly getting influxes from the field and FTA that can't be predicted," commented Termotto. "We end up working long hours and seeing many more patients that we would back in the States. We had 42 patients with pressing problems from FTA in one day, which is our one day record so far."

Termotto explained that a dentist's worst problem in Vietnam is the same one he faced back in the States. "Our primary problem is motivation in keeping teeth clean and good oral hygiene generally. We get two grunts from the same unit out of the field, one will have clean well-kept teeth, the other will have a horror story because he didn't take the time to brush his teeth."

Spec. 4 Ralph Stirling, Termotto's dental aid and a student of mouth problems, denied that dentists haphazardly pull teeth. "We definitely try to avoid extractions," he insisted.

Probably the biggest difference between the Army and a civilian dentist is an added responsibility of keeping all the teeth in a specific division in shape. And he is expected to keep the 1st Cav's teeth in order, despite all the sodas.

It Hurts Doc!

New Skytrooper opens wide during examination at FTA. Hopefully, nasty dental problems won't flare up out in the bush when no dentist is available (US Army Photo by Pfc. Conrad Leighton).

This is the dental clinic story in full, partly because I no longer have the picture.

I also talked to Lt. Col. Labrossi, formerly the commanding officer of 1/7th and now the assistant brigade commander. He said he was flying out to several 1st Cav. units, working training popular forces (PF) troops to zero in their weapons, spot booby traps and just generally get a feel for warfare in a modern vein.

Today I went over to the 1st Brigade TOC and learned they didn't have a bird for us so we took a jeep down through Long Binh and Saigon, checking out the activities of Cav. The only unit we had a chance to see was Charlie, 1/5th Cav, which isn't in my brigade but since they're under men from our brigade, I collected a story anyway.

Saigon just leaves me limp although it's entertaining watching faces. Watching Vietnamese faces, I see significant intelligence. In fact I find them more interesting than American faces, more exotic to me, I suppose. It is hard to take their pictures in a moving jeep through traffic, especially from the back seat.

Lt. O'Daly is leaving for home tomorrow. He said he is going into the advertising business when he gets out of the service and said he wishes he could get fellows from our office into his agency that he'd set up. It sounds like an interesting line of work but in the middle of New York City?

Well, time marches on—only 205 days to go, at the most.

Dog Food Grubbing

January 23, 1971

There is still news around and I'm going to find it. More dog stories. More "what-the-units-are-doing-in-the-rear" pieces and still an imaginative article now and then. I can't be allowed to fall into the laziness trap that the Army's set.

Talking of dog stories and my inhibitions, I find myself digging in the mess hall's garbage cans, searching for dog food for our beloved pooches. When I first started the practice, I was all alone and felt embarrassed like it was a personal humiliation to be seen sifting through garbage cans. Now I kind of enjoy it and even make other guys feel guilty enough about their starving hounds so they search with me.

Today I was in Phuoc Vinh and was introduced to the first new man that's come into our office in some time. He's a grunt who was pulled out of the FTA because of his artist background. He's from Mobile, Alabama, and seems a nice guy and a talent. I hope so; we need some fresh faces around here.

Dave Lewis took a shot of me, which he liked and printed several copies for me, which I'm sending you. It's a pretty characteristic photo that could have been shot anywhere, on a firebase most likely.

Celebrating Tet; Nixon's Speech

January 24, 1971

We were just invaded by five guys, either DEROSing or going on R&R.

The dentists were celebrating Happy Tet in a party put on by their Vietnamese office workers. The food was good generally. Then I went up to 15th

Administration Company with the lieutenant and Don Fry and had steaks at the company's party. I'm a member of 15th Admin by the way and attached to Headquarters and Headquarters Company for food and lodging. That doesn't mean I can't eat at 15th Admin though. They had free beers and sodas, not a bad idea on a hot afternoon.

Lt. O'Daly was able to pawn off the CKC going out of Saigon—he bribed someone. He gave me a fan for my room, a good one that can cool me nicely. It is more practical than a CKC, which just sat gathering dust.

One of these days I'm going out with Colonel Stevenson to take pictures of the 1st Brigade firebases, which might prove quite a job. I've fallen behind on my firebases; I still know the main ones but I'm not sure about the mini-firebases.

You said something about my spelling disintegrating. Maybe it's because I'm typing too fast and not checking my work. I've been rushing and let questionable spelling pass. Pardon me, please.

We keep hearing wild things about us going back into Cambodia—we'd better not, especially after what President Nixon said last night in his State of the Union Address, which I listened to. I thought it was a great speech if he can come through with what he says. It sounded almost liberal in spots; it was refreshing compared to his old rhetoric. His ideas about cabinet department changes, curing cancer, and a fresh approach to welfare sounded good.

I found it hard to swallow his dismissing the Vietnam War as "over." We have a lot of our country's money and troops tied up in this little country. I agree that the U.S. is more important but I don't want to be forgotten, although I doubt Nixon has forgotten us. How was the speech taken in the U.S.? Did the cynics carry the day or was there really a refreshing new breeze in the country? I'd like to believe there is a glowing future for the U.S.

THE FEMININE MYSTIQUE

Comparing a female dog to a provocative human woman was a stretch. When presented in this fashion, the alluring woman looks pretty silly, undoubtedly my intent. The February 17, 1971, Cavalair *used this article with the headline "Tiger Owns All the Traits of a Woman."*

BIEN HOA—That men have never completely penetrated the mystique of women is one of the joyous facts of human life. But how about the dogs? Do the female dogs lead the males around with their feminine air of mystery? After careful examination of dogdom, it does appear that some female hounds do have that something extra. Tiger, the mascot of the 40th Dental Detachment, is such a dog.

Although most of her admirers are human American males, it is still hard to resist her animation, imagination and style. "She has a mind of her own," insists Spec 5 Garland Tiner (Odessa, Tex.), a dental lab technician. "She chases and catches everything: lizards, frogs, rats and mice. She plays with them and kills them. She loves to ride jeeps. She also gets a big kick out of chasing rocks thrown by her boys and eating them. She's also very playful and friendly with GIs."

Tiger has a few hang-ups and has been known to make a lot of noise over nothing. "She can't stand the garbage truck people," said Spec 4 Ronald Cullum (Johnson City, Ill.), "especially the Vietnamese men. She'll sit and bark." So far she hasn't attacked a garbage collector but mercy if she does.

Like all bewitching women, she has a delightfully different favorite pastime. "She loves mud," disclosed SFC William Hopson (Modesto, Cal.). "She likes mud so much she lives in it. We have to wash her down sometimes to live with her."

Tiger has a dogged sense of purpose that is astounding, a must for any female with designs. "She stayed in one place for a week to catch a mouse," related Tiner. "There isn't a thing she can't catch given time. She's even been known to dive underwater in pursuit of a frog." She's a triumph of endurance over her obvious limitations.

As if these coveted traits aren't enough, her boys had the ultimate tribute to her femininity. "She's a smart dog who just does things differently," maintained a loyal admirer.

So far, the response from the male dogs across the street is in doubt but there is agreement among the dental people that Tiger is the coming dog. With her many exotic ways, everyone agrees she should be the belle of the neighborhood and the object of every dogfight.

Upcoming Jungle Outing; Ice Plant; Pot Head Attack

January 25, 1971

I got thrown into something else today. It appears that my bush experiences with Echo Recon, 1st Bn., 7th Cav aren't over. You know that I've been talking to Lt. Lynch about going out with Echo Recon again. It seems that *Infantry Magazine*, the magazine of infantry officers with some prestige, wants a photo feature done on an infantry lieutenant. Because Lt. Lynch is one of the most successful leaders around and I'd been out with Echo Recon before, I was asked to go out and do the story.

It's the kind of challenge I don't feel I can turn down. I know you've counseled me not to go out again but I'm curious and know this unit. It's a good gung ho unit that could keep me safe and provide, very possibly, another good story. I know many of the guys. And I probably won't have another time in my life when I can try out some real live adventure, my Nikonos, and my new boonie hat.

This will be a drastic switch from my first outing. It is the dry season and I won't get wet like I did last time. I may have to do some hard humping, something I was saved from last time because we found the caches. I think taking the chance is worth it. I'm restless and feel unused in the office despite doing my job.

Lt. Lynch and Lt. Col. Labrozzi, two men I've mentioned in past letters, are in an article in *U.S. News and World Report* in an issue toward the end of January. I went on a merry chase with the lieutenant looking for an issue he could read and have. Lynch tells me the article is pretty accurate. Labrozzi was really put out that I couldn't find the black and white pictures of the first Echo Recon mission. I'm taking plenty of film and taking no chances this time.

I worked on a story about the local ice plant today, compiling notes. It was another slow day that I spent smoking the pipe and walking around. I'm postponing my wisdom-teeth extractions and the sortie to Saigon until another time.

In February, part of the units will begin to stand down but it won't stop my bush thing. Everyone is waiting eagerly for the process to start. The Army wastes our time with hurry up and wait routines and GI's aren't famous for their patience.

Ed Howard was set upon by three potheads about three nights ago and then, after beating them off, was arrested by the MPs. Why anyone would want to tackle Ed I'll never know. He didn't think the attackers were racially motivated but rather, needed money and tried to take it from him. The three were whites. Ed was much madder at the MPs—they put handcuffs on him first and one of the three muggers busted him in the mouth. It was particularly humiliating because Ed is a Chicago policeman on a leave of absence from the police force. "I'm going to catch that MP and beat his young ass!" Ed threatened menacingly. He did see the funny side of it though. By the way, the three potheads were arrested too. Dad, you say you're unimaginative but less imagination is required here—the outlandish is commonplace.

Anti-Freeze Makes Ice

Where ice comes from in the tropics was a mystery to me until I uncovered this ice plant. It reminds me of making homemade ice cream—in this case, ice— on a big scale. The February 17, 1971, Cavalair *and March 22, 1971,* Pacific Stars and Stripes *used this brief piece.*

BIEN HOA—What is one way to use anti-freeze in Vietnam? To make ice, of course.

3. Into the Jungle: January 1, 1971, to February 27, 1971

Water in steel tubs is frozen into 300-pound ice blocks by the action of an anti-freeze brine solution circulating around the tubs. The solution is part of a process used for creating ice in a country that is devoid of frozen matter.

Capt. John A. Hardman, HHC Rear S-4, is in charge of giving out the ice. "The ice plant, which is run by Pacific Architects and Engineers, produced 96 blocks of ice a day," explained Hardman. "Mess halls and medical dispensaries are the only people authorized ice from the plant."

Most of the mess halls have their own ice machines so they don't always draw their allotted block. Two units that do take their full are the only combat units receiving Bien Hoa ice.

"The 2nd of the 19th Artillery and the 1st of the 12th Cav are the only forward units we supply," remarked Hardman.

"They're authorized 6 pounds per man per day on the firebases, and three pounds per man in the rear.

Generals; 1st Cav Patch; Davy Crockett Story

January 26, 1971

About all I did was work on placing canteens in my rucksack and watching Brig. Gen. Hyman give out the Unit Safety Award for December to 15th S&S along with a few token bronze star medals. Hyman, I'm told, is the only one of the three generals in the Cav with West Point training; Putnam is OCS and Burton ROTC. Hyman is a hard ass, not surprisingly. Hyman is infamous for surprise sorties into enlisted-man-held territory and the serious losses perpetrated on EM hides. He blacklisted Jim Locker, one of our best photo lab men at Phuoc Vinh, because Jim's hair was too long. The general said as Jim got into his chopper, "get a haircut." To which Locker replied, "Right now?" The general called our major later saying that this was blatant insubordination. I'm going to have to work for Hyman and don't look forward to it.

You should have watched Hyman at the awards ceremony. He was the epitome of the blindly ritualistic lifer that enlisted men dislike. I've heard a lot of officers talking about resigning their commissions. I asked a captain over at 15th S&S today if he was staying in the Army. "Now?" he asked. "Hell no." He sounded like O'Daly, who is already out of the Army and, I suspect, overjoyed by the freedom.

The "Old Foes" story was by far my favorite too, although I was a little upset with the editor for what he thought was my error. The Chieu Hoi, Davy Crockett, didn't ask for mercy when he lost the trail. He asked to be shot. This was a huge difference in his psychology; I wasn't sure myself until I asked Lt. Lynch about it. He said I'd been right; he'd been asking to be shot and the lieutenant was shocked when the Chieu Hoi made the request. The story had soul and the fellows felt just the way I wrote it—it wasn't contrived.

Mother Dorcy and her husband, a now long deceased colonel, designed the 1st Cav's patch, which is plastered all over the 1st Cav's AO (area of operations). She is old, tired and losing her memory. She writes these horrible letters, asking for a kind word and a memory of the past. She wants to die and the letters we put in the *Cavalair* are far from what our staff wishes she says. All her letters are good for are tears for a sad old woman.

I'm sorry you feel a fear for my hide that I don't feel. I'm tired of playing it safe, leading a sheltered life, writing irrelevant fluff stories. Echo Recon held out their souls to me in the Davy Crockett story, that they can follow their hearts and principles even when their lives may be threatened. Nobody in Echo Recon has died in a long time so they're working on the assumption that they will survive. I don't want you to worry too much.

Chieu Hois; Logging Bird Crash; Night Intruder; Reporter Arrested

January 27, 1971

I flew out to FSB Green today and talked with Echo Recon 1/7th about their last couple of weeks. It's just been one thing after another for them. They found 118 Chieu Hois coming down a road, which was not a big deal as far as surprises go, once they stopped the Montagnard mob, determined they were friendly, and they wanted to rally to the Allies' side.

They also had a logging bird crash as it was coming in with supplies. Nobody, either in the chopper or on the ground, was hurt seriously but one GI playing cards was shook up as the Huey hit five feet from where he was sitting. It was nightmarish, they said, the engines of the bird whining a high scream as everyone prepared for the chopper to explode with men trapped inside. The engines were silenced without an explosion and the trapped men saved. One of the trapped men, Carl Shipp, was in Echo Recon when I went out with them the first time. He felt very fortunate to escape with a few cuts in his scalp. The platoon wasted several days securing the crash area and having the twisted bird's body removed.

They also got into contact several times. One night was particularly frightening for them. Often out in the bush you can't see the enemy who is trying to kill you. A firefight will often take place without either side getting a good look at the other. Two Jesses were sleeping in a little tent: Sgt. Mike Jessee and Sgt. Jesse Reed, both from Tennessee. They heard something and called in movement to the other squads.

A figure came within five feet of the tent and then moved off. Mike played dead while Jesse prepared for them the second time the enemy moved in. It sounded like there were about ten of them looking around.

Then a spot that Jesse had been watching where moonlight lit the ground became dark with the shape of a man bending over, looking into the dark. Jesse fired and the phantom fled with a moan.

Because it was dark, no one made a move to check out the area until morning. They had Cobra gunships working out close, making sure that no more enemy soldiers invaded the camp. Next morning they found the body of the enemy soldier that Jesse had shot—through the heart by the way. It was about a hundred pound black bear.

The platoon was understandably surprised and embarrassed by the bear incident. I wonder what would have happened if Jesse had just nicked the bear and the bear left some blood as his calling card. They might have claimed the poor bear on their body count. I didn't know there were bear in Vietnam or that they traveled in groups.

I got a fast ride back from FSB Green on a Huey; it's been several weeks since I had a Huey ride and enjoyed it.

Now for a flashback of times past. Last night we had eight extra bodies visiting from Phuoc Vinh. Mortimer (Don Fry) was drunk and making a noisy pest of himself until 1 a.m. With his old Phuoc Vinh drinking buddies, he reverted to his old drinking self. Along with the Phuoc Vinh bodies, we had a visitor from the USARV PIO in Long Bin who was going out to do a story on a night ambush at FSB Jupiter. I guess he got enough sleep but he got out late because our jeep wouldn't work. Jupiter is the replacement for FSB Ares, which is where CBS had that shocking documentary on marijuana among the troops.

I got back from FSB Green and Lt. White asked me if I had heard the word about Spec 4 Peters, the USARV guy's name. When I said it was all new to me he explained that the Command Sergeant Major at Jupiter did a marijuana check on Peters and found a kilo of marijuana on him. White had to fly out to Jupiter to get custody of Peters and handed him over to his company commander down at USARV. What a mess—that man is in for trouble, how much I'm not sure.

I'm heading off to bed early to make up the sleep I lost last night.

ECHO RECON PLATOON RALLIES 117

My friend Bruce Gottsche—who was involved in rescuing these people—showed me pictures of them on a firebase afterwards and their clothes were rags, in an advanced state of decomposition with many holes in them. The story was in the February 17, 1971, Cavalair.

Perplexed and unnerved, skytroopers of Echo Recon, 1st Bn., 7th Cav. watched and waited as the sounds of a large group of people moved toward them.

Appearing anything but menacing, the noisemakers came into view. "A little kid was walking point with five Chieu Hoi leaflets on a stick," explained Sgt. William Cribb. "He was about 20 feet ahead of the rest." Following him was a noisy but friendly mob of 117 Montagnards.

"We didn't know whether they were ralliers or VC at first," said Sgt. Doyle Desmond. The real problem was speaking to them since none of the GIs spoke Montagnard. The Chieu Hoi leaflets promptly made their intentions clear.

The ralliers were making too much noise now for the GIs' comfort. "Somebody mentioned the word 'VC' and they quieted down," explained Desmond.

Some of the children needed a doctor, so the medic did what he could before flying them to FSB Green on choppers.

As luck would have it, taking the ralliers out took no time at all. "We were only 100 meters from our insertion point," said Desmond.

SERGEANT CALLS COBRA PROTECTION FOR GRIZZLY AFFAIR

At the first Echo Recon reunion I attended, I was fascinated with the different soldiers' memories of this night's events. They had fun comparing recollections but they couldn't entirely agree on what happened—their memories were a bit suspect too. This piece was in the February 17, 1971, Cavalair *and in the May 1971* Garry Owen *orientation issue.*

NEAR FSB GREEN—Firefights can begin and end without anyone ever seeing the enemy—one of the horrors of a guerrilla war in the jungle. And what is worse is when infiltrators penetrate the perimeter at night. Not long ago, Echo Recon, 1st Bn, 7th Cav was set upon by such an onslaught.

"I was asleep when I was awakened by something sneaking around my tent," recounted Sgt. Mike Jessee (Kingsport, Tenn.). "I could hear other prowlers nearby."

Jessee, wide-awake by now, whispered, "Get me a frag!" to which his tentmate called up the other squads, reporting movement. The noisy interlopers moved off, giving the GIs time to come up with a strategy.

"They started moving back toward us," commented Sgt. Jesse Reed, Jessee's partner. "Jessee stayed on the other side and played dead with his weapon. I was watching a spot where the moon lit the ground when it suddenly got dark. I could see the silhouette of a man bending over, peering into the dark. I opened up on him, the phantom moaned and fled into the dark."

Everyone was wide-awake by now and no one slept the rest of the night. Cobra gunships were called in to work out close to the camp, trying to protect Echo Recon from the NVA infiltrators.

Next morning, they discovered the body of an enemy soldier, shot through the heart. He was a five-foot, hundred pound black bear.

Reed was shaken by the whole bear affair. "I've never killed a bear before and I didn't know they had any in Vietnam," he claimed.

Reed, an old time Tennessee hunter, probably didn't know he was in a hunting stand when he shot at the prowler. His partner, Jessee, probably was afraid of the wrong thing: he should have been afraid of being mauled. And the ultimate indignity for Reed was that he'd never had to call in a Cobra to shoot his wild game.

FSB Green Contact; Newbie Shot

January 28, 1971

Today was briefing night for me. They had a nice hot action up with Delta, 1st Bn., 7th Cav this afternoon that's still in progress. Four men were wounded in the contact and we in the rear still aren't sure who initiated contact, them or us. A MEDEVAC bird, trying to take out the most seriously injured man with a sucking check wound, was hit. The pilot, the door gunner and a medic were all hit and they split the scene. The Charlie Charlie (Lt. Col. Fry's command and control) bird was shot up when it got too close and is now grounded at FSB Green. It will be pulled out by a bigger helicopter, probably a flying crane. Col. Stevenson's command and control chopper is being used and he missed tonight's briefing.

Before I forget, yesterday had some action too while I was out there. A newbie from A Co., 1/7 was setting up an automatic ambush some distance from his platoon when an enemy soldier walked up to him and shot him twice. On FSB Green, the 155s were sending out rounds in support although what good I don't know. They tried to get the injured man out but the MEDEVAC chopper didn't have a sling that would work. Before long, it didn't matter. The newbie, shot in the chest and throat, was dead. Pretty grim. The grunts were understandably upset, a little irrational about the MEDEVAC bird's inability to save the man. MEDEVAC choppers have it pretty rough; they lead a precarious existence.

New Hooch Lost

January 30, 1971

Our PIO castle, our new hooch, was abandoned by direct order of his majesty the base commander, Col. Spawn—the dirty son-of-a-bitch. He held a surprise inspection and decided that EM swine shouldn't live in former officers' quarters, and threw us out without warning. We no longer have our own rooms or any privacy—what a blow.

This was humiliating for Second Lieutenant White who turned First Lieutenant today. He was helpless against a chicken colonel. We have become nomads as we are thrown from hook to hooch. What's a real bummer is that we know we will have to move again within another month. We have a hard time making and keeping friends. Al and I have sworn that we will revenge ourselves on Spawn somehow: stop writing stories about Bien Hoa and snub him. Tomorrow Al is going home for two weeks and I'm off to mess around with Echo Recon for a week. Spawn couldn't have hit us at a worse time, psychologically.

The *Cavalair* had four of my stories in it. Notice all the animal stories—we've hit a new low in action out there and I hope it stays that way. Tet has gone with a whimper instead of a bang this year.

I am looking forward to escaping from the rear out with Echo Recon. I need a change from the drudgery of rear lifer warfare.

Hooch Loss Upset; War Won?

January 31, 1971

I didn't go out to FSB Green and Echo Recon today; they finally moved the 1/7th's old firebase Jupiter out all together. All the Chinooks were tied up moving Jupiter's gear to Powder Ridge, the new LZ. Not a single Chinook sortie was sent up to FSB Green and anyway, Green wasn't the place I wanted. Echo Recon, unknown to me, moved to FSB Noble, 1/7th's small new firebase. I'm going out tomorrow.

I was still steaming over being thrown out of our old hooch. Our major was down today so I asked him if it would be possible to get a release from the office if I could find a job somewhere else, down at MACV or USARV maybe. The major, who is above all a disarmingly friendly guy, just grinned at me, which kind of blew my argument. He said that I'd probably stay and said in effect that there was no real reason why I should leave, which is true I guess. Lt. White, later on, tried to cool me off. I was polite so I don't think I ruffled any feathers but at least they know that I take this affront seriously. The major didn't stand up for us on the hooch business and with a full bird, he didn't have any options other than silence.

As medicine for my heated nerves, I went swimming with the FSSE crowd and had a ball paddling around, playing king-of-the-air-mattress and bouncing volleyball-sized balls off people's heads. Swimming pools make it like stateside or better, except for the lack of females.

Lt. Lynch's claim that we have won the war befuddled me. It's true, the Vietnamese are prosperous now but I believe it's dependence on a rich nation's war machine. It is corrupt and many of these businesses will fold when we leave, even with continued aid. There will be chaos when we leave—it's inevitable. I allowed myself to be swayed for an hour or two into things that I don't believe, which I recognized once I had a chance to think. We certainly haven't won this war and the Vietnamese in their hearts still don't like us.

Stuck on FSB Green

February 1, 1971

Some days it doesn't pay to come to a firebase, like today. I flew out bright and early on a Huey. Then I found that Echo Recon was on FSB Noble instead of FSB Green, where I am now. I spent the rest of the day trying unsuccessfully to reach Noble.

I made poor use of my options. I could have taken the lieutenant colonel's chuck chuck bird but I was too proud to do that. Instead, I waited for a Chinook that was layed on to carry water to Noble.

I was stalemated thanks to a 3 million dollar skycrane. I watched the crane go over Green on the way to Noble with a bulldozer dangling beneath it. When it made it to Noble, it crashed although no one was killed. One of the men from Echo Mortars was only about 10 feet from the falling bird. It must have been quite a spectacle; I'm told there are bits of the bird all over the west forty so my Chinook couldn't come in.

I'm sleeping with Echo Mortars tonight, some of whom I know. Tomorrow I'll see if I can link up with Echo Recon. I should get plenty of sleep if the local cannons will politely keep their traps shut. I looking forward to tonight—I've never slept overnight on a firebase.

It was hot out here and shade was scarce. As was my theory, late afternoon is the nicest time of a firebase's day; most chores are done and neighbors chat about how short they are. Because choppers have bedded down for the night, the dust also has a chance to settle.

I took two rolls of film today so you can have a look at Green, my local press territory. This base has been in War Zone D longer than any other battalion firebase, more than 2 months after its rebirth. Green was here when I first started working in Bien Hoa. Oh, the nostalgia. Today was a long fruitless vigil but tomorrow should be better. I'm sleeping in a hammock. Whee!

Skycrane Wreck; Echo Recon Outing

February 2, 1971

I finally hit Noble about 10 a.m., in plenty of time to link up with Echo Recon 1/7th. I saw the remains of the skycrane. I'm flabbergasted that no one was killed. It's a complete loss to the Army. I took a number of shots, which I'll mail home.

I got an inkling of what happened to the crane when our slicks (helicopters) came in to take us out to the LZ. Dust in a blinding cloud momentarily hid the choppers. We had the red dust caked onto our faces—what an untidy mess we are now.

I'm now about 2000 meters from FSB Noble in my little hooch with a mosquito net roof. I'm enjoying how dry it is. It's about 5:30 p.m. and the sun is already low. I'm in the bamboo, which goes 30 or 40 feet above my head.

A small fire started in our jungle LZ is giving off a popping sound similar to rifle fire. It sounded like B-40 rockets a couple of times, shaking us up. It was decided the explosives probably came from dud rounds from the Cobras that worked out before we CAed (combat assaulted) in.

We're in the same general area that Delta Co. had its contact several days ago; nobody's happy about that. Except for the bears, Echo Recon has never been attacked at night so I can relax now. My pack is pretty heavy with nine quarts of water and all the supplies I'm carrying.

It becomes remarkably cold during the nights. Last night, with Echo Mortars, I nearly froze up with the 55 degree temperature. It's hot during the day and cold at night, like the deserts.

We did very little today but tomorrow we'll probably start serious humping. Steve Harbeck says he feels we'll find something although he doesn't know what. Lt. Lynch, when I asked him what we were out here for, said we were out to kill gooks. Great, just plain great.

I'm staying nice and secure with the platoon CP (command post). No Audie Murphy–style bravado for me. It's like an amplifier out here. I can hear choppers, planes and artillery firing well off in the distance. We're much noisier during the dry season. The husks off of bamboo when they've dried crackle loudly when stepped on, like the finest crackers.

I was searched today for marijuana and harder drugs except alcohol of course. I didn't have anything on me and it was a monumental waste of time. They frisked me, the whole works. They've been catching GIs right and left with the stuff. They're trying to break the habit by frontal assault and I assure you, it won't work. It a rerun of prohibition and it's destined to fail.

First Day in Jungle

February 3, 1971

I'm now 2 clicks away from last night's position. It was a very slow day: I'm told this was an ordinary day in the bush. We were walking on "high speed" NVA-made trails. We found American and NVA night positions—the NVA camp being used more recently. The NVA camp was near a small stream.

Last night I slept about eight hours, a superb night's sleep. My only trial during the night was when I got lost in the dark. I made one wrong turn and

3. Into the Jungle: January 1, 1971, to February 27, 1971   191

The poor skycrane was clearly totaled.

FSB Noble was a new firebase and dust was everywhere. Helicopters turned the landscape into a dust bowl.

flailed around the camp 20 minutes trying to find Harbeck, the guy I was waking up to take night guard.

I was telling the fellows, Harbeck—the sniper—and Demond—a squad leader—that I was somewhat embarrassed working for a lieutenant my own age. They laughed (Harbeck's 24 and Demond 26) because Lt. Lynch is only 21.

I've been watching small lizards all day when we took rest breaks from humping. I can't catch them though. I've seen few other wild specimens. I heard a strange bird call a few minutes ago.

I've been spending much of my day talking to Steve Harbeck, a former law student at Cornell University who was drafted away from his studies. He's got a great mind. He's the kind of guy the CID sees once a month because he was once affiliated with the SDS. He was also a McCarthyite in 1968 which I think better represents his views than the SDS. Tom Preece has left the bush for home and Steve is my replacement peer. Being a sniper, he's also part of the CP. His views on the war jive with mine—we both see the insanity of it.

I heard a fuck-you lizard call ten times, which I'm told represents superior lizard lungpower. Thirteen is the recognized record.

The bamboo is interesting stuff and not structurally as strong as deciduous trees. It bends when it grows too tall and rots rapidly on the ground. I've seen it used for everything from roofing and hooch walls to making musical instruments.

Many grunts use hammocks instead of air mattress beds. They aren't as low to the ground as ground bound beds but they are farther from the ants and other pests. This mission is slow; nothing compared to the last time out with them.

Lost in the Jungle

February 4, 1971

We went two clicks more. If I never see a giant bamboo forest again, it won't be any too soon. We continued down the NVA trail and by noon were setting up our night base camp and sending out small patrols. I went out on a patrol which was a mistake.

We left our "heavies" behind at the camp and headed off towards a small stream. We moved down the stream, found nothing and broke brush up to what we thought was the trail we'd been going down. It was a different trail at least as heavily traveled as the other. On the mistaken notion that it was our trail, we walked way out around our camp and got lost. It was all bamboo and it all looked the same.

They sent out another patrol to find us and, wouldn't you know it, they found us. Then the two patrols started back and we both got lost although

3. Into the Jungle: January 1, 1971, to February 27, 1971   193

When tramping was done for the day, tents were set up and the men talked. Harbeck is in the upper left and Lynch the lower right, holding a spoon.

through the power of high intellect and finding the right trail, we finally found the camp.

Becky, I saw a monkey today. I thought he was going to crash and burn as he hurdled through the bamboo but he somehow survived the plunge. He pulled out at about twenty feet and disappeared. I'd disappear too if I'd gotten a gander of ugly GIs moving through the jungle, leaving refuse as they go.

We see many old NDPs (night defensive positions), both American and NVA. Although NVA soldiers are slobs, the Americans are in a class of their own as far as clogging jungle trails with garbage.

I picked up another giant land snail shell of another type. This is a more colorful shell than the other with a different kind of swirl.

You would think that GIs, ready for a gook hiding behind every bamboo clump, would have a single-mindedness about survival. Although they are interested in remaining intact, after patrol hours the guys follow a relaxed schedule. They cook their personalized chow, play cards or just sit and talk. The only concessions to the war are keeping the noise down and not listening to radios.

I came out here to relax and grow a beard to intimidate the hardened REMFs. Lights are always out after dark. It could be a worse life.

Restful Jungle Day; Writing by Moonlight
February 5, 1971

We had another nice quiet day. We made our biggest finds of the operation so far which isn't saying much. We found an old NVA company-sized night camp along a large side trail. Farther along the trail we ran across several small bunkers protecting a small hooch in a serene bamboo forest setting. Besides that and humping another click or two, it was a restful day.

Days are much cooler here than in Bien Hoa. We set up early in the afternoon and relaxed. Our night position is a particularly good one with a stream and an open area we can use for a set-down logging tomorrow. I should leave then for Bien Hoa without the excitement of a big find like the last outing. The day after, the word has come down from highers, Echo Recon will be moved to help build a new 1/7th firebase.

We aren't suppose to us C-4 explosives for heat tabs but everyone uses it anyway. The unit stole bars of C-4 from the engineers on FSB Noble and has been heating water with it ever since.

Just to prove it can be done, I'm writing this in the moonlight. The forest is lit by a nearly full moon, casting bamboo-leaf shadows over this paper. I've been listening to what we think are wild pigs which one of the squads saw earlier today. I saw a wild turkey too.

Until dark (and moonlight) I was talking to the Jesses of the bear episode. Jesse Reed made me a bamboo pipe in which I was smoking cherry blend tobacco and gagging on. It was sport jabbering with them.

This little bush jaunt has done great things for my sanity. I've been telling the guys that I'm shamming from the rear—they like that. Night-night, I could keep this up but the mosquito squadrons are moving in and I've got to get under the mosquito net pronto.

I'm awake for night-guard radio-watch and the moon still is shining in its glory. You can find beauty anywhere and these jungles aren't an exception—moonlit nights are a mysterious beauty the world over.

It sounds like an ultra quiet barracks with snores and shuffling bodies, spiced up with the jungle's sounds. This peace disguises that we are imprisoned by a wall of protective claymore mines and trip flares.

Night Condensation
February 6, 1971

I froze last night, fickle jungle. About two hours after night guard ended, I heard the steady drip drip of what I thought was rain but I stuck my head out from under my poncho liner and noticed that the stars were out but it was cold. Then it dawned on me that the droplets off the trees were condensation. It was 60 degree at the most—cold for these parts.

I've decided to stay out another day and CA into the new firebase location to shoot up my remaining rolls of film.

I just learned they have a mailbag out here so I'm sending this now. Don't worry about me. I'm having an invaluable experience and enjoying it to boot.

Digging Up Grave; Monkeys

January 7, 1971

Echo Recon's plans were changed after I missed the last bird out—now they're humping another 4 days. The remains of yesterday were taken up playing hearts and a rap session on such unlikely subjects as physical education and the financial conditions in colleges, not to mention teaching sex in health class.

Today we were in the process of digging up an NVA grave when we heard noises like chopping and building hooches. I was with Steve Harbeck and Lt. Lynch; they were certain it was NVA building a hooch until we started seeing movement in the trees. For a second I thought I saw a man walking down a trail. Then he leaped onto a tree and went up it hand over hand so fast that I thought he was running up a hill. I realized then what I was looking at; it was a group of orangutans, chimpanzees or some other large primates. For a while we looked for NVA—it seemed too good to be true. A squad reconned the area and found nothing so we went back to digging up the grave.

It was a long, hard, rocky grave we found that took us 30 minutes, several of us shoveling, to find the body. About a month old, we could see only his grisly face—he'd been shot in the mouth and was ripe. Because our NDP (night defensive perimeter) was nearby, we made sure to cover him up. We added an NVA body to someone's body count. We joked as we dug.

In moving the 2 clicks today we saw fresh "slick" tracks, Ho Chi Minh sandals, along a stream we walked by, then through. We were walking on squelch down most of the trail. We went out of the bamboo into higher ground. It was hardwood jungle terrain with trees easily a hundred feet tall.

I just got an order from the rear, probably Lt. White, to catch the bird at the next logging and beat it back to the rear. I'd been planning to go back anyway.

Nightmare; Thatched Hooches

January 8, 1971

Lt. Lynch had a nightmare last night; he was haunted by the NVA in that grave. He put a cross on the grave, which was incongruous considering the NVA was in a Buddhist grave. What bothered the lieutenant, I think, was that we broke the NVA's neck when we rifled through the grave.

Today we found 25 thatched hooches, recently abandoned, a big find. Delta, 1/7th's contact was less than a click away so this probably is what the fight was about. At its height it's estimated this village held hundreds of people. It's rare in War Zone D to find thatched hooches. It was Lynch's theory that the gooks were near the streams—that's where he looked and he was right.

This village had such refinements as a large fish trap in the stream and notch in a tree, which filled up with sap that burns. This may have been a hospital complex.

I may get extracted tomorrow because the brass is invading then to have a peek. This is such a large hooch complex that the platoon has scouted only part of it. We're holed up in a small section the farthest up stream. It's in the bamboo again.

I've got some shots of grunts with an NVA roof over their heads. I'm sleeping under a hooch roof too. In some respects this is as good as the cache find. I still can't say I've been in a contact, thank God.

The moon has been out every night making guarding early in the night easier. I have guard late tonight so I won't benefit from a well-lit landscape.

Enemy Complex; Eye Injury

January 9, 1971

We've moved to the middle of the second section of the hooch complex. It's at least 700 meters long. It was a cold night sleeping on an air mattress of bamboo in the center of a rat-infested NVA hooch.

They're building the LZ I hope to leave out of; this should be it for this outing.

What a bummer. We had to blow the LZ and had 3 cases of Bangalore torpedoes kicked out to us. A smoke grenade started a small fire in the grass and for some reason, the blasting caps were set off. There were two explosions: the lieutenant was nicked by the first bang, Demond got a gash above the eye when the second bang caught him off guard. He's being MEDEVACed.

One of the guys told me Demond was hit in the eye. A Ranger-type LOH helicopter made an amazing landing and took out Demond. Then a log bird came in and, without telling anyone, dropped TNT and other explosives, which set off the lieutenant. Lynch was so mad that he was shaking—this was adding insult to injury. This obliterated the fun of finding the hooch complex.

The people in the rear thought the blasts were Lynch's and Demond's fault—they should have known better than to play with blasting caps near fire. I was there and can testify that they were working frantically to protect us from having the torpedoes themselves explode. They're heroes in my book. Demond's only thanks may be to lose an eye [*he didn't*].

3. Into the Jungle: January 1, 1971, to February 27, 1971

I'm back in the rear (Bien Hoa) now and it's too late to answer all your letters. I'll write tomorrow, I promise.

1/7 RECON FINDS COMPLEX

I did considerable work in the jungle to get this story, which was a bigger deal than the story suggested—the complex was extensive—but you wouldn't know it from what I wrote. There was a story with several pictures as the centerfold in the March 2, 1971, Cavalair. *It was also on the front page of the March 26, 1971,* Observer.

NEAR FSB NOBLE—It isn't very often that grunts sleep under a roof in the boonies. They virtually have to capture a roof, which seems unlikely in the middle of nowhere, but that is what Echo Recon, 1st Bn., 7th Cav did recently.

About 100 NVA had built thatched-roofed hooches, an unusual permanent type of structure for this remote a section. For some reason, the NVA left the large hooch and bunker complex. The hooches at one end of the complex were much newer than at the other, leaving indications that the enemy had used the complex until recently.

For six days Echo Recon had been walking along a large NVA infiltration trail. Fresh slick tracks along one stream and the suitability of the terrain for the NVA kept the GIs alert and quiet.

First Lt. John Lynch, platoon leader, had a definite hunting ground in mind. "We know that during the dry season small streams dry up," explained Lynch, "and the enemy has to find large flowing streams to survive. By staying on the trails and staying near water, we think we can find the NVA."

As it turned out, his theory was correct. On the sixth day into the mission, the lieutenant sent a squad up a trail along a stream and hit paydirt, eleven NVA hooches. He then moved up the platoon to the small village, and after a thorough search of the area, sent out another squad, which found two more parts of the village up the trail.

Thus the skytroopers found accommodations for the night. GI air mattresses, mosquito nets on bamboo matting under a thatched roof and a built-in bunker below provided more comfort. This still wouldn't compare with stateside standards, but for Echo Recon this was the life.

What follows are captions for the photos that accompanied this story. The pictures are indistinct and thus not being shown but the captions provide added details so they're included.

When an enemy complex is discovered in the midst of the jungle, the reconnaissance platoon moves cautiously at first, then more boldly as it becomes apparent that the enemy has vacated. After each hooch has been checked out and cleared by the platoon members, the men secure the area for the night and break for chow like the four recon members in the sun-dappled clearing below.

At bottom right and left: Echo Recon members check and clear vacated enemy hooches. Above, a skytrooper who has found a seat among the abandoned enemy living quarters takes a welcome moment of relaxation after a day of carrying a heavy load of provision and ammunition through the jungle.

Mountain of Mail

February 10, 1971

I found a mountain of mail when I got back and was greatly encouraged by the tone; it's a refreshing reminder that there's another world when I leave Vietnam.

Today I was on what I would describe as a "shit detail." Not literally, burning human waste is done constantly here. What I'm talking about is completing the story on Operation Scrub.

Lieutenant on Warpath; Uncle Larry; Operation Scrub

February 11, 1971

What an unnerving day. Our Lt. White was at his worst. He has been on one of his campaigns—which I still think is at least subtly racist—to get Ed Howard out of the office. I was the only one in the office that wasn't under attack. Al Brown is lucky he's gone because he'd be a whipping boy too. Don Fry was given a particularly bad time but kept taking it. I'm seriously thinking about asking to go to Phuoc Vinh to escape.

Uncle Larry [*Coyte*] called today from Saigon, wondering if he could come up and see me or vice versa. I said I'd love to but Saigon was too far and a place I didn't understand. He called me just as White was getting into a tirade. I'm so pooped from the bush and so tired of White that I didn't have anything left for seeing Uncle Larry. It's extremely frustrating.

Also, I've been told to write a favorable story of Operation Scrub, which finished recently. I'm plodding away; I have no enthusiasm for the idea. Scrub is a project the Army should have thought of years ago and used with imagination. Instead it seems a lot of senior officers want to get their names worked into the paper. I'm making a hypocrite of myself and writing a favorable story with plenty of higher-up quotes to please everyone.

I just finished going to the briefing for the first time in ten days. The 2nd Bn., 12th Cav is finally part of our brigade. They're stationed in Phuoc

3. *Into the Jungle: January 1, 1971, to February 27, 1971*   199

Vinh. I got through half the briefing before realizing that our brigade AO was way too big; that's how I found out 2/12th was ours.

There was a vicious firefight in the 2nd Bn., 7th Cav today. We won the battle but suffered one dead and four wounded. They suffered at least three dead and our company brought the world down on the NVAs' heads. The war is growing hotter; it's livelier now than it's been for several months. I wonder if the Cav will really be able to get out of Vietnam?

Psyops Bird

February 13, 1971

I didn't write yesterday because I got into a strange run-in with Lt. White, which ended up with both the lieutenant and I going up to the Major at Phuoc Vinh to try to straighten things out. I kept my cool even when I was giving White a bad time and was polite to the Major. I had enough of White's harassing the others in the office and since I was the least touched by his onslaught, I felt it my duty to speak to the Major and at least have him talk to White. I was moderately successful—at least the problems were opened up to the boss.

White wants to work me hard, which I don't mind.

Dave Lewis got sick up at Phuoc Vinh so I was given one of his assignments: to go up with an Air Force Psyops bird and take pictures. Today I went flying in a tiny Cessna Super Skymaster, an 02B, built in 1967. We started off taking pictures of an old C-47 dropping leaflets to the wind, in color for the supplement that is being put out for the 1st Cav History Book.

Then I played the part of my pilot's co-pilot. We played Chieu Hoi tapes and threw out pamphlets and, predictably, I got so airsick with all the circling that I nearly threw up. It was interesting nonetheless. The 02B has 1800-watt speakers, if you can imagine. They are loud enough to be heard out in the bush, which I can testify to from my last outing.

The NVA and VC have put a few holes in the plane but no one has been hurt so far. My pilot, Capt. Myron Loss (Middleburg, Penn.), and I talked over the intercom headsets and I must say, he was an easygoing type of officer. Part of the fun in dropping the leaflets is finding which way the wind is blowing so a certain area is being hit. We chased our clouds of leaflets, what he called "drop spotter charges" and observed where they landed. The leaflets, if we were up a couple of thousand feet, would take 10 minutes or more to come down.

I went to an Air Force briefing that was more humorous and relaxed than the Army version. We had three lieutenant colonel pilots listening calmly to a young enlisted man giving the briefing in a calm fashion that wouldn't have been allowed in the Army. The Air Force officers were such gentlemen compared to their Army counterparts.

I've been looking at other people's camera equipment, a dangerous business for me. Ron McCowen was showing off his color slides up at Phuoc Vinh last night from his Nikon F and I was pink with envy. Which reminds me, I'll send those rolls of film to you.

Psyops Missions Spread Word

I generally wasn't airsick in helicopters but fixed-wing planes were a different matter. This was the closest I came in country to losing my lunch. The following was in the March 2, 1971, Cavalair.

BIEN HOA—The Cessna Super Skymaster (02B) flew alongside the much larger C-47 to have a good view of a leaflet drop. "A C-47 can drop a million leaflets in a day," said Capt. Myron Loss, the 02B's pilot, "they can really flood an area." The big bird's paper trail was vivid testimony for what he said.

The 02B pealed off and started on its own mission as part of the 9th Special Operations Squadron. After finding a target on the map and spotting it below, Loss set up his tape recorder and started giving the countryside his selection of tapes through a 1800 watt speaker system. He circled around the target area, giving its inhabitants his best sound and this Army passenger's stomach began to curdle.

Loss is proud of the response he has gotten from the enemy. "They shoot at us," he said, "our program makes them mad. We've had some hits but we haven't suffered any casualties."

"Sometimes we get a quick-reaction tape mission," he added. "We have an aircraft make a tape directly from the radio and broadcast it or we can broadcast it directly from the radio without making a tape."

After several hours the last part of the mission, the leaflet drop, was started. This passenger went into the back seat and prepared to throw out the Chieu Hoi pamphlets, his stomach in turmoil. A few pamphlets were cast to the wind.

"We drop what we call spotter charges of leaflets to see where the wind carries the pamphlets," explained Loss. "It's hard to judge because heat rises from the sun-heated ground or a moist rice paddy. I think I know how the leaflets are falling today."

With that, the 02B made a long bombing run, littering the ground with paper. This passenger, in the advanced stages of losing control of his digestive system, hung his head out of the window. The plane returned to its home airfield, its mission complete.

Memorial Service

February 14, 1971

I finished the SCRUB story, the Psyops pictures, and flew over to Bearcat in a LOH for a story on the opening of a new chapel. Bearcat is a bleak place near Long Binh, which looks like a huge square firebase with a large fleet of helicopters. The chapel opening was another in a string of stories special to other people who go to a great to deal of pain to get me to write.

I forgot that on February 12th I took a LOH to a memorial service out in the field with Chaplin Workman for a man who died in the A, 2nd of the 7th contact the day before. It was an eerie scene; a whole squad in prayer for their lost comrade.

Al Brown got back from New Jersey today after his two week leave home. He is still readjusting to the heat. It was very cold at home but when I told him what he missed with the lieutenant, he agreed that he was better off away from the office. His leave seemed like it lasted five days instead of two weeks because of the travel time.

I've got an envelope with 8 rolls of film, part of the rolls from the bush, ready to put in the mail to you.

Tomorrow is six months in Vietnam.

I haven't been able to relax the way I did while O'Daly was here. In two weeks Lt. Field and his PIO crew from Song Be are coming down when they close out Song Be and hand it over to the ARVNs. Once they arrive, I wonder who will control this office.

When Don Fry leaves for his two week leave in about three days, I change my job to jeep driver and photographer although I'm well on the way to being a photographer already. It's discouraging given my interest in writing. When talking with the major the other day, he seemed to care less what happened to the PIO office or me; he cared more about becoming the executive officer of a grunt battalion when the division PIO changes to a brigade PIO.

Hooch Theft

February 15, 1971

I collected my pay and shammed the rest of the day—not much day was left after the time-consuming flight up and back from Phuoc Vinh and the waiting. I got a look at the bushy shots that I'd taken and there was hope for some of the flicks although as a whole, they were underexposed. I sent the 10 rolls I've collected so far home for you to develop, Dad. They should give you an idea of what's going on here.

I talked with one of the Echo Recon fellows about Doyle Demond. He is being taken to Japan. His eye will not be the same although he won't be completely blind. It's a rough way to leave this country; there are better ways to get out of the bush.

Our hooch is grand central without any privacy at all. The PIO is at one end and Special Services, the potheads and drug freaks, at the other end. There isn't an easy way to lock your room like there was in the old hooch. Several days ago someone got at my wallet which was semi-exposed and cleaned it out, all $10 worth. It is frustrating; I heard the guy looking through my stuff but I was too tired for it to register what was going on. It was petty theft but it's frustrating. The Army doesn't seem to accept our need for privacy.

The Air Force is getting its money's worth out of the airfield next door; it seems to be alive with all kinds of activity these days.

Ping Pong; Operation SCRUB; Freedom Bird

February 17, 1971

I was just playing ping-pong with a Black E-6 who may be a hair faster than me, although we always seemed to be tied near the end of the game when he'd pull most of the games out. I'm really tuckered out, my arm sore from swatting that small white ball like I was trying to hit a homer. Ping-pong is a pleasant change from sitting around.

I talked to Colonel Richard L. Harris, Division Support Command (DISCOM) commander, about operation SCRUB. He's a high-minded guy taken with collections of words out of which I've tried to make sentences somehow. He was a friendly man who gave me the clincher to the SCRUB story.

I was taking pictures of GIs getting on the Freedom Bird and GIs getting off. The ones getting off didn't seem to have a rank below E-6. I did some checking and confirmed that they had taken advantage of the two-week leave program—turned it into a program for lifers. They are the people who can most easily afford the cost. I thought it was a good program for the grunts that want a break from the field.

I've enclosed another Army newspaper that sometimes uses our stories. The story of mine is one I've never seen anywhere else, probably because it isn't much of a story. This paper is put out by USARV with a small staff compared to ours.

Tomorrow I'm flying with the Special Services Band to FSB Audi and FSB Sally, both in the second brigade. Because the band works and flies out of Bien Hoa, Lt. White thinks we can claim them as ours. I've always been curious about Audi and Sally—they're firebases I never got a chance to see while I lived in Song Be. They both are near the Cambodian border, I think. I know Audi is.

It's been quiet here; you really begin to wonder if the war is still in

3. Into the Jungle: January 1, 1971, to February 27, 1971

progress. Up north it is, I guess, although we don't hear much about it down here. We only know what's going on in our own division and now, just in our brigade.

Scrub Nets $12 Million

I grumbled endlessly when writing this story but now find the topic of excess equipment interesting. Collecting surplus probably was a good idea and there was nothing wrong with officers pushing for the program. What surprises me now is that they only netted $12 million—that was chicken feed compared to what was spent on the war. This story was on the front page of the March 10, 1971, Cavalair *and in the March 31, 1971,* Army Times.

BIEN HOA—One of the 1st Cav's biggest campaigns ended recently with the closing of the last collection yard for Operation Scrub, a division-wide effort to "scrub clean" units of all their unnecessary supplies and equipment. Scrub lasted only four months but it resulted in more than $12 million worth of equipment to be salvaged.

The project's success and size came as a surprise even to its organizers. "We expected people to be reluctant to turn in equipment," commented Lt. Col. Robert B. Hoppe, the Division Support Command S-4 (DISCOM), "because they were fighting a war. But with bad experiences with unit moves in the past, where units were weighted down with equipment, they took advantage of the program."

Scrub's start was a shaky one. "Scrub was slow at first because people were getting rid of their worst equipment," said Col Hoppe. "But as the emphasis on the program grew, so did the amount of equipment coming in increase. I don't know how many times we filled up that yard but we often couldn't keep ahead of the volume."

"The coordination between the five or six different elements were crucial to the program's success," added the colonel, "since several of the elements were outside the 1st Cav."

The 15th Supply and Service Bn. took the brunt of the equipment invasion job, and the initiative in sorting and dispersing the incoming gear. Once 15th S&S saw the amount of equipment involved, Battalion Commander LTC Clifton A. Horn provided 25 men to work full time on the job.

"We don't have the trucks in the division to move the equipment," said Capt. Jerry E. Simpson, in charge of Scrub for 15th S&S. "We picked up additional trucks from the 4th Transportation Command. The semi-trailer requirements for us had to be doubled from eight to 16 a day at the height of the operations. Transportation was a key factor in Scrub."

The 79th Maintenance Bn. in Long Binh was at the receiving end of the

1st Cav's collection drive, putting reclaimed supplies back into the Army's supply channels. 1st Lt. Gary Askim was appointed as liaison officer for scrub between 15th S&S and 79th Maintenance, to bring order to the transfer of the stream of supplies, which included everything from trucks to helmet liners.

The 27th Maintenance Bn. checked the equipment coming in and the Forward Service and Support Element (FSSE) handled turn-in yards in Phuoc Vinh, Song Be and Mace. Equipment from the forward yards was convoyed to the main yards in Bien Hoa.

In his final action report on Scrub, Capt. Lawrence J. Becker, DISCOM project officer, outlined another facet of the program: "Because of the relaxed turn-in requirements, the popularity of this operation made it an overwhelming success, requiring that Operation Scrub be extended three times."

The report also gave an indication of the immensity of the undertaking. "During the period of Oct. 6 to Dec. 28," Becker noted, "595 vehicles, 398 trailers, 514 generators, and some 36,000 miscellaneous items were turned in."

The majority of equipment in the $12 million total went to Collection, Classification and Salvage (CC&S) at Long Binh. Redistribution within the 1st Cav accounted for $298,484.73 worth of supplies while $517.067.18 worth of gear was turned over to the Property Disposal Office.

Col. Richard L. Harris, DISCOM commander, explained Scrub's role in the larger Vietnam picture: "Project SCRUB started off as the 1st Cav's effort toward the USARV goal of cleaning up the battlefields and returning materials and unneeded equipment back in, to supply channels or for disposal as was appropriate. This type of program is new to the Army, where a unit is still in the fields of war."

The Scrub concept was originated by USARV as "Project Scrub" but the Cav's Operation Scrub represented a broadening of the program, extending it to TOI&E equipment not needed for the unit mission as well as excess gear.

"The relative stability of the 1st Cav's area of operations," Col. Harris continued, "allowed us to look into economics of retrograding certain excess items. What made Scrub unique was that it went beyond excesses of equipment on property books, which could be turned in without many of the formalities associated with turning the items in."

"An airmobile division," the colonel concluded, "should try to keep itself as light as possible. And not having moved the division in some time, it was time we looked into this area. Scrub provided the format for such a program."

So ended another 1st Cav campaign, this one within the First Team, directed against the cluttered supply yard and the forgotten CONEX instead of the NVA.

Special Services Band

February 18, 1971

Today I flew out with the 1st Cav's Special Services Band. I had a good time although from a photo standpoint it was a bust. We flew up to FSB Audi (5th Bn., 7th Cav.) and FSB Betty (1st Bn., 8th Cav.), getting my first look at the 2nd Battalion in 4 months. Audi was small but the band had a good audience. The music group called "The Sounds from the Other Side" was the best group I've heard on a firebase; they were real pros. Betty was a full battalion sized firebase and yet the crowd was much poorer because General Burton had a compulsory wards ceremony going at the same time. Betty's crowd was small and unenthusiastic but the electrical power going out didn't help.

I came back with the band, enjoying the Huey ride but got hot. For the first time I was riding in a Huey with its sliding doors closed. I like the doors open with the wind blowing. I hitchhiked back to the office and unloaded my camera, only to discover that the film hadn't advanced so I got no pictures—what a blow. At least I had a story to write.

It's really growing hot, almost unbearably so. I felt like an egg frying as I sat out at Betty listing to the rock group. Bien Hoa, if anything, was even hotter. There aren't any trees in Bien Hoa and the tin roofs act like hot plates, cooking the people beneath.

The Army band would set up in the middle of the firebase, often with a nice crowd like this one.

I talked to the 2nd Brigade men and stand down proceeding start in about ten days for them. Things will start to snowball, Bien Hoa will become a zoo full of disintegrating units and our office, a month after standdown begins, will become the main PIO office.

"Sounds from the Other Side"

Live music was available in Vietnam thanks to Army bands. Though firebases constituted truly challenging venues, I saw several bands performing on LZs and was impressed. This story was in the March 17, 1971, Cavalair.

BIEN HOA—Music has always held a touch of the sentimental, especially for the young GI in Vietnam. Canned music from radios and tape recorders bring back some of the warm feelings, but a live band is the best instrument for awakening a memory, especially with the rich rock sound. In this spirit, "The Sounds from the Other Side," the 1st Cav's Special Services Band, has brought live rock music to the firebases.

The band members set up in the dust of the firebase, in this case FSB Audi, connecting their instruments and mikes, testing their drums and eyeing the crowd. With everything in order, they swung into the show.

"25 Miles," sung by the music director and organist, Spec. 4 Chuck DiModeca, had noticeable impact on the audience sitting on sandbag and culvert hooches. SSgt. Ernie McClelland, in charge of the band, gave the listeners a charge with his soul sound. The six-member band created the mellow sound like the professionals they all at one time were. Somewhere along the line the band plucked the right string and the crowd at FSB Audi felt it.

Pieces like "I'll be There," "Who's Maken Love," "Love Bones," "Funky Chicken," "Proud Mary" and "My Girl" are the staples of the group's success. FSB Audi's show was a glowing success with the small but friendly audience.

FSB Betty's show, on the other hand, was typical of what can stand in the way of a show. An awards ceremony was held at the same time and the electricity went out, dissipating the sound and the crowd. "Sometimes," said McClelland, "we have to stop the show altogether because of a fire mission."

"Nonetheless, all the band members agree that it's worth it. 'Spooky' and some of the other songs remind the guys of good things they were doing back home," said Robinson and that is success itself.

Reporter's Death; Dog Dies; Hospital Visit
February 19, 1971

I took the jeep up to get the brakes fixed and ended up "dead lining" it, in other words letting it sit until we could scrounge parts. It took me most of the morning to get away from the jeep.

3. Into the Jungle: January 1, 1971, to February 27, 1971   207

Lt. White told me he had to have the jeep because General Abrams was giving an award to a sergeant from B 2/8th who, while he was in the 25th Division, was a hero in Cambodia. As luck would have it, the day before he was to receive the Distinguished Service Cross, he was wounded on a firebase when the enemy mortared the place. I was sent down, hitchhiking, to get a story and take pictures. The sergeant, named Wood, had frag wounds on his chest and a tube in his mouth, making it hard for him to talk. I couldn't get the story from him so I sat and waited three hours for the generals to arrive.

SFC Lebus, a senior sergeant in our office, came into the ward where I was waiting. He was sent down to make sure the pictures were taken. He then floored me with news the likes of which I've never received in Vietnam. As you know, I've never lost a friend in Vietnam. He told me that Steve Werner from USARV PIO, who also carried a Nikonos camera, went up to Khe Sanh with the 1st Brigade, 5th Infantry Division with a group of engineers on a road. He was hit with a B-40 rocket in an ambush and died, probably instantly.

Steve was the only guy I knew very well in the USARV PIO. He would aggressively go after stories like me. Unlike me, he had the run of the whole country so he could find more trouble than I've found in the 1st Cav. You may remember me telling you about Steve and Roger, whom I talked with in the club a short while after hitting Bien Hoa. I talked to Roger a great deal that night but it was Steve that I really got to know the best in later meetings. Steve was an ex–Boy Scout, well known for giving out Boy Scout mirrors to the grunts (and me). What shook up guys in my office was that Steve was short with about twenty days left in country. He volunteered to go out, the wrong choice in retrospect.

Taking Abrams' picture was anti-climactic after that. He is an old man—he must be at least 65 years old. I thought he had kind of a funny face—the hospital didn't seem to bother him the way it bothered me. He had his herd with him, colonels on down. He was there about five minutes, big deal. Before I knew it, he was winging his way away from the 24th Evac Hospital to who knows where.

The hospital is a depressing place I discovered again as I sat for the three hours. One guy was particularly shocking for me, mostly because he kept smiling despite being badly wounded. He was from the 25th Division and the VC had turn his claymore mines on him and blown them. He was hit in the chest and heavily in the legs. He was a big strong fellow who reminded me of my cousin Gordy. There is a horror for me in seeing someone who will live with whopping scars.

Snatch, our homeless pup, got run over by the MPs last night and had to be shot. She was a pooch without a future. It may be all for the better but I never like to lose friends, even smelly stupid little dogs. There's no future for our dogs when we're gone. The Vietnamese savor dog flesh but how could anyone eat a friend.

Vietnamese Band; Strippers; Operation Keystone
February 21, 1971

Dad, I remain loyal to the bear story—Vietnam has bears. A platoon from 1/12th killed another bear in an automatic ambush so bears are not uncommon out there.

Yesterday I hitched into Long Binh and back, then I hitched to the Air Force side of Bien Hoa and finally hitched to Phuoc Vinh when I couldn't catch a bird at the Air Force. It was sweltering all day and I was out in the rays long enough to develop a farmer's tan with a big V down my chest where my shirt doesn't protect my skin. I find my boonie hat does a good job of cutting the sun that hits my head. I got my long ride to Phuoc Vinh from a major and a captain from MI (military intelligence). After picking me up they picked up a fellow from Radio Research, another area I'm not allowed to write about. I got to talking with the radio research guy and made one remark so radical that the officers in the front seat half-seriously said they'd let me walk. We were way out in the middle of nowhere so I shut up promptly.

I went to Phuoc Vinh to see a real live Vietnamese Band and Strip Show. I also talked to some of the boys before they come down to Bien Hoa. The band was surprisingly good with competent musicians. Band members showed a good deal of individual character—they were real people on stage, not "gooks."

Sodas and beer were free because the club had been making too much money, this being the PIO's own little club in the civilian press hooch. They'd had problems with several dishonest sergeants taking money out of the club's pot so they were partying, trying to make the club unprofitable or, at least, broke.

The strippers came on toward the end and I have to hand it to these loose Vietnamese women—they left absolutely nothing to imagination. After their prolonged cast-off-the-scanty-garments routine, they pranced off the stage with everything open to view. It was almost too much for a number of horny GIs—it was funny.

Our paper came out today without a single story of mine. In fact, they were so short of copy that they didn't even have much Cav copy in the Cav paper.

When I hitched to Long Binh yesterday, it was to pick up pictures of Operation Keystone and the yellow hats heading the program. Operation Keystone is same-same division standdown and the units will drive in to Long Binh, one by one, and in as orderly a fashion as possible, turn everything in. The 11th ACR (Armored Cavalry Regiment) and the 25th Division's last brigade in Vietnam are all pulling out at the same time with turn-in points near the Cav's. It's quite an operation. This turn-in point is in a section of Long Binh I've never visited before—Long Binh is even bigger than I'd thought.

Arguing with Officers

February 22, 1971

Starting 6:10 yesterday afternoon, I was having a bad day. I didn't go to the briefing after telling Lt. White that I would, a major blunder on my part. The lieutenant was quick to catch me as I was playing ping-pong. He warmed up on Al Brown for something and then really lit into me.

"Why don't you stop acting like a child and take orders like a man," he said. "I'm going to give you some advice. You are going to be in the Army a lot longer than I am and you had better settle down or you're going to be in trouble." He had me virtually at attention. He threatened me with an article 15 in his humorless insulting way and said he'd send me up to see the major. Then I made a further blunder, not know the major, and insisted on seeing the major.

So I went up to see the major this morning carrying a note from Lt. White. The major read the note, called me in, and proceeded to not only back up White but cut me off from what I was trying to say. He said I'd lose some money (get an Article 15) if I kept rebelling. And then he said, "If you're being raped, at least you can lay back and enjoy it." That weasel can kindly fuck himself. He lost all the respect I had for him with that remark—he's so much the lifer despite being a cute little man. I'm going to lay low and do my job despite White, the whole point right along.

I did a story yesterday, before getting into my quarrel with White, on the dedication of a new athletic field. The field was dedicated to Spec 4 Hall who died along with 7 other men in a mid-air collision in late September. With the standdown coming up, athletic fields are being built all over in preparation for the idle grunts coming out of the field during standdown.

White called Brown and me into the office late this afternoon and we thought we were in for another grilling. He said instead that the Song Be PIO is coming down and, starting next week, Al and I are to work exclusively for the 1st Brigade. Sadly, we are still working for him. We are moving hooches again, possibly back to the same one we were kicked out of. It's unlikely that the major will be around long because as the Cav shrinks, his job will be done away with and he hopes to go out to a grunt battalion. White, on the other hand, could be around a while. He keeps forcing my hand in these squabbles by insulting me grossly as he does everyone he can get some control over. My stock may have gone down with White and the major but everyone else in the office sees my side. I can't remember ever getting cornered like this before and getting this mad.

The lifers wonder why they get gassed and fragged. They wonder why the enlisted swine rebel. They don't understand why drugs are rampant and nobody salutes officers. It is more their fault than they know. They refuse to listen and are far too quick to jump on rankless peons like me mercilessly. Saying that officers as a class are smarter than the enlisted man is rubbish. It feels like being in an insane asylum with the insane in charge. I'll be damned if they'll destroy my will and won't forgive them for their thoughtlessness.

HALL FIELD DEDICATED

I would report on ceremonies on Bien Hoa Army Base for our paper, in this case an athletic field dedication. The bulk of dedications—the names of firebases particularly—were to fallen soldiers. This brief piece was in the March 17, 1971, Cavalair.

BIEN HOA—Hall Field, the 229th AHB's new athletic field, was dedicated recently in memory of Spec. 4 Donald Allen Hall, who died Sept. 27, 1970, in a helicopter accident.

Col. James F. Hamlet, 11th Aviation Group Commander, and Col. Richard Maeder, Bien Hoa Army Base commander, were among the dignitaries taking part in the ceremony. After a number of speakers decried the misfortunes of war in which men such as Spec. 4 Hall die, the battalion had a moment of prayer. Then the softball game began to the music of the 1st Cav Band.

Keystone; Echo Recon Ambushed

February 23, 1971

I had no run-ins with anybody today—White was playing it cool for a change. Maybe he thinks he made his point, whatever it was, and is willing to let me work in peace.

I hitched down to the Keystone Operation headquarters for the 1st Cav today. It's a complicated matter moving out a division and this section in Long Binh is only part of the operation. They handle the turn-in of all equipment except helicopters, avionics, medical equipment and cryptographic equipment. About 80% of what is turned in to them is disposed of in Vietnam. Dad, from your India days you're familiar with the rationale for it being too expensive to ship old equipment home. I guess they'll set up a kind of personnel turn-in at what was the FTA for sending people to other units outside the 1st Cav. Some of the units are being completely disbanded, losing all their equipment. Other units are returning to the States (Ft. Hood, Texas) with their equipment but without most of their men. And a few units are staying until the bitter end.

About a week after I left Echo Recon, they were hit in an ambush. One guy whose name I don't recognize was killed; he was walking point. Spec 4 Snow, whom I knew well, was MEDEVACed with two broken legs and sent back to the world. Sgt. Jesse Reed was wounded lightly and one other GI was hurt. I left just in time but wouldn't have been hurt in the CP anyway. The NVA blew a claymore mine on them—Echo Recon's luck went sour.

Psyops stands for psychological operations—psychological warfare, if you like. It's also known as S-5 or G-5 at the brigade and division levels. The Air Force, because it doesn't cost as much to fly a small plane as a chopper, has been given the mission of dropping leaflets and broadcasting infuriating and enticing messages to the enemy.

I'll make it yet despite the all-pervading hassles with White. I don't feel a bit guilty or sorry for standing up for what I think is right.

Shyness

February 25, 1971

I've just been sitting, talking to Dave Lewis, who just got back from Sidney, Australia. He suffers from the same disease I do, shyness as far as the girls go. He was looking at the Australian girls for almost a week and was flabbergasted by their beauty. He was impressed by the aborigine's bark paintings and spent his money on that. His nose is peeling but he looks happy enough. He is looking forward to leaving Vietnam, leaving me drooling. Not only is he leaving but is ETSing—escaping the dumb dumb existence of military discipline and stupidity.

The latest rumors sound better than the old one. I hear someone else doesn't like White and he's not going to stay with the office. Also, although General Hyman will be living in the HHC Rear for the next month, it's General Burton who's going to be in command of the last brigade to stay, which would be an improvement.

I flew up to Phuoc Vinh and made out a caption sheet for my bush color slides which turned out well. I'm going to see if I can grab the ones they don't use. Phuoc Vinh looked good to me. The staff was there, sunning as I nosed my way around the office, and sunning until I left. In Bien Hoa we'd never get away with such shenanigans: White and the lifers would spot us in no time.

Lost Reporter

February 27, 1971—a year and a day in this man's army

I find the thought of your blizzard experience incredible. I miss the sweeping changes in the weather; it's always the dust or the mud and the heat here.

Talking of what the dog dragged in, here comes Al Brown. We thought he was lost for good. As I suspected and what I'm always afraid of in these firebase-hopping expeditions, Al was caught out on a remote firebase overnight—it's about 50 minutes (about 80 miles) by Chinook from Bien Hoa. He stayed last night and most of today before catching a chopper. He was frustrated no end. I don't blame him a bit if he's cynical about his visit to FSB Powder Ridge.

You talk about strange incidents. I get into a routine of what to expect and the kind of stories you find out in the bush. Today's action was for the 1/12th unit was shockingly different. An enemy sniper shot two GIs through the heart, killing them both. I'm used to us giving a good fight but this was so one sided.

I'm glad to hear the film arrived.

Colonel Maeder is no longer the Bien Hoa Army Base commander as good fortune shows itself. That's one less man for the PIO to have an unhappy working relationship with. Now maybe we can find a decent hooch. It looks more like the rest of my tour won't be under the thumbs of Hyman and Maeder.

The jeep finally is fixed and running. Lt. White was running around franticly trying to come up with brake shoes. It was a day of triumph for him since this jeep is the only one in the PIO now that Phuoc Vinh's jeep is gone. White has been friendly of late and I'm staying out of his way, successfully so far.

I talked with Dave Lewis again and he's approaching ten days to getting out. He's the guy I'm most sorry to see go although I'm glad he is getting to leave the Army. He's the first person I worked with in Vietnam—it will be the end of an era when he departs. He was on a short tour; he hit country about a month before I did. The stampede out of the office for fellows DEROSing starts early next month.

I'm growing short myself. Another three and a half or four months and that will be it if a two-month drop works out for me. I have high hopes. Cheers, don't let the snow get you down—feel privileged.

Chapter 4

The Audience Shrinks: March 1, 1971, to April 30, 1971

I was still plugging away, reporting on myriad topics. The division shrank to a third of its size, a brigade, with parallel shrinkage in the information office. There was restlessness among the remaining troops, with a serious fragging taking place. There was more involvement with the civilian press, including Sam Donaldson. I was given a bit more responsibility with handling stories and photos.

Hooch Mobbed; Saigon Driving; PFC Tucker; Captured Money

March 1, 1971

Most of the Song Be crew is down now and have mobbed our little barracks. It will make our haunts unpopular with the drug freaks, which isn't bad. But now we have a little mosquito netted bed and wall-locker cubicle per man, a not very satisfying set-up. Don Fry is back; his money ran out because he took personal checks along instead of traveler's checks. He had a great time.

I got a chance yesterday to drive in Saigon traffic, which I've heard so much about. "What a trip!" as a head would say. I did all the things that a driver instructor would have fits about. I tailgated and was tailgated, passed into the other lane and was accordingly passed, and had a ball. I enjoyed it; it's like a war. I really liked going off the launch pad (the stop light—there were a couple of lights) and weaving among the motorcycles. The only problem was that I wasn't confident that the jeep was going to hold its bolts together long enough to make it back to Bien Hoa. We picked up the *Cavalair* without much trouble and headed back. And I thought Iowa roads were bad. The only thing that bothered me was the smog. I'll have to try it again.

Enclosed is a *Cavalair*. I'm unhappy with my centerfold—it doesn't show what the hooch complex looked like.

I was talking with Steve Harbeck for about an hour at lunch about the claymore they had blown on them. I was wrong; their pointman walked past the ambush. It was what we so eloquently call a cluster-fuck situation; the guys were too close to each other. One American claymore did four guys a job. PFC Tucker was killed (I'm enclosing a picture of him) and three other guys were pretty thoroughly punctured. I guess the point man, Mike Jessee, grew up five years in the moment the claymore went off. He didn't spot it and it's doubtful that anyone would have. His best friend, Jesse Reed, was one of the wounded. Mike ended up in tears and I don't blame him a bit.

I did a story on the 1,000,000 in piastras found on five dead NVA and how the company that found them missed the fact that 1,000 $50 bills were interspersed among the piastras. The grunts didn't get any more of a reward than ice cream for their find. There has been much speculation on what a competent unit with an understanding leader would have done. They would have divided the greenbacks among the platoon that found the money, illegally. There is general contempt for a platoon that would turn in that much money; it's a trophy of war and the Army doesn't adequately pay its grunts for their risky line of work (if it's possible to pay anyone enough).

This letter must end; Al Brown wants the typewriter to write a story.

PFC James Edward Tucker, Jr., is shown as I saw him when I was out with Echo Recon two weeks before he died.

4. The Audience Shrinks: March 1, 1971, to April 30, 1971

NVA Purse Strings Cut in 1/7 Firefight

There was unseemly fascination by the troops with this capture of a hoard of NVA money. This article was on the front page of the March 17, 1971, Cavalair and in a short truncated version in the April 30, 1971, Observer.

NEAR FSB ARES—The NVA have become so adept at hiding their valuables that sometimes GIs don't even notice what they've captured. Recently the 3rd Platoon of Alpha Co, 1st Bn. 7th Cav robbed the NVA and it required the backhauling of the loot before it was clear how thoroughly the platoon had done Charlie a job.

The platoon had killed five NVA in a claymore ambush and a search of the bodies produced four AK-47s and an M-1 carbine. But the biggest find was virtually a portable NVA bank. The enemy soldiers were carrying two bundles with 500,000 piasters per bundle plus a five-piaster coin.

Overjoyed by the rare find of one million piasters, the grunts called in a report on the money over their radio and a backlog bird promptly appeared and flew the captured material back to Ares.

While checking through the piasters on the firebase, something odd was found mixed in. There were familiar-looking green bills with Benjamin Franklin's face on them. There turned out to be a large collection of these American fifty-dollar bills, a thousand of them, interspersed among the piasters.

The money was turned over to the division finance office in the rear and the $50,000 was sent back to the U.S. Treasury after a check was run on the bills' serial numbers.

The piasters were turned over to the government of South Vietnam.

Theories on the mission of the waylaid currency vary, one of the more prominent being that the dead enemy soldiers were members of an NVA pay team. It's also possible that they were acting as couriers, playing the role of a human Brinks truck.

The Viet Cong and North Vietnamese forces use American currency in large denominations to buy supplies, according to a recent article in *Stars and Stripes* concerning the Cav's money capture. The American green is readily accepted as payment for rice, medicine and munitions through underground channels, frequently in the Saigon black market.

Pizza; Medals; Soldiers to 101st

March 2, 1971

I went over and had a pizza with my Echo Recon buddies, Steve Harbeck and Tim Payne. I had three beers, which tanked me up for the day. Steve was telling me about the sniper instructors at his sniper school. They had a man who was a crack shot with a pistol at 300 feet. They are some of the best shots in the country, Steve said, and they are rifle addicts. I keep having trouble spotting my old buddies from the bush in the rear. Without their plumage of dirt and long hair, they just don't look the same. I didn't recognize Tim until after arriving at the pizza shop. Tim was his old comical self with 37 days to go before he ETSes; then he gets to see his wife and his new baby that he's never seen.

Today was the first day the 1st and 2nd Brigade PIO staffs worked together, nominally. There was great confusion with little work getting done. The officers kept us wasting away in the office or running down awards ceremonies.

I covered an awards ceremony for the 1/30 Artillery. They gave away a mass of air medals, bronze stars and Army commendation medals. They had about 50 artillerymen that were given all three. How worthless can an award become? These guys, most of them, had never seen combat or been on a firebase being attacked. Few had done more than their jobs although feed howitzers is a hard and thankless one. And these guys are more deserving of medals than people in the rear. The only attacks we've experience have been drug raids by our Army.

Tomorrow is the first day that a unit, 5th of the 7th Cav, an infantry battalion, will actually send some men out of the Cav to another unit, the 101st. I get to pick up a movie crew from a Long Binh Army outfit to take pictures of the processing of the first large group of men. The 5/7th has already turned in their equipment.

I've enclosed some slides from the second bush outing with Echo Recon.

Standdown Begins; Shakedown Inspection

March 3, 1971

Today was the first day that 1st Cav units officially began to stand down. I was dispatched to SEAPC (South East Asia Pictorial Center) in Long Binh to pick up four photographers to film the ceremony. I acted as a guide for the truck drivers who didn't have the slightest idea of where to go. That was all I did all day.

This office is a zoo where the lieutenants are jabbering and giving conflicting orders and the far-too-numerous enlisted men do what work they can find. Travel is becoming harder, especially for fixed wing flights. Choppers aren't as numerous either. Al Brown expects us to have problems moving in the 1st Brigade the way we used to.

We had a silly shake down inspection at 6 a.m. this morning for drugs and guns conducted by lieutenants White and Field for some obscure reason.

They didn't find anything because they'd said something was up the night before. It reminds me of basic training, this kind of nonsense. They don't trust us and never explain anything they do. We're not even sure they were within their legal rights. They've taken all M-16s away from those of us in the rear because they are afraid of shootings. They also are afraid that someone will be fragged—hand grenades are watched closely.

I have little control of what is going on. This breeds the frustration and mix-ups that result in my putting out only six stories last month, my all-time low.

I was talking with Sgt. Jim Parker, a soul brother who's taking Ed Howard's place for the time being. We agree that our officers' dependence on an authoritarian approach is self-defeating. Jim, it turns out, is unhappily married. His wife took all his money, ran around with another man, and influenced him to make unwise decisions. Then she asked for a divorce with him paying for everything. It's far more complex than that but he's upset. He wants to get out of the office with Field and White. He wants to go back to the bush where the action is up north. He spent a tour in the bush and must have liked it.

Firebase Design; Military Police; Officers Squabble

March 4, 1971

I went out to FSB Sherman, which used to be a 2nd of the 7th firebase but was taken over by the 1st of the 12th two days ago. I did a story on how battalions build firebases differently and how the 1/12th is rebuilding a 2/7th firebase. The officers think it is a good idea to have the same old kind of firebase the 1/12th is used to. The enlisted men like the idea of keeping what's there intact and not working so hard. But the 1/12th is dogmatic about having a "showy" firebase. They say their most showy firebase so far was Jupiter, which was a well-built-up place on top of a hill. But again, I feel it's appearances as opposed to substance.

I talked about this firebase rebuilding with a young lieutenant who seemed familiar to me. It turns out he was the platoon leader of Echo Recon, 1/12th few months ago and is now working on the firebase. I wondered if he was the guy whose platoon on a "riverene" operation (rubber rafts down a river) had three guys drown in an accident. I asked him whether his platoon was the one and was immediately sorry when he grimaced. I think he must have lost his zeal for the bush since I saw him the first time. The bush, in the final analysis, is a horrible place. It's likely that only once a month will a platoon get in trouble but that day can be living hell. I keep talking to ex-grunts who bear this out.

I had to go to Phuoc Vinh but birds from Bien Hoa were in short supply.

I decided to hitch a ride down from Phuoc Vinh to Bien Hoa and see if this is a viable alternative to the fixed wing. I sat two hours talking to the MP (military police) at the Phuoc Vinh gate before I got a ride.

MPs have a thankless job: they harass and get harassed from both top and bottom. The guy I was talking with was an ex-grunt from 5/7th who was bemoaning the fact that if he'd stayed in the bush longer, he'd be going home with 5/7th now instead of in forty days. We talked about the idea of creative harassment. Since MPs are forced to hassle people, I thought it would be an admirable idea to make harassment as painless and honest as possible. He liked the idea after a while although for a few moments I thought the idea ludicrous.

He said that GIs he gave DRs (disciplinary reports) were the guys who lied to him; he respected those who were honest with him. If he had a quota of DRs to give out and didn't see any reason for giving them (this happens, he said), he'd finding someone like a grunt going to the PX to pick up a hat and give them a DR for not having a hat, going on the assumption that the grunt's commander (the one who takes the action) would rip up the DR when it came to him. The MPs, known as "Ps" for short over here, are as human as the rest of us.

I finally caught a ride—a bumpy, airy and generally uncomfortable ride—in a deuce and a half truck. I sat in the back talking with the other guys, gabbing away, looking for information.

It seems that two MPs were taking a guy back from Phuoc Vinh after he was court martialed. He had gotten six months at hard labor and a dishonorable discharge. They said he was a good guy nonetheless. He had been AWOL for two years in Saigon—I couldn't see how such a feat was possible. He married a Vietnam gal and the girl's parents ran one of Saigon's big clubs. His wife had a child and the fellow sooner or later would have had to face trying to legally get his wife and child home. Another Vietnamese got jealous and turned him in. His crime is usually punishable by spending no less than three years in jail but in a pretrial agreement, the prosecution and defense agreed on the lesser sentence so the trial was a formality.

About five miles down the road from Phuoc Vinh two human bodies were by the side of the road. Someone, it appeared, had killed two VC and left them as a warning on the road. There they rotted, grotesque reminders of the barbarism in this foolish war. After an hour and a half ride at breakneck speed, I made it to Bien Hoa.

I walked into the office and caught the tail end of a tongue-lashing that was taking place over the phone. Captain Runkle was bawling out Lt. White for the lousy support he, Capt. Runkle, had received while in Bien Hoa today. The lieutenants were off in the jeep all day and Runkle was florid. White was a whining mouse, objecting weakly, and Lt. Field was looking over his shoulder trying to get all gist of the bawling out since he was the other lieutenant at fault in Runkle's opinion. I made a hasty retreat. I hear that SFC Lebus came into the office earlier today, off-handedly asking for the jeep for a couple of hours, and was turned down pretty flatly by White. He dislikes White more than just about anyone in the office. What catfights—this is called leadership?

Dave Charlton has four days, he tells me, to ETS. Dave Lewis follows him by four days. Charlton is from Wisconsin and a pacifist with a master's degree in English. He doesn't like the Army and does as little work as possible. He is a good man although far too intense for me. He's been here about 13 months—he's an old timer. He is famous for not going out to the bush or the firebases. That may be wisdom—I don't want to pass judgment on him. Peace to him and in four days, maybe he'll get a chance to find real peace.

1ST OF 12TH SELF-STYLES FIREBASES

There were differences in the way battalion commanders handled their units. Usually it was hard for soldiers to compare commanders' approaches—constructing firebases was an exception. The following was in the March 24, 1971, Cavalair.

FSB SHERMAN—It's hard to accept a firebase as being home but once there is a grudging acceptance of the mud and the dust, a battalion comes up with a personalized setup. Because the firebase is moved often, the GIs end up rebuilding the same design base in different corners of the Cav's AO.

Consequently, there is a clash of styles when one battalion takes over another battalion's firebase, whether the bunkers are the wrong shape, the gun pits the wrong width, or whatever.

For instance, when the 1st Bn, 12th Cav replaced the 2nd Bn, 7th Cav at FSB Sherman not long ago, changes were made to provide base layout more to the liking and tastes of the new resident battalion. With past architectural triumphs such as FSB Powder Ridge, Timbuktu, Jupiter and Ares, the battalion set out to rebuild FSB Sherman so as to conform to an SOP [*standard operating procedure*] dating back through many Vietnam campaigns.

"You're faced with methods of organization conflicting with what you're accustomed to," explained 1st Lt. John Austin, the assistant S-3. "They split their mortar crews while we don't, for example." But the new battalion had some consolation in not having to start from scratch; the prefilled sandbags helped expedite the renovation.

"We always insist on a good firebase," commented SFC Thomas Stockman. "Jupiter was our show base. This will be a good one too once we get it built up. We're also enlarging it."

That an individual style of firebase design will ever be attributed to a single battalion seems unlikely, but the rebuilding will still go on. For, like a family renovating a new home, the battalion rebuilds the new fort to resemble the old fort.

FSB Ares; Dust Control; Frag Fishing

March 5, 1971

I flew out to FSB Ares, which is now a 1/7th firebase. Steve Harbeck and most of the Echo Mortars crew who I know were there. I was out most of the day and am nice and warm with a glowing sunburn. I had a relaxing time talking about old times, collecting stories, and drinking beers and sodas because they hadn't gotten the water point functioning. Steve was shamming, a little crestfallen at the news that he was going to stay in the bush at least another month because the battalion was not going to Phuoc Vinh before Bien Hoa and standdown. He was the usual aristocratic drinking buddy I enjoy.

I'm developing a story on penepriming the firebases to keep the dust down. Peneprime is a molasses-like tar used to make surfaces resembling asphalt—fuel oil can be used for the same purpose. Firebases have a real dust problem when choppers hang around, blowing particles into food and hooches so that nothing can be kept clean. By weighing down and jellying the dust, the peneprime (or fuel oil) are much appreciated by the LZ inhabitants. This admittedly is a half-jesting story to get the names of a few of my friends in the paper.

I talked with the 4th Platoon of Charlie, 1/7 about what they'd been doing and came up with a promising yarn. The company had a six day log (six days' worth of food) and discovered on their sixth day out that they weren't going to be resupplied because they were in a dangerous area and near the end of their mission. So, on the 7th day out, they took a chance in making a little too much noise and went fishing in typical grunt fashion. They threw five frags into the water, stunning the fish and bringing them to the surface.

They were fishing in a good-sized stream 10 to 12 feet across and about 6 feet deep. The NVA had set up a dam with a fish trap in it but this was too slow a method for catching supper. After exposing the bountiful fish supply, about a hundred fish, 5 or 6 GIs dove into the water and grabbed the fish as they floated past the dam. Using NVA cooking utensils, they'd found they cooked up the fish with the hot sauces and spices that grunts use heavily.

One of the fellows involved in this crude form of fishing said that this method came out of their pangs of hunger. Usually well fed, the GIs were quick to find a way to fill up. They caught catfish and a fish similar to perch. The lunker of the lot was between 18 and 24 inches long. They were logged (fed) on the 8th day.

4. The Audience Shrinks: March 1, 1971, to April 30, 1971   221

By noon I had two stories and decided to spend the rest of the day talking around. I should note here that Ares was closed for a month or so. The new Ares was built on the old flattened clearing of the old firebase and is far smaller than the battalion-sized firebase of the 1/12th. I plan to go back with a camera because I can get practically a full view of the firebase without taking to the air to do it. I sat around until 6:30 p.m. waiting for the Charlie Charlie bird to take me home.

OIL BITES THE DUST

Using oil on firebases to suppress the dust traded flying dust for an oily smell, generally considered an improvement. The March 24, 1971, Cavalair *used this story.*

FSB ARES—LZ inhabitants are veteran dust eaters, though they've never had much of a fondness for the stuff. The dry season has again created plenty of dust and therefore plenty of work for the peneprime and diesel fuel spreaders.

There are definite preferences among the detail people about which they think does the better job.

"I like the diesel better than the peneprime," professes PFC Juan Kellogg, a member of Echo Mortars, 1st Bn., 7th Cav, "it's not as messy and it still keeps the dirt down." Sgt. Charles Wall, on the other hand, extols the virtues of the gooey tar. "I like peneprime because it last longer," he said. Wall, it should recorded, was splotched with tar.

It is impossible, short of an acre of asphalt, to completely halt the onslaught of the dust. A Chinook pumps enough dust with its blades on oilless earth to nearly suffocate an entire firebase.

"We were eating dust at FSB Green before we peneprimed it," commented SSgt. Eddie Robinson in charge of part of the oiling activities. "It's one of our ongoing projects."

And eating dust is meant literally. "It gets into the chow, hooches, mortar tubes—you can't keep things clean," added Sgt. Edward Kilgore. As if to make the point, a Chinook coming in disappeared in its own cloud, reminiscent of the Dust Bowl of the 1930s.

At the price of tar on the boots, the dust can be kept in place on the ground. Until the monsoons and the mud save the firebases from the dust, the GIs will continue oiling down the firebases.

1/7, EXPEDIENT FISHERMEN

Fishing wasn't done much in the 1st Cav—this was my only story on the subject. And it's a shame the fishermen cheated. The following was in the

Top: Firebase outhouses were pretty basic. Excrement fell into cut-out barrels and the contents burned, as shown here. The outhouse is in use and the occupant has a paper stuck out of the door—it's likely it was the one I wrote for. *Bottom:* Artillery pieces needed regular maintenance and, as I recall, this 105mm howitzer was being pulled out for repairs.

March 31, 1971, Cavalair, *with a shortened version in the* Army Times *of June 16, 1971.*

FSB ARES—Because of the 1st Cav's efficient logging methods, grunts can rarely complain of going hungry. However, in rare instances where resupplying becomes difficult or an impossible task, the boonie travelers resort to ingenuity for food.

Finding themselves in one of these rare instances, elements of Charlie Co., 1st Bn. 7th Cav decided to go fishing.

The company discovered a 10 to 12 foot wide stream about 6 feet deep with a dam-like fish trap built by the NVA. The GIs soon realized the fish trap was far too slow for the feeding of two platoons, so they experimented with a field-expedient fishing trawler.

"We threw five frags into the stream," remarked PFC Marty Kielawa, "and five or six guys jumped into the water to scoop up the stunned fish. Using the dam as a trap, we caught enough fish to feed two platoons."

Although the old-time anglers were mildly upset by this mass fish hunt, the platoons made a large catch. "We came out with about a hundred fish," said Kielawa. "We caught mostly catfish and something similar to a perch. The largest fish was 18 to 24 inches long."

"We used some NVA cooking utensils we'd found, along with whatever else we could find," explained Sgt. Gary Dake. "Then we mixed in our hot sauces and spices and fried them up."

The verdict is still out on the palatability of the fish, although there was widespread agreement that it was an adequate stomach-filler.

Slow Day

March 6, 1971

Today was extremely slow. I wrote up my three stories and no mail came today.

A 50-year-old E-8 just clobbered me in a ping-pong game. He didn't look that formidable although I was warned beforehand when he polished off the E-6 I've been having so much trouble beating. It was pleasant and exhilarating.

The *Cavalair* had my Scrub story in it. There were a lot of officers' names—that's why the general and such like it. Good propaganda for them. I've never written anything quite like it before and must say, I haven't missed much.

Since I've grown my mustache and consistently wear my granny glasses, the enlisted men have gotten along better with me and even the lifers have been suspicious but friendly so far.

Special Story; New Job?

March 7, 1971

The future shows promise—Lt. White will only be in the office another two weeks. He got himself a job working with the Saigon Support Command. He is looking forward to it, even told me that we all ought to get together down there, which is as unlikely as can be.

Also, I get to cover a special story starting tomorrow down at the beach at Vung Tau with D Company, 1st of the 12th Cav when they take a three-day in-country R&R. Being the first of its type out of the Cav, it ought to be great sport. I'm taking only twenty dollars so I have money when I go on a real out-of-country R&R. In fact, I have two sore arms, especially the left, from immunizations shots I need to escape the country.

We're going to lose a battalion from our brigade but I don't know which one. If it's the 2nd of the 12th, I won't be able to get together with Mike Payne who you want me to meet.

White said something about me taking Ron McCowen's place when McCowen leaves in early April. He's one of the heads running the paper but I already had the job by default. There will only be about 12 men in the office by the time Phuoc Vinh's PIO come down here. Dave Lewis is down here, leaving for good.

We've got some big bats flying outside, at least six of them. It's up to 12 bats now.

Vung Tau

March 9, 1971

I feel like a crispy critter, what we call NVA burned up by a napalm drop. I stayed on the beach too long and glow red now.

The grunts think this Vung Tau beach area is a great idea. Not only are they away from the war and the tedious chores on firebases but the city of Vung Tau is on limits with its bars and prostitutes at semi-reasonable prices.

This tiny resort is on the South China Sea a few miles from Saigon. We were flown in by Chinook from Bien Hoa. One minute the soldiers were in the bush, five hours later they were minus rucksack on the beach or in the village.

This place has been open as a resort since March 1 and there are still many bugs in the operation. We stay in tents, have a club with a bar and snack bar, which seems overpriced and poorly run. As long as I stay out of the village I won't spend much money.

The captain of D Co. 1st Bn., 12th Cav got very drunk and bought himself a regal python for 30 bucks. Yes, Becky, it's a beautiful snake. The captain showed it to General Putnam, who grinned broadly and asked the captain what he was going to do with it. The general seemed impressed by the operation here, so far.

The sun was so bright yesterday that I got a splitting headache. I slept fitfully until I walked outside and threw up, which eased my head pains enough for me to sleep.

The sea wasn't very good for body surfing—the waves were breaking too soon. Also Vietnamese gals are not a fair trade for American girls as far as I'm concerned.

Inflation is hitting the whorehouses here as more GIs start arriving. I won't embarrass you with what buys what but in just a week the prices rose 30%.

The Army's got everything, even its own skin paste for sunburns, which, although probably effective, is virtually impervious to soap and water. Sand sticks to the stuff, creating a walking sand creature.

I feel a little guilty taking R&R in country with grunts that, I feel, earned the right to come here. Maybe I'm too sensitive.

Vung Tau End

March 10, 1971

Tonight's my last night in Vung Tau. I've had enough of the beach and don't feel I've gotten away from the Army. Living in crude tents and wearing OD green are reminders of the ever-present Army. The wind has been blowing steadily off the sea, buffeting the tents and putting sand into the air. Sleeping here isn't nearly as comfortable as back in Bien Hoa and I can't keep the sand off me.

The grunts have spent most of their money although it's not accurate to say they're ready to go back to the bush. They are hoping the ground troops really are going to be taken out of the field and they'll be able to stay in the rear.

I couldn't get my hands on the Vung Tau negatives so I'm settling for the front page and the story with a few of the pictures.

Mr. Nice Guy

March 11, 1971

I made it back to Bien Hoa around 11 a.m. and have been coping with the madhouse that is the PIO since. I'm looking forward to going on a real R&R soon. I don't want to see fatigue-clad GIs while I'm there. Getting out of here will be a last-minute scramble.

I guess my saving grace as far as a lot of the guys are concerned is that

A Skytrooper's paradise

Story lengthened

Story and Photos by Pfc. Conrad Leighton

BIEN HOA — "Boonie" weary, bearded, still decked in battle gear and brushing the dust from their fatigues, grunts from Delta Co., 1st Bn., 12th Cav trudged from the choppers here, with a promise of a three day rest and a plunge in the surf at Vung Tau.

Exchanging rucksacks and "sixteens" for cutoff fatigues, the men combat assaulted the South China Sea beach. Others, less interested in a watery relaxation, found the nearby Vung Tau Village worth a unique recon mission.

Delta was the first of the 1st Cav units to participate in this new program of well-deserved rest and recuperation.

Capt. William Hink, the G-1 project officer coordinating the R&R operation, explained that the Cav had been looking for such a site for some time, so when the property became available the Command grabbed the chance.

The program is intended for support units as well as the infantry, but Hink said, "The grunts natually have the priority, because they are the ones who most need the rest."

"There is a bar with beer, mixed drinks and sodas," added Hink, "a snack bar and a chow tent serving from 8 to 10 in the morning and 3 to 5 in the afternoon. Malaria pills and mosquito nets are the only routine things we have down here," said the project officer. "The men are here to rest and relax."

The "Ville", as the GIs have dubbed the village, naturally fascinates the men who spend most of all their tour in the bush and don't have the chance to come in contact with the Vietnamese people and their culture.

With buses making regular runs between the "Ville" and the Cav resort area, GIs seem to melt into the village between the hours of 6 in the morning and 10 at night. "The girls aren't half bad," insisted one GI.

Just about anything could be found in the small village, as Company Commander Captain Lee Davidson could attest. During one of his excursions, the slim bespeckled Captain bought a three-foot baby royal python. The pair became the sensation of the standdown and provided continuing wonderment as the young captain explored the beach area with his pet.

Among the onlookers was MG George W. Putnam, Jr., there to review the center's facilities. Though a bit taken aback, Gen. Putnam smiled broadly and politely asked what the captain was to do with his pet.

Except for the fatigue bathing suits, one would hardly realize that these sandy beaches were indeed part of Vietnam. Lifeguards patrol the beach, a bathhouse is handy for securing valuables and suntan cream is parcelled out free.

The three days passed for the Delta Company Skytroopers and another company was ready to replace them. Possibly lighter in the pocketbook, some tanned, some maybe a tinge on the raw side of tan, but all more relaxed after this brief rest away from the tensions and pressures of living in the bush, the men reluctantly boarded the bus for the return trip to Bien Hoa.

Baby Royal

Captain Lee Davidson, company commander for Delta Co., 1st Bn., 12th Cav and friend step up to a bar at Vung Tau — two whiskey sours please! (U.S. Army Photo by Pfc. Conrad Leighton)

Soaking Up Sun and Surf

Two Skytroopers from 1st Bn., 12th Cav. soak up sea and ski on a stretch of beach at Vung Tau, the 1st Cav's three-day R&R spot (U.S. Army Photo by Pfc. Conrad Leighton).

I'm non-abrasive, I don't hassle people and usually stay calm. Talking with Jim Parker, who keeps buttering me up, says I'm one of the nicest guys he's met even though he's black and I'm white. This embarrasses me but may be true to a point. People aren't as quick to jump on my back—this is true even of White. It's one of the few pleasures of the Army to have made more friends than enemies. I won't let this praise go to my head.

Our souvenir issue of the *Cavalair* came out and I had leafed through a copy. I'm in it, swimming in a water hole at the firebase when I went with Ramlow to the place months ago.

All kinds of stuff came from you today—three letters and the contact prints of the negatives I sent you. I'm encouraged by the contact prints—I should be able to come up with dandy prints when I get home. I'll mark up the sheets and send them home.

Would it be "peals of laughter"? Would it be "banana peels"? I require a competent editor; all I need is for them to make me an editor. Then we'll be in real trouble.

Several GIs were atwitter about a monstrous snake they'd seen in "the Vill" (Vung Tau Village), which I couldn't believe until I saw a Polaroid of it engulfing one of the guys in its grasp. It was either a python or boa—I don't know my snakes, Becky.

New Lieutenant; Intimidating Dogs

March 12, 1971

Today was an incredibly slow day—I did nothing but type up the "Bush to the Beach" story and thought what I'd do on my upcoming R&R. The office was the usual madhouse and junkyard. Field, the 2nd Brigade's lieutenant, has been scrounging madly and the office has filled up with his prizes. There's no news on a larger hooch for the PIO enlisted men.

We have a new lieutenant about to become a captain who is going to be in charge of our new consolidated information office after Phuoc Vinh comes down here. He seems to be a pleasant enough guy but I haven't seen him in action yet. White will probably be gone by the time I return from leave. I don't know who will be in charge. I don't look forward to working for Field. You work for him, not with him. He's the kind of guy who will mail home the office refrigerator or go swimming while leaving the enlisted men to hold down the hot office. He's little better than White in his own way.

The Blacks in the area have a strange campaign going to intimidate the dogs that bark. They don't try to make friends; they throw rocks instead. Blanche, since we've moved to the new hooch, has become hyper-nervous when one of the resident Blacks comes in. She growls and they return the compliment with a kick or the stab of a broom handle. Displaced aggression maybe—probably. Needless to say I give the Blacks a wide berth too. With the notable exception of Ed Howard and Jim Parker, I've made few friends among the Blacks. We live in different worlds.

I hear the 2/7th is standing down soon from the 1st Brigade. I don't understand the planning, which is classified and out of reach to me. What I do know is that men are beginning to leave in some numbers now. The 1st Cav is no longer intact.

The *First Team* magazine should be out March 22nd, the day I return from R&R. I have high hopes for my Echo Recon cache article.

Officers Disagree

March 13, 1971

I officially signed into the R&R-DEROS Center today although I'm still staying in the office. I have decided to take a standard leave on standby, which is riskier but cuts the cost of my flight to Hong Kong by about 130 bucks. I'm keeping my cool and hoping I can make it out okay. I can convert my money to traveler's checks tomorrow and then make the 7:45 a.m. briefing on the 15th. After that I can start my vigil at Camp Alpha in Tan Son Nhut and hope to get a flight.

You ever find yourself in the awkward position of supporting someone you just finished trying to tomahawk? I find myself supporting White against Field's flagrant misuse of what the 1st Brigade PIO (my brigade) has built up. White decided he'd had enough of Field's gymnastics with the office and called up the major. I listened to the conversation and had to admit that White was right. Field has turned our tiny office into a warehouse for his useless scrounged items. The jeep is gone all day with Field. He tries to play the hard taskmaster with his men and then presents the poorest example possible by never being here and never doing his job. It'll be interesting to watch; the major is coming down tomorrow. We were hoping that Field would go down to Saigon for the night like he has recently but White, out of the kindness of his heart, admitted to having called the major to Field's face. Field was indignant but is warned so he's staying here for the night.

Otherwise, today has been just another day sitting, everyone tracking sand into the office and living in the small space that isn't occupied with office junk. It's virtually impossible to work in this kind of atmosphere. General Hyman ran off with one of our desks so we have very little space left for the job of writing with twice as many writers to use the typewriters.

There is one thing about the 2nd Brigade writers: they're used to writing one story a week plus a few photos. They've never approached the output that Al and I have routinely produced. It looks like Al and I are going to be put on layout at least part of the time in a half-month or so. Al, by the way, just extended his tour in Vietnam by a month so he could have less than 150 days left in the Army and ETS out of the 1st Cav. That means I may leave well before he does.

I can get ahold of a tape recorder to play the cassette you sent me. I can send you cassettes in return if you like although I'm growing attached to the typing keys which give me the time to think. I'm afraid a tape I send home would be aimless. I could give you a feel for the place—sounds from the airfield and all.

Dad, it's choppers—not planes—that fly to firebases. A few firebases like the now defunct FSB Snuffy had landing strips but I can't remember ever seeing the caribous land. The war I've experienced has predominately been by choppers, whether they be a Huey, Cobra, Chinook or LOH.

Basic training was my closest approximation of hell week and I won't allow myself to go through that sort of nonsense again. I'm sure you've heard of what veterans think of fraternity Mickey Mouse games. I'm no masochist—I've got enough trouble with people who think they aren't playing games and are to wear rabbit ears.

Hong Kong?

March 14, 1971

Tomorrow I'm going to Camp Alpha with hopes of making it to Hong Kong. It's possible I will have to hit another R&R site if Hong Kong isn't open although that would be a last-ditch affair that I'm not expecting.

I went to *The Graduate* this afternoon—it's quite a flick; I can see why it's popular. I still like the movie *MASH* more but then I'm still in the OD green machine.

Mortars hit Phuoc Vinh's Service Club where GIs go for entertainment the other night and one medic was killed. The fellows didn't have the sense to hit the turf after the first round landed. So for the next couple of weeks the artillery will be allowed to fire as much as a thousand rounds a night to keep the VC ducking—I wonder if that'll work. Phuoc Vinh is coming down here late this month for good and Bien Hoa will be the only brigade headquarters except maybe Mace. Phuoc Vinh will fade into the past like Song Be. That's fine with me—no more fixed wing flights up there anymore.

Al Brown wanted a couple of pictures of himself. He's particularly interested in the pose with Blanche, our pooch, like the one you mailed me. I'd rather have the negatives at home but I'd appreciate a print every once in a while to see what's there. The prints are great and I thank you for spending the time on them.

I'm lucky that getting out on leave or R&R is so simple because I flubbed in waiting until today, Sunday, to pick up my traveler's checks; the bank is closed Sundays. I'll have to rush tomorrow but shouldn't have any trouble. Steve Harbeck is going on R&R to Sidney on the 17th so I'll probably see him at Camp Alpha if I don't see him here first. I'll go to the 7:45 briefing tomorrow morning, come back for the bank opening at 9 a.m., and hope I get back to the R&R-DEROS center in time. I can hitch down if all else fails.

The office will be in turmoil just after I return with Phuoc Vinh's staff invasion and Phuoc Vinh itself consigned to oblivion. I'm not going to come back early, that's for sure.

It's almost cool now because it's so windy. The dust is blowing around and the atmosphere gets so dust ridden than the sun turns red and disappears behind the dust. In a month or so it will begin raining again and the dust will disappear.

Camp Alpha

March 15, 1971

I made it to Camp Alpha and start waiting, hoping to fly out tomorrow morning. It's been an odd experience.

We had what I'd call a horn freak for a bus driver, sounding his whining horn at every vehicle in front of him. He was driving fast and thoughtlessly, irritating everyone on the road. One Vietnamese pedestrian who was upset at the bus spat contemptuously on the ground and pointed at it. The bus driver wasn't improving relations with the natives.

Once I arrived here, I went in to have a snack at the compound's little club. I added another strange character to my list of con men. He wanted me to buy traveler's checks and let him sell them on the black market for a $75 profit. I was appalled but kept listening out of curiosity.

I've heard better pitches before. He was a friendly-enough spaced-out dude who started by asking if I minded if he sat at my table. The club was dark for some reason, lending an air of mystery to our dealings. He obviously was deep into drugs and, although always polite, his story didn't make sense. I couldn't figure out his motives—it looked like more than just greed to me. After telling him I didn't want $75 that much, I walked off.

It's a pretty fair layout. The room accommodations are good: the mess hall is within 100 yards as is the PX, the club and the terminal.

I'm taking about $800 of my money and $325 from others to buy camera equipment in Hong Kong.

I've really looked forward to this break; I was suffocating in our muddy office setup with multiple bosses. The civilian clothes—the ones originally from home—feel odd. They don't have enough pockets, are too tight, and they're hot. I do look neater now without all the draped cloth of fatigues.

It's Hawaii, Not Hong Kong

March 16, 1971

One of the frustrations of stand-by leave is that sometimes you're left standing one or two people short of making the flight. And that about sizes up this morning.

So, instead of Hong Kong, I'm going to Hawaii, which isn't bad. What this means for my camera purchasing campaign is that I buy the equipment by catalog after I get back. I'm leaving most of my money here at Camp Alpha.

It's a much longer flight to Hawaii but I still get out of country for a week, which is great. I've been told that I'm almost sure to make this flight. This was my only option now that I'd decided to come down here on standby instead of paying my way.

I slept maybe 7 hours last night, fitfully, wondering what I'd be in for today. Now I wish I'd brought the Nikonos along; how was I to know?

I've always wanted a Hawaiian shirt. Cheers!

Hawaii

March 16, 1971 (on a post card)

I made it after a long flight and it's gorgeous. It's the States. It's clean and prosperous with non–Vietnamese vegetation. It's not as gaudy as Miami Beach and far more attractive. I rented a large single room for $10 a night with friendly management that doesn't snarl when you ask a question. I will rest in peace tonight. The time change hasn't hit me that hard. I've gone native and bought bright print shirts, shorts and sandals. Looks good to me.

Sleepless

March 17, 1971 (very early in the morning)

I can't sleep because of the time zone changes so I just finished a stroll along the main drag. This place is filled with the longhaired youth of the hooked generation. Two panhandlers, one shaggy trippy fellow and a scantily clad girl, stopped me separately on the street. The guy wanted a quarter for fare to the airport (unlikely) and the girl wanted a dollar towards her plane fare home to Frisco. I thought the girl's line more believable but I didn't have a dollar, just change. The dude got his quarter. It didn't bother me giving them money. I can't help envying them, especially the girl, because they're unfettered by the Green Machine.

Most of the GIs have their wives or sweethearts here. I was embarrassed to walk into the lobby of the R&R center with all those beautiful women and none were fair game.

I'm not far from the beach, maybe five blocks away. Tomorrow I'm checking out the surf scene. I've been down to the beach once but found the sand granulated, not fine and good for bare feet like Vung Tau's. I'm hoping to find somebody to socialize with—I didn't come here to be a hermit.

Surfer; Longhair Bar

March 20, 1971

I haven't written for two days because I was too gloomy and yesterday, because I waited until it was too late.

I went to the R&R-sponsored luau, which was a treat. I was taken by the three-woman musical group providing most of the backup for the show and some solos on the side. What struck me were their ages, probably 45 years plus. That's one age group I've never seen loosen up enough to keep a vocal-instrumental group going. One portly lively member was plucking a bass fiddle. They were good. I wish we'd see more noise out of the oldsters in such a creative vein. Yeah, Mom, start a group.

I rented fins and a facemask, and then swam out to the reef. I nearly got cut on the coral when a wave caught me off guard. It didn't strike me as the classic reef—not enough color. There were a wide variety of bluegill shaped fish.

I was wondering about the life of a surfer so I paddled out to where the waves were breaking and gabbed with a surfer. The waves were slow so I had time for a mini-bull session. At times he'd paddle off after a wave. The young man, who obviously was an Island native, was friendly. He said there wasn't much talking among the surfers, just occasional growls when the competition got thick for spots on the waves. He said he was on welfare and on and off about college. It looked like real sport to me.

They have a new smaller surfboard that they say is faster and more maneuverable than the big boards of old.

Yesterday I rented a Dodge Dart for a day and drove about 25 miles outside of Honolulu to have a look at the beaches but I forgot my bathing suit. I'd forgotten how much I dislike driving cars without 4 speed transmissions—it was a real drag. It's beautiful country if a bit civilized. It's clean, not dirty like Vietnam. I only kept the car four hours.

Last night I went to a college hangout, a longhair bar, and must have picked the right one. The first five guys I talked with were veterans. They looked like I want to look when I grow up and get out of the Army. Their hair was down to their shoulders with full beards. They were freaks despite their appearances.

I can't remember having such a good time drinking. We were buying pitchers of beer and playing pool. Keith, one of the veterans, was my pool partner and we managed to win only one game. They said they'd had knives and 45s pulled on occasions but it was a friendly drunken crowd this night.

Keith was trying his considerable charms out on one of the visiting pretty girls, Nancy, as the gab centered about the pool table. His strategy fell short although Nancy and Keith left as friends. Keith by the way was decked out in hair to the shoulders and a magnificent long black beard.

My luck with the girls was so so—they were friendly but not close. I had the feeling of being among friends. I wonder if I could find such a group in Fremont, Nebraska?

Keith said that he wouldn't mind going back to Vietnam if the country was at peace. For six months he worked with Montagnards near Pleiku and enjoyed it. He was in Vietnam about four years ago.

Hawaiians are traditionally a friendly people, a change from the distrust of the typical Vietnamese. A typical small-town American like me is hard pressed to compete with his Hawaiian countrymen. Part of it is their tolerance of different race in the Hawaiian melting pot.

4. The Audience Shrinks: March 1, 1971, to April 30, 1971   233

Back in Vietnam

March 23, 1971

I'm back at Camp Alpha. You should receive a box full of Hawaiian clothing, mumus and shirts. I left Hawaii at 8:15 a.m. March 22 and now have no idea what time it is. On our hour-long stop at Guam I eyed a couple of B-52s and bought a box of Philippine cigars.

I spent seven hours on the trip back reading *Everything You Always Wanted to Know About SEX* by David Reuben, M.D. Boy, was I ignorant—he gave me all kinds of wild ideas.

I'm not particularly glad to be back—I was repulsed by my first glimpse of seedy Vietnam.

Magazine Out; Fragging; 1st Brigade Gone

March 24, 1971

I reached Bien Hoa with mixed feelings. I was pleased by the stack of your letters waiting for me. I was taken back by Field who is now the boss of the Bien Hoa PIO staff with the exit of Wonder Boy White to SSC. The magazine finally came out and I was fairly happy with my article and photos. It looks like we're moving hooches, the Almighty only knows where.

Field and White had a monumental falling out while I was gone just before White left. White wanted Field's help and Field was damned if he'd give it. This has been building between these two stubborn power-blinded characters. The spectators, Brown and Fry, said it nearly ended in a fistfight and lasted 30 or 40 minutes.

I mailed off the magazine, another *Cavalair* that came out while I was gone, and my fifth article in *Stars and Stripes*, a small one. I like the magazine—it's the best put out by our office since I arrived. My article was extensively rewritten and frankly, I wrote it so fast that I'm not sure what was changed. There was one point where caches two and three were mixed up. I wrote that article an awfully long time ago and would do a better job now. I doubt the photos could have been better.

We had a fragging in 2/19th Artillery while I was gone, a bloody one. It appears that a soul brother threw a grenade into a hooch belonging to three new lieutenants, killing two of them and wounding the third. I guess the MPs and CID gave the suspect a going over when they found gloves and a grenade pin in his pocket but then, I also heard the suspect wasn't being friendly himself. Throwing a frag is the ultimate display of your barbarian tendencies. It was just a matter of time before something like this happened.

It took me nearly a half hour to catch up on the letters you'd written. I find your third blizzard hard to believe.

The 1st Brigade stood down which means I'm not sure what. I guess now the five remaining battalions are part of the third brigade or the division. I'm not in a division any longer; I'm in a brigade called the 1st Cav Division. Very confusing.

Tomorrow I'm going up to the 2/12th Cav and might get my hands on PFC Paine [*also from Fremont, Nebraska*].

Ed Howard is gone and more bodies are descending on the office at week's end. We still have about 35 people in the PIO.

Standdown Details

March 25, 1971

I flew out to FSB Ares (1/7th's) today where little was happening. I talked to A Co. 1st of the 7th about what they'd been doing in the bush. The 4th platoon killed six gooks last mission and trotted out all the gory details, which turned me off. The 3rd platoon hadn't done much since they killed the five NVA (with only two claymores) and found all that money. The second platoon had the prize find in one of their claymore automatic ambushes, a dead chicken. The platoon is now known as the Colonel Sanders platoon and predictably, their lieutenant is now known as chicken man. Lt. Lynch from Echo Recon is now the company commander and about to become a captain. The grizzly killers of the 4th platoon didn't make for much of a story.

The firebases are getting to bore me—everything is a repeat performance. I'm now officially working in the 3rd Brigade. I've heard that Col. Stevenson (1st Brigade CO) is going back to a job in the Pentagon and his responsibilities for the mean time belong to the colonel of the 3rd Brigade. Both Mace and Phuoc Vinh are moving down to Bien Hoa next week. The operational scheme is a mystery to me. When Brigadier General Burton comes back from shamming in the States, he will have to face working in Bien Hoa. I don't see there will be much left to do for us Americans.

I'm suffering from the post R&R dumps. Vietnam doesn't look so good after Hawaii, a civilized American place where I wouldn't mind playing soldier. I'm out of place, playing reporter to units that still think like killers. Body counts are meaningless to me.

I'm already looking forward to an R&R—not a standby leave—to Sidney in May. And after my Hong Kong disappointment, my luck should be better.

The office remains a madhouse with Field nominally in charge; there are far too many bodies to keep the workload straight. I've heard that White, before he left, blighted me in my efficiency report to DINFOS, which bugs me but doesn't mean much. He wasn't my peer—he was the dud. DINFOS has no influence over my Army career but it's sad they'll now think they failed with me. I haven't done that badly despite still being a PFC. If they want a volunteer Army, they could start by making honest incentives for doing a good job.

I've been liberally encouraged to slack off and lately I have little choice but to comply. Spec 5 Jim Ventrillio was telling me he was looking at the logbook of the 1st Brigade's work output. He said we had months we did more than he's done in his entire time in Vietnam. I don't doubt it but then, he's a Spec 5 (E-5) while Al Brown and I are PFCs (E-3s). Jim's been in the Army longer but this still is unfair.

The weather is about to change. The monsoons are on the way—there have been sprinkles recently and more clouds in the sky. As far as I'm concerned, Vietnam doesn't have a pleasant time of year. And Bien Hoa, I'm told, is one of the least attractive sections of this country.

I keep hearing GIs say that Vietnam is going to be another Korea. I don't see how we can keep troops stationed here, even as advisers. We're not wanted here. You say that a poll taken indicated that 70% of Americans want out of Vietnam immediately; is this saying we've finally admitted defeat? It'd be great to admit one of our mistakes for a change.

Hooch Move

March 26, 1971

Today we learned that the enlisted swine are going to move again, this time to hooches on the other side of the base. It'll be a 15-minute walk to our office every morning! Not only that but we may end up with guard duty because 15th Admin is our home outfit—what a drag.

You've never seen such a group of rebellious men as when the lieutenants informed us where our hooch was being moved. Our last semblances of freedom may be gone. The PIO has been a proud office but its liveliness is in danger of going down the drain.

The gutless wonder, our major, failed us again. The selfish old coot long since forgot we existed. So the panicked lieutenants nominally in charge have to watch as we're screwed over. The major is looking out for his career and forgetting the PIO.

The 3rd Brigade PIO at Mace was forced to leave when some wise guys from the brigade started gassing the PIO hooch. No one would help them; it seemed that the terrorist's moves were sanctioned. The PIO was believed to be enjoying too much of a special status at the 3rd Brigade. I doubt they had it that good but the PIO's work output has never been as visible as ours. The 3rd Brigade boys are down here now and the most rebellious of us all.

I've been spending my time typing out labels to send envelopes off to the troops who have already DEROSed. We've thousands of them to do and it's a slow business typing them manually.

The division stood down today—I'm not sure how much of it. All the generals, Abrams on down, were here. I was fortunate enough to miss it. I was collecting my paycheck and ordering my Nikkormat from Pacific Mail Order. Al Brown, who had to do a story on the festivities, said that Abrams gave an exceedingly uninspired speech. Al said he saluted Putnam and Abrams—Putnam returned the salute but Abrams didn't.

They were going to have the ceremonies at Phuoc Vinh but decided to change to here. The reason most likely was that a couple of days before the VC walked mortars up right into the area where the ceremonies were going to be held—they could have 20 generals wiped out at once. I toyed with what that would have done for the war effort—probably removed a lot of bad advice.

The magazine, which I had great hopes for, had its significance lost in the standdown. Our paper is fading as well—it will be published only every two weeks. The vast majority of our staff is short, leaving next month. Al and I, together and removed from the rest of the office for so long, may find ourselves alone in May.

Hooch Move; Visiting Soldier from Home

March 27, 1971

As soon as we were awake this morning we were moving. Starting about 6:45 a.m., we threw our footlockers and assorted trash into a truck and hauled it the ¾ of a mile to 15th Administration Company's housing. We have our own rooms along with a number of 15th Admin's clerks. My new roommate works with a computer at one of the offices. We've timed the walk to the office; it indeed is 15 minutes. It's good I'm an ex-hiker from Glacier Park or this would be tedious.

I spent part of today typing labels in addition to moving my household goods. People are leaving right and left. Ron McKeown is down here and ready to leave with a 24-day drop.

The battalion stringer, kind of the battalion's press contact, came in from the 2/12th today. This stringer is well known in the office as one of the most aggressive stringers in the division as was his predecessor. I asked him if he knew a guy by the name of Mike Paine in Bravo Company. "Sure," he said, "I know him but he's in a small unit in Echo Recon." I asked him where I could get my hands on Mike and he explained that the unit was in standdown at what used to be the FTA. So I rushed down, prepared to see him for the first and possibly last time. As luck would have it, he's being reassigned to the 1/12th Cav so he'll be around.

Mike's a slightly taller huskier fellow than I am and has the look of a proficient grunt. Talking to the battalion stringer, it seems that Mike was a better than average bush beater so they transferred him from Bravo Company to a more elite Echo Recon five-man ranger team. Mike explained it somewhat differently: "Bravo Company is accident prone; I wanted to get out of there." He was counting his days and not enjoying being one of the longest people in the 1st Cav.

He threw in one remark indicating that the bush hadn't desensitized him. He said his unit had torn up a mortar outfit of VC who'd been mortaring Phuoc Vinh. His unit accounted for four of the seven people in the mortar crew and one of them was still alive. One of the grunts threatened to kill the VC but Mike was against it. Mike said the MEDEVAC bird was slow and the VC could have died—the VC *was* a human being.

Mike was in the area of the service club the night the VC mortared it when the medic was blown away. He said all the grunts hit it (fell to the ground) while the REMFs hightailed it out the back way and were hit before reaching the bunkers.

Mike's parents will be glad to know that Mike is looking healthy and cheerful, although he's counting the days (a few over 200) before he comes home. He apologizes for not writing; I told him I'd write something to my parents so his parents wouldn't worry too much.

I'm going to meet him tomorrow at noon and do that story I promised you. I'll get quotes from Mike and me to send you, Dad. I'll get some film and take a roll of the two of us. Mike doesn't know what he's to be doing at 1/12th yet but says that it's better than ending up in the 101st Airborne. Mike said he's been reading the papers and they're taking most of the casualties up north. I work with the 1st of the 12th Cav so if I wander around their firebases, I may run into Mike.

Tell Mike's parents to stay cool.

Shooting with Mike

March 28, 1971

I typed labels all morning and this afternoon took a roll of film of Mike, his friend George, and me near the FTA repelling tower, near a Huey chopper, near a bunker and near an accident on the highway.

I took down some quotes from Mike although I'm not sure all are toned down enough for public consumption. "I'm proud to be a grunt but nobody really wants to be a grunt. I'm counting the days until I leave Vietnam. I don't think we should be here; I'm just fighting to stay alive." But maybe in a way Mike's had better luck being in the bush. "I survived a mortar attack at Phuoc Vinh Service Club when I was in the rear. Three days later we ran into the VC that had fired the rounds out in the bush." Along with yesterday's letter, maybe you can piece together something. For quotes from me just use part of letters, they shoot the gamut of my feelings on the subject of Vietnam. You can say we've both been in the same brigades with me here earlier. He went out in smaller patrols than I did although I was on one light patrol with only five men the first time I went out. He's an engaging guy. I'm going to the floorshow at the FTA tonight if I can finish this soon enough.

Mike got a letter from his parents yesterday so he's filled in on what's going on at home. Mike was an M-60 machine gunner with B Company and an RTO for the month he was with Echo Recon, 2/12th. Tomorrow he becomes part of the 1/12th. George, his close friend, is going up to the 101st and isn't happy about that. George says the 101st is going to have its shot at killing him, a gloomy way of looking at it. This is his second tour in Vietnam so he should have a good chance but he does envy Mike for staying where the action isn't.

The *Cavalair* came out today with two of my stories and three photos including one on the front page. The paper has no substance; no one is working and it shows. I'll package everything up now, then go off and see Mike.

P.S. I just accidentally exposed part of the Payne-Leighton roll of film—let's hope I didn't lose it all.

Medals; Joe Freed

March 31, 1971

I discovered that I was awarded an Air Medal yesterday along with three-quarters of the rest of the office. Today I got my first Army Commendation Medal, an ARCOM. I'm not sure how meaningful these medals are but I suppose I've earned them if anybody has in the office. The ARCOM said Spec 4 Leighton on it— I'm hoping that isn't a mistake.

Joe Freed from the *New*

I'm standing on the left with Mike and George underneath the rotor blade of a Huey helicopter.

York Daily News was doing his interviewing today. He does it by having us round up New York GIs and get them on the phone. I guess some of these civilian correspondents have a way of taking advantage of the Army. Talking to Master Sergeant Garcia, it seems that at one time the Army did a lot of shooting for the civilians. But about two years ago the military stopped helping out the civilian press when relations went sour. Garcia said he thought CBS in particular had abused their favorable relationship. Garcia has few illusions about Vietnam now and he's been here before. I think he sees that both sides, the military and the civilian press, share part of the blame for no more photography by the military for the civilians.

We have civilian press coming through Bien Hoa constantly but my view of them is peripheral at best. A correspondent for the *Wall Street Journal* just called but I was no help—I didn't know anything. I am valuable to them at times. As an example, we needed another photographer from SEAPC and I was the only one who knew where to go. I probably know this area better than anyone else in the PIO except maybe Fry who, in his role as an inveterate drinker, gets into corners of the base where I never tread.

The official configuration when standdown (the 1st phase) is complete: 1/7th, 1/17th, 2/5th and 2/8th will remain; all the rest will go. I will become part of a detachment of the 3rd Brigade. It should be fun. It looks like our new Lt. Laudner is an easy going type that shouldn't be too hard to work for. Field has become noticeably more relaxed. There is hope for the future.

Sgt. Long—one of ours—is a disappointment; despite his rank he is hopelessly lacking in the skills required in the PIO. He can't type and has a peculiar inability to open combination locks. He can't talk and think fast enough to keep up with the rest of us. And I seriously doubt many of the things he tells me. He also has tried to establish this holier-than-thou relationship with me. I tire of listening to him in one-way conversations that never develop into anything. He's dull and isn't doing a thing in the office because he can't. I can hardly wait for him to leave.

Calley Verdict; Moving PIO

April 2, 1971

Mail call was a bonanza: three letters from you. This Calley verdict has the grunts up in arms; the body count psychology has taken a staggering blow. We've found ourselves guilty in Vietnam, they say, and why the hell don't we sky up out of this Vietnam hole!

The *Weird Harold* [Omaha Herald *newspaper*] articles you sent me are something, the Wally Provost one in particular—the grunts would laugh. Too bad he can't be drafted and go eleven bush. He'd lose his enthusiasm pronto, and maybe his life. [*Dad was a liberal in a conservative state—Nebraska—*

and sent me clippings demonstrating how conservative the state was. Wally Provost was a well-known Herald *sports writer.*]

Today we moved the Division PIO office, the hardest physical labor I've done since hitting Vietnam. Boxes of magazines are heavy. The major, his bland self, was down and even helped throw books around. The lieutenants were having fun with him; he's hopelessly inept at dealing with problems any more serious than how many shots he ought to have at the officer's club. The office is in utter chaos.

I was given my air medal for "active participation in more than 25 aerial mission over hostile territory in support of operations against Communist aggression..." and so on. All the medals except the backdated ARCOM are giveaways.

I've caught a cold that's hobbling me. I blame Hawaii's "cold" air. If I catch a cold that easily then what will happen when I go home and it's freezing cold. It's the hottest time of the year so I dream of cold. It's so bad that I dream of a cold shower.

My roommate tells me that he's seen the orders come down on me so it's official—I'm a Spec 4. Enclosed is the front page of the *Observer* with my story the lead one—gag.

Shrinking PIO

April 3, 1971

It was another day whittling down on the division's PIO junk to accommodate the lesser needs of a brigade. Lt. Launder told me the office would only be allowed two officers and 7 enlisted men including MSG Garcia. Al Brown and I are the obvious choices to stay because of our experience and the relatively long stretch of time we have left. Lt. Field seems to be on the way out. The Chief of Staff, a full bird colonel I think, is coming over around noon tomorrow for an inspection. They're down on the PIO as of now. When the office shrinks, we hope to become less conspicuous and probably will do more work for our size.

Another skimpy *Cavalair* came out. There were no stories from me; just a centerfold with a bunch of old photos in an elegy to the departed 1st Brigade. There is still one more to come; then there will be virtually a month of no paper at all until the office is straightened out. The paper's name will change after the transition.

I'll send you 30 or so copies of the magazine with my cache article in a few days. I agree, the cache story will have the widest appeal to the 1st Cav readers and has the most to do with what the division was and to some extent still is doing. I thought some of the other articles were more spectacular but I probably put myself further out on the limb for my story than any of the other photographers.

4. The Audience Shrinks: March 1, 1971, to April 30, 1971   241

I haven't seen my orders yet but I'm pretty sure I'm a more illustrious and richer Spec 4. I'm thinking of buying a car but I'm afraid I'm still too poor. If I'm stationed back in the States, maybe then I'll buy a car.

FSB Mace Visit

April 6, 1971

I've been sidetracked for a day by an unforeseen trip to FSB Mace, still the home of the 3rd Brigade. I only stayed there a day—what a waste of time. It's about 40 miles from Bien Hoa next to a mountain. It's a seedy surprisingly small and dusty base. I still can't figure out why they sent me out; there was nothing there and within days the whole base is moving to Bien Hoa. The second squadron of the 11th Armored Cavalry Regiment will take over the base. The 11th ACR is "opcon" to the 3rd Brigade, which means that the brigade has operational control of the 11 ACR's tracks.

I talked to a couple of grunts about a contact I'd heard they'd gotten in, a bloody costly 7 hour firefight. Six GIs were killed and 19 wounded when the NVA pulled an ambush on B Company, 2nd of the 8th Cav. Bravo Company has a name for itself as the non–DEROS company. The ultimate blow for Bravo Company in the contact was that a LOH, trying to help, threw white phosphorous grenades on the Americans' position killing three GIs. This is the battalion, 2/8th, that our major is going to in a week or two. He's all they need.

After a poor night at Mace, I decided to duff out of the area. After a mild reprimand from the major, I got back to work in the office in Bien Hoa.

A number of guys in the office have taken advantage of the move from Phuoc Vinh to escape working by staying away from the office. About six of them have been written up as AWOL and the major insists that they'll get Article 15s for their troubles. It would be a justice of sorts; the shammers haven't helped.

The office should quiet down in a few days.

Money Troubles

April 7, 1971

You remember that $160 that Lt. O'Daly wanted me to buy cameras with. Well, Spec 4 Russo who I sent the money off with to Hong Kong only gave me $140 back. At the same time, Lt. O'Daly sent a letter inquiring about the money or the camera equipment. This was a parting favor to Lt. O'Daly and it's a good lesson in when not to give a favor. My solution is to send the $140 to O'Daly and give Russo the address of O'Daly for the $20 he promises to send. I wash my hands of this affair, which walks on the edge of illegal. I feel like I've been had.

I'm relieved to hear the film came out. Thanks, Dad, for the quick printing session you did for me.

CBS Interview; Hooch Mates

April 8, 1971

I've got CQ (command quarters) tonight, which means I hold down the office building and keep an eye on the phone and watching over what little the PIO has that can be stolen.

A CBS team was over this morning interviewing GIs about what President Nixon was saying about getting out of Vietnam. Six of the biggest hams in the PIO aired their views to the media. I doubt if anyone said much kind about Nixon; most of us agree that we should have duffed out the back door long ago. We don't have to be charitable to Nixon just because he's our ultimate boss. He's supposed to work for us a little anyways. I missed the whole thing, I'm sorry to say. The press has been out of sight in Bien Hoa for several weeks but now it's back, at least for a visit.

All I have to do on CQ tonight is sleep in a bed but it's only 8:15 p.m., hardly bedtime. I can rest peacefully.

Al Brown and I have put in a request for R&R in Sidney for late May which should be real sport. It will be winter there but only in the 50s, not the sub-zero Midwestern winter.

I was talking to one of our young (21-year-old) tiny (80 pound) hooch mates today about the mama san business working for GIs. She said that she expects to be out of work soon but has been able to save enough money to live for some time. GIs are careless and carefree about the way they throw their money around. I've seen some mama sans take $10 MPC a month for doing their job, a small fortune over here. She's my second hooch mate.

With my hooch mate now it's $4, converted to piastres. And from what my tiny hooch mate was saying today, $4 is a king's ransom, especially when 7 or 8 fellows are all paying her $4. American money and its awesome possibilities for corruption have completely corrupted some of these poor girls. It's not uncommon to see a hooch mate pregnant with a GI's child. It's a sad commentary on the wisdom of our having Vietnamese cleaning ladies.

Rich Werner took his Nikkormat down to Saigon with him two days ago, a major blunder. A "cowboy" on a motorcycle grabbed it off Rick's neck and made a fast getaway. Rich was beside himself and galled by the Vietnamese spectators who laughed uproariously. He was the laugh of the street and it will cost him the $150 to replace the camera. Vietnamese enjoy seeing GIs hurt—we aren't loved.

Fragging Interest

April 10, 1971

I don't know why I started typing on a big sheet like this because I have nothing to say. I haven't done anything today or yesterday, not voluntarily.

We've had two correspondents, one from CBS and another from *Overseas Weekly*, trying to get information on the fragging incident where the two lieutenants died. They wanted to see the scene of the explosion and we (the Army) flatly refused to allow it. I'm hoping the fragging was an isolated incident. It's no surprise that two of the Army's biggest critics wanted information on an incident that's embarrassing and horrifying to the Army.

I have four medals that I know of so far: 1 air medal, 2 ARCOMs, and a bronze star—all giveaways. I'm told they will mean something when I get back to the world where people are gullible. They're meaningless unless you get a bronze star with a V (for valor) or medals above.

Enclosed is the final copy of the *Cavalair* to be put out. The bi-weekly brigade paper has been dubbed "Garry Owen News."

Movie Disappointment

April 12, 1971

I didn't write yesterday because nothing happened. Today too. But tomorrow I'm going to do something. I'm going out to one or two of the firebases. I've taken out a Pentax with a 70 to 150mm zoom lens on a hand receipt. I'm going to try interviewing people on what they thought of Nixon's program to end the war. Maybe our editor, who suggested the interviews, is deciding to say something for a change in the paper.

I went to see the movie *MASH* for the 4th time last night and was disappointed. The projectionists in past showings had mutilated it so much that its continuity was lost. I got so tensed up waiting for the film to scramble the message that I missed some of the best parts. Every time they changed a reel they lost about 10 minutes of footage. The movie was free but I almost walked out.

Grunts Take on Calley's Conviction; Soul Brother Troubles

April 13, 1971

I went out to FSB Charles today and talked to the grunts. With sandbags lying about, the grunts gave me the old sob story about being overworked and having a lousy job which was nothing but the truth—common knowledge. Then I interviewed them about the war and such tidbits. I made the mistake of talking about the Calley conviction and they got downright upset. They came up with stuff such as: "He should be freed—definitely. He was trained to do his job. The minute he came into the Army, he was trained to kill. He's suffering for everybody." I could find only one guy, a lieutenant oddly enough, who would stand up for the conviction.

I had the feeling that they wanted the whole Army to hang for it, which I can understand. Everyone thought we ought to get out of Vietnam immediately but didn't particularly blame President Nixon for the war. The said he'd been saddled with it. I felt this was one of the less enlightened groups of bush GIs—I know someone like Harbeck wouldn't have said the same thing. But Calley's verdict was the big thing. This was Delta Company, 1/7th Cav.

Again, it was the soul brothers that were the most intractable. I'd say the blacks are too stubborn for any kind of conversation to take place. I have invariably taken more guff from them than anyone else, even the lifers, and it hurts. They refuse to see any side of an issue but their narrow own. I was accused by them of my ignorance of matters of the bush—which isn't so—and of being a REMF of the first order. It was like changing the mind of a brick wall—they weren't listening.

The brigade is in a strange extended situation. First Support Base Charles isn't within artillery range of any of its units. I went to the briefing for the 3rd Brigade tonight to try to figure out what was going on after returning from Charles. I'm convinced the brigade will have to consolidate its position—it just can't hold down the turf of more than half a division.

The phantoms of the departing—yet not departed—PIO bodies are still to be seen near the PIO hooches. We still have more shammers than workers.

I've heard that our new colonel (lieutenant colonel actually) is coming up with some real winners for rules. I'm part of the Combined Service and Support Battalion (CSSB) and this man is in charge, of our hooches at least. He wants to tear down all the partitions in the hooches, making open bay billets. He doesn't want white shirts or boonie hats worn in the Bien Hoa Army Base area. And, he wants to shoot most of our pet dogs. This means more trouble for us.

Tomorrow I have to get a haircut and come up with 3,000 to 10,000 address labels.

Grunts Get Fill

Sandbags were a critical element of the defense on firebases but the bane of a grunt's existence—sandbags after all weren't prefilled. Once two-thirds of our division left the country, the remaining brigade started a smaller version of the Cavalair *called* Garry Owen. *This piece was in the first* Garry Owen *issue on May 7, 1971.*

FSB CHARLES—"Don't put us down as sandbag fillers. We're grunts," insisted PFC Dan Hanley, but the seed of doubt was planted. Around him were a thousand or so sandbags he and his colleagues had filled.

In a country noted for its millions of sandbags, these seemed even more evident than usual. A superficial inspection explained the thousands of extra sandbags, since there wasn't a metal culvert in sight.

Metal culverts, used as one and two-man hooches on firebases, allow for less digging for a safe home and a large degree of mobility. But with the digging of deeper log-beamed bunkers, sandbags multiply like mice.

"LZ Charles has been built by the 3rd Plt., D Co., 1 Bn., 7th Cav," Sgt. Bob Larson proudly commented. "We've been here for ten days. Ten minutes after the bird landed, we were filling sandbags and haven't stopped since."

"Another 1000 sandbags and we'll be done for the day," explained Hanley.

"All these sandbags instead of culverts will make it easier to tear down," said Larson as if he could hardly wait.

GIs Advertise; Self-Declared Heroes; PIO Doghouse

April 15, 1971

We were almost had by the press but they blew it for a change—not that I blame them for nailing the Army to the wall on occasion, like on FSB Ares and FSB Dragonhead. It seems that 29 GIs took a $5000 ad out in the *New York Times*, saying they were sorry they couldn't attend the peace demonstration because they were still in Vietnam. They said they were from the 1st Air Cavalry, which threw the press and us for a loop. After checking a few of the names with USARV, who has an index of all the people in Vietnam, it appears the men are from the 7th Squadron, 1st Air Cavalry—not a 1st Air Cavalry Division unit. That unit is based in Vinh Long near (or possibly in) the Delta. There was a sigh of relief among our information officers, although I was sorry to miss a good fight.

My old friend Lt. White may be in the thick of it. I've been told he's not part of SSC but the 1st Aviation Brigade PIO, which will get the brunt of the flack for having guys in their unit backing an anti-war column. It's unlikely much will be done to the guys involved legally. They may be in for harassment but it's likely the press will get on the lifers' backs if anything is done to the protestors. I think it was a brave move on the protestors' part although I can't see how they came up with the money. Personally, I would be embarrassed to be a martyr for misguided Vietnam.

I am disgusted by all the GIs, especially REMFs, who make Vietnam sound like a super hardship and the home of the only true manhood. The fellow with the "I know I'm going to Heaven because I've spent my time in Hell" on his lighter who's never been out of Bien Hoa is worth a laugh. The army journalists, especially the shammers in our office, who have "OFFICIAL ARMY WAR CORRESPONDENT" sewed above their Cav patch, are a version of this nonsense. Anybody in the rear knows it isn't necessarily that bad. It's common for GIs to extend in Vietnam to get away from the lifer harassment of the States and make the extra money. The bush can be that bad—I'm not referring to the grunts. That's a different hard world.

I hear stories about the General's Mess, where the generals have chow. They have the best cooks with air conditioning. It's more like a feast than the daily chore of the enlisted man's mess. Privilege and rank are synonymous in the Army. In the States the contrast probably isn't as bad but here, where we can't escape the Army, privileges show.

Our office is one big PIO doghouse. We can't keep feeding all these dogs—they're getting hungry despite our attempts to fill them up. They probably are getting greased to death like the GIs over here, eating all this oily food. I dream of a nice low fat meal, Mom.

Newbie Search

April 16, 1971

I found out where the rear of the 2/8th Cav is located so I could find where the logging bird and chuck chuck bird leave Bien Hoa for FSB Fontaine. The birds leave around 6:30 a.m., too early but I'll make the bird tomorrow.

Also, I went out hunting for newbies, new troops coming in straight from the U.S. Predictably, there aren't many of them. I'm writing up what I consider to be a good story on newbies starting off, "The newbies in the 1st Cav have become the whooping cranes of Vietnam, an endangered species." Catchy—huh? They've already stopped giving the Cobra and MEDEVAC demonstrations for the lack of bodies to make it worthwhile.

Fontaine should be interesting; it's the hottest firebase in the brigade. I've never been on a 3rd Brigade firebase. 6:30 is too early—I'll be sleep walking—I'm spoiled. Others have formations every morning at that hour but that doesn't mean I have to like it.

Lt. Field was just telling about hitching a ride with a bus full of soul brothers. One of the brothers asked Field if he was sure he wanted to ride on the bus. Field said that he could stand it if they could, and cracked up. There's the suspicion that the blacks are riding around in the bus just so they can reverse the bus segregation of old.

NEWBIES RARE BIRDS

Now that I was a grizzled 1st Cav veteran, I noticed there weren't that many new recruits to lord over, so I investigated. I located this story in the May 1971 Garry Owen *orientation issue.*

BIEN HOA—The newbie in the 1st Cav has become the whooping crane of Vietnam, a species in danger of becoming extinct. At one time not so long ago, long disorderly lines of these brightly dyed patchless men marched about Bien Hoa. Now, however, it takes good eyes, patience and an understanding of their work details before these rare birds can be identified.

Standdown nearly dried the flow altogether. "We've always had newbies, though we may have spent a few days without some coming in during standdown," noted Spec. 4 Robert Henselman, a clerk. "We've had as many as 22 in one day recently, our biggest day. We've also had as few as three."

An exhaustive search couldn't track down the newbies reportedly in the area. They finally appeared at the 4 p.m. formation—all eight of them.

With only a brigade left, it is unlikely that the 1st Cav will ever see the large migrations of fresh faces crossing the Army base as in yesteryear. In fact, newbies have taken on a value of sorts—no one will take them for granted here again.

FSB Fontaine; Crocodile

April 17, 1971

I didn't have much trouble making it out of bed at 6 a.m. without an alarm clock, then found the right bird in time to make the flight.

FSB Fontaine is a big firebase near the mountains and not too far from a main asphalt-covered road. The number of palm trees in sight surprised me; the terrain is remarkably different from War Zone D. I couldn't come up with much for stories from either C or D companies of the 2/8th Cav. I missed the action that Field just happened to hit at Fontaine two days ago when Echo Recon 2/8th fired up some NVA and found a cache. Field should have a good story if he was on the stick—I could have done something with it in his place.

I had a good time though; I'd forgotten how much I enjoyed flying around in Hueys. The companies are working in the foothills and the mountains—grueling work. Several fellows from Delta Company insisted that their platoon had seen a crocodile in a stream; I'm writing up a story expressing my doubts about it. I've been taken in before, why not again?

I did get the $20 from Russo and mailed it to O'Daly so I'm home free. Talking of money, I will have to have another $100 for R&R in Sydney. Hopefully that will be the last money I have to take out of savings.

I thought I heard a Phantom jet's whine and sure enough, I just spotted it while standing outside the door. They make a distinctive sound that once heard is hard to forget. He just landed. It's not as handsome as an F-5 but it's much bigger, capable of bigger loads. They're at home in Tan Son Nhut, not Bien Hoa.

I'm beginning to feel short and don't like the feeling. It's ridiculous, worrying about my skin more than I used to. I'm not changing my habits of flying to firebases and I'll remain careful. I can't see quitting work when I get short; time goes faster when I'm doing my job.

CROC KEEPS DISTANCE

Gullibility has always been an issue for me. I'm proud that I was appropriately distrustful of the grunts—there's a good chance their tale was a crock. The May 7, 1971, Garry Owen *included this yarn. The* Pacific Stars and Stripes *also used it on May 26, 1971.*

FSB FONTAINE—The boonies sometimes seem like a haunted house filled with goblins. One of the latest spookings came with the report of a crocodile lurking in a pond upstream from where a platoon had just taken a bath.

The grunts of D Co, 2nd Bn., 8th Cav were worried that this crocodile might add a Skytrooper to its body count. Surprisingly, no one was willing to admit they actually saw the reptile, reportedly five feet long.

It all started after a long day of humping with a late afternoon skinny dip in a small stream.

"While setting up upstream some guy spotted this crocodile in the water," related Sgt. James Adams. "He didn't say what it was doing. That kind of got our imaginations going."

"The crocodile didn't come after us because we didn't go after it," added Adams. "We were afraid it would come waddling through our NDP."

Whether fact or fancy, the crocodile exists as far as Delta Company is concerned. Insists Adams: "If we had security to make sure that nothing would jump in with me, I'd go swimming there again. Otherwise—no way!"

Sick GI Leaves; Mule

April 18, 1971

I'm sitting on CQ, listening to the radio. It's about 8 o'clock. It's been another slow day.

Al Brown and I checked about our R&R in Sydney and we've got the orders for May 19th in hand. It will be winter there in May where the temperature averages about 60 degrees—cold. I will take the Nikonos along so I can show you what I see.

Listening to the news, I wonder if the world will ever be quiet again—it really sounds violent. I can't figure out what's going on in Washington, D.C. I wonder if we'll ever see anything happen over here—it's so slow?

I was talking with Bruce Leonard today. He's a long-time member of

4. The Audience Shrinks: March 1, 1971, to April 30, 1971   249

Echo Recon 1/7th and finally DEROSing and ETSing, a bit to his surprise. He was jubilant at finally making it out of the bush for good yet strangely ambivalent about the bush—he's been in Vietnam two years, a year of it in the bush. He's a competent grunt and a talented guy. I wonder what he'll do when he's free of the Army.

Steve Harbeck is driving a deuce and a half truck somewhere in Bien Hoa—I should see him soon with any luck. There is not much left of the Echo Recon I knew. Nearly everyone is in the rear that I knew—I'm feeling old. The response to the cache story in the magazine was rave reviews from the platoon, which is gratifying. It's too bad the article was months late—many of the guys are long gone.

I went over to FSSE last night and got about as polluted as I've managed to get in Vietnam. I managed to stumble the half-mile home to my hooch.

Rich Werner went to the 90th Replacement for shipment back to the States—his new assignment is Ft. Knox. Last night he threw up about a dozen times and we're afraid he's got malaria. He was so frantic to get home to his wife that he literally escaped from the 15th Med Dispensary to make it to the 90th. Enough's enough, he ought to go to the hospital and be late getting back to his wife; he's no good to her sick. He admitted he hadn't been taking his malaria pills although I suspect he may have what I had—that vicious ten-day fever that was going around. His problem might be mental—he's been in hyperactive state this last week waiting for his orders. I hope I can be cooler when I finally escape 'Nam.

It's been peaceful on CQ so far. I hope some idiot doesn't roll me out of the sack at 2:30 a.m. like my last CQ—I'll throttle him.

I got a ride on a mule today, a four-wheeled motorized platform used for carrying everything. It's small enough to be carried inside a Chinook. They are wheeling around all the firebases carrying everything that a skytrooper could want. Riding it on a paved road was an experience. It felt like a motorcycle and it's no safer. With a highly geared motor that whines shrilly at all times, it's quite distinctive. I'll take a jeep anytime.

GI Thieves; Roving Prostitute

April 19, 1971

My roommate, while he was moving out, attempted to run off with my fan. The hooch mate in the room was all that stopped him, bless her. It's still a stab in the back. Thefts have been rampant—stereo equipment and refrigerators have disappeared almost daily from at least one room in the area. They're just plain dishonest, though my hooch mate's sticking up for me was encouraging. We have a descriptive vulgar term for these crooks: buddy fuckers. The Army has assembled the very best and worst of what is the U.S.

I was supposed to have the day off but I got so bored and disgusted with my hooch that I retreated to the office—a long safe distance away. I rewrote the 2/5th Bn. stringer's story about a chaplain. It was awful and I couldn't do much to help it except to chop out the redundancies, about half the story. I had a good time with it. This guy suffers from the inability to see men as anything but "troops."

It was hotter than a pistol today, which brings to mind your crack, Mom, about turning off the air conditioner when I get home—don't you dare! I've gotten used to it but still don't like it.

Garry Owen is a good old-fashioned drinking song, which somehow got attached to the 3rd Brigade. I'm going to find out what it means yet.

I get this paranoid feeling every time I enter my room. I hate to lock up what little I have. As "African Genesis" points out, territory is a strong drive. Maybe I feel uneasy by not having a safe territory. At least that misguided attempt at discipline, tearing down the walls in the hooches, has fallen through. Now the question is whether there are enough people, 14 to a hooch, for 15th Admin to keep what hooches they've got. I could find myself homeless.

Some goofy-looking old bird with Mississippi Air National Guard written on its side landed at Bien Hoa's Aerial Port. I wonder what it's doing here? It looks like a small prop-driven C-5A—it's an overweight fat plane.

Now we've got roving prostitutes, probably hooch mates trying to make a fast buck. I was propositioned *in my room*—it was comical. This tiny chubby Vietnamese girl came in and slyly mumbled, "boom boom" and, not understanding, I asked her if she was looking for someone. Then it dawned on me what she'd said. I just said no and grinned. She had this odd naughty devil-may-care look, then made a grab for my family jewels, taking me by surprise. She quickly di di moued (left quickly). I was embarrassed but glad her last move hadn't been serious. After my roommate's trying to steal my prized possession, my fan, this was almost too much.

Guard Duty; Scout Dog; Fuel Specialist; Civilian Press

April 21, 1971—8 a.m.

I had Quick Reaction Force duty last night, which turned into Green Line Guard. This means that I spent a night guarding Bien Hoa. They issued the three of us an M-79 grenade launcher, a M-16 and a M-60 machinegun. I got to carry the M-60. I got a ride out to the berm but had to carry it the quarter of a mile back to the arms room this morning. What a chore. One of our mortar tubes was sending up aerial flares so we could see the expanse where the infiltrators might come.

The other PIO man on guard with me was a new photographer named

4. The Audience Shrinks: March 1, 1971, to April 30, 1971 251

Bunker who was just acquired from the 25th Scout Dog Platoon. He brought his German shepherd out with him, just for the hell of it. His dog's name is Charlie and he's a veteran of Cambodia with a Bronze Star for killing an NVA with his teeth. He was a friendly dog nonetheless; I felt more secure knowing we had a keen nose and sharp teeth working for us.

Guard on the berm is *the* most likely place to find a pot smoker. It's the boring sort of duty where a joint speeds up the long night and lightens the load. We tried one "J" without much effect and took turns on guard the rest of the night. I was feeling hungry because they'd had us come for guard before suppertime so we missed the meal. As a whole, the night was a new experience for me and a total waste.

Yesterday I worked on a story about POL (Petroleum, Oils, and Lubricants), specifically a guy who checks all the fuels coming into the brigade. It can be critical because if water or sediments get mixed in with the fuel, the fuel is no good. Sometimes a filter system goes bad, ruptures, and the fuel gets contaminated. I talked with the guy about upgraded and downgraded fuels that have gotten mixed. The Cav uses many thousands of gallons of fuel a day so a small fleet of trucks is kept busy supplying the fuel points, forward and rear.

Enclosed is a story written in memory of Steve Warner—I'm not about to let his fate happen to me.

A colonel thinks Sherwood Dickerman, a New York reporter of some note, is a troublemaker. Lt. Launder (my boss) thinks we may have blown it by sending this guy out with a recon platoon. I said that all civilians were troublemakers to which Launder replied that he wishes *he* was a civilian. It'll be fun to watch. Dickerman is said to be in his forties, maybe too old to go out in the bush. USARV Liaison seems to think he's in good shape for his age. I wonder how much trouble he'll stir up.

92 CHARLIE MOS A GAS

The quality of fuel is something I took for granted but, especially given the vast quantities of fuels we used and depended on, it makes sense to have someone checking to make sure the gas was good. The June 16, 1971, Garry Owen *included the following story.*

BIEN HOA—The continuous high quality of fuels cannot be taken for granted in Vietnam. Consequently, an MOS for a petroleum products analyst has evolved to make certain that fuels are clean. This specialist, a 92 Charlie, is as close as fuel will come to having a doctor.

Working in the 1st Cav Petroleum Laboratory, the Cav's only working 92 Charlie, Spec. 5 Arthur Bailey, tests all the fuels coming into the 3rd Brigade.

Contamination from water is a constant danger. "Condensation can't be avoided in 10,000 gallon bladders, so fuel goes through a filter separator," said Bailey. "The filter has a maximum life expectancy in Vietnam of six months. If not tested, the filter will rupture and water will get into the gas tanks."

To avoid this, samples are taken—usually on a monthly basis. The most care is taken with JP4, chopper fuel. If a chopper runs out of fuel while in flight, chanced are great it will crash. Bailey's job is to make sure this never happens.

Thankfully, he rarely finds anything wrong. "About once every two months I find something contaminated," Bailey estimated.

The Cav's Supply and Transportation Co, of which Bailey is part, handles approximately 60,000 gallons of JP4, diesel and mogas daily.

Like a doctor who has kept his patient alive and active, Bailey finds much satisfaction from his job. He can take pride in watching choppers fly and his fuel burn.

Boom Boom Girl Attack

April 22, 1971

Tomorrow I'm going down to Saigon to see how our paper is laid out so that I can be a last minute substitute if something goes wrong. I'm curious to see it but I don't think it's a layout man's dream. I'm told it's a small room we work in with a number of others also doing layouts for other brigades and divisions.

I grow tired of what we can't investigate or say. Our paper never alludes to what's going on in the States. We never admit a mistake or mention anything controversial. It's only Army messages of self-congratulations. I guess I should be grateful I could find and write as much as I have.

A captain who I gave a ride to in the jeep told me about what he considered his classic Vietnam experience. Two battalions had changed places on palace guard in Phuoc Vinh within a day. The old battalion hadn't told the new battalion about the special arrangements that had been made with some of the villagers to come over the berm during the night. So the GIs—thinking they were enemy infiltrators—open up on the prostitutes as they came from the village. The shocked whores hit it and then shouted, "We've come to screw you, not to shoot you!" The TOC that night was thrown into hysterics, laughing uproariously once it was determined that no one was hurt in the snafu. By the next night everything was back to normal—everyone knew what was going on. This, in a way, is a classic tale of the good times for a typical GI.

The place can be corrupting for a GI. I don't feel this is hell but it often shows humans at their worst. And I don't think prostitution is all that bad—killing is on top of my list.

DINFOS Classmates; Britisher; Paper Layout; ABC Rebuffed

April 23, 1971

My day in Tan Son Nhut gave some rewards I didn't expect. I discovered when I got there, for one thing, that I've been living virtually next door to four or five of my old DINFOS buddies and didn't know it. They're stationed in Long Binh and I met one of them, Mike Roche, laying out a paper down in the Observer Office in MACV Compound. He said another old classmate had showed up a few months ago after getting grabbed by a levy from a stateside assignment. I'm going to contact them and find out what they've uncovered.

Another fringe benefit of the trip was talking to a real civilian, a Britisher, whose home seems to be the world. He is fascinatingly snobbish, something the British are famous for. He is a petroleum technician, meaning he advises people on how to set up, add to and run their petroleum operations but he talked little about petroleum.

He started off by expressing his disgust for Vietnam. "This is a terribly dirty country," Mr. Houston (that's his name) said, putting his nose almost literally in the air. "This place (Saigon) hasn't changed since 1937 when I was last here. The trash, except for more American cans, is still the same. Now Singapore is a civilized place; they have stiff fines for littering." He had sold his house in Colorado and leased a new home in what I think was the Lower Antilles. He has a bachelor's degree in English literature and went through the U.S. Army language school in Chinese (Mandarin). He's still a healthy 62-year-old; I'd say he's worth many more years. I was fascinated by his accent—I wonder if this is the type of Britisher that made the British Empire the viable enterprise it once was. I can't remember meeting anyone quite like him.

Setting up the work of the paper wasn't nearly as interesting as the extras. It's a cramped place and three of us was a crowd. Other papers worked in the same area simultaneously. It's an offset layout and capable of a good deal of sophistication except that the Army shuns its possibilities as a rule. I'm just not tempted by the idea of laying out a paper in a crowded office with only a few months left to go. Lief Hansen is already doing it and I'm content to let it stay that way.

The Military Assistance Command Vietnam (MACV) in Tan Son Nhut is a baronial setup with stateside-like facilities. It has a huge swimming pool, air conditioning everywhere, a gymnasium with an entire basketball court, and one of the fanciest weight rooms I've ever seen. It's by far the best facilities I've seen in Vietnam. I'm really roughing it by comparison. If the grunts could see it they'd shrivel up and die—or get hopping mad. And I've never seen this many officers at one time, except maybe at USARV.

Back home at our office in Bien Hoa, I was told the lieutenants wouldn't give a well-known ABC news commentator peanuts. Sam Donaldson, whose beat is usually Washington, D.C., is visiting and wanted to go out and find out what the troops thought of the veterans' peace march in the national capitol. They said no, gave him a lousy excuse, and he left mad when they ignored him. Another triumph for the 1st Cav PIO for the moment. It's CBS that's been burning us, not ABC. Now they're really in for it, I hope. Anyway, I'd like to know what the grunts think. I think I'll go out and find out for myself tomorrow.

I find your letters a consistent joy—it's worth it to hang around for mail call. Cheers from your fan in Vietnam.

Sam Donaldson

April 24, 1971

Sam Donaldson came back today and this time, I got a chance to see him. He got a little of what he wanted and it looked today like it was the higher ups, not our lieutenants, that were causing Donaldson trouble. He struck me as rather pompous, though interesting for all his talking.

At first, he was calling up ABC in Saigon to tell them that he had missed his bird to go to FSB Fontaine because it left early. He suspected that it had left early to avoid having to carry him. But he calmed down after the lieutenants in an appeasement gesture got him interviews with members of the 229th Assault Helicopter Battalion. Much like the Britisher yesterday, he was interesting despite my doubts on how much of what he said was for show. He does have a stage presence that follows him even into a cluttered unimpressive PIO office. He seemed naïve about Vietnam but catching on fast. He said he'd come over to Vietnam because this has been the biggest news story going for a long time and he thought he ought to get a part in the picture by doing a little reporting on it.

He explained that when he was first getting into journalism back in the early 1950s, it was the World War II correspondents who were the "old pros." They had been in on the invasions; they had been where it was at. And I think his comparing that war with this war is valid. Vietnam has had a monumental, even catastrophic, impact on the U.S. Donaldson impressed me although his hamishness bothered me; he did far more talking than listening.

We have a couple of guys here typing their own travel orders because the MPs have been hassling them at the Air Force Gate, won't let them go over to the Air Force side that has vastly superior facilities to anything the Army has to offer. They aren't from our office; they work on the sniffer birds that detect the enemy through a secret process known to only a few. This one fellow from Maine has a magnificent mustache—one of the best I've seen. They'll make him cut it off sooner or later—a tragedy in the making.

4. The Audience Shrinks: March 1, 1971, to April 30, 1971   255

I'm moving my gear to another room and handing my old room over to the mamasans. Maybe now I can sleep late and get some peace. I'll have a PIO roommate, Jim Ventrilio, with similar habits to my own. This should be an improvement from my old room.

NCOIC

April 27—14 months in the Army

I dropped in on the digs of my old DINFOS classmate, Norbert Langbecker. He never did show but I did get some idea of how the other half lives. He has his own personal room that he doesn't have to fight for. His office is air-conditioned and his outfit stable. His one drawback is he's got a tedious job that brings him no closer to the realities of Vietnam. I'm getting a far better education in the war than he is. But for the material comforts and the security, his job is superior.

It looks like our office is going to move again and the enlisted man hooches moving—what a mess. And for some reason lost to me, the PIO has to put out an introductory issue to the *Garry Owen*. The work of writing (copying) the histories of the different units was divided between Al and me. It won't be much fun.

Tomorrow our senior junior enlisted man—who is leaving—will show me how to run his little operation although I'm not sure I'll get the title NCOIC (non-commissioned officer in charge), not that it makes much difference. They probably made the right choice in me—I'm going to be here the longest and have the talent for being around at the wrong time and getting caught for details. This is another detail.

Last night I listened to Lt. Launder for more than an hour bullshitting on everything from Mosby's effect on the Civil War to the ungodly firepower of the 11th ACR's tanks. Launder has a beautifully organized mind—what he said was interesting and I was impressed. He would make a fine teacher. I wish I had his talent for talking at length and in detail plus his knack for expressing his excitement. He seems the right man to be in charge of us, a welcome change.

It rained hard today for the first time in months. The weather has changed suddenly—yesterday's clouds of dust may be the last. The mud is about to make life miserable for us.

Maybe now I can get my money's worth out of the Nikonos—it's great in rain. I'm missing the darkroom work that used to make photography so enjoyable [*all darkroom work was done for me in the Army*]. I think I could get more out of my camera if I could see the results from it firsthand and make adjustments.

New PIO Office; Colors Ceremony; General's Briefing

April 29, 1971

I'd be typing this but we locked ourselves out of our new office, which we moved into today. It's a far better setup than our old office. It had a built-in darkroom from the 20th Engineer's PIO, its former occupants.

I'm getting my own desk and taking over part of the responsibilities. I managed to pass over some "authority" to Al Brown so I won't lose him as a friend. I'd rather have him stay an equal than become a lonely despised PIO czar. I'm not sure they'd want me as czar anyway.

Tonight I was saddled with the task of writing up the return of the colors to the States. When our new photographer Bunker showed up, I agreed to play photographer too. He wanted to dry out his room instead, which was flooded in a cloudburst this afternoon.

The ceremony was sunset and 94 bodies were lined up to carry the colors home. All clad in new fatigues, the skytroopers stood at attention. They were a happy lot of GIs—many of them had gotten hefty drops from their Vietnam tours and looking forward to returning from the war. The sun was setting as the ceremony of uncasing and recasing the colors was completed. I hate to admit it but it was stirring.

I drove a SEAPC photographer back to Long Binh tonight. I've never driven a jeep to Long Binh at night before and enjoyed it. The lack of road signs nearly threw me once and I stalled the jeep in the middle of Route 1. I nearly got run down by a Lambretta, had he dared.

I miss the typewriter—my handwriting has disintegrated noticeably. Maybe my typing has improved enough to offset the loss.

Yesterday I sat in on a briefing General Burton and his aides gave to a visiting Thai major general. The briefing reaffirmed what I'd always thought about what an airmobile division (brigade now) does. A battalion, using intelligence indicators, is brought to sit on top of an NVA/VC troop concentration and headquarters, then chase them all over the countryside. From the briefing, it is evident that there aren't many replacements coming into the NVA regiments from Cambodia. There don't appear to be many enemy forces in our area—good news for us.

General's Mess; Turtle Race

April 30, 1971

I'm typing on sheets with the letterhead of the unit that preceded us in our new office so you can get an idea of their grand style [*which read: DEPARTMENT OF THE ARMY, HEADQUARTERS, 20TH ENGINEER BRIGADE, APO SAN FRANCISCO 96491*]. They seem more tightly organized than we

4. The Audience Shrinks: March 1, 1971, to April 30, 1971

The 1st Cav colors leave Vietnam.

are but their approach to PIO work was (and still is in Long Binh) more conservative than ours.

I just finished a ping-pong game with a soul brother with fine reflexes who beat me once. I ended up beating him about four times but they were good volleys all. In this humidity I sweat so much it looks like I stood out in the rain. It rained again today, hard. And this pattern of showers after a humidity buildup should continue.

I ran down the grunt battalions' histories (the four of them) in Cambodia. I walked all over the post and only got four paragraphs for my trouble.

Much Later (8:30 p.m.)

I just finished pulling duty. They needed a photographer and I was the only "photographer" in sight so I was grabbed. I got to see how the big leaders live; I went to the General's mess and used this beat up Mamiya-Sekor 70mm camera with a Polaroid back on it. The only picture that didn't come out was the one we wanted, the one of his honor, Brig. General Hyman, who was back for a visit. I got a classic of him after receiving the award with his mouth wide open. Even the other officers liked it in an irreverent way.

I took a number of shots of the ex-grunts working as waiters in the mess and every single one of them came out. I was afraid I'd have troubles with the Polaroid back but it's so easy to use. I'm not tempted though—I'm faithful to my Nikonos and the Nikkormat (which I hope to get soon).

Not surprisingly, the ex-grunts didn't like the waiter job. Promotions were slow and there was no excitement at all. One guy even admitted that he'd been thinking about becoming a door gunner or a grunt again. He's sick of playing spiffy trooper and besides, he's a pothead and feels like a hypocrite playing strack-trooper.

Commenting on your three letters I haven't commented on, I listen to the Armed Forces Vietnam Network (AFVN) when I listen to the radio or watch the tube. That's all we've got and they're definitely better than nothing. FSSE stands for the Forward Support and Service Element, which used to be the forward representative of a number of service battalions in the rear. Now it's part of CSSB, working in the headquarters. Its function is a bit hazy. Dave Armijo and SFC Wilson, two of my old buddies, are in FSSE; their hooch used to be next door to mine when I was in the 2/19th Artillery's area.

I keep my camera locked up all the time and am not ostentatious with what I've got. I have a footlocker to keep it in. I don't know anything about an M-060 machinegun other than it's simple to load and fire although I wouldn't want to clean it. It can be fired from the hip or a tripod or a built up bipod on the machine gun itself. I slept part of the night on top of the bunker and stayed up, watching from the top the rest of the time. I was actually on guard only three or four hours.

So our pet Harvey is in a big turtle race. We'll have a celebrity in our

4. The Audience Shrinks: March 1, 1971, to April 30, 1971

midst if he survives the ordeal and wins. I see turtle racing as a great commentary on our sports nuts. It demonstrates that intellect isn't required to be a winner. I'd love to write up this event. I'd go wild about Harvey—taking it for granted he wins—as the epitome of courage, integrity, ingenuity, drive, brains, and brawn that make a true champion. Can you imagine being turtle of the year or an immortal turtle? This is a great idea, right up there with worm wiggling races and frog broad jumping. I wonder how expensive training would be? I can imagine cheating, a turtle with a waxed bottom to his shell being disqualified. I suppose you could have a duped turtle—waxed unbeknownst to its small mind. This is no sillier than how we faun over our premier athletes.

Those six Americans killed 21 miles north of Saigon were probably from the 2nd Squadron of the 11th Armored Cavalry Regiment. They've been hitting the shit lately to put it mildly. Two weeks ago they were opcon to us; now they're getting blown away in battles where the 25th Infantry Division used to be. Over near Mace the 1st of the 7th Cav has been hitting it too but I don't think they've lost six men in one day.

All is quiet here. I'm sorry to miss the tulips.

CHAPTER 5

Nearing the End: May 1, 1971, to June 29, 1971

Pickings were limited but there were still stories and photos to be had. The brigade worked with the Australians and a battalion was embroiled in a bloody battle with a stubborn enemy.

Military Police Firefight

May 1, 1971

The clouds are forming and the daily monsoon is about to do its thing. The only thing I did today was write a little yarn on the MPs which I don't want to take credit for because I copied most of it.

I did come up with a little dirt while I was talking to one of the MPs. A patrol was ambushed down in the village (Bien Hoa City, I think) and one MP from another MP detachment in Long Bin was shot through the head and killed. A car from the 545th MP Platoon (ours) came to the rescue and got shot up by an AK-47-wielding VC although he didn't get them. One of the MPs returned fire with an M-16 and perforated one of the VC, killing him, but the damage was done. One of the MPs from the 545th got an AK round through the hand and will probably lose two of his fingers. I've been told that this is the pattern: a large unit leaves and the NVA-VC harasses the last units to leave. It happened with the 4th Division according to Jim Ventrilio and it looks like history is repeating itself.

I watched a phantom jet coming into the runway today and then take off again at the last moment. I don't know what he was doing but I got a glimpse of its fabled speed—it's an awful lot bigger jet than the usual on the Bien Hoa airstrip. I like the F-5 Freedom fighter better for looks. Phantoms have been more in evidence here lately. I wonder why?

I mailed a copy of the FIRST TEAM SUPPLEMENT that used some of my photos. The new *Cavalair* we're planning will rerun a number of old stories from the past, preferably some that Al Brown and I did on the lighter side of things. Because it's an orientation issue, I doubt if much of the orientation material will be that inspired.

Guard Duty Capture

May 2, 1971

For the third night in a row I got grabbed for something but last night was the worst yet. Capt. Ladner, the Det. 5 company commander, captured me just after finishing the letter to you. Ladner in his usual irreverent way had come in and given us twenty-five seconds to decide who was going. After our time was up, he picked me out so I spent a sleepless miserable night on the Green Line. They didn't put a flair in my area the whole time I was on guard—I would have been a sitting duck for any sapper in the area. The only thing I could take consolation in was that the sapper wouldn't waste the explosives required to blow my bunker away. Again, I was the lucky recipient of the M-60 machinegun, which I had to tote all over the place. I'm going to leave early tonight although nothing worse can happen than getting caught for perimeter guard. Ladner, by the way, is different from Lt. Launder—don't get them mixed up.

Our new first issue of *Garry Owen* came out as you can see. We had a lot of fun with it. I like the front page although I wonder about the front man's bare foot—that isn't typical and sticks out. But the picture of the 1st of the 9th fellows with their silly black hats is a classic. My contribution to the paper was uninspired but it adds a little copy. Lt. Field added a good deal to this paper, a pleasant surprise.

This morning I slept off the bunker guard and this afternoon stuffed envelopes with PIO magazines that fellows that recently left missed. This is one of the chores that the Major said he'd have us do and left for us. We don't have the setup for this kind of work. Everything is done manually and we waste gobs of time doing it. Lt. Launder is helpless to do anything about the task so we've decided to do it and leave it well enough alone in the future.

Our office is finally settling down. MSgt. Garcia is back from his month of reenlistment leave in Alaska. We've finally reached the point where everyone has to work although we're not overworked.

I'm glad to be part of the *Garry Owen* because it's a marked departure from the typical Army paper. We are playing with it, making more use of our artists. I doubt it will win any awards. We might get a little more readership for our troubles, something the Army never seems to worry about.

I'm plugging away with 17 days left before my leave to Australia starts. It ought to be a "really trippy experience" as a skag freak would put it.

Layouts; Gifts; Vonnegut

May 3, 1971

    I talked to one of the guys who writes up the orders for ETSing and DEROSing. He said the standard drop being given now is forty days, which would mean I'd leave July 4th or so. I'm going to do a story on the people who do up the orders in a day or two. That would mean I have two months left—not bad at all.

    I was pleased with the way pictures of the Division Colors going home April 29th came out. I'm sure the lifers will like them and it is an impressive shot of the flag bearers walking down between two rows of skytroopers. I doubt if they'll come up with much of a layout for the pictures. The photofeature layouts are all the same—dull. Even the best pictures get lost in the layout.

    Mom, I don't know if I can come up with another of those sleeping shirts. I hope Dad realized that's my authentic genuine war trophy given to me by a live grunt about to ETS. I'm glad Dad liked it; I'll keep my eyes open. Technically, it was illegal to send it but big deal—it's a common thing to do and it's better to make use of it at home than throw it away here, which would have been its fate. I'll send more illegal goods home because some of it will come in handy back in the world.

    I read Kurt Vonnegut's *The Sirens of Titan* last night until 12:30 and now have a roaring headache, which I suspect was caused by this strange, perplexing and savage book. He has such an unusual style of blockbusting surprises that he's hard to adjust to and thus the headache.

Typing

May 4, 1971

    I may have done more typing today than I've ever done before—I'm pooped out. It was all copy work; no real thinking except an eye for errors in style. I'd say I typed 19 pages doubled spaced in about 4 hours. This is what I'd expected to happen with fewer people remaining to do the work. But I'm not against working and this day was done almost before it began.

    I started typing up mimeograph stencils for news releases of stories we've done in the recent past. I'm out of practice so I make mistakes; I look at the keyboard too much, get lost in the keys, and flub it.

    Tomorrow I'm going over to the Air Force photo lab and print up the ceremonial shots of the Division colors going to Ft. Hood. I was unhappy with the prints that SEAPC got off the negatives so I'll try myself. These would be the first prints I've made in Vietnam using a photo lab myself. I hope I haven't forgotten everything when I get home. I haven't seen any darkrooms that can compete with ours at home for reliability.

Demotion?

May 5, 1971

I went over to Air Force photo lab but they had no power while I was there so I finally quit the vigil and admitted defeat.

I got my pay voucher for the month and didn't get paid as a Spec 4 so, in a huff, I went over and discovered the problem. I am a Spec 4 but the orders weren't produced until April 1, which means they won't show on the pay vouchers until next month's end. The date of rank is March 1 so I should get a hefty addition for that period in June 15th's pay.

Then I noticed they had my MOS wrong: they'd changed it from a 71Q20 to a 71B20, which means I'd be a plain old clerk if I didn't do something about it. I went over and had an amendment put on the orders keeping my 71Q20 MOS, back where I started from.

I was assigned to write a piece for the chaplain's column so I wrote what may be the most dreadful article of my career, making an ass out of myself, I thought. It's so humorless and bad that it's funny. I'd make a lousy man of God.

Dogfight

May 6, 1971

Coco and Ben, two of our dogs, just got into another dogfight in the middle of our office. Coco has been proving his manhood, getting in at least four scrapes today. That's all the action we've had for the day.

It looks like the PIO finally gets a hooch of its own; I moved in two days or so. No rooms are allowed anymore, just dividers between our spaces without doors. I'll have to lock my valuables in the footlockers I've got. All this moving bugs me.

After I return from Australia, getting my orders will be the big thing.

Mailroom Dedicated

May 8, 1971

We did move yesterday. It's hopefully our last hooch and definitely a step in the wrong direction facility-wise.

The only thing I did today was take pictures of a 229th Assault Helicopter Battalion ceremony. A mailroom was dedicated to Mr. Reuben Grauer, the chairman of Rally Support Vietnam Personnel (RSVP). He has been packaging 200 to 300 pounds a month filled with cheeses, cigars and selections of pocket books. Many packages have been received by the 1st Cav where the sender wasn't identified—RSVP is probably behind them. 227th AHB had a sports award given in Mr. Grauer's name. Mr. Grauer doesn't seem that politically rabid from his letters. He's probably a throwback to the World War II days when GIs were routinely supported.

Yesterday some lifer E-7s came in and ran off with our air conditioner and today it's back. Lt. Launder raised a stink about it so the office is cooler although it isn't big enough to cool the entire office. This office is naturally cooler because we have two roofs instead of the usual one so we're insulated more against the hot roof. It's still warm.

229TH HONORS

Soldiers appreciated support from home, particularly care packages. I'm sure the honor for Mr. Grauer was heartfelt. This story was in the June 2, 1971, issue of Garry Owen.

BIEN HOA—Rueben Grauer, who has consistently and generously supported the 1st Cav, has been further honored. Besides the Reuben Grauer Sport Tournament held by the 227th Assault Helicopter Bn. several months ago, the 229th AHB has named its mailroom after him.

In naming the Reuben Grauer mailroom, the 229th mailed him a plaque reading: TO REUBEN GRAUER (R-S-V-P) "A MAN WHO CARES," which summed up the sentiments of the men of the battalion.

A salesman in Columbia, S.C., Grauer has turned his home into a virtual warehouse to keep the packages coming to Vietnam. As the chairman and driving force behind Rally Support Vietnam Personnel (RSVP), he ensures that his organization regularly sends packages to the 1st Cav.

Sending 200–300 lbs. of assorted gifts a month for 52 months in a row, Grauer's group has helped add a little spice to the life of the average GI here. Cheeses and cigars or selections of pocket books regularly appear without a great deal of fanfare. About the only giveaway on a package is RSVP.

The *Columbia Records*, a daily newspaper, recently chose Grauer for the city's "Live Wire Award," spotlighting his enthusiasm and energy as a member of RSVP. He has also received a letter of recognition from the White House and a former 1st Cav commander, Gen. George I. Forsythe, made him an honorary member of the 1st Cav.

FSB Sherman; Strange Bedfellows

May 10, 1971

Today I got charred out at FSB Sherman, although I managed to get out and back by 1 p.m. It's a good-sized firebase although maybe all the firebases

5. Nearing the End: May 1, 1971, to June 30, 1971   265

are that big, I don't know. It's been weeks since I was out to a firebase. The Chinooks were only going to one place so Big Al and I, against our better judgment, went the same place. As luck would have it, two companies were on Sherman so we both got stories. I took some color slides for the magazine that will be put out in about two months.

My story was on strange bedfellows. A grunt woke up to find himself in bed with something. With a whoop he rolled out of bed and started dancing around, trying to extricate himself from whatever had a hold on him. It bit him and slithered to freedom. This guy thinks it was a snake; most of his buddies vote for a lizard. Another guy claims their man was a crocodile wrestler who'd just lost his first match. It ought to be a good yarn and possible *Stripes* material.

Big Al was prancing around after getting his "Watch This, Fellas!" story into *Stripes* yesterday. I thought it was a dandy story and it did make it as both Al and I predicted it would.

Last night Don "Mortimer" Fry, Greg Goodwin, Al Brown and I were stealing Polaroid film out of the refrigerator and shooting the enclosed flicks. A Polaroid is more fun than a picnic because we knew immediately whether we goofed or not. And it was such fast film that available light shots were a simple trick. My favorite is the sex education shot.

Mortimer still hasn't left although he was supposed to make his exit 11 days ago. He gets drunk and misses his plane every night before the big event. He's already got two amendments to his orders and may be working on his third round—I hope not.

Being the NCOIC doesn't mean much. It is a good thing to have on my record but it's practically worthless as far as real power goes. Al Brown does as much as I do. I send out stories to different papers, magazines and wire services but am still primarily just a writer.

Our new hooch is working out fairly well. We have enough privacy to survive but it's still a public gathering place unlike our hooches of old.

The monsoons are going fitfully: we get heavy rains every two or three days but it's nothing like August and September of last year.

ODD COUPLE PART

Soldiers were vulnerable to attack by night intruders. It's even worse if you can't see them and get bitten. This was in the Lighter Side column of the June 2, 1971, Garry Owen. *It also was in the June 8, 1971,* Pacific Stars and Stripes.

NEAR FSB SHERMAN—Odd couples aren't found only on Broadway. Spec 4 Darrell Auby of 2nd Plt., D Co., 1st Bn., 12th Cav can testify to this.

Auby was snoozing peacefully inside his platoon's night defensive position until awakened near midnight by something that had crawled into bed with him. With a whoop, he rolled out of bed and started a hopping dance, desperately trying to escape from his newfound bedfellow. His buddies thought he'd captured something but it was the reverse—something had captured him.

His slippery antagonist inflicted several superficial wounds on Auby's body without suffering so much as a bruise itself. Having completely outclassed Auby, the thing slithered to freedom, leaving a shaken victim in the dark.

"The guys keep saying it was a lizard but I'm sure it was a snake—and a big one," commented Auby, "and I'm afraid of snakes."

One of his buddies came up with an even more outrageous answer to the riddle of the reptile sparring partner: a crocodile wrestler who lost his first match.

WATCH THIS, FELLAS!

I really like this story, which was written by my partner Al Brown, so I'm including it; it's written in the same style as many of mine. This story was used in the May 7, 1971, Garry Owen. Pacific Stars and Stripes *also used it although I can't date it.*

BIEN HOA—Mother Nature often has fun playing tricks on unsuspecting grunts. PFC Dale Hebdon of Bravo Co., 1st Bn., 12th Cav., learned this the hard way.

He and his buddies were swimming in the Song Dong Nai River recently after a hard day of humping in the sweltering Vietnam jungle. Hebdon, who had gained a reputation among his friends as being highly imaginative, spotted a sturdy tree along the bank of the river and decided to play Tarzan.

Fetching a long rope from his rucksack, he climbed the tree and tied the rope to a large branch, with all intentions of swinging into the cool, refreshing water below.

Shouting "Watch this, fellas!," Hebdon heaved forward on the rope and, to his shock and bewilderment, brought the entire tree down into the river with him. The top half landed on his head, but fortunately the water broke the impact and Hebdon escaped injury.

After the mishap, Hebdon said, "It seems the ants had hollowed out the tree and all it took was my weight to bring it down."

"My desire to show off made me the laughing stock of my platoon," he added with a grin.

If the weird experience taught Hebdon just one thing, it would undoubtedly be not to take anything in the bush for granted—including the reliability of trees.

Hungry Dogs; Ages

May 11, 1971

I researched our most recent Medal of Honor winner and wrote a story. We have about five candidates still waiting for this medal.

The dogs around here are all underfed. Nobody is willing to pick up scraps at the mess halls and there just aren't as many guys as there used to be to take care of our pooches. Our office has four dogs without that many to feed them. The commanders of CSSB have decided to pick up dogs, which isn't a bad idea. The GIs are holding onto their dogs because they are attached to them, not because they're feeding them.

It's raining at this moment in a late afternoon thundershower. The monsoons still haven't hit in force the way they were going when I first hit country. It's muggier than it was during the dry season and just as hot besides. I was taken in by some of the guys who claimed the dry season was the worst. When I hit country was probably the worst time to go out and I didn't realize it.

SEAPC got my color slides from yesterday done and back by this afternoon. That's amazingly good service. The slides came out well; the Nikonos is a fine camera with a lens that is second to none. Our darkroom is finally getting set up and it's just a matter of a week or two before it's in operation. I collected a number of negatives from the past out of our files. They would have been thrown away had I not intervened. I'll send them home as soon as possible.

I was playing softball (throwing the skin-covered egg) with Pat Deatherage, our clerk of odd jobs. In ten short minutes our sweat soaked us both. The sun and the humidity coupled up to make us look like we'd been dunked. The lieutenants are trying to come up with a softball team. I doubt we'll amount to much but we'll have a great time losing.

I'm finally dispatching the last of my 3-cent cigars, which were simply awful. I've been giving them away madly and smoking the remainder. I'm down to eight and counting. I get so bored here that I have to do something for my nerves. Cancer may get me because I smoke but my nerves may get me first if I'm not careful.

Mortimer should have left by now, an end of an era. Now Big Al and I have nobody that's been with us more than two months. Mortimer was with us for five months. I get the feeling of advanced age but I'm far from the oldest fellow in the office. Big Al turned 24 yesterday, Tumulty is 25, Launder is 25, and Field is 26 or 27. I'll be younger than many of these guys in two years when I ETS (exit the service).

Congressional Medal of Honor Awarded

We would be assigned stories we researched in the office rather than in the field. We had learned a major medal was being awarded and this piece reported it to the brigade in the June 2, 1971, Garry Owen.

BIEN HOA—The 1st Cav's 21st Medal of Honor award was given recently for a Cavalryman's bravery and unselfish sacrifice in Tay Ninh province on the morning of July 18, 1969.

Sgt. Rodney J. Evans, a squad leader with D. Co., 1st Bn, 12th Cav was taking part in a bomb damage assessment mission when his unit ran into a firmly entrenched enemy. One claymore was blown on the point element of the unit, wounding several skytroopers.

Then Evans spotted a second mine. Crawling forward on the ground, he yelled, "Mine!" and leaped onto the claymore. The mine exploded but Evans' body muffled the blast, saving a number of men. Evans died shortly afterwards from his wounds.

President Nixon gave the Medal of Honor to Evans' family.

Stringer's Story: Frag Booby Trap

May 13, 1971

We have a new battalion stringer from 1/7th Cav who may be starting the process of taking my job when I leave. He's my age, my height and an English major in college (Penn State). He looks like a good man. I showed him how I'd write up his story from the notes he had. It happened that the story was one of the newest harrowing experiences of former lieutenant and now Captain John Lynch. He's now the CO of A Co., 1/7th, formerly of Echo Recon, of course.

The NVA nearly got him in a booby trap. He was turning over a dead NVA that had been shot and blown by a claymore moments earlier. When he turned the body over and there was a live frag with the pin pulled underneath. He only had time to turn the body back onto the frag before it exploded. He was thrown into the air but suffered only a burst eardrum. His RTO, seeing him thrown into the air and covered with blood, called a MEDEVAC. The RTO said the Captain was a "line 1." He thought Lynch was dead. Happily, Lynch wasn't dead though about the only thing he could say about the experience afterwards was "wow." Again, he's lucky to be alive; God must be on his side. If I were him I'd quit—he's pushing his luck.

Anyway, back to our new writer, I helped him write up this yarn, doing it in my format. I've never written a story quite like it. I've got great hopes for Joseph C. Lamont, the stringer's name. By the way, the reason the NVA put the frag under their dead comrade was obvious—to blow away a stupid American.

5. Nearing the End: May 1, 1971, to June 30, 1971

I sent home the negatives this afternoon that I salvaged from our files. You'll recognize some of the shots; others are new even to me. I'm not sure of everything on those rolls. I still haven't found some of the black-and-white cache shots and probably never will.

It's now less than a week to my R&R to Australia. The office is about as tolerable as it's ever been so in a way I'm sorry to leave. We don't have to work all the time. We can play ping pong some afternoons and don't have to report what we're doing, a refreshing change. And not surprisingly, we're doing just as much work as we used to.

I'm going out to the 2/5th Cav's firebase bright and early tomorrow morning. I don't even know what its name is; I've never been to a 2/5th firebase. After tomorrow, I'll have visited at least one LZ (firebase) of all four of our remaining maneuver battalions.

DEAD NVA STILL DEADLY

I wrote this story from another writer's notes, showing him how to do it. What was odd was that I knew the principal in the story—the victim really. For a man who had suffered so many battlefield traumas, this experience couldn't have helped Captain Lynch. Joe Lamont was quite rightly given credit for the story in the June 2, 1971, Garry Owen. *It also made it into the* Pacific Stars and Stripes *on May 27, 1971.*

NEAR FIRE SUPPORT BASE MACE—An NVA literally blew up in the face of the commanding officer of A Co., 1st Bn., 7th Cav., 3rd Brigade recently.

Set up in a defensive position with claymores out, Spec. 4 Lonnie Miller opened up on seven NVA passing through the area with his M16. He killed one of the enemy. Capt. John Lynch came up, joined Miller and together they blew the claymores so they could recon the area.

Lynch approached the dead NVA. The captain carefully turned over the body and then almost leaped out of his shoes.

"Ah ... there's a hand grenade under the body!" he yelled and had enough time only to roll the body back on the grenade. It blew up and threw Lynch into the air.

Lynch's radio telephone operator called in a medevac bird immediately. Seeing Lynch flying through the air, covered with blood, his RTO called the captain in as a "line 1" (killed in action).

Fortunately, the RTO was a little premature in calling Lynch out. Other than a burst eardrum, the CO was unharmed.

In commenting on the gory encounter, Lynch admitted this was one of the biggest shocks he'd had in his long time in the bush. It all happened so fast that afterwards all he could say was "Wow!"

FSB Evelyn; NVA Kills

May 14, 1971—tomorrow's 9 months in country

    I got out of bed too early and started the day grumpy. I did get out to the 2nd Bn., 5th Cav's firebase, Evelyn. I went out with the battalion stringer who may do stories out there for us. The firebase, near the mountains, is at least 50 miles from civilization. I ended up giving the stringer what I consider a good story. It seems that one of the companies, as much out of self-defense as anything, killed five NVA.

    D Co., 2/5th was walking in a hilly area not far from Evelyn. They spotted one NVA carrying a rifle. The NVA tried to "duff the AO" but was shot dead before he could escape. The platoon, the 3rd Pn., moved up and decided not to walk up a draw—luckily for them. They found a bunker complex, received some fire from it and ended up throwing frags into each of the bunkers. One explosion killed four NVA hiding in one of the bunkers. This was one of the heaviest contacts of recent days and for once, the Americans didn't blow it and lose a man. I didn't want to write a hard new story so I let the stringer cover it when the company comes onto the firebase in two days, when I'm getting ready for Australia.

    There wasn't much going on at the firebase today so I decided to fly out on a logging mission to A Co., 2/5th. They hadn't done anything to write home about. I took a number of shots of them eating chow and relaxing, the typical log day. D Co. spotted some more NVA today and so, as we sat around and relaxed, Delta Co. was calling in Cobra gunships, artillery and, from what the RTO said, even thinking about bringing in an air strike.

    It was a quiet day; I decided just to take pictures and forget about a story. The air traffic out of Evelyn was almost non-existent—I was lucky to make it out at all. I almost got kicked off the bird. I'd have had to stay the night—not something I relish.

    Big Al went to the 2/8th's new firebase, Fanning. He picked up a crocodile story—maybe my croc story wasn't so far fetched? The same GIs also caught a turtle and stamped it with "Government Inspected" on the back of the shell.

    Field's 2/8th cache story and a picture made *Stars and Stripes*. We may not be able to live with him. The picture was the only one sent out to anyone in our last collection of releases—we sent it to the right paper.

    Al and I are going to work together on the inoculation of the Bien Hoa Army Base dogs tomorrow. CSSB and BHAB Garrison have a program to inoculate or get rid of all the dogs in the 1st Cav's area. Hopefully, they'll have long lines of dogs waiting for vaccination. Maybe we can make *Stripes* with that. I'm taking the photos; I decided to let Al write the story.

    Now I prepare for leave and go through nightguard on May 16.

5. Nearing the End: May 1, 1971, to June 30, 1971

From multiple references to my taking pictures—like the ones above—it's clear I didn't get the negatives and slides I took for the Army for the second half of my tour. I wish I'd had the foresight to take more photographs for myself.

Dog Vaccination

May 15, 1971

This morning Big Al and I covered the dog vaccination program and our own dogs had their distemper shots. Blanche took it calmly but Coco nearly went into shock and howled like a banshee. It didn't seem there were many dogs in evidence. After tomorrow, when shots sessions end, the MPs and other volunteers will start picking up stray dogs. There should be a large number; this place is full of hounds.

Another short piece got into *Stars and Stripes* today, a follow-up on the $50,000 and a million piaster story. This shows our new releases do work.

Colonel Hamlet, who used to be the commander of the 11th Aviation Brigade, is being promoted to Brig. General shortly. He's hard core Army and his color means very little.

I found some films in the files, this roll from the Mamiyaflex of the grunts climbing a ladder into a Chinook at a 2/7th firebase.

Sapper Attack Preparations

May 17, 1971

The disruption from the green line guard is over. I couldn't see much last night, even when the moon was out. I got two hours of sleep, not nearly enough.

Today we had a special meeting at the 15 Admin orderly room. Bien Hoa Army Base may go on yellow alert. Intelligence is predicting a sapper attack soon. It may come to the point where everyone wears flak jackets and takes a gas mask everywhere they go.

I'm glad I'm leaving for Australia soon. We won't leave for Camp Alpha until the morning of the 19th. That evening we'll get on the big bird and wing it to kangaroo country.

It looks like I may not get that drop I'd hoped for. I might get only a week or two. I might make it back in early August—not so hot. I'm still hoping for July.

Enclosed are experimental shots taken by Pat Deatherage. Notice how my build has expanded. It's this Army food—too many potatoes and starches with not enough vegetables or well-cooked meats.

I didn't take a bath or change my clothes from last night so I'm a real mess. I'm about to take a shower and change.

Orientation Issue

May 18, 1971

Our orientation issue finally came out and I like it. We had some extra money to play with in these issues and used some of it on this paper. They didn't list me as NCOIC but did put a picture of me swimming. Flattering.

I spent most of today typing stencils for news releases plus some rewriting. I'm coming up with more stories that are a half or a third mine that I've reorganized and rewritten.

Tomorrow Al and I are off to Australia. I'll keep writing and use my camera while there.

There has been all this talk about the impending Communist attack. I doubt that anything will happen.

Australia

May 22, 1971

Australia is quite a place: gorgeous girls and delightfully cool weather. I've got a hangover from mixing drinks—mostly scotch—last night.

The first night I went to sleep. Last night I went to the Texas Tavern and tried my luck with the women. I picked the wrong one—that's why I've got the hangover. I got my comeuppance for going after the belle of the place. Unfortunately, she had this thing about John Wayne—the epitome of masculinity she thought. I had to admit that I was no John Wayne and didn't want to be John Wayne. I don't know if that's what did it but she told me off in an odd sort of way. I walked out in disgust.

One mistake I'm not repeating tonight: I rented a suite last night and went formal. I may have looked good but didn't feels like myself. Tonight it's bell-bottomed blue jeans; I'll be my old informal uncouth self.

I'm on Macleay Street in a motel by that name in the King's Cross area, supposedly where the nightlife is to be found.

There are many little things different about Australia including they drive on the wrong side of the street and their accents are delightful but odd. They do speak English, which helps.

Sue, the girl at the motel desk, is a fine example of a Sidneyite. She's about my age, blond and beautiful. She's an immigrant from New Zealand. She said New Zealand is good for newlyweds and old folks. Being in neither category, she left for the big city.

Hyde Park; Distinguished Old Man

May 24, 1971

Things have calmed since the last letter. The weather has become fair and I'm a little wiser; I've tried to find peace and happiness in places other than bars.

Last night I went on a horseback riding tour. Most of the time we sat around eating and doing some drinking. For socializing, it was mostly a letdown. It was fun to get away—25 miles out of Sidney. Each of us guys shelled out $25 which provided us with a girl (1:1) invited by Mermaid Tours out to this little "ranch" (I use the term loosely) out in the bush. Nothing was done to ensure the boys and girls were compatible. A few were happy; the majority suffered.

Yesterday I walked around, taking pictures of the harbor, found their Hyde Park and walked about. The Salvation Army had a parade and I watched a chess game. I walked farther into the park and found the political nuts taking advantage of the park's free speech policy. At first I listened to a hard core communist—the crowd thought he was funny but I found him so bitter that he wasn't worth listening to.

Then I found Webster, a character that emigrated from England some time ago. He's a clever impressive authority on the definitions and intricacies of sex. He was delightfully witty and obscene. Australia—like the U.S.—is a prudish country with a great deal of censorship so Webster is considered an unacceptable extremist although not politically.

He was a master of the putdown with an extensive vocabulary of dirty words and sayings. He kept the large crowd in stitches.

A hippie I gave a few coins to—he was hitchhiking around the world as a bum—was telling me about Webster. Webster's life is as passionate and sexually mixed up as he says it is. He's for racial equality because it allows him more variety in bed.

Webster is steadfastly against working. He was all for bigamy, homosexuality, heterosexuals, and lesbians. He is reputed to make a living from the paper he sells at his Sunday harangues. The majority of his crowd was young and not particularly shocked by what he said. I'm sorry I didn't buy his paper; I kind of identify with him.

Today the weather is warm (65 to 70 degrees) with a deep blue sky. I went back to Hyde Park but because it's Monday, there were no speakers. I found the Botanical Gardens, which were huge, extending around a small bay. There were plants from all over the world and because of the mild climate, the gardens had everything from palms and cacti to oaks and northern pines.

While standing in the park, watching a group of oldsters play a variation of bowling with lopsided balls, I got to talking with a distinguished-looking old man. It turns out he is an executive in the Prudential Insurance Company. He introduced me to Dennis Knutsen from Virginia, Minnesota, who works for him. Dennis, who is about 29 years old, got married and graduated as an economics-business major in college. The couple traveled about the world. Being loyal to home, he's going back to Minnesota to settle down in 60 days.

I had a good time touring their building and taking pictures from its roof. I wondered why the old executive was being kind to me and discovered the reason, I think. He spent a long and incredibly rough time in World War II and felt a kinship with a soldier like me.

I'm going to go to the Whisky A Go-Go with Big Al and an acquaintance. So far their findings have been mediocre and mine nil.

Last Day of R&R

May 25, 1971

This will probably be my last letter from Australia—I go back tomorrow.

Nothing much developed in the bars last night. I had a hard time staying interested amid all the smoke, booze and noise. As I suspected, it's hard to set up a meaningful relationship with a girl in less than a week.

I took a ferry across the bay for 15 cents Australian to the zoo and my feet got sore from the long walk up the hills, past cages and pens.

Once I adjusted, the time rocketed by. This country in many respects is too American, influenced by our TV, music, clothes, freeway construction, cornflakes and wasteful habits. And despite what I said in my earlier letter, Australian girls have nothing on ours.

Streetwalker

We had a brief encounter I didn't tell my family about just after Big Al and I arrived in Australia. We were approached by this streetwalker who propositioned Big Al. This woman must have been six feet tall and Al was taller. He told her he wasn't interested and I piped up, all five feet seven inches of me, "I'm not interested either."

"I didn't ask you," she snapped, then all three of us laughed.

Flying Back

May 27, 1971

We made it back to Camp Alpha last night and Bien Hoa this morning. It seemed a much longer flight back. It took us 3 hours to cross the desolate center of the Australian continent and clouds started closing in when we stopped

5. Nearing the End: May 1, 1971, to June 30, 1971

in Manila. Big Al was upset when he was asked for a dollar for washing his hands with a bar of Dial soap in the Manila terminal bathroom—what a racket. This was an example of the rampant corruption in the Philippines.

We took off to a sunset spectacle like I've never seen before. The sun shown orange in a patch of sky beside the thunderheads we had to avoid out on the flight to Saigon. It was a strange color seeming larger than life. The Philippines' vegetation looked even lusher than Vietnam's.

Sydney was worth it—I came home with $125 out of the $310 I left with.

The lieutenants have been writing stories while Al and I were gone. I'll bet there's a sigh of relief from them when we get back to work—running down stories is harder than it looks.

Back to Work

May 28, 1971

I'm readjusting to the office today but tomorrow morning I'm taking a convoy out to Mace and possibly farther. The battalions are being supplied more by truck than they use to be.

Australia's cool fair weather seems like heaven now. My room was cold there but I refused to turn on the heater. Here it's the muggy monsoon heat I contend with.

That much heralded sapper attack never materialized. It would have had to be a small-scale attack because our intelligence has a good idea of the number of enemy troops out there. It is quiet. It's now pretty conclusive that the Cambodian incursion, at least its limited objectives, was a success. You will note how quiet it's been here since I hit country.

FSB Fanning Road Trip; Toting Guns

May 29, 1971

I rode out to the 2nd of the 8th's Firebase Fanning this morning after awakening far too early. The ride to the firebase didn't add much except perhaps some good rain shots. I also got soaked to the skin for laughs. Happily I had my Nikonos—impervious to rain. I'm curious to see how the pictures came out. I ought to have some great shots of wet and miserable GIs. I should have taken a self-portrait—I was a mess too.

The ride back was drier and the jungle fatigues are fast drying. By the time I got back to Bien Hoa, it was hard to tell I'd been soaked two hours before. The firebases of 2/8th now are supplied almost completely by convoy. Fanning is completely supplied from the ground. FSB King, their mini-firebase, has supplies brought to a town called Riviera and is flown by Chinook from there. Although firebases can be supplied completely by air, it's far cheaper and faster to move goods by convoy. Chinooks cost thousands of dollars an hour to run; trucks don't cost nearly as much.

Your college's recent involvement with the police makes your police sound like our MPs. Our MPs try to maintain order and become unpopular like your town police. I wonder how that policeman who had that thing about always having his guns would feel in Bien Hoa. Most of us have no guns anymore and this is a combat zone. I go out to firebases and on convoys without a weapon. I've never been shot at and we lose more than a few men in the field from firearms accidents. The gun-toting mentality is scary.

Jeep Mechanic; Convoy

May 30, 1971

I was captured this afternoon and put to work on our jeep. I think I now have sunburn underneath all the grease I collected while working under the jeep. I liked my Cushman scooter better—it didn't have as many places to grease and it was more reliable. I don't trust the jeep as far as I can drive it.

I can make a good story out of the convoy I went out with yesterday. I collected facts from a warrant officer about the majority of supplies going to the forward firebases by truck. Along with my own experience, a half decent story is developing. The film from yesterday came out; apparently the Nikonos can shoot through a layer of water.

Things are beginning to crawl again, Becky. Enclosed is a fly of some kind. They've been all over everything, including me—why can't this country have a civilized dead season like our winter and I'm bored by Vietnam going from dry summer to wet summer.

Monsoons

June 1, 1971

Today I was typing stencils for press releases and retyping stories. Because no one else can type as fast as me, much of the typing lands on my shoulders, which doesn't bother me—I like to type. And being able to write on the typewriter instead of typing from handwritten stories also helps.

The lieutenants are doing the best stories now. Big Al and I haven't accomplished much since getting back—our enthusiasm is waning after ten months.

Tomorrow I'm going to use my new 200mm lens for the first time to take pictures of EOD (explosive ordnance disposal) blowing up tons of defective ammunition. A long telephoto lens is the right thing for this job, believe me. They blow stuff about once a week and everyone knows when it happens. A mushroom cloud forms to the north.

5. Nearing the End: May 1, 1971, to June 30, 1971

Trucks log all but H2O

by Spec. 4 Conrad Leighton

FSB MACE – The trucking business is flourishing in the 1st Cav. In the past, firebases were logged completely by air, but trucks are now proving far more economical and almost as fast when conditions are right. Much of the resupply of the forward firebases near here is now being done by convoy.

On a recent morning, two trucks and several escorts started down Route 1 toward this firebase and FSB Fanning. Missing the large CSSB morning convoy, the trucks traveled alone past rubber plantations, charcoal sheds, banana groves, bustling villages and other developments in the countryside.

Typical of road supply operations is the 2d Bn., 8th Cav's setup. "We're moving nothing by air now except water," commented CW2 David Rienzie, battalion property book officer. "We send out two of our trucks and two Supply and Transport Co. trucks a day to the fire bases."

Rain drenched a dozen GIs in the open back of the truck. Flack jackets and M-16s lay strewn about the truck in case of an ambush, always a possibility. Beer and soda, mail and numerous odds and ends provided seats for the travelers.

Except for the misery of the downpour, the 65 mile trip proved uneventful. Two hours after setting out, the small caravan pulled into FSB Fanning.

The trip back was equally quiet. By this time the sun had dried out the GI's soaked fatigues. The only excitement occured when the fuel pump of an escorting gun jeep conked out and one of the trucks was forced to pull it.

Keeping the trucks and jeeps maintained is a constant headache. Parts wear out quickly because of the heavy use and constant pounding the vehicles are subjected to. However, 2d Bn., 8th Cav is showing that compared to the complexity of maintaining helicopters, trucks are easier and cheaper to keep running.

The 3d Bde. remains airmobile but that doesn't mean the brigade has done away with ground transportation to the firebases. There are still many jobs for which trucks are preferred--even if they can't fly.

Piggy-back

Piggy-back doesn't refer only to pens. In this case, it's a 3/4 ton truck loading off of a semi-trailor truck as part of the operation to build FSB King. Supplies were trucked into Riviera, a firebase near the South China Sea. From there, Chinooks flew them into the firebase. The new 2d Bn., 8th Cav firebase replaced FSB Donna, another mini-firebase (U.S. Army Photo by Spec. 4 Phil Siebert).

I wrote the story and caption but the story's picture isn't mine.

You ask about our best selling magazines. *Playboy* and *Penthouse* are popular for their striking nudes. They are the outstanding examples of a mostly tasteless collection of girlie magazines. The Army seems to know what the boys want. I don't see magazines such as *Saturday Review* or *The New Republic*. And the comic selection is poor.

I ate poorly in Australia. I didn't care for the way most of the food was served and it cost too much. I'm waiting for a refrigerator I can rifle when I get home and cooking more to my liking. It was almost a relief to get back to the Army fare, tasteless but filling.

I haven't found my calling as a writer. I rarely get a chance to write a long article and feel like a starved writer, only skimming the surface. I need so little information for my typical stories that it only takes about two minutes after finding a source to finish taking notes. I doubt I'll go into journalism. As Ray Stannard Baker [*Dad's uncle*] told you, Dad, there's no money in journalism.

That sunburn I got while greasing the jeep is still bothering me. Tans are touchy things—maybe I can keep the one I have until I get back.

Not all units had flashy war jobs but I saw the dental units in action on firebases and feel they deserved recognition.

This rain is acting like fertilizer; between the time I left for Sydney and getting back, the grass went from a golden brown to a vigorous green. They'll be coming up with grass cutting details soon. Bien Hoa Army Base never allows enough green stuff to grow for someone to hide behind. Right now Bien Hoa is being practically washed away by the monsoons. Deep gullies are forming along many of the major roads. If you're not careful at night, you can break a leg or a neck falling into ditches. There are pretty trees in Vietnam but not a one on our base.

EOD Explosion

June 2, 1971

I spent most of the day watching EOD blow tons of ammunition. They have a firing range about a mile outside of the BHAB berm. The largest contributor to today's explosion was the Air Force, who brought in a semi-tractor-trailer truck full of unusable 20mm rounds, 50,900 rounds. But the explosion included everything you could think of: 500 pound bombs, M79 rounds, barrels of NVA weapons, and C-4 explosives to make sure the collection went up properly.

The collection was thrown into a small crater. Other craters in the area testified to the explosive force of past bangs. The site was in an area that had been flattened by a Rome plow a year or two back to give the Bien Hoa berm a clear field of fire. The jungle is already growing back. With the monsoons, the craters are filling with water.

We stood off about ¾ of a mile away and watched it go. They had a detonation cord that doesn't just burn but literally explodes and moves at an amazing rate. It took less than a second for a cord ½ mile long to detonate the C-4 on top of the explosives. The shock wave took several seconds to dissipate as we watched the mushroom cloud form.

I went in to examine the aftereffects and was impressed. This explosion was much more powerful than the one when we blew up the Echo Recon cache. A crater was dug 60 feet wide and 35 to 40 feet deep, like a B52 bomb crater. I had fun with my camera and can hardly wait for the results.

I got a farmer's tan around the collar and overall cooked again.

MACV Visit

June 5, 1971

You've had two days of silence from me. I was down at MACV headquarters to lay out the *Garry Owen* with Lief Hansen. I could go crazy putting the paper together. About all I was doing was working on the headliner machine, which was acting up. Being a novice didn't help. I must have wasted a full spool of tape before the day was done. I hadn't realized how little I learned at DINFOS. I think I could be an editor after a couple of disastrous issues.

I took advantage of MACV's facilities while visiting. I saw *My Fair Lady* for the third time in air-conditioned comfort. I went in the Olympic-sized pool and worked out in their fantastic weights room. I had a choice of two bands last night, one in the Service Club and one in the EM Club. I'm sure it's so plush because there are so many high-ranking officers. I saw 20 lieutenant colonels, 10 colonels, three brigadier generals and one major general. I walked around for a few minutes and found a parking place for General Abrams, no less. The entire MACV work building—which is huge—is air-conditioned.

Enclosed is our newest magazine. I think the cover is simply awful—it would have been better in black and white. I'd rather put out an inexpensive

EOD has monthly blast

BIEN HOA – The crowd of onlookers stood tense and quiet as it awaited the explosive spectacle that would soon occur nearly a mile away.

The men stared across the open field from their perches on trucks and jeeps. Then someone pressed a claymore firing device and, less than one second later, a thunderous blast followed by a gigantic black mushroom cloud filled the air. The 42d Explosive Ordnance Detachment (EOD) had accomplished its monthly mission.

That mission, according to 1st Sgt. Lawrence Klees, is to summarily explode four to six tons of rockets, mortars, artillery projectors, bombs, grenades, claymore mines, flares, C-4 explosive, small arms ammunition and dilapidated weapons.

On the morning of the big day, numerous trucks and 25 men brought nearly five tons of unusable ammunition out to a deep pit and spent the whole morning unloading their wares. One flatbed alone contained 50,900 Air Force 20mm shells.

Upon completion of the long and arduous task of carefully placing each rocket, mortar, shell and bomb into the pit, a long detonation cord composed of PETN explosive was stretched out nearly a mile away. Shortly afterward the formidable pile of destruction was blasted into the heavens.

A few seconds after the initial shock impact, which was felt miles away, it began to rain, as if nature itself had been affected by the EOD Team's spectacular mission.

Booming Business

A gigantic mushroom cloud fills the sky as the 42d EOD team explodes six tons of ammunition and explosives outside of Bien Hoa (U.S. Army Photo by Spec. 4 Conrad Leighton).

A story about the EOD monthly blast.

quality paper with something to say *in copy*. I like lively copy and well-chosen pictures, not eye-wrenching extravaganzas. And pink is not a particularly manly color. And the photo pages don't have enough pictures of people in them.

The transient sleeping facilities aren't bad at all. About all you need is a pillow and a sheet—nights are too warm for more. The mosquitoes weren't as bad as they were at Camp Alpha. You go by mosquito count, the number of welts the next morning and the number swatted when awake. I've always been big on a mosquito net and a fan—the perfect combination.

I'm cleaning my weapon (M-16) along with everyone else tomorrow—

what a waste. I'll have to do it again before I leave. The PIO tries to stay as far away from our parent Admin Company as possible. It doesn't pay to get caught during the day in the company area. I'm glad our office is outside the company's prison camp or we'd really have troubles.

Sergeant-Lieutenant Flap

June 6, 1971

MSgt. Garcia and our lieutenant editor are mad at each other. The Sarg is mad about the paper and the LT's taking off weekends to visit Saigon on "official business." Also the Sarg feels the paper is falling apart—hard to disagree with after the last issue. I'm more on the Sarg's side because I don't do much of the Sarg's job but the LT is always piling work on my lap. I'm not directly involved but saw this coming. I'd say a master sergeant is about equal to a lieutenant in power—I'll be curious to see how this develops.

I'm wondering if *I* should get counseling when I get home. I'm in the old rut, Hawaii and Australia bearing that out. Getting out of the bars was all that saved me. Australia was too much like the States, reminding me of home in an inadequate way. Maybe a counselor could come up with fresh ideas. I don't want an Army counselor—I'll be damned if I entrust my future to an Army shrink. An army counselor would be impotent with my Army problems. I'm looking past the Army and I don't like what I'm seeing.

I was to go off to cover a joint Australian–2nd of the 8th story this morning but Lt. Launder couldn't get it arranged. The Australians think they have an enemy unit trapped so they're coming in on them from several sides. The 2nd of the 8th Cav is providing support.

I wouldn't mess with the Aussies—they're far more serious about jungle warfare than Americans. Maybe on Wednesday I can get out there and cover it. Our Army had been chasing this unit all over the southern part of Vietnam and now it's the Aussie's turn.

Aussie Casualties

June 7, 1971

We got some distressing news about the Aussie–2/8th operation: the Aussies suffered 5 killed and a number wounded. They must have hit something. I thought no one messed with them and got away with it. I'll make it a point to keep a safe distance from the action. They may have found an element of that headquarters they're after, which would lead to a bloody fight.

This afternoon we had a compulsory attendance meeting where only half the PIO guys showed up. The subject was green line guard duty. A major told us they're boning up the defense just in case something unexpected happens.

Brig. Gen. Burton has asked an engineer brigade for lights on the perimeter but he wasn't all that optimistic of getting lights in our time. Things have been quiet but we've grown lax. There hasn't been a major sapper or ground attack since Tet 1968. In his droll manner, he said he wanted to make sure our defenses weren't weak just in case. I'm glad they care but I doubt guard duty will change. My next guard duty is on June 10th—yuk.

Operation with Australians

June 9, 1971

I got out of the sack at 6 a.m. in the midst of a lavish dream about girls. By some quirk, I awoke at exactly 6 a.m. as if I'd had an alarm clock. I managed to find the right chopper at Lassiter Pad and flew out to FSB Fanning.

After scouting around, I discovered a six-man LNO (I couldn't find out what the acronym stands for) team running the radios in liaison with 2/8th and the Americans in general. I was sent out to cover this big joint operation.

The 3d Bn., 33d NVA Regiment and D445, a VC Bn., were discovered to have settled in a bunker complex in the Aussie's area of operations near the American-Aussie borders. The 3/33 is a battalion the Cav has been chasing for years. D445 was the lively sister battalion of the defunct D440, who was shattered by the Aussies in Tet 68 and forced to disband. The Aussies and Yanks hope to seriously hurt the two battalions.

Two Australian battalions and 3 American companies have sprung a trap on the enemy. The Aussies are moving in by ground and the Americans on a river bordering Phuoc Tuy Province, the Aussie country, acting as a blocking force. So far the Aussies have the one bloody contact I mentioned but only lost one man on the ground. One of the Aussie's 15 Huey choppers in Vietnam crashed, killing two men inside. By bringing up their armor, the Aussies wreaked havoc in the enemy's ranks although most of the VC-NVA's dead were dragged off. They found what they figure to be the 3/33rds 32 bunkers with 129 bed spaces and D445's 100 bunkers. The Aussies feel they have a sizable force trapped.

I spent most of the day talking to the fine Australian chaps. They spent most of the afternoon taking coordinates of different units. You could see the trap slowly being closed tight. They struck me as more gung ho than the American GIs—they weren't as sorry to be here. All the guys I talked to were enlistees. Their rank structure is different than ours—they say they get rank because of their proficiency and training in their job, not because of their time in service. Because these men had specialized skills, they were making as much as lieutenants despite being enlisted men. They seemed very different soldiers from us; I'd rather be in their army and take more pride in what I'm doing. This is the biggest operation I've been involved with since hitting country.

The Australian force is the majority of the 1st Australian Taskforce, the main Aussie fighting force in Vietnam. They've been in Phuoc Tuy Province since early 1965. They've taken to tanks—they think tanks are great once they're in position.

Their idea of a body count is actually standing on a body, nothing else will do. They know that in their first encounter two days ago, they killed 8 or ten enemy soldiers but only had one body that couldn't be dragged away because a disabled tank was resting on it. The other bodies were scarfed up by the Vietnamese who take great pains to drag away their dead. Today they found two bodies in a bunker complex.

The firing range was open today so the Australian signalmen decided to try out their weapons. They fired the SLR (self-loading rifle), an Aussie version of a 7.62 cal. NATO weapon. Much the same size as our M-14s, it's a heavier round than that of the M-16. The Aussies insist that they shoot at targets and make their rounds count instead of shooting thousands of lighter-caliber rounds in a general direction.

I almost got trapped for the night at FSB Mace but managed to catch a bird back around 6:30 p.m.

It's like there's a war going on. I get a little of that gung ho isn't-war-glorious feel. I still think we've blown it over here; even the Aussies see this. They don't think they could have won this war in our shoes.

Blanche is in heat again. Yesterday there was a titanic struggle between two of her suitors, Coco and Zero. Coco kicked ass (to use the local vernacular) and left the slightly larger Zero panic-strickened but unhurt.

Enough writing. I'm hungry and going to buy something at the snack bar outside the Service Club, if they've got it.

Aussies Talk

June 10, 1971

In talking with the Aussies, it appears our Armies are similar but there are differences. Their food is better—they have professional cooks who take pride in what they feed troops. Their firebases have trees on them so they're not so hot. They don't waste ammunition on questionable targets. Instead of moving men around their units, they send whole units over and back—they remain together.

The liaison men were fascinated by our *Playboy* magazine—they can't get it uncensored in Australia. They may be a more prudish country than ours.

Their lieutenants are trained much the same way as ours with similar spotty results. The Aussies are proud drinkers although they claim that when they get in brawls, they don't escalate like American brawls. Their uniforms have pockets in their sleeves, among other places.

Their Army, as does their country, stresses cleanliness and order more than ours. They seem to have more respect for rules. They don't leave the jungles quite the mess as the Americans. They show more respect for rank. From what they said about their colonel, their officers can be as haughty and downright stupid as ours. They seem more British than American.

Al Gregory, a new photographer of ours, went out to the Australian side as I was working on Fanning. He had a chance to see the larger of the two bunker complexes. He said they were the equivalent of an R&R side, elaborately constructed for comfort, gook style. Most of the complex was demolished before Al got there. He said he thought the enemy had escaped the trap when the Aussies hit the complex. If the opposition doesn't want to fight in the jungle, they can thumb their noses at large forces like the Allies have assembled and escape through a hole in the line less than a hundred meters wide. I have doubts about the success of this operation except that the NVA-VC have been uprooted again and will take several months to dig in and rebuild.

I got a flak jacket so now I'm legal when I guard the berm. We're supposed to have a helmet and flak jacket plus our weapon in case something happens. The moon will be full tonight, helping us see.

I bought 12 comic books this week—some are pretty good. The incredible Hulk is Big Al and my favorite. Comics make as much sense as many of the "facts" we live with.

No Drop

June 11, 1971

Guard duty was a real drag but tolerable—I'm getting used to being uncomfortable. The moon was out during guard so I could see something. It rained only half-heartedly so I stayed fairly dry, except for my fanny, which was soaked because I had to sit on something wet.

The lieutenants, contradicting themselves, decided we didn't want a long article. They now want superficial short stories on the operation with the Aussies. I was crestfallen; I'd looked forward to doing something of substance.

I received two of your fine letters. So long hair is the thing in college—that's no surprise. I want to return to college and grow my hair long, my delayed rebellion.

I'm pretty much in despair of getting a drop. In 4 days I'll be eligible for a drop but because no units are leaving now, nothing is being given. I may take another leave to Hawaii, be away from here for a week and try to do it cheaply.

Dogpile

June 13, 1971

    I got bawled out yesterday for not getting enough photos into print in outside media, which is unfair. I was tempted to point out that no one has been taking pictures the way we used to. I'm no magician; no one has shown much interest in doing their jobs as photographers.

    When I get back, I'm going to avoid Vietnam veterans for at least six months. I keep getting drawn into conversations where these hardcore liars tell these hardcore war stories. And in those unlikely instances where they're true, there's no reason to glorify Vietnam.

    I'm the reigning ping-pong champ of the office. Big Al beat me three games to eight a week ago but hasn't won since. I keep coming from behind, which bugs him no end.

    We nearly had a twelve-dog dogfight pileup outside. After our chicken barbeque this afternoon, our trashcan became a big nuisance. Many of the dogs were hungry so there was a small battle over the scraps. It might be more humane to have no dogs.

    I'm working on the photos for release tomorrow.

Photos

June 14, 1971

    I worked most of the day looking for photos to release to the press. We found some stuff I didn't know existed and was finally given the right to pick what I wanted, I went ahead and picked. I was only nominally in charge; the lab crew printed up what they liked although I agreed with most of what they did. We'll see if we can get these pictures into anything.

    As I should have expected, our lieutenant editor looked at the Aussie stories and gagged today. He wants them rewritten by tomorrow. I've got CQ tonight so I'll do it then. The lieutenant never worried about the paper until it's too late. He doesn't look at a story until the day before layout begins. He ordered me to turn the three stories into one.

    Lief Hansen just looked at some of the shots I'm about to release; he was astounded because he'd never seen them before. We do have some decent photographers and should use them.

2/5th Hit Hard

June 15, 1971

    Last night I worked until 9 a.m. on the Aussie story, getting it into palatable form after rewriting it until I was blue in the face. I wrote all the captions to the photos going out tomorrow. Part of them will go out by mail and the rest will be hand-carried to Long Bing and Saigon, probably by me.

Some poor company of 2nd Bn., 5th Cav got their asses kicked yesterday. They were hit so hard that they were forced to leave their dead behind. They made the mistake of sending a light patrol across a river, thinking the enemy was on the side with the majority of the unit. They weren't, of course. The light unit was hit hard and the rest of the unit was forced to cross the river to get to their besieged buddies. In the process they lost more men. It was a demonstration that the enemy, the bush phantoms, are dangerous.

I just learned that there are only four people with information MOSes in the 1st Cav: Big Al, MSG Garcia, SFC Lebus and me. The Army has a hold on MOS changes while it reevaluates the system. It means that most of our staff is working in their secondary MOS and conceivably could be thrown back into their primary MOS, mostly 11B20 (infantry).

Sergeant's Past

June 16, 1971

MSG Garcia was telling about a peculiar secondary MOS he's got. He was once an MP working in prisons in detention of prisoners. He was telling about a special ultra-rare (it may no longer exist) hangman. Garcia in his time in European prisons handled only one prisoner who was on the way to being executed. This man was hanged for raping, murdering and cutting up a woman who had spurned him. It was hard to feel for this damned soul. Garcia said there have been only two hangmen in the Army at any one time. It sounded like Garcia was glad to escape to the PIO.

Big Al wrote five stories this week and I wrote one although I rewrote everything in sight.

The 2nd of the 5th is at it again with some big enemy force they found so the killing goes on. I'll find out about the killing results, perhaps tomorrow. I'm not looking forward to this news.

Photographer in Bush; 2/5th Fight

June 17, 1971

Blanche is in heat and it's really degrading for the males—they have troubles controlling themselves. They beg, whimper, bark and fight among themselves while Blanche tries to hold them off. She has ten suitors in the immediate area.

The 2/5th did get into it. Their count now has gone from yesterday's total to 31 wounded and 6 dead. Larry Buehner, our top photographer, was sent out to take pictures in a general visit. Instead, he was sent out into the bush and virtually stranded. He was lucky to get a bird out.

5. Nearing the End: May 1, 1971, to June 30, 1971

To hear him tell it, he was the most pitiful of sights, carrying a 45 at his hip and a Nikon F in hand, drenched by the rain. They called in air strikes and a section of max (Cobras) just a few hundred meters from where he stood. The company commander thought Larry was going to hump with them—nobody had told Buehner this.

He finally got a helicopter back when they found the body of a man lost in a contact yesterday—he got to escort the body.

The NVA battalion they'd found was penned in by about four companies. The NVA the day before had captured 8 individual weapons and ample ammunition for us to classify it a major defeat. The fighting is still going today from what I heard. The gooks were firing on automatic during the firefights that have been raging out there, something seldom seen. This is the first time we've had this violent a fight since I hit Vietnam ten months ago.

I just threw Blanche and Coco out of the office after they somehow crept in. It was easy to remove them; I just threw Blanche out and her most ardent suitor followed hungrily. To give you an idea of the dog pound we run, I've seen Coco, Ti Ti, Ben, Fang and Zero all going after Blanche. And that doesn't include the fly-by-nights. Thank God human females don't have such a captivating smell—perfumes are bad enough.

2/5th Fight Continues

June 18, 1971

That enemy battalion that's been giving us so much trouble near FSB Mace is giving us more trouble. Now we have most of 5 companies from 3 battalions surrounding the bunker complex where the enemy resides. B Co., 1st of the 7th Cav was mauled today only an hour after hitting the ground. Al Gregory went out to one of the 2/5th companies and got some grunts ready for action. Our next issue should be pretty warlike.

MACOI, the office that clears all our war stories, killed one of our stories about a new method of setting up claymore ambushes (automatics) and sent Hansen into a fit down in Saigon. We sent him down some substitutes today. My Aussie story made it through so page 7 should be all right.

Your care package of books came in the mail. Big Al was hoping for food but I was pleased.

I'm enclosing my old combat correspondent card. It's always been pretty worthless. It's impressive for people who don't know any better but most of the people over here know better.

We are resorting to brutal tactics, grabbing and throwing dogs out of the office. The 1st Cav Dog Pound ought to start collecting around here. Blanche is causing a catastrophe—I didn't know dogs could get this bad.

Also, I'm enclosing some stamps which I hope are useable when they get there. This is the way Pacific Mail-Order refunds money. I can't use the stamps and they're beginning to stick together—what a mess. I'm passing the buck and hoping you can use them.

The editor of *Army Report* just called and wanted to know if we were going to send him anything. We've pictures ready but everybody keeps passing the buck to me when it comes to getting it done. I'll send him what I've got and hope it's enough. He must be as short on good copy as our paper is. It must be frustrating to be in charge of his paper. We've got more freedom but don't take advantage of what we can do.

Aussie Press Release; Letter to the Editor

June 19, 1971

I'm writing this on the back of one of our news releases, this one the Aussie-American offering. I'm finally getting out my news releases; what a chore considering MACOI dragged their feet to the point where I just gave up on one of the stories.

I spent most of the day driving back and forth to Long Binh. Driving a jeep can become tedious down the same road if that's all you do.

I lost the flip with Big Al so I have to go out and cover the 2/5th operations. I'm afraid of what I'll find—I may not even be able to come up with a story. How do you cover up heavy loss when everyone knows the truth?

This promotion business seems to involve all luck—it doesn't seem to involve what you can or can't do. Big Al went to the promotion board but was humiliated to discover it was a practice board, not the real thing. Even worse, he was asked a bunch of stupid lifer questions, which were meaningless. They didn't ask him about his job. I hate promotion boards—it seems to be duds who pass judgment.

I got a little piece into our paper's Horse's Mouth column asking about snakes. I can ship a snake home if I can find one. The rub is that snakes are found for sale only in Saigon and prices are through the roof. I would rather buy a snake at home and not just because it's hard to package a snake. Snake diseases and Nebraska's relative dryness wouldn't be good for a Vietnamese snake. And I can't get up the nerve to pick one up. I'm hopeless, Becky; you'll have to capture your own snake. I can tolerate lizards better but they're harder to transport and buy here.

That new move of President Nixon of checking all the GIs leaving Vietnam for heroin addiction might be a good idea if it's run well. They may come up with thousands of troops before a few months are out. There's a guy who wants me to write a story on addiction; he's been on and off skag three times. He's like a reformed drunk who is not fixated on his addiction. I'm not all that interested. Everyone is tired of the problem; we're all aware of how widespread the addiction disease has become.

I saw a newbie today and was startled by how different I am now compared to when I first hit here 10 months ago. My fatigues are faded, I'm not worried about being blown away in my sleep, I'm not that curious anymore, I know my way around and I'm psyched up to leave.

MAKING COMMON CAUSE

This was my only chance to work with the Australian forces and I found them refreshing. And this was a big if not bloodless deal, attempting to trap large troublesome enemy units. This piece landed in the July 2, 1971, issue of Stars and Stripes *and the July 14, 1971, issue of* Army Times.

FSB FANNING—The Aussies and the Yanks recently got a chance to size up each other as they concentrated their forces in a gathering brought about, not so oddly, by the enemy.

A VC battalion the Australians had been chasing for years and a NVA Regiment the 2nd Bn., 8th Cav, 3d Bde, 1st Cav Div had been trying to destroy were both settled in the same area. The operation was started to root out the two unwanted enemy units.

The Aussies found the most action as they moved into a suspected enemy hideout. Their infantry and armor got into a daylong firefight with a determined, desperate enemy. They captured a pair of elaborate bunker complexes, one of 32 bunkers with 129 sleeping spaces and another of 100 bunkers with proportionately more room.

The Americans, for the time being, acted as a blocking force as the Australians moved through their home area of operation towards the Americans' home territory. The 3rd Brigade contributed FSB Hall to the operation and the 1st Australian Task Force FSBs Trish and Pamela.

The six-man Australian liaison team worked with the 2nd of the 8th in promoting communications at a unit and a personal level. Differences in unit locations were mapped as details on the human side of life were swapped.

"In building firebases we don't cut down the trees the way you do, we cut only for the artillery," pointed out Lt. Mick Castle, a member of the liaison team on FSB Fanning, "but then we've only got a few helicopters in the country."

The differences between the Australians, who take great pride in their armor, and the airmobile American 1st Cav, with its profusion of choppers, were many. The Australians have been in Phuoc Tuy Province since 1965 while the 1st Cav has hopped throughout Vietnam.

The Australians even showed differences on the firing range at FSB Fanning. They showed off their 7.62mm self-loading rifle (SLR) to the curious

GIs at the range. "The Tommies (British) use their model of this weapon," said Sgt. Blue Joseph, the senior NCO in the liaison team, noting the British influence on his Army.

Spec. 4 Al Gregory, a 1st Cav photographer, had a chance to visit the Australians in the field. Having problems with the Aussie lingo himself, Gregory got the chance to help the Aussies with U.S. Army abbreviations and acronyms, a form of speech in itself.

The Aussies had found an NVA history book of an American unit that had been giving the NVA trouble. The NVA, couched in U.S. Army jargon, referred to the American unit as "1 ACD," which puzzled the Aussies. The moment Gregory was presented with the all-too-familiar letter he blurted out, "Hey, that's my unit's abbreviation, the 1st Air Cavalry Division."

Relations remained cordial. "This is the first time I've been associated with Aussies," explained Capt. Ronald Druener, 2nd Bn, 8th Cav's S-3. "If this opportunity to work with the Aussies came again, I wouldn't hesitate."

The trading of information and men between the two Allies proved the two forces had much in common. What was proving a very unhappy gathering for the enemy has been a pleasant gathering for the Allies.

The Horse's Mouth

Dear FTHM:

My kid sister raises snakes and wants one from Vietnam. She's already got a five-foot boa constrictor. I'd like to know what kind of non-poisonous snakes Vietnam has. Personally, I'm afraid of snakes and am willing to settle for a lizard, which wouldn't bother me so much. What I'd like to know is what kind of snakes does 'Nam have and how can I get one of these critters back to the world?

Dear CML:

We've got good news for you. According to a veterinarian at the 4th Veterinary Hospital in Long Binh, they will gladly register your snake, weigh it, box and mail it for you at a rate of $2.30 per kilogram. However, we're sorry to say we have no idea how many varieties of non-poisonous snakes there are in the 'Nam. We advise you to go to the post library and check out a book on snakes, which might help you out.

Sweet Sunday

June 20, 1971—55 days left.

It was a very slow day. It's Sunday and everybody—almost literally—was off except for me. I sent out our stories and pictures. Big Al went down to Saigon with the material destined for UPI, AP and *Overseas Weekly*. I'm sitting at a newly cleaned desk, cleaner than I've ever had it. All this newfound space—it's great. I'm working on a system to log in all our stories from now on so I know what is going on.

Your letter # 218 showed up. I think I've done pretty well staying out of the trouble areas. This new fight that started when 2/5th discovered the battalion headquarters of the unit they'd been trying to nail for months was a fluke. I'll make every attempt to stay out of the bush, realizing now the size of the enemy units out there.

Fake Stories

June 21, 1971

Al Gregory is going out with me to the 2/5th tomorrow. Things have quieted down for them now. Al was trying to talk me into going out to the bush in a logging with him. I told him to forget it—I'm too short. I have gone on my last outing into the bush if I can help it. The operation started by the 2/5th when they ran into those bunker complexes netted 30 NVA dead in all, not to mention our own dead. I'd say the winner was in doubt although we did capture their bunker complexes. Instead of me, Al recruited Larry Buehner and they will go to the bush while I sit on the firebase.

One of the guys came back from Saigon to report having a good time in bed last night with a full-blooded Chinese chick. Now he waits to see if he develops the clap, an occupational hazard of the horny GI.

I tried writing a fake war story today. It was pretty good—it probably would have gotten in. Selby Hannah, one of our old timers, wrote a story about 5 months ago just before he left. It has gotten into everything since being released for public bafflement. I heard he did this in response to the lack of scratchings he was getting from the writers in the brigades. I wonder how much fiction I'm writing when I'm writing about "facts." At least I try to write funny stories—it's easier to take if you're joking to start with. Professional liar artists like Art Buchwald tell more than the truth by stretching the truth. And I'm afraid the Army's truths often are lies. It makes you wonder what it real.

It's raining now, as usual. Our air conditioner is still keeping the office moderately cool (85 degrees or so). I'm starting my summer mustache.

Forklifts

June 22, 1971

You'll be glad to hear that I didn't get out to FSB Furr this morning. They were closing Furr and moving to some other dog-forsaken place.

There were ten people who wanted to go on the Chuck Chuck bird this morning so I said forget it. I probably could have gotten on but didn't think I'd come up with the story I was after. So I sat around and shammed all morning.

This afternoon I went over to the Supply and Transportation Company for a story on their forklifts. They have ten 6-ton-capacity forklifts that they work into the ground. They are big noisy irreplaceable machines. The huge machines move virtually everything in the supply yards. The operators have to be tough, patient and quick to learn. Most of the drivers are trained on the job to do a very delicate task.

During standdown they worked 18 hours a day moving CONEXes (the all-purpose containers offices keep their supplies in and move stuff to and from the States in). I asked them if they counted CONEXes instead of sheep in their sleep. They claimed not. However, what was required for drivers were people with good manual dexterity and considerable common sense.

These machines each weigh 29,000 pounds and could easily back over a jeep or a Lambretta without noticing it much. They have all kinds of controls for shortening their turning distance, pitching 15 degrees to either side, two or four wheel drive, moving the forks on the front and many other things. Watching them move 300 pound ice blocks using their fine touch is something that's always fascinated me up at Sandy Pad, in readying loads to be slung under Chinooks. I enjoyed talking to the drivers—they do deserve publicity.

Big Al had an equally hard time getting out to FSB Sherman (1/12th) which is being moved too. Only two skycranes came in hauling tractors and we aren't allowed to get rides on them. He attempted to do a story on the CID (Criminal Investigation Department) and drew a blank. They should be called the Confidential Investigation Office—it's more fitting. I don't know why Al didn't realize there was no story there but I've done the same thing.

We have newspapers put out by the Defense Department that we receive every two days made up of clippings from the foremost papers back in the States. Today I was reading about the secret origins of the Vietnam War that had become all-too-public. I had to stop reading—it was too depressing. I'm glad for the disclosures but it's painful to see what stupidity our government is capable of. Goldwater seems delighted to call Johnson a liar and have facts to buttress what he was saying.

Cav Gets a Lift

Forklifts were an unsung backbone of our division. They were also big and nimble enough to entrance me. I found this article in the September 8, 1971, Garry Owen.

5. Nearing the End: May 1, 1971, to June 30, 1971

BIEN HOA—For the 1st Cav, the forklift holds as important a position in the supply yards as the helicopter does in the field. In the world of CONEXes and economy-size containers, the forklift is irreplaceable.

The 3rd Bde. Supply and Transport Co. has ten forklifts here and others at forward bases. Most of them are the 29,000 pound model, capable of lifting 6,000 pounds at a time.

"When we're out of forklifts, we're out of business," maintains 1st Lt. Garry Askim, the officer in charge of the company's supply yards.

The small group of drivers, saddled with the responsibility of working their monsters, were trained on the job as a rule. "Not everyone with the dexterity to drive makes a good forklift driver," explained Askim. "We've got to have a calm level-headed guy with common sense."

Asked how many CONEXes they'd moved since starting to run the forklifts, two drivers, Spec 4s Jerry Keating and Antonio Aguilar, just groaned. "During standdown, all we handled were CONEXes," said Keating. "CONEXes, CONEXes, 18 hours a day."

They demonstrated the selection of controls on their machines. They came up with 15 degree lists to each side, 2 and 4 wheel drive, 3 different steering modes for turning in a small space, moveable forks, adjustable forklifter and many finer points that a non-driver couldn't understand.

They consider peneprime their least cooperative item for loading. "If the barrel bursts, you get peneprime all over your forklift," said Aguilar. With pre-stabbed barrels, a tarred forklift becomes the inevitable result.

Working long, erratic hours, the forklift drivers keep the supply yards in order and the convoys and Chinook pad in business. Although not thought of as the heart of the airmobile brigade like the chopper, the forklift is often just as important. Army containers are made for forklifts as much as for choppers, and there are few other pieces of equipment in Vietnam capable of moving them.

2/5th Contact Details; Hitching Rides

June 24, 1971

I flew out first to FSB Gail and finally to the one Al Gregory and I wanted, FSB Evelyn. We talked to C Co., 2/5th about that big contact they got into. Everything I heard was true—they went through hell. It was easily the bitterest battle since Cambodia for anyone in the 1st Cav. The NVA stood and fought for 3 days in some of the best dug-in bunker any of the grunts had ever seen. The bunker complex was a klick across! D Co., 2/5th took most of the dead; Charlie Co. took most of the wounded. Most of the wounds were suffered when Blue Max (Cobras) brought their rockets in too close. I was a mess.

I talked to a guy who had a bullet bounce off his steel pot. He usually didn't wear a helmet—he's lucky he did this time. I'm writing a hollow little yarn about that since our paper is so short on copy.

Both D and C companies were in shock most of the time they were fighting. Delta's dead were horribly messed up; it was a real shock for the GIs to carry out their dead. D Company was combat ineffective after the initial ambush by the NVA. They had a medic wounded only slightly die of a heart attack back in 24th Evac. It was the NVA all along who dominated the fighting.

Getting back presented a problem. We took a Chinook to Bearcat, our big helicopter base, and hitched a ride by truck to Long Binh. Then we got a ride to the other side of Long Binh and finally caught a ride to Bien Hoa. It was too much like work—Bien Hoa is just too far from the 3rd Brigade firebases. I'll spend more time in the office now that I've had my outing for the week.

He Keeps His Head

This is a small side story from the big battle of the 2/5th. Being shot in the head is not something to trifle with—this GI could celebrate his good fortune. The Army Reporter *used this article on July 19, 1971, and it was in* Garry Owen *on August 11, 1971.*

FSB EVELYN—Third Brigade has a new steel pot champion. Spec. 4 Terry Smith of Charlie Co. 2nd Bn., 5th Cav was never attracted to his helmet until recently when his company got into a prolonged ferocious firefight.

Smith found himself pinned down by NVA firing AK-47s on automatic. Prone on the jungle ground, he blasted away with his M-60 machinegun at the dug-in enemy.

A B-40 rocket-propelled grenade went off 15 feet away. "A few seconds later something hit me in the helmet," said Smith. "I thought it was a piece of shrapnel." Despite his new headache, he tried to retaliate.

Somehow, the trigger mechanism fell out of his M-60 as he was about to fire back with a fresh belt of ammunition. He was forced to drag his useless weapon and himself out of the fight.

His curiosity was aroused later when he could relax. Smith separated the helmet liner from his steel pot and several pieces of an AK-47 round fell out. His helmet had saved his life.

"We always had trouble getting him to wear his helmet," said SSgt. Troy Saw. Newly decorated with a Bronze Star for Valor, Smith will probably never object to his helmet again.

Writing 2/5th Story

June 25, 1971—50 days left

I just came back from "eating" at the mess hall—how I've survived on this fare I'll never know. The cooks start with decent food and cook the vitamins and taste right out of it. I realize you saw people in India starving, Dad, but a rich army like ours should do better. I've even seen the dogs turn down meat the Army expected us to eat.

I spent all morning trying to figure out how to write the 2/5th contact story without mentioning all the dead and wounded. I came up with what I thought was about as well as I could do, although I got a headache for my efforts. We'll get the story down to MACOI for clearance and get it out in a news release with photos, about two weeks after the fact.

I'm a good 70 miles from the bloody contact so I was safe but it scared me too. As I was writing out the story, I came to realize that the line units bring it on themselves. They were out looking for the enemy and a fight, and found both in abundance. Their call for help once they discovered the enemy was straight out of the airmobile strategy. We're coming up with a very warlike press release, our most warlike since the 1st Cav stood down.

One of our photos from my last photo release was in *Stripes* today so things are working out well now. The next release should do even better although at the price of grunt lives—too high a price. Al Gregory did a good job on the pictures. We'll see what develops.

Dave Bunker, our photographer who came to us from a scout dog platoon, is working to get his old dog for a pet. His dog went through Cambodia before Dave hit country. This is the dog that was out with Dave and I on bunker guard my first night of guard duty. He's a huge German shepherd. Dave says the dog is getting too old for Army work. Dave wants to take him home, understandable also because the dog saved Dave from death on several occasions.

Testing for drugs before leaving Vietnam strikes me as a good idea, if the goal behind the project is rehabilitation as they say it is. It should make the smuggling of hard drugs more difficult when GIs leave Vietnam. This is still a stopgap—leaving Vietnam is the best way to start a cure.

Photographer Sees Casualties

June 26, 1971

Joe Lamont was on FSB Mace when the dying and less seriously wounded were coming through from the 2/5th action. The doctors wanted him to take pictures of it but Joe couldn't force himself to do it. He watched them working on mutilated GIs and couldn't believe it was happening. Those are guys like you and me, he was saying. It reminds me of when I was trying to work up stories in the hospital in Long Binh. It was different for Joe, in that the men's wounds hadn't been bandaged and the sedatives hadn't been given for pain. What a horror.

Outage

June 27, 1971—48 days

Al Gregory was trying to talk me into going out to some new bunker complex and cache that someone found in the field. No way, not even. Keeping my promise to you in mind, I told him to kindly forget it.

There's three weeks that can be taken in leave while I'm in Vietnam. I've taken two and I'll see if I can take the last shortly. As you say, it's better to spend my remaining time out of country, anywhere.

The power for our hooch went out last night and a miserable night followed. Having a fan and lights has spoiled me. The transition to having neither was hard. I'm not sure we have power yet. I felt discriminated against: the hooches next door had lights, stereo and everything.

Hoochmate Sacked

June 30, 1971

I made it through guard duty last night. There was no wind and I could hear the mosquitoes. Usually, they are sneaky and don't hum but last night, maybe because they were a different species, they kept me awake most of the night with their buzzing and nosing around. Otherwise, I didn't spot anything. I had a chance to talk to a guy who enlisted originally as a grunt, a rarity. He now works in the post office and has been in country something like 18 months. He was ETSing the day before I DEROS from Vietnam. He was a grunt when they had a real war, not like the one we have now. He was in Tay Ninh Province where the NVA were all hard-core cases who made it a point to shoot back.

Our hoochmate, Ohn (alias Babysan), got thrown out of our hooch when some lifer caught her in bed with another lifer. Everybody knew she'd been in dereliction of her duty and messing with this sorry E-6. So I'm out of clean clothes for the time being until we get a new maid. The E-6 is the one who should have been fired but he's got diplomatic immunity, Army style.

Dad, do you realize that for a stretch you weighed more than I do? I'm about 145–150 pounds now. I've been running on one of the dirt roads near the berm trying to keep my weight down. I'm trying to stay off of potatoes.

A fellow by the name of Head who came into country the same day I did has been trying to kick his drug habit. I don't think he's succeeded yet.

5. Nearing the End: May 1, 1971, to June 30, 1971

At FSSE he was always the stranger who moped in the corner. I thought he disliked me but I've learned since that it's more probable that human relationships weren't his thing. He probably didn't know I was there—he was living in his own world.

You remember that congressional investigation about half the guys in Admin Co had going? Well, those of us who signed the thing went before the new Admin Co. CO and signed a statement acknowledging that we realized somebody was watching to make sure our complaints hadn't gone unnoticed. It's already clear that our new company commander is as big a dud as our last CO. Our new CO is the guy who used to give Big Al and I nothing when we were out on the firebases. He was so above such low creatures like us. Some improvement.

Chapter 6

Being Short: July 1, 1971, to August 15, 1971

Being short was practically a disease process, making soldiers with only a few days in country less effective. There were lurid stories of GIs dying only a few hours from leaving Vietnam for good; Steve Warner's death was the only example I personally knew. And you can see from my letters I bought into it. Although I stayed active to the end—my last, longest and probably most enlightening story was about Chinook helicopter maintenance—it was common for men to use being short as an excuse for sloughing off. Many of my subsequent letters are short—I've spared readers my unattractive wringing of the hands and whining.

Politics

July 1, 1971

I rewrote that god-forsaken 2/5th contact story for at least the 4th time. I never want to see it again. The 2/8th got some men killed about two days ago in another contact. Things are warming up although they aren't about to overrun Bien Hoa yet.

I went out and had a couple of beers with Big Al and Teddy Wempe, our lab technician. Teddy is a member of the *Young Americans for Freedom* and a wild-eyed follower of William F. Buckley, Jr. He trots out all the conservative line yet, with his Bronx accent, he's fun to listen to. We get along surprisingly well. He was reading *The New Republic*, an opposition rag, and enjoyed it. He even agreed with part of an editorial in the magazine about the "Top Secret" disclosures. He especially liked the part about Goldwater. Teddy's a 26-year-old who lives in New York State and drinks too much beer. His plump self looks much older than his years. He's very much of an individual and friendly. I won't tell him, Dad, that you are a member of the ACLU.

6. Being Short: July 1, 1971, to August 15, 1971

Teddy infuriated me with one of the last quotes from the old NCOIC of the paper. This fellow, a self-proclaimed radical, Teddy told me that he thought of me as the epitome of all that is square. You know: small town, quiet, doesn't smoke many Js, and doesn't join. I've always felt this guy thought this and didn't like him. He's a city boy, an outspokenly snobbish head who joins anything that will help sell himself. I find myself closer to Teddy although my politics supposedly are closer to the other guy.

Big Al and I have been feeding sardines to the dogs. The mess halls are barely keeping us humans alive. Being constantly hounded by hungry dogs, we've taken to supplementing their diets. In the long run it's foolish—in 60 days both of us will be gone. But what can you do when your dog is hungry and you're still around. Very sad.

I suggested in my letters home that we had lost this fight. What I now realize is this battle was a throwback to the hot war of the past and what was still happening further north. The casualties were bad—there was no question there—but it was to be expected when a big enemy unit chose to fight instead of run. I now recognize we did win but not without major cost.

MEN OF 3RD BRIGADE UPHOLD CAV TRADITION

This article was in the August 1, 1971, Garry Owen. *A version with a different open made it into the July 15, 1971,* Pacific Stars and Stripes. *A third version close to the* Stars and Stripes *one was in the July 19, 1971,* Army Reporter. *I'm going with the non–1st Cav open, which I'm sure I wrote. The 1st Cav open included the word "fightingest"—I would never use that word—and written in a style that's alien to mine.*

FSB FURR—Exposing the enemy's position and quickly calling in enough friendly forces to overwhelm them is the essence of the airmobile concept of warfare. The red Brigade mobilized such a classic counterattack recently when D Co., 2nd Bn,. 5th Cav. discovered an NVA headquarters and was hurled back.

What developed into some of the toughest fighting for the 1st Cav. since Cambodia began when D Co. took enemy mortar fire during the night. The following morning a squad checked out an automatic ambush set up across a jungle stream After retrieving the claymores, they walked further into the bush and cleared and patrolled the trail

Hidden NVA unleashed B-40 rocket-propelled grenades and AK-47s on a light patrol from Delta Co., 2nd Bn,. 5th Cav, forcing the patrol's retreat and a call for help to the parent company. Facing withering fire from hidden bunkers a few minutes later, the company realized it was dueling with a force fielding superior firepower from impregnable positions. The FO (forward observer) then tried to pin down the enemy with artillery, Cobra gunship fire and airstrikes.

Meanwhile, the company commander called for reinforcements. By the next day, six infantry companies were in the immediate area.

Charlie Co., 2nd Bn., 5th Cav was the first to arrive and became embroiled in some of the worst of the fighting. Charlie Company managed to reach its embattled sister company through a test of endurance, moving through five klicks (5000 meters) of jungle in two hours.

Next day, with Charlie Co. support, Delta Co. took more fire and pulled back. Charlie Co. then made a sweep. In rapid succession, a claymore was blown on the company, the men were raked by heavy fire and ended up pinned down.

"I've been here 11 months and I've never been in a fight like that," said 1st Lt. Albert Vaxmonsky, looking back on his experience with discomfort. "We took them by surprise, to our surprise. They weren't prepared for where we came in. We could see the NVA heading for cover."

Charlie Co. thinks they were battling a .30 caliber machine gun, although it was hard to confirm with all the AK47s firing automatic. "We had 30 or so B40s, 30 mortar rounds and countless AK47s rounds fired our direction," said Vaxmonsky. Charlie Co. threw out its own heavy volume of fire, keeping the situation from deteriorating.

Charlie Co. finally pulled back with the FO still calling in fire support.

Next morning, Alpha Co. 1st Bn., 12th Cav made contact on another side of the klick-wide bunker complex while other companies were closing in from other angles. Finally, the NVA abandoned the bunkers as the Cav pressure became too great.

"Our company swept through and discovered 25 command bunkers in our area alone, the best bunkers I've ever come across," said Vaxmonsky. The companies now occupied a battalion-sized bunker complex, newly-built with some parts still under construction.

The well-camouflaged bunkers had four feet of overhead cover, and were protected from anything but a direct hit. Between 75 and 200 NVA were estimated to have lived in the complex before it was captured.

Afterthoughts in Charlie Co. were numerous. "Everybody said they (the NVA) couldn't be there after three and a half days, but they were," noted Vaxmonsky. "It just doesn't happen."

"We've never had a fight where they stood and fought," claimed Spec. 4 William Germann.

SSgt. Troy Shaw, a two-tour veteran of Vietnam, exclaimed, with a note of disbelief in his voice, "I was pinned down, getting shot at from three sides." He received a Silver Star for Gallantry in Action for his part in the engagement.

The NVA unit sent packing is thought to be the same one the 3rd Brigade has been chasing around for months.

Bus Incident

July 3, 1971

I just got back from taking the bus around Saigon. It's a lot of work to get our releases to UPI, AP and *Oversees Weekly*. I finally made it to JUSPAO (Joint United States Public Affairs Office) after changing two buses from MACV compound in Tan Son Nhut. Much of the hour-long drive was taken up going in circles and waiting for the bus driver to show. I finally got to see the Tudo Street area with all its bars and hotels. I was approached by hawkers of gross photos, skag, pot and some other things I couldn't decipher.

I'm developing my brush-off but an armless war veteran gave me the most trouble. He showed me a little card that said he'd once been normal but the war hobbled him and didn't I feel sorry. I had trouble shoeing him away. I did feel sorry for him but he took my brush-off with a jaunty air I couldn't help respecting.

JUSPAO isn't a place that sticks out but is in a district hard to confuse with any other. A modern building inside, it's guarded by a Marine guard who was really spiffy. The guy had a great salute—I was really impressed. He's got 52 days left in Vietnam and wants to go either to Helsinki or Kenya. He said he'd really like Kenya. I think he's got a thankless job. His establishment was bombed two weeks ago.

The trip back was somewhat eventful. On the bus from MACV Headquarters to Long Binh, we made a stop and picked up three GIs. Another man, a taxi driver, boarded and wanted money from the soldiers. It was quite a scene with several other bus riders coming to the aid of the hapless or dishonest GIs, whatever they were.

Taxi drivers aren't uniformly honest but then, neither are GIs. I thought the passengers acted in a bigoted fashion—it reached the point where they nearly threw the taxi man out the door before I could leave the bus. Finally, the bus pulled out, the taxi driver still fuming. A couple of urchins threw rocks at the bus although they didn't break anything.

Independence Day

July 4, 1971

Sunday is a day of rest for me and it's July 4th. There were two outdoor barbeques that I found today so I stuffed myself, even came up with a fine hunk of steak. I played ping-pong and watched our new Service Club girls.

Spec 4 Dan Evans, who has been writing for *Stars and Stripes* as long

I'm standing at the door of a bunker on the edge of Bien Hoa Army Base, wearing my periodically controversial wire-rimmed glasses.

as I've been here, went out to 2/8th and wrote about the same action I've been working on. What bugs me is that he can say so much more than I can. He can give intelligence data, the statistics on our dead and wounded, and do a more balanced job. He's a better journalist because he's allowed to dig for muck once in a while—I never can. He works for the Army nominally only.

I slept poorly last night; I think Saigon disagreed with me. It's a place I'm not enthusiastic about. There are pretty streetwalkers and feverish street businesses but I dream of the clean openness of home.

Sleeper

July 6, 1971

I just got back from FSB Mace. Nothing much was going on there; it was just raining. I went out by convoy and returned, finally, by chopper. The grunt battalions are suffering through a drought in replacements to the point where they are almost half strength. Either an awful lot of new men will have to be sent over or we're leaving. I'm betting on the later but not soon enough to help me.

I developed a story on a new warrant officer, a chopper pilot in country only a few weeks. I'm going to make the point that warrant officers are not

6. Being Short: July 1, 1971, to August 15, 1971   303

such obvious newbies. They don't ask funny questions about their job, they don't look unhappy (and aren't) and their uniform, a special one made of fire resistant cloth, doesn't fade. I had to ask to learn whether he was a newbie or not. I'm also going to outline a little of what's special about pilots.

My other yarn I picked up from some grunts from B 2/5th about how their company captured a POW. To put it simply, they heard him snoring inside a bunker. Some hardy soul jumped into the bunker and found him asleep. The NVA solder was tapped on the shoulder. He awoke, grasping instantly the helplessness of his position, and started hollering so heatedly that the GI didn't need an interpreter. Being mercifully bloodless, it should make a good story.

The *USARV Report* and the *MACV Observer* both had the Aussie story in full in their sheets so I made a complete slam—wow.

I've got CQ tonight. Guard duty has asked for more men from our office so I'll have it every 9 days now instead of every two weeks.

SNORE JOB LANDS A POW

Not waking up in time was a disaster, as this man could've testified, had you been able to understand Vietnamese. What follows was in the July 28, 1971, Garry Owen, *while a modified version appeared in a July 1971* Pacific Stars and Stripes *issue, and a short version was in the* Army Reporter *on August 2, 1971.*

NEAR FSB FURR—Snoring claimed a victim recently when 1st Plt., B Co, 2d Bn., 5th Cav discovered an NVA. Caught napping, one very unhappy enemy soldier found himself among new companions.

Bravo Co. moved into an extensive bunker complex the enemy had abandoned only a few hours before. A map found in one bunker gave the location of another set of bunkers a few hundred meters away.

I like the cartoon

Header of my snore story.

The 1st Platoon was sent to check it out. On finding the fortifications, the GIs started methodically going through the area. Suddenly they heard someone snoring inside a bunker. The noise was surrounded and a hardy soul jumped into the bunker.

The explorer found an enemy soldier stretched out on a mat, fast asleep and without a weapon. The GI nudged his adversary, who awoke with a start. Knowing instantly the helplessness of the situation, the new detainee started using all kinds of language. The platoon didn't need an interpreter to tell them how angry their POW was.

The detainee was marched off to the company's command post, where the 2nd platoon learned about the episode. "They said they had a POW," said Spec. 4 Ken Dierdorf, "but we hadn't heard any shots."

"I'd sure like to have seen his face when he woke up," said PFC Archie Martinez, another member of the 2nd Plt.

As first-rate opportunists, the men of 1st Platoon should be pleased with themselves. Yet they must have the nagging suspicion that their detainee could qualify as a Hoi Chanh who was turned in by his own snores.

Lost Newspaper

July 7, 1971

Pat Deatherage tells me we're way up on column inches in outside media. We got one photo in Army News Features (ANF), an Army-side clipping service for news of Army-wide importance. That's a first for us.

The dogs kept me up part of the night. With five dogs taking turns barking, I was ready to throttle the ornery beasts. Coco, the chocolate wolf, has started making it a habit of sleeping during the days on top of the poncho liner on my bed and spreading sand throughout it. What a pain.

My ping-pong game is improving; Big Al couldn't lay a paddle on me today. The only night he clobbered me was when I'd tried some pot and my reflexes slowed up. The service club has two new girls working in it, an improvement over the old ones. At least one of the girls came to us from 1/5th Mech, which was working the DMZ. It's a relief for her to come down here I hear.

It seems that we lost all the copies of the *Garry Owen* newspaper. It's already 10 days late. Somebody said they had it at the 8th Aerial port but this sighting wasn't confirmed. It's frustrating having two weeks of work go down the drain. It gives you an idea of the shipping problems we have here.

I went to the Medical Company today to have a wart on my foot checked. I'm going over to 24th Evac tomorrow—it's wart day at the dermatology clinic.

Bad Time to Be a Grunt

July 8, 1971

I hitched over to Long Binh this morning and had acid put on the wart and with repeated treatments, the wart will be eaten away. A staff sergeant instead of a doctor treated me but this medic knew what he was doing.

Captain Medina and his lawyer came through here yesterday morning. They came into the 8th Aerial Port and three of our guys went over about 3 a.m. and got shots of them. I wonder what they're after. The 1st Cav should stay out of that situation. The 1st Cav in the past has been accused of atrocities like that but in the area we're working right now we don't come across the hard-core VC villages found farther north.

Whatever happened to Mike Paine—have his parents heard from him? I've lost touch with him. I last saw him on 1/121th's FSB Sherman. He was with C Company, 1/12th. His battalion is about the only one that's managed to avoid the heavy fighting. It's a bad time to be a grunt; I hope Mike gets out of the boonies soon and gets a rear job.

Philippine Band; Helicopter Maintenance Incentives

July 10—35 days left

About the only thing we did today was stack sandbags around our hooch, which didn't take much time. Everyone has been grossly shamming. I was working today and completely alone in the office for several hours. Lt. Launder is getting upset because the staff is never around, even when there's work to do.

I tried getting high on some Thai grass last night and all the other guys seemed to be hard hit. I thought I was affected but played ping-pong with Big Al and walloped him six straight games to his disgust.

We then sat down and listened to what at first we thought was just another Vietnamese music group. It turned out to be the best band I've heard in Vietnam—one of the best anywhere for that matter. They had a repertoire that was out of this world. They didn't pause between songs like other groups to pad their shows. They didn't mispronounce English—their accents were flawless. They must have done 45 songs and their agile dancers were almost as good as the band itself. The audience left exhausted and happy. The band was Philippine, not Vietnamese, playing American and British music.

Tomorrow night Big Al and I have the misfortune of both having guard duty. I'm getting used to it but it's uncomfortable compared to the usual night we spend with a fan, a well-lit room, and a comfortable bed.

I did a story yesterday on A Co, 229th AHB with a lieutenant for a photographer. He was too lazy to do the story so I was his luckless victim. The helicopter maintenance people are some of those rare birds who can get $60 pro-pay or something like that with their specialized and critical MOSes. They said that everyone in their company was extending their stay in Vietnam because of the high morale in the company. It's probably because they're so well paid they can't afford to go home. [*I wrote an article on helicopter maintenance which was published in the February 12, 1971, Observer.*] The Army has gone to some wild extremes to keep people here. There are bribes like 30-day all-expenses-paid extended leaves to anywhere in the world, $60 a month combat pay even if you're in a secure area, and the PX. R & R is another. The two-week-leave to the States is still another. Hard-core Army men will be sorry to see the ever-so-profitable Vietnam War end.

Keeping Choppers Flying

Helicopter maintenance was one of those vital jobs that most skytroopers rarely witnessed. And not being a mechanical sort myself, I was impressed by the skills these fellows had. I located this story in the February 12, 1971, issue of The Observer.

It takes more than gas and a pilot to keep a chopper airborne. Besides gas, a helicopter needs a steady diet of oils and greases and requires a working over every hundred hours of flying time to give constant smooth performance. It's hardly something to be taken for granted, especially for the men of "North Flag," C Company, 229th Assault Helicopter Battalion.

Even the 13-week school that a helicopter maintenance and repair man goes through is only the beginning of learning the trade. PFC Lorenzo Perez of Fremont, Cal., had a lot of learning to do. "It took me six months to figure out what I was doing. You really don't know how it's done until you've worked on one. It's on-the-job training and preventive maintenance all the way."

"We like to get three birds at a time," explained Spec 4 Dava McCall of Detroit, Mich., "though flying scheduling doesn't always allow us to have our way. We have 19 birds to keep in condition. It just depends on how badly messed up a bird is to how long we keep it. A new bird takes no more than 3 or 4 days. Messed up—a week."

Technical Inspection (TI) takes responsibility for everything being right. Experts on helicopter maintenance, they are the quality control team constantly watching the maintenance crews.

The ground maintenance crewmembers agreed that, as McCall put it, "It's the pilots that make our job easy or hard. We've got good pilots here."

Helicopters become known by number and reputation although they're somewhat hard to tell apart because they are all the same Huey. "Number 150 has 170 bullet holes in; it's a good 1969 bird," explained McCall. "Number 274 is probably our oldest bird from 1966. All the choppers in the company are kept in good shape and we've been painting them, so that their ages now don't show so much."

With the aid of a competent ground crew, a bird with plenty of gas and a good pilot can do its job easily. As the backbone of the 1st Cav's troop movements, repairs can't be left to chance.

Night Scope; One-Upmanship

July 12, 1971

For all the hollering Big Al does about being shafted, last night it was my turn to suffer, nothing fatal, mind you. We were both on guard duty but he got Quick Reaction Force (QRF) for the third time—I've never had it—and I got the M-60 on tower guard. We got the extremes. I carried an M-60 a good quarter mile. He had a much shorter walk with an M-16. It wasn't *that* bad really.

I got a chance to use a special night scope on an M-16 called a "starlight scope." About $8,000 worth of optics and electronics, it can see in very weak light. Everything has a green cast to it. The gizmo wasn't up to full snuff but I had fun with it. The tower was about 40 feet off the ground so I didn't have trouble with the mosquitoes. I could see about a half mile of the green line and talked to the Bien Hoa TOC every half hour when they had a commo check. I had first watch so it wasn't too bad.

The rain didn't fall during the night but about an hour after I got back to the hooch and bedded down for a few more winks, it let loose. It's raining hard now.

I went down to Ton San Nhut this afternoon to drop off a couple of stories to be cleared at MACOI (Military Assistance Command Office of Information) plus try to run down what they call the "tear sheets" of the lost issue, the parts of the now infamous issue that never made it back alive.

On the way back I talked to several GIs from the 1st of the 5th Mech, the armored unit up at Quan Tri on the DMZ that is standing down. They had all kinds of harrowing tales of how bad it was up there.

The gabbing degenerated into a form of one-upmanship. There's nothing stupider than claiming an armored cavalry unit is better than an air cavalry unit—they function entirely differently and for different purposes. I was willing to admit that their territory was rougher than ours but they clearly don't understand how an airmobile outfit works. I was tempted to accuse them of being newbies but that would have done no good.

I was over drinking with Dave Armijo night before last and decided to walk to my hooch. Some guy I didn't know heard us talking about how things had been warming up around Bien Hoa lately. The guy growled, "You don't have no right to talk about action, you don't know what you're talking about. I've been in country 17 months."

Dave and I were dumbfounded. Dave has 15 months and I have 11 so we've been around. Dave replied hotly that he'd had a friend get his head shot off only a couple of yards away from him in Cambodia. He said he'd been out in the bush and been shot at. I didn't feel I needed to say a thing. We walked off in a huff and decided afterwards we should have bashed the stupid mudhen's head in. There are things you don't say in Vietnam and some sick fools who say them.

I've got to go to a drug and safety class tomorrow morning. It'll undoubtedly be another demonstration of the Army's "Don't You Dare!" approach to drugs. I'll be two hours wasted, just watch.

Slack

July 13, 1971

In the immortal words of SFC Lebus, "You can be replaced by a PFC." I think he was kidding but it's still true. Someday a PFC will replace me if I'm lucky. In fact, maybe an E-1 will replace me. A guy came down from 1/5th Mech. as an E-1 because of dereliction of duty.

I now have my leave orders so I'm going on July 19th on R&R for a week, probably to Hawaii.

The drug and safety class this morning only lasted 15 minutes. Capt. Gimian did relatively well, didn't throw around that many clichés, and let us out without much ado. I'm not doing anything now except writing and didn't do much of anything today. This is a slack period. By the time I return from leave, I expect to have 18 days left.

Snow

July 14, 1971

I got my orders for leaving Vietnam!

All those snow pictures you sent make me homesick. The Vietnamese wouldn't know what to do with a snowflake if they saw one. I remember how homesick a Vietnamese DINFOS classmate was during our training in June and July. I can imagine what he'd feel like in our December or January.

I'm going to *Catch-22* at the Air Force Theater tonight.

Big Al and I are getting restless—leaving will be so soon.

Civilian Affairs

July 15, 1971

I went over to Long Binh this morning to have my warts worked over and had quite an experience on the way back. I got a ride with a SSgt. Kim

6. Being Short: July 1, 1971, to August 15, 1971

Potaozala, a member of a civil affairs team working for the Long Binh Post. We got to talking and he asked if I could spare a few minutes because he had to pick up some stuff in Long Binh village. My curiosity aroused, I decided to go with him and have a look at how the other half lives.

I stopped halfway down a quiet street and was greeted by a young Vietnamese interpreter who lived there. He asked me in and we sat and talked. He asked me to have lunch with them, Vietnamese style. It was a real eye-opener.

Kim, the staff sergeant, is Australian, not American. He switched from their army to ours when he was up north. He's been in Vietnam for 5 years—he's 24 years old and looks 30, and is married to a Vietnamese gal who lives up in Tay Ninh. He's a real spellbinding character.

He said the war started because the Vietnamese did ask for help and Kim said the Americans have given the wrong kind of help. He was bitter because the Americans have stupid regulations about staying on post and not getting involved with the Vietnamese. Kim said that the Vietnamese, 90% of them, were good people with a basic streak of honesty. Very few Americans had a chance to learn what Vietnamese, the real natives, were like. Americans' involvement is with drug pushers, prostitutes, and bar maids. Kim thinks his native country, Australia, could have done a better job in Vietnam like they did in Malaysia.

We talked for two hours. I had a chance to taste nuoc mam, the staple Vietnamese sauce, along with their rice, an omelet, dried fish and some greens. I liked the food—it was much better than I expected. Talking to the young interpreter who was my host, I was impressed with how friendly he was. He wasn't after my money. He explained his relationship in his home. He is a corporal in the Vietnamese army and the man whose house he lived in was a captain. Yet he, the corporal, holds a superior position in the family. His relatives call him uncle. His extended Vietnam family is big and successful, he said.

Kim asked me if I wanted to do a madcap story on his outfit in a resettlement of the refugees from the war. It would be great sport with someone like Kim at my side that speaks fluent Vietnamese. Kim said one reason for the failure in Laos was that there were no American advisers with the troops. The role of an American adviser, according to Kim, is to direct artillery, air strikes and other heavy American assistance. Without advisers as RTOs, the Vietnamese can't communicate with the Americans' firepower. This is what Kim did for a long time, working as an adviser, and he liked it. He says he feels he's accomplishing something over here. He changed to the American army, not because he thinks it's better than his native Army but because that way he could continue his role advising the Vietnamese.

Kim said his youngest son had just died in Tay Ninh from double pneumonia. He noted that the first two years are the roughest for a child here. He said he found the Americans a very ignorant people—they had no respect or interest in learning Vietnamese customs. The first time he'd gotten in a fight with a GI, he was walking down the street with his arms around his interpreter, a standard show of friendship in Vietnam. A passing GI called Kim a queer. Kim responded by knocking the guy out cold. And I take it that wasn't the last time Kim got mad at an American.

I have doubts about doing a story on Kim's program. The 1st Cav deals only with tokenism I feel as far as pacification and Vietnamese relations go. I'm hoping I can come up with a tenuous link with the 1st Cav so I can do a magazine story on this relocation and kill two birds with one stone.

So, by following my curiosity and keeping a moderately open mind, I had an experience that makes more sense than most of my Vietnam experiences. I've always been surprised that the Vietnamese, who I thought were unfriendly, smile a good deal. They seem a happy people if given a chance. Inflation (500% in 5 years) has made the cost of living for the Vietnamese almost unbearably high. At the same time wages have remained the same. Corruption has become the alternative to going broke and we Americans have fed the corruption.

Kim doesn't care for the Vietnamese cowboys or the American press. He doesn't like the REMFs who have never been out of Long Binh (or Bien Hoa or whatever) and seen Vietnam. I told him I hadn't seen much of Vietnam myself except for Song Be. Somehow Army tacticians feel soldiers shouldn't know those they're theoretically fighting for. Absurd!

Kim said the Americans have done a few things right. Helicopters are a logical answer to the problems of mobility. Advisers are logical helpers for the Vietnamese. Kim was different from virtually all Americans I've encountered so far in his profound respect for the Vietnamese. He has no doubt they are worth fighting for. He sees himself as fighting for the people, not hazy principles.

Technically what I was doing today was illegal although I was with an official, Kim, who was legally visiting Long Binh village. Few Americans like me are allowed to go down to the Vill so only those doing something illegal visit.

Today was a good day as far as stories being picked up by the outside news media went. The 2/5th story that I'd predicted would make it into *Stripes* made it. I didn't claim we had won the fight, only that we pushed them out. The Aussie story made it into *Army Times* in its entirety. I'd say the 2/5th story was better written, despite its slant.

This is the big day, 11 months in Vietnam and payday to boot. I now have money for Hawaii next week.

Slow News

July 17, 1971

I've had two nothing days in a row. I put out a news release but wrote nothing new. The fellow working with the pacification program hasn't called so I guess that's dead. He hit me at the wrong time since I'm about to go on leave.

The lieutenant I'd mentioned in the past no longer works at the PIO. He got DXed (turned in as useless) and because he's short he'll not end up doing much. He's been without function really, less than useless, the whole time he's been in Bien Hoa. Lt. Launder wouldn't stand up for him, in fact was one of the prime movers to his exit. Launder said the guy had made more enemies in Vietnam than he, Launder, expected to make in his life. The artists were particularly upset with our old lieutenant because when he left, he cleaned out several drawers of art supplies belonging to the office.

MSgt. Garcia made it back today. He said he hit it just right in Alaska with gorgeous weather in the 70s and 80s.

Several of my stories made it into the *USARV Reporter* today and since the *Garry Owen* seems to be a fading memory, I'll send you a couple of pages from USARV's paper. Our own paper hasn't been out in more than a month—incredible. It's hard to keep writing without my own paper.

Marking Time Until R&R

July 18, 1971

It's a profoundly dull day but tomorrow shows promise—I'm off to Hawaii and maybe I can call you once I get there. I'll be home soon but I'm finding the wait hard—I'm a little homesick.

I talked with MSG Garcia about two Alaskan scout battalions in the National Guard. They're unique to the Army in that they're Eskimos. They patrol the Bering Strait and other icy masses. They are made National Guardsmen so they don't have to go into the Army. They are superb warriors for the job, the Sarg says.

Hawaii

July 20, 1971

I'm in Hawaii after an awful jet ride. I have no idea what time it really is and went to bed at 3 a.m. So far I've spent $55 including my room and clothes—amazingly cheap by local standards. Living in some "barracks" in Fort Derussey has worked beautifully; the price of a room a mere $26.

I spent the day haunting the beach, watching the girls go by. I saw one who looked black—what a spectacular tan. I'll be an optional red later in the day if lay on the beach too long.

Sunburn and Heartache

July 21, 1971

I'm sitting at a table near a food and drink stall, taking cover after my optional suntan developed into a glowing red burn.

I was playing volleyball and one of the women I talked with after a game was on a rest break from the hospital. She'd found her husband hanging in their garage, dead. The shock had given her a heart condition, she said. She's from New York City, the Bronx specifically. I loved listening to her rib her fellow patients, who were hospitalized for "head and heart" problems. I suspect she's really being treated for heartbreak, not a cardiac condition.

People Watching

July 22, 1971

I've come to the conclusion that it's the people, not the beach, that draws people to a beach. The shared experience is what counts and since I have nobody to share this with, it's a waste. I look at it as high-class Vietnam shamming and although dull, awfully safe.

Only Watching

July 23, 1971

There was a concert on the Ft. Derussey lawn by a Christian rock group.

I was miserable for a while but the pain from my burn wore off and now I can sleep. I find it an agonizing experience watching all the women in bikinis—watching only is hollow.

Men of Service

July 24, 1971

I just finished calling you—I still recognize your voices.

I went to the concert by that Jesus Group, the Certain Sounds. They had a good crowd but played the same stuff as yesterday. They aggressively proselytize; each getting up and telling what Jesus has done for them. One gal called those who didn't embrace Jesus Christ fools and hypocrites—she gave a lesson in ineffective proselytizing.

The guy I told you about on the phone, who claimed he was a professional photographer because he did it for money, was back on the raft, chasing the same girl he's been after for some time. I thought the girl was worth the trouble.

6. Being Short: July 1, 1971, to August 15, 1971   313

This is the same fellow who told me he didn't associate with servicemen, as though he was a superior species. His girl had left before this remark, which left both a Navy dude and me laughing. His intended love is a service brat.

I fly back tomorrow. I can't wait to get back so that I can leave.

Office Coup

July 27, 1971

I came back to an office that has been turned inside out. We have a new head information officer, a captain, who has completely changed the place to suit his whims. He told the staff that if they didn't work, they would be thrown to the dogs. For a number of our men who had been in the infantry, it was a cruel thing to say. He was on an ego trip. Lt. Launder, who came off of R&R a day before I did, had an even worse shock. The captain took over the office in less than an hour, a military coup. I'm glad I'm leaving but I'm not yet convinced the captain is actually bad.

The *Garry Owen* paper finally came out; it's one of our better ones. This paper has much of the content of the lost issue. I like the cartoon with my snore story. The snore story made it into *Stripes* although they cut out my conclusion. Our centerfold had better pictures than usual because of the shots I'd successfully splashed in other Vietnam papers.

Our dog Blanche is pregnant again—that's all we need, more dogs. We still don't have replacements for Al and me although we're assured someone is on the way.

I spent $82 in Hawaii and even that was too much.

Aerial Heroics

July 28, 1971

I talked with the new captain for almost an hour—it's more like he talked. He expressed what I consider enlightened thoughts. He said the military was well equipped to invade Vietnam but not withdrawing. He thinks the words such as mamasan, papasan, dink, and gook should be expunged from military speech. He thinks well of Nixon's novel approach to Red China. As a whole, I was impressed by what he said.

I spent the afternoon writing a story on a warrant officer in an LOH who was shot through the leg while flying. His doorgunner climbed up front into the copilot's seat to help. With only two men on board, the doorgunner was doing a courageous act, especially considering he's 5'10" and 230 pounds of muscle. The doorgunner had to climb outside the bird to get into the front. He then worked the floor pedals while the groggy pilot did the rest. They managed to land the helicopter. The lucky shot from an enemy soldier almost did them in. I talked with the pilot at 24th Evac in Long Binh.

Regarding the papers I've mentioned, *Stars and Stripes* is literally a Pacific edition. The *Army Reporter* is the biggest strictly Vietnam military paper. The *Observer* is one of the oldest papers in Vietnam. *Army Times* is an Army-wide publication. And then there are lesser papers, our *Garry Owen* is one of them.

Gunner's Aerial Daring Saves Their Lives

The men of this piece showed what adrenalin and daring could accomplish in a desperate situation. It was printed in the August 25, 1971, Garry Owen *and a version rewritten by Alan Brown (according to a message he scrawled on the clipping) that made it into the August 25, 1971,* Stars and Stripes.

BEARCAT—Enemy ground fire opened up from below, hitting the low-flying American LOH scout chopper. A bullet passed through the LOH's floor, the pilot's right leg, the instrument panel, and punctured the glass bubble windshield. An H Troop, 16th Cav. pilot, WO Thomas Burnett, and his doorgunner, Spec. 4 Michael Perry, found themselves scrambling for their lives.

"It was just a lucky shot," claimed Burnett afterwards, "the sniper's first burst seriously hampered my control of the LOH. Had it not been for the daring of my doorgunner, all might have been lost."

Burnett, whose use of the chopper's pedals, was slowed because of his injury, fought to keep the craft airborne. "Don't pass out, I'm coming up," Perry yelled to his pilot over the headset.

Within 15 seconds, according to Burnett, Perry managed to climb into the copilot's seat by scrambling from his seat in the rear, via a precarious route outside the bird's cabin. Burnett was amazed.

"He's about 5'10"," explained Burnett, "and a good 230 pounds. We're always teasing him about being 'the Chunker,' too heavy for a small bird. At the 90 knots we were escaping, his moving up was no small feat." Perry, at that point, took charge of the pedals.

Burnett began to recover from his initial shock. "We were going to land it in a field," said Burnett, "but when we got close to the ground we found the land was marshy and realized the bird wasn't hit badly."

With Perry, who had some training in flying choppers, working the pedals, they managed to land at LZ Rock about 15 minutes after Burnett had been hit.

"It wasn't a real smooth landing but we got the bird down without banging it up too badly," said Burnett.

6. Being Short: July 1, 1971, to August 15, 1971   315

Don't Judge a Book ...

July 30, 1971—15 days left

I got my first compliment on my mustache. MSgt. Garcia said that it was destined to droop, which is gauche (even illegal) as far as the Army is concerned. He was kidding and growing a mustache is challenging for me—bad facial hair genetics, you know.

You're going to have to brace yourself. I've been told I look like a typical head by the local heads. It hurts them, it seems, to see a guy who fits right into their stereotype do it without drugs. I get along well with the heads so I don't know whether I should be shocked or not.

My clothes are giving out; I may have to DEROS naked if I don't watch it. I ripped out some of the only pants I have that fit me. I'm down to three shirts, which are sufficient but they're all frayed around the collar. Considering the beating they'd taken, they've held up remarkably well.

I'm seeing more replacements; the PX seems particularly filled with these newbies. My heart bleeds for them but I still want to leave. It's not so much that I'm a smug short trooper but it's more that I'm getting bored.

Fue-Gas Explosion

August 1, 1971—13 days

I had tower guard last night and was dually bored. Thankfully the monsoons are slowing down although it was stifling last night until it began to drizzle. Lightning set off a fue-gas barrel, causing a little stir. Fue-gas is napalm set off by a grenade placed inside the barrel of the liquid, a rough but effective variety of flamethrower. I've never seen one used but have seen it demonstrated. It is one of the most effective battlefield expedients. I had the middle watch from midnight until 3 a.m. with nothing to see.

The *USARV Reporter* came out with two nice large 1st Cav photos and that snooze story of mine. I liked the way they used the photos but there were no bylines.

I've decided to do a final magazine article on Chinooks, which no one has done a story on for an amazingly long time. I'll probably take a hop out to Bearcat where the big goofy-looking birds are based, to gather information. I'll probably take photos too. I'll have a copy of it sent home—it'll be published long after I leave.

Chinook Maintenance

August 3, 1971—11 days

Today I flew out to Bearcat and started work on what I hope is my last story in this country. The 362nd Aviation Company, which used to be B Co,

228th AHB, has 16 Chinooks and puts up 3 or 4 birds a day to work for the brigade, sometimes a few more. The maintenance and repair problems are mind-boggling—a Chinook has more moving parts than a jet. Nearly everyone gets pro-pay, an extra sum added onto their checks because they're in a critical MOS.

I was talking to one Spec 5, who was complaining because he was working in an E-6 slot. I was sorry for him until I figured out that he was making more than the typical E-6, about $730 a month, twice what I make. He said he ought to be making $800 a month—bully for him. I tried to shut that conversation off, crybaby. He knew what he was getting into; he reenlisted until 1975.

I got a ride over on a Huey and back to Long Binh in a Thia 2½ ton truck plus two other rides to Bien Hoa. I made amazingly good time on the route back. That may be my last jaunt anywhere near the boonies.

Our new captain wants satire and comic spoofs on enemy activity for the magazine. He claims he has support for such a radical approach but MSgt. Garcia doubts it. I like the captain's idea but doubt whether it will work out, having seen the system stomp on such ideas. I feel the captain is right that our paper has to say something but Garcia is also right that it won't happen. I'm sorry I'll miss this. I've been writing some zany articles for the captain—they'll send them when they get published. We'll see if they really get published.

Awaiting a Replacement

August 4, 1971—10 days

Today I finished my Chinook story. With all the retypes, I probably wrote 16 or so doubled spaced long sheets like this one. The captain is a horse of a different breed. I'm not slacking off for his benefit. I spent last night writing up a spoof on a VC for our paper, one of my better humorous bits, I thought. The Chinook story is certainly meatier and longer.

I've got CQ tonight, the last duty in the office. There are no replacements yet. I'd feel more comfortable if there was an orderly transition before I leave.

CHINOOK

I flew in Chinooks many times and took them for granted. I knew they were important but never realized the work necessary to keeping them in service. This long article was my contribution to our fall 1971 First Team *magazine, printed long after I left Vietnam.*

The passenger sits in ear-splitting silence, wondering how anything could be as noisy and shaky as a Chinook and still fly. He watches one of the

6. Being Short: July 1, 1971, to August 15, 1971

doorgunners unconcernedly opening a C-ration can and is vaguely aware of the pilot's presence when a nomex-clad hand appears and turns a knob on the instrument panel. The passenger also notices a fifth crewman is lying on the floor, resting atop cushions, staring intently through a square hole in the floor.

Little can the casual observer imagine the talent and training required to keep a Chinook flying safely. The apparent ease with which the flight crew carries out their duties is deceiving, simply the tip of the iceberg. For example, to the passenger's fleeting glance, the man on the floor barely serves a purpose, he's a feather-bedder. But, in fact, he's a highly trained Chinook flight engineer, as essential as the pilot to ensure maximum efficiency from each mission.

As the "hook" floats into a firebase, the flight engineer relays the distance between sling load and the trees to the pilot, with an accuracy acquired through long experience. Grasping the quick-release handle or "pickle grip," all the time in the air, the flight engineer can jettison the load by remote control if it is too heavy, a tree snags the swaying cargo or some other danger presents itself. A second pair of eyes for the pilot, he is the master of a critical blind spot.

Along with the pilot and the maintenance crew, the flight engineer is one of a new breed of Chinook specialists who have emerged since the aircraft's introduction into the army twelve years ago. Accordingly, they have become a critical part of the 1st Cav's air mobility and logistical capability.

By using this tremendous backlog of experience and six years with the First Team in Vietnam, the 3rd Brigade's Chinook company has developed an effective, albeit complex, operation. When two of the 1st Cav's brigades stood down, two of the three Chinook lift companies left also. The remaining company, the 362nd Aviation Co, was formerly Bravo Co, 228th Assault Helicopter Bn. Along with assistance from the 1st Aviation Brigade, they furnish the heavy cargo lift capability for the Garry Owen Brigade.

The company has 16 Chinooks and 200 men. In their busier, divisional days, they launched 8 birds daily. With the decreased demands for the brigade, in relatively close proximity to Bearcat, their home for the past two years, the company normally launches only 3 or 4 birds now. Even with this reduced commitment, they still lift 3,500 tons of supplies and 6,500 pax (passengers) each month.

However, the tremendous capability is not achieved without considerable effort and expense. CW2 Charles Michael, the company safety officer, commented on the high cost of Chinook operations, "For a typical load of beer and soda, it costs approximately $67 to deliver each full can to a firebase." Although the army is not in business to make money, careful attention is given to all the contributing factors to the high cost of operation.

First, the pilots cost more to train. "It takes a special rating; you have to have CH-47 transition training at Ft. Rucker, Ala., for six weeks after flight school," Michael explained. "Also, we have to keep our instrument rating current, where other pilots don't."

Michael emphasized that the extras were necessary because of several peculiarities of the hook. "We have a depth perception problem because of the height the pilot sits and because he can never see his load. It takes several months of flight experience to get the back wheels to hit when you expect them to," Michael added.

A second factor is the high initial cost of a Chinook. The 362nd flies the older "A" models, which cost $1,674,561. According to Michael, this doesn't include armor plating or armaments. Losing one bird is a costly experience. As a result, "We're not supposed to be the first in or the last out," Michael said.

Another contributor to the high cost is the expense of operating the hook in flight. Because a hook swallows 75 gallons of fuel in 15 minutes, a full load of cargo is vital to economic operation. "It's ideal to have something on the hook at all times, going and coming, Michael commented. "Passengers usually aren't on mission sheets. They're scheduled only on LZ moves. But we do carry a lot of unscheduled pax," he concluded.

As irreplaceable as the pilot himself is the large crew of mechanics. Talking to SFC James Remington, the company maintenance supervisor, a Chinook is a mind-bogglingly, complex collection of intricately balanced machinery. Working with Chinooks for ten years, Remington has been with the 1st Cav since it picked up its first Chinooks in March 1963, except for a one-year lapse.

Remington underscored the final cost factor: "It takes 12 hours of maintenance for every hour of flight. We have a five-man general-mechanics team start work on a bird and call in as many of our seven specialized shops as necessary."

A tour through their formidable shop complex impresses the observer by the scale of the undertaking. Even though his shop is filled with highly trained technicians, requiring specialized tools and machines and an oversized supply room, Remington said he still couldn't put a Chinook together from scratch. Many of the parts are pre-balanced at the Boeing factory and never touched in Vietnam.

With six rotor blades, three motors, transmission, hydraulics and tubing that one mechanic called a plumber's nightmare, it is surprising that maintenance personnel can figure the ships out. Remington said the problem of finding experienced replacements for his crewmen is a constant one. Most of the crews receive special pro-pays for their critical MOSes.

An all-pervading sense of caution dominates the entire company. Flight engineers, trained as maintenance men also, will sometimes ground a bird in the field because of something relatively small. The company has a fine safety record but they say it's the small things that will go sour in the long run.

On unhappy occasions, a Chinook will be stuck on a firebase or some similar remote spot. Parts, mechanics and whatever else is required are flown to the downed bird and a spirited attempt is made to fly it out.

In rare instances when repair isn't possible, the competition, a CH-54 "flying crane," is called in. "In those cases, usually there isn't enough left to do much with," commented Remington.

The maintenance crews are loyal to the Chinook, despite its faults. "You always have competition between aircraft but to us the flying crane is a mosquito," said Remington proudly. In fact, most of the crewmen have worked exclusively on hooks.

One of the TI (technical inspection) men had worked on jets before going to hooks. When asked how the two compared mechanically, he maintained the Chinook was far more complicated than a jet, because it has more moving parts. Electronically though, the hook is less complex.

For the cavalrymen who think of a Chinook as simply a bone-rattling ride to a firebase or Vung Tau, the bird fully deserves a second look and perhaps a bit of admiration. For the 362nd Aviation Co., who take pride in it being mathematically impossible for a hook to fly, it's a very involved, demanding business.

Ford Jeeps

August 5, 1971

When I finally settle down at home, I'm *never* going to buy a Ford. [*I should have taken my advice. I bought a Ford Maverick—and it was an awful car—a few months later.*] The jeeps here used to be Willys but now they're Fords with predictable results. The rear axles, especially the U-joint areas, are bad. The larger horsepower is unnecessary and dangerous. The wheels' independent suspension system is a poor one. MSgt. Garcia says McNamara got Ford the contract—I have to wonder about McNamara. I'm mad because I was robbed of half a day because of our jeep. I went to the motor pool at 7:20 a.m. and spent the rest of the morning and part of this afternoon trying to free it from the motor pool's clutches. Somebody did an inspection and the jeep didn't pass, as usual.

Big Al got inspected by some major last night and reported to the orderly room for not having his flak jacket. The major asked him condescendingly what he would do if an attack came. Al retorted that the flak jacket would get in the way when he jumped out of the tower and ran. The utility of a flak jacket is debatable.

I got a haircut today. Now my mustache has the longest hairs on my head. The Vietnamese barber was overzealous.

Medical Records Hunt

August 7, 1971

I went on a hunt for my medical records. I was told that I don't have to have my medical records to DEROS but if anything goes wrong with my health because of the Army, it's a hopeless case unless I can show the medical records. After checking with three company orderly rooms, I finally hit it on my last hope, the Medical Company. I'd made the mistake of turning them in at Phuoc Vinh last August. Records seem the only way the Army knows you exist. Horrible things happen when you lose your records, especially your financial records.

You wonder about the veterinarians in Vietnam; who will treat GI animals? For one thing, the scout dogs have an elaborate program of care and there are hundreds of K-9s in the Bien Hoa area. They are constantly being tested for worms and given special dunkings for ticks and fleas. The Vietnamese pets get some of the spin. The Army does many things to keep the GIs happy over here, much more than you'd suspect back there.

My writing is deteriorating, as I get shorter. They've been rewriting everything I've done recently, in particular the story about the warrant officer and his copilot scrambling to stay alive. I've attempted to be diligent to the last but it isn't that easy. With seven days to go and only four of them in Bien Hoa, my drive is shot. I don't start clearing Admin Co. until the 9th and leave for 90th until the morning of the 11th. So I'm functionally unemployed and out of work.

SFC Lebus is finally leaving Vietnam and the Army. He tells me that the comic books I've been buying are in fact OCS (officer training school) manuals. They might as well be. With heretical views like that, he'd better get out of the Army fast.

Going-Away Meal

August 8, 1971—6 days to go

Big Al and I hitched over to Long Binh and ate at the Mandarin House, the Chinese restaurant. We were celebrating leaving country, kind of a last lunch. We discovered that two of the main gates on QL 1, prime routes into Long Binh, were closed, possibly for good. There had been too many accidents at those gates we were told.

We had a relaxing meal of varied Chinese dishes. The shrimp and beef dishes were out of sight! We both ordered a hodgepodge of foods although it reeked of Army Orient. We had orange soda out of cans and ate our dessert with a plastic Army spoon. They offered us chopsticks, which we declined. The dessert was worth mentioning, candied mushrooms. Al had one kind and I another but I got a raw deal: his tasted like fruit cocktail, mine like candied mushrooms.

The new *Garry Owen* issue arrived. I like the rewrite of the 2/5th story. I didn't like the layout of the front page but I got a byline, no small ego trip.

I can hardly wait to get home, oh boy!

Clearing Begins; Last Letter

August 9, 1971—5 days to go

The way I figure it, today I clear the company (it's done), tomorrow I clear the brigade, the day after I clear 90th Replacement Bn., the next day I clear out of Vietnam, the next day I clear out of Oakland and I'm home to Nebraska. Notice the orderly progression—I take it day by day and stay sane that way.

The only scandal for the day was discovered in the unofficial Army critic, *The Overseas Weekly*. They lit into us (story enclosed) and did a "number 10" (poor) job. They got my 2/5th story confused with the 2/8th one. Yes, we're covering up but they could at least pin us for the right coverup. I have no trouble defending myself from such shoddy muckraking. I don't mind taking a few lumps if they attack the right area but they missed the whole point— we weren't allowed to mention our casualties or how poorly the battle went for us.

I'm pretty sure I sent out the 2/5th story with pictures. A baby could have found inconsistencies between the two stories and pictures that weren't correctly matched.

I'm encouraged by the prospects of beating this letter home. Tomorrow is my last full day in Bien Hoa. It won't be long now.

Afterwards

I made it home without incident, and after a leave, was stationed at the Brooke Army Medical Center Public Information Office in September 1971. I discovered in late 1971 that I could get out of the regular Army, which I promptly did, and immediately returned to college. In December 1973, I graduated from college with an English major and a near art minor.

I found a job doing Social Security Disability claims in 1974, which I did for 36 years until I retired. People wonder why I didn't go after a more glamorous career rather than staying a stolid bureaucrat but it gave me the foundation for the great adventure of my life, having and raising a family.

A lovely woman married me in 1977 and we now have four children and three grandchildren. The marriage and our family remain the most satisfying part of my life. In addition to family activities, I do many things including maintaining my orchard, baking bread, singing in choirs, fiddling with various kinds of photography, reading too much, gardening, and now writing. I've lived in one house for 30 years and Minnesota for 40, nourishing my need for stability following an unsettled childhood.

Regarding what I took away from Vietnam, I'm still not sure. As best I can tell, I turned my back on the experience and never looked back—"the world" really was better. After getting reacquainted with my 22-year-old self while transcribing my old letters 45 years later, I know that I'm surely a more stable and wiser person. I don't attribute much of what I see as my success to my Vietnam experience—it didn't change where I was headed.

Maybe someone can divine some everlasting truths from this book but such revelations elude me. And after all, I wasn't in command and suffered no traumas of note. I was a junior enlisted man writing little stories whose primary value, I see now, was to record life in a distant war.

Index

Numbers in ***bold italics*** indicate pages with photographs.

1st Australian Taskforce 282, 283, 289
1st Cav colors exit the 'Nam ***257***, 262
1st Cav leaving *see* Standdown of division
1st Cav patch 184
1st Cav Petroleum Laboratory 251
1st Cav Special Services Band ***113***, 114, 205, 210
1st Cav Supply and Transportation Company 252
1/5th Mech 307
1/7, Expedient Fishermen 221, 223
1/7 Recon Finds Complex 197
1/9th 261
1/12th Self-Styles Firebases 217, 219
1/14th Artillery 115
1/21st Artillery 116, 117, ***118***
1/30th Artillery 216
2/5th 286, 287, 291, 293, 295, 298, 299, 300, 321
2/8th Cav 246, 281, 282, 289, 290, 298
2/12th battalion stringer 236
2/19th Artillery 126, 127, 157, 163, 173, 233
3rd Bn. 33d NVA Regiment 282, 287
3rd Brigade Supply and Transport Company 292, 293
3rd Field Hospital 120, 137, 140
4th Veterinary Hospital 290
5/7th Cav 216
7th Squadron, 1st Air Cavalry 245
8th Aerial Port 127, 305
8th Engineers 40, 42, 169, 170
8-inch guns 101, 103
11th Armored Cavalry Regiment (ACR) 173, 208, 241, 255, 259
11th Aviation Group 210
15th Administration Company 5, 180, 236, 250, 271, 297
15th Medical Dispensary 249

15th Supply and Service Battalion 203
20th Engineer's PIO 256
24th Evac Hospital 137, 207, 294, 304, 314
25th Division 208
25th Scout Dog Platoon 251
27th Maintenance 173, 204
40th Dental Detachment 177, ***178***, 180, 181
42nd Explosive Ordnance Disposal Detachment 280
79th Maintenance 204
90th Replacement 82, 249, 321
92 Charlie MOS a Gas 251
93rd Evacuation Hospital 46, 47, 90, 99, 100, 137
229th Assault Helicopter Battalion 157, 254, 263, 264, 306
229th Honors 264
290M tractor and scraper 12, 13
322nd Aviation Detachment 51
362nd Aviation Company, formerly B Co., 228th AHB 315, 316–319
495th Veterinary Detachment 59
545th Military Police Platoon 260

A Company 1/7th 147, 187, 215, 234, 268
A Company 1/12th 300
A Company 15th Medical Battalion 175, 176
A Company, 2/5th 270
A Company 2/7th 40, 41, 42, 49, 80, 201
A Company 8th Engineer Battalion 103
ABC news 254
Abrams, General 207, 236
Adams, Sgt. James 248
Address labels 244
Aerial Heroics 313, 314
"African Genesis" 250
After Vietnam 321, 322
Aguilar, Spec 4 Antonio 293

323

324 Index

Air conditioner stolen 264
Air Force Rocketed 95, 134, 135
Air strike 27
Airbase 5, 30, 95, 127, 134, 135, 138, 202
Alaska 4
Alcohol 18, 90, 97, 111, 112, 136, 148, 284
Alpha Co. Bulldozes Heavy Guns Through 103
Alpha Troop 1/9th 21, 24
Ambushes on abandoned firebases 84, 85, 86
American Civil Liberties Union (ACLU) 298
American dead 37, 38
American flag 50, 51
Anderson, Sgt. Joseph 13
Anderson, Lt. Roger 119, 120
FSB Andre 90, 91, 97, 140
Anlin, Sgt. John 130, 131
Anti-freeze 182
Ants 6
Arclight (B-52) mission 43
FSB Ares 64, 65, 86, 87, 95, 108, 169, 215, 220, 221, 234
Armed Forces Vietnam Network (AFVN) 358
Armijo, Dave 258, 307, 308
Armor Vehicle Launched Bridge (AVLB) 103
Army Reporter newspaper 141, 288, 294, 299, 303, 314
Army Republic Vietnam (ARVNs) 138, 140, 201
Army Times newspaper 170, 203, 289, 314
Army vs. Drugs 95
Arquello, Spec. 4 Marcos 132
Artillery *4*, 10, 11, 14, 42, 55, 86, 87, 101, 116, 117, *118*, 134, 145, 152, 157, 158, 177, **222**
Askim, 1st Lt. Gary 204, 293
Associated Press (AP) 301
Auby, Spec 4 Darrell 265, 266
FSB Audi 202, 205
Austin, 1st Lt. John C. 62, 219
Australian army 281; liaison team 282, 289

B Battery 1/21st Artillery 115
B Battery 2/19th Artillery 42, 53, 55
B Company 1/7th 68, 74, 132, 287
B Company 1/8th 20
B Company 1/12th 131
B Company 2/5th 303, 304
B Company 2/7th 55
B Company 2/8th 207, 241
B Company 2/12th 237, 238, 266
Bad Day 22
Bad Night 25
Bailey, Spec 5 Arthur 251, 252

Bailey, PFC Larry 147
Baker, Ray Stannard 278
Bare Feet Get Bitten, Ranger Says 90, 91
Barracks 4
Bartlett, WO John C. 13, 21, 24
Battalion surgeon 78, 86
Bear 185, 208
Bearcat 201, 294, 314, 315, 315, 316–319
Becker, Capt. Lawrence J. 204
Becomes Proud Papa 97
Bees 26
Being Short 298
Belanger, Spec 4 George 44
Benton, Susanne 109
Berguist, Capt. Kenneth 80
Best CO We've Ever Had 20
FSB Betty 205
Bible 6, 67
Bien Hoa 3
Bigoted GI 103
Bitten Foot 90
Black Hats 42, 111
Black Horse Brigade 9, 28
Black Market 16, 44, 229
Blackmore, Spec 4 John 172
Blacks 146, 227, 244
Blackwell, Spec. 4 Mike 112, 114
Blank, PFC Bill 74
Blough, Steve **70**
Boat missions 54
Bomb craters 55
Bookelaar, WO Geoffrey 13
Boom Boom Girl Attack 252
Borovey, Jim "Rapper John" 122
Boutzil, Alex 28, 29
Braun, Sgt. Doug 38
Briefings 14, 51
Britisher 253
Brown, Spec 4 Alan 45, 64, 78, 102, 119, 120, 121, 122, 123, 137, 150, 158, 162, 168, 169, 188, 201, 209, 212, 214, 229, 233, 235, 236, 242, 248, 256, 265, 267, 270, 271, 272, 274, 275, 286, 288, 291, 292, 297, 298, 299, 304, 314, 320, 321
Buchwald, Art 291
Buckley, William F., Jr. 298
Buehner, Spec 4 Larry 286, 287
Bug Wars 161
Bulldozer 189
Bunker, Spec 4 Dave 251, 295
Burn Accident 145
Burnett, WO Thomas 314
Burton, Brig. Gen. Jonathan R. 137, 205, 211, 256, 282
Bus Incident 301
Bush League Entertainer 166
Butterflies 6, 63, 123, 148, 162

Butteris, Spec 4 Marvin 96, 98
FSB Buttons (Song Be) 3, 9, 10, 11, 12, 13, 14, 16, 18, 20, 21, 22, 28, 29, 201
Buying Liquor 90

C Company 1/7th 115, 122, 132, 139, 220, 221, 223
C Company 1/12th 155
C Company 2/5th 293, 294, 300
C Company 2/7th 37, 38, **39**, 53, 54, **63**, 90, 92
C Company 229th Assault Helicopter Battalion (AHB) 172, 306
Cache magazine article 70, **72–75**, 249
Cache newspaper article 70, 71, 95
Caches 67–75, 89, 93
Calley's Conviction 239, 244
Calvitti, Spec 4 Joseph 79, 80
Cam Rahn Bay 4, 5, 30
Cambodia 9, 10, 13, 14, 20, 27, 47, 120
Camp Alpha 228, 229, 233
Campbell, Spec 5 David 172
Can, Duong Cong 33
Caribou 18
Carrell, Alan 43
Cartoons 108
Castle, Lt. Mick 289
Castle Pad 150
Catch-22 movie 308
Catholic Mission 9, 11, **16**, 29
Cavalair 12, 13, 20, 21, 24, 30, 38, 49, 55, 57, 59, 61, 63, 80, 85, 87, 91, 97, 98, 100, 102, 103, 104–110, 114, 116, 117, 131, 141, 146, 147, 151, 153, 155, 161, 166, 169, 171, 174, 175, 176, 180, 181, 182, 183, 185, 186, 197, 200, 203, 206, 208, 210, 213, 215, 219, 221, 223, 233, 236, 238, 240
Cav's High Wire Act "Digs In" 110
CBS news 82, 87, 88, 89, 92, 104, 239, 242, 243
CBS's FSB Ares Pot Party 92, 104, 111, 169
Central Highlands 11
"Certain Sounds" rock group 312
Chaplains 38, 78
Chaplain's column 263
FSB Charles 243, 244, 245
Charlton, Spec 4 Dave 219
Chieu Hoi 30, 31, 35, 76, 86, 138, 183, 184.199
Chinook 6, 8, 13, 15, 17, 18, 27, 41, 65, 69, 75, 76, **112**, **113**, 114, 316–319
Chinook Maintenance 315, 316
Christian rock group 312
Civil Affairs team 308, 309
Civilian press relations 239
Clark, Sgt. Kelly 117
Claymore mines 39, 41, 62, 268
Cobra gunship 8, **11**, 15, 21, 55

Collection, Classification and Salvage (CC&S) 204
Colors Ceremony 256
Combat assault 40, 41, 42, 43, 85
Combined Service and Support Battalion (CSSB) 244, 258, 267
Comics 160, 284, 320
Command quarters (CQ) 242, 249, 285, 303, 317
Confused patient 90
Congressional inquiries 145, 297
FSB Connell 73, 87, 160
Convoy 276
Cooking 146, 147, 193, 220, 295
Cooks 166, 169
Cooper, Spec 4 Ronald 170
Cotton, Cecil 43
Court martialed 218
Coyle, Capt. Michael P., Jr. 78, 79
Cribb, Sgt. William 186
Criminal Investigation Department (CID) 292
Croc Keeps Distance 248
Crockett, Davy 138, 139, 141, 183
Crocodile 248, 270
Crossbows 11, 15
Crow, PFC Donald 79, 80
Cullum, Spec 4 Ronald 181
Currency exchange day 44
Custer, Sgt. William B. 21

D-9 bulldozer 101, 102, 103
D Company 1/7th 99, 100, 126, 187, 196, 244, 245
D Company 1/12th 160, 161, 224, 225, 226, 268
D Company 2/5th 270, 293, 294, 299, 300
D Company 2/8th 247, 248
D445 VC Battalion 282
FSB Dacus 101, 103, 139
Dap 167
FSB Darby 169
Date Eligible for Return from Overseas (DEROS) 130
Dasenbrock, 1st Lt. Tom 41
Davidson, Capt. Lee **226**
Davidson, Lt. Gen. 96
DDT 35
Dead NVA Still Deadly 269
Deatherage, Pat 267, 271, 304
Defense Information School (DINFOS) 3, 43, 123, 152, 234, 253
DEROS Center 34, 150, 227, 229
DEROSing 93, 130, 177, 179, 212, 235, 249, 262, 296, 315, 320
Defenseless children 132
Defoliation **42**

326 Index

Deisley, Sgt. Steven 35
Delaney, Spec 4 Robert 59
Demond, Sgt. Doyle 186, 192, 196, 202
Demotion? 263
Dentistry 48, 59, 60, 177, 178
Dexter, Sgt. George 124, 140, 141
Dickerman, Sherwood 251
Dierdorf, Spec 4 Ken 304
Digging Up Grave 195
DiModeca, Spec 4 Chuck 206
DINFOS Classmates 253
Disciplinary reports (DRs) 218
Distinguished Old Man 273
Division swimming pool 175
Doctor 8, 39
Dog Food Grubbing 179
Dog Vaccination 270, 271
Dogfight 263
Dogs *see* Pet Dogs; Scout Dogs
Donaldson, Sam 254
FSB Donna 277
Draft deferment 3
Draft lottery 3
Drake, Sgt. Gary 223
Drops 262, 284
Druener, Capt. Ronald 290
Drugs 5, 18, 26, 50, 95, 104, 107, 111, 112, 114, 127, 164, 167, 175, 177, 190, 216, 288, 295, 296, 297, 308
Drunken major 143
Duffy, PFC Joe 119
Dump accident 18
FSB Durall 76, 83, 85, 87, 88, 100

E Company, 2/7th 42
Echo Company Mortars 1/7th 126, 189, 190, 220, 221
Echo Recon 1/7th 31, 65, 75, 77, 83, 85, 86, 95, 126, 138, 139, 141, 164, 165, 166, 177, 181, 183, 184, 185, 186, 189, 190, 192, *193*, 194–198, 211, 214
Echo Recon 1/12th 48, *56*, 61, 62, 91, 217
Echo Recon 2/7th 54, *57*, 58
Echo Recon 2/8th 247
Echo Recon 2/12th 237, 238
Economizing 81, 82, 87, 92
Elephants 174
Enemy body count 24
Enemy propaganda broadcast 63, 64
Enemy Thatched Hooches/Complex 196, 197
Enlisted man 1, 9
Enlisted man's club 35
Epstein, Lt. 116, 171
Euphemisms 155
Evans, Spec 4 Dan 301, 302
Evans, Sgt. Rodney J. 268

FSB Evelyn 270, 293, 294
Example of Our Newspaper 104–110
Exit the Service (ETS) 267, 296
Explaining Art of Horseshoes 153
Explosive ordinance disposal (EOD) 18, 19, 69, 74, 75, 276, 278, 279, 280

Fake stories 291
FSB Fanning 270, 275, 277, 282, 289
Fatigues fatigued 315
Feminine Mystique 180
Field, Lt. Stan 201, 216, 217, 218, 219, 227, 228, 233, 234, 239, 246, 247, 261, 267, 270, 311
Fire support bases (FSB) 18, 66, 67; *see individual FSBs by name*
Firebase Christmas 125, 126
Firebase *129*; design 217, 219; dust suppression 220; outhouse *222*
Fireworks 148, 149
First Day in Jungle (second outing) 190
First Impressions 7
First Mission Hot for Sergeant 85
First Sergeant Hassles 133
First Stinging Defeat 155
First story printed 33
First Team Academy 5, 82
First Team magazine 227, 316
Flying boxcar 5, 18
Flying Circus 40, 76
Flying cranes 18, 41, 319
Flying PX *40*
FSB Fontaine 246, 247, 254
Foolish war 1
Football 84, 158
Forklifts 292, 293
Fort Hood 210, 262
Ford Jeep 319
Fort Lewis 5
Forward observer 86, 87, 177, 300
Forward Support Service Element (FSSE) 111, 114, 148, 153, 154, 159, 204, 249, 258
Frag Booby Trap 268, 269
Frag fishing 220, 223
Fragging 146, 164, 217, 233, 243
Freed, Joe 238
Freedom Bird 35, 82, 83, 159, 202
Fuel-gas Explosion 315
Fry, Lt. Col. Alfred E. 187
Fry, Spec 5 Donald "Mortimer" 127, 159, 168, 185, 201, 213, 233, 239, 265, 267
FSB Furr 291, 299, 303

FSB Gail 293
Garbage dump 126
Garcia, MSgt. 239, 262, 281, 286, 311, 316
FSB Garry Owen 37, 38, 39, 40

Index

Garry Owen newspaper 155, 243, 244, 245, 246, 247, 248, 251, 252, 255, 261, 261, 264, 265, 266, 268, 269, 272, 277, 279, 280, 292, 293, 294, 299, 303, 304, 313, 314, 321
Gates, Spec 4 Jerry 55
Gaudet, Spec 4 John 119
General's Mess 246, 258
Germann, Spec 4 William 300
GI Thieves 249
Giae, Chief Division Scout Nguyen Cong 32
Gibson, PFC Shannon 165
Gimian, Capt. 308
Girlie magazines 277, 283
GIs advertise in *New York Times* 245
GI's child 96, 97
GI's 4-legged War Trophy 123
GIs Prefer Theirs "On the Rocks" 146
Goldwater, Sen. Barry 292, 298
Goodwin, Greg 265
Gottsche, Sgt. Bruce 66, **70**, 185
Graham, WO Tyrone 13
Grauer, Reuben 263, 264
Grease gun 32
FSB Green 30, 31, 32, 35, 66, 69, 75, 85, 115, 117, 128, 132, 133, 138, 141, 145, 146, 147, 148, 154, 164, 165, 166, 184, 186, 189, 221
Green grass 278
Green line guard duty 250, 261, 271, 284, 296, 305, 307, 315
Gregory, Spec 4 Al 284, 287, 290, 291, 293, 295, 296
Gromar, 1st Lt. Robert 14
Grunts Dislike Entomology 161
Grunts Get Fill 244, 245
Grunts vs. Insects 160
Guard duty 68, 250, 251
Gunner's Aerial Daring Saves Their Lives 314
Guns taken away from GIs 217, 276

H Troop, 16th Cav 314
Hackett, Capt. Jim 130, 131
Hagler, Capt. 27
Hair 14, 284
Hair musical 164, 177
Haircuts 128, 244, 320
FSB Hall 289
Hall, Spec 4 Donald Allen 209, 210
Hall Field Dedicated 210
Hamlet, Col. 271
Hamlet, Col. James F. 210
Hanley, PFC Dan 245
Hanna, Spec 4 Selby 291
Hanoi Village 6
Hansen, Spec 4 Lief 253, 279, 285, 287
Harbeck, Sgt. Steve 84, 85, 86, 126, 190, 192, **193**, 195, 214, 215, 216, 220, 229, 244, 249

Hardman, Capt. John A. 183
Harris, PFC James 147
Harris, Col. Richard L. 202, 204
Harvey, PFC Ronald 170
Hawaii 230–232, 311–313
He Keeps His Head 294
Helicopter crashes 8, 37, 184, 189, 190
Helicopter hitchhiking 159
Helicopter Maintenance 172, 306
Helicopter maintenance incentives 306
Helicopter pilots 302, 303
Helicopters 4, 6, 8, 9, 10, 17
Henselman, Spec 4 Robert 247
Heroin 111, 112
He's a Clutch Performer 87
He's a Tumbler 131
Hink, Capt. William 226
Hitchhiking 136
Hladik, SSgt. Delbert 154, 155
Hlavacek, John 133
Hong Kong 153, 229
Hooch housing 14, 114, 158, 163, 187, 235, 255, 263
Hooch Loss Upset 188
Hooch mates 29, 30, 50, **88**, 103, 242, 249
Hooch Mobbed 213
Hooch theft 202
Hoochmate Sacked 296
Hope, Bob show 134, 148, 149, 160
Hoppe, Lt. Col. Robert B. 203
Hopson, SFC William 181
Horn, Lt. Col. Clifton A. 203
Hornets 154
Horse's Mouth 290
Horseshoes 153
Hospitalization 46
How Dog Story Began 123
Howard, Ed 111, 116, 167, **168**, 171, 174, 182, 234
Huey 6, 9, 15, 28, 40, 51, 136, 185, 189, 127
Human bodies by road 218
Huntley, Spec 4 Gary 176
Huong, Thach 33
Hyde Park 273
Hyman, Brig. Gen. 183, 211, 258

Ice 144, 145, 146, 147, 182
Ice Plant 144, 182
Incentives to stay in Vietnam 306
Independence Day 301
Infiltration Becomes Evident 13

Japan 4, 99
Jeep 9, 10, 22, 47, 64, 122, 134, 136, 137, 162, 168, 206, 207, 212, 256, 276, 288, 319
Jeep Mechanic 276

Index

Jessee, Sgt. Mike 184, 186, 194, 214
Jets 5, 27, 135, 138, 158, 159, 174, 247, 260
Johnson, Pres. Lyndon 292
Joint United States Public Affairs Office (JUSPAO) 301
Jones, Spec 5 Harold D. 78, 79
Jo's Operation Telephone Home 44
Joseph, Sgt. Blue 290
Jouanicot, Capt. Maxwell 44
FSB Jupiter 108, 130, 131, 140, 155, 161, 169, 170, 185, 188

Keating, Spec 4 Jerry 293
Keeping Choppers Flying 306
Kellogg, PFC Juan 221
Kennedy, Sgt. Thomas 58
Kennedy, Capt. William 59
Kielawa, PFC Marty 223
Kilgore, Sgt. Edward 221
Killed Stories 152
Killer Helicopters 14, 15
FSB King 275, 277
Kit Carson Scouts 7, 31, 32, 33, 48, 99, 101, 139
Klees, Sgt. Lawrence 280
Knapp, Spec 4 Billy M. 154
Knutsen, Dennis 274

Labrossi, Lt. Col. 178, 182
Ladner, Capt. 261
Lamont, Spec 4 Joseph C. 268, 269, 295, 296
Langbecker, Norbert 255
Lankhorst, PFC Steven 90, 92
Larson, Sgt. Bob 245
Lassiter Pad 282
Latrines 5, 120, **222**
Launder, 1st Lt. John E. 239, 255, 261, 267, 281, 305, 311, 313
Lawrence, Jack 37
Leaving (DEROSing) Vietnam 321
Lebus, SFC 207, 219, 308, 320
Lee, Capt. Gordon 94
Leeches 67, 69
Leighton, Conrad **238**, **302**
Leighton, Jim 129
Lemn, Spec 5 Edgar B. 33
Leonard, Bruce 248, 249
Leopard, Sgt. Don 57
Levesque, PFC Jerry 162
Lewis, Spec 4 Dave **10**, 17, 25, 26, 27, 127, 132, 137, 179, 199, 211, 212, 219, 224
Light Observation Helicopter (LOH) 13, 15, 24, 43, 155, 201, 241, 314
Lizards 6
Locker, Jim 183
Lodate, Sgt. James 35
Logging Bird Crash 184

Long, WO Robert B. 21, 22, 24
Long Binh 28, 46, 51, 119, 320
Long Crow, Sgt. Alvin 48, 62
Longhair Bar 232
Loss, Capt. Myron 199, 200
Lost in the Jungle 192
Lost Newspaper 304, 307
Luau 231
Lynch, 1st Lt. (later Capt.) John 177, 182, 188, 190, 192, **193**, 195, 196, 197, 234, 268

M-16 9
FSB Mace 173, 235, 241, 269, 277, 283, 287, 302
Maeder, Col. Richard 210, 212
Mail 64, 127, 163, 198, 226, 233, 239
Making Common Cause 289–290
Malaria-like fever 37, 43, 45, 46
Malloy, Lt. Col. 140
Mandarin House Chinese restaurant 320, 321
Manila terminal bathroom 275
Mano, Tom 43
Marijuana 18, 26, 34, 89, 92, 95, 104, 111, 112, 127, 169, 182, 185, 251, 258, 304, 305, 315
FSB Mars 48, 51, 52, 59, 60, 61, 62
Martin, John Alfred **167**
Martinez, PFC Archie 304
Martinez, Capt. Ray 38
M*A*S*H movie 243
Materne, Sgt. Vinc G. 20, 21
Mays, Sgt. Clay "Cowboy" **94**
McCall, Spec 4 Dava 306
McCaw, WO Stanley C. 24
McClelland, SSgt. Ernie 206
McKeown, Spec 5 Ron 224, 236
McDonnel, Josephine 44
McKnight, Capt. Paul 172
McMillian, PFC Ronald 34, 35
Med Colonel Regarded as the Top Dog 175, 176
Medal of Honor (Congressional) 267, 268
Medals 238, 240
Medevac 8, 18, 56, 78, 136, 155, 156, 187
Medical Civic Action Program (MEDCAP) 17
Medical Records Hunt 320
Medical ward 45
Medics 48, 78, 86, 99, 100, 101
Medic's Job Includes Being "Just a Grunt" 100
Medina, Capt. 305
Mekong Delta 46
Men of 3rd Brigade Uphold Cav Tradition 299
Michael, CW2 Charles 319
Midland Lutheran College 321
Military Air Radio System (MARS) 44

Index 329

Military Assistance Command Office of Information (MACOI) 287, 288, 295, 307
Military Assistant Command Vietnam (MACV) 253, 279, 301, 303
Military Payment Currency (MPC) 36, 44, 45
Military Police (MPs) 18, 19, 182, 207, 218, 233, 254, 260
Military Police Firefight 260
Miller, Spec 4 Lonnie 269
Mimeograph 262
Miscarriage 123
Mr. Nice Guy 225, 226
Money 44, 122, 214
Monkey 173, 193, 195
Monsoons 13, 52, 65, 131, 260
Montagnard Viet Cong (VC) 24
Montagnards 9, 11, 15, 16, 19, 24, 25, 28, 33, 184, 186
Moore, Spec 4 Ron 147
Morale 164
Morrison, Sgt. Dale 120
Morrison, Spec 4 Dick 60
Mosquitoes 66, 144, 194, 197, 199, 213, 280, 296, 307
Moth 7, 162
Movie Disappointment 243
Mules (motorized) *113*, 114, 249
Mulligan, Capt. William E. 13
Musgrove, Helen "Patches" 120, 121, 133, 136, 137, 138, 139, 140, 146
Music 101, *113*, 115, 155, 171, *205*, 206, 208
Mustaches 22, 28, 224, 254, 291, 315, 320
My office *38*

Nagamine, Sgt. Brian T. 13
FSB Nancy 140
Napalm drop 27
NCO-EM Club System Provides Fun, Refreshments 170, 171, 172
Nebraska 6
New PIO Office 256
New Republic 298
New Year's Celebration, Brawl 157
New York Daily News 239
New York Times 245
Newbies 302, 303, 315
Newbies get checkup 178
Newbies Rare Birds 246, 247
Night guard in jungle 194
Night Intruder 184, 185
Night Scope 307
Nixon, Pres. Richard 180, 242, 243, 244, 268, 288
FSB Noble 188, 189, 190, *191*, 197
Non-commissioned officer in charge (NCOIC) 255, 256, 265, 299

Norris, 1st Lt. Allen 56
North Vietnamese Army (NVA) 14, 21, 33, 54, 58, 74, 84, 85, 89, 105, 138, 139, 165, 190, 192, 195, 197, 199, 215, 220, 223, 268, 291, 294, 303
Not Shoot First 90
Notra Dame des Mission *see* Catholic Mission
Nui Ba Ra 9, *12*
NVA Money Hoard 214
NVA Purse Strings Cut in 1/7 Firefight 215
NVA Rice Cache Falls to Cav 105

Observer newspaper 197, 215, 253, 306, 314
O'Daly, Lt. 45, 64, 83, 115, 116, 153, 155, 158, 159, 162, 179, 180, 241
Odd Couple Part 266, 267
Office Coupe 313
Ohio Wesleyan University 3, 84
Oil Bites the Dust 221
Olathe, Kansas leaves 144, 149
Old Foes Become Friends 141, 183
Omaha Herald newspaper 239
One-upsmanship 307
Open Mess System 170
Operation Keystone *see* Standdown
Operation Scrub 92, 93, 94, 143, 198, 202, 203, 204
Operation with Australians 282
Orders to leave Vietnam 308
Orientation Issue 272
Osborne, Spec 5 Barney 148
Our Poor Jeep 82
Overseas Weekly 243, 301, 321

Pacific Architects and Engineers (PA & E) 144, 183
Pad Serves 1st Brigade 114
Paine, PFC Mike 176, 224, 236, 237, *238*
FSB Pamela 289
Paper layout 252
Parker, Capt. James R. 13
Parker, Sgt. Jim 217
Pash, PFC Billy *105*
Patches *see* Musgrove, Helen
Payne, Spec 4 Timothy 74, 141, *142*, 215, 216
Peneprime 221, 293
Penland, Spec 4 Harry 59
People Sniffer 105
People watching 312
Perez, Corp. Frank 91, 99
Perez, PFC Lorenzo 306
Perez, Spec 4 Rey 130
Perrier, Kevin 1, 40
Perry, Spec 4 Michael 314
FSB Pershing 40, 41, 42, 53, 55, 59, 80

Index

Personnel Action Can Solve Your Problems 151
Personnel Action Office 149, 151
Pet dogs 11, 49, 50, 56, 59, 65, 104, 123, 134, 136, 157, 158, 161, 166, 173, 175, 176, 179, 207, 227, 244, 246, 263, 267, 270, 271, 283, 285, 286, 287, 295, 299, 304, 313
Peters, Spec 4
Petroleum, Oils, and Lubricants (POL) 251
Phantom jets 247, 260
Philippine Band 305
Photo lab 52
Photographer Sees Casualties 295, 296
Photographer Wants to Write 77
Photography 9, 16, 35, 40, 41, 69, 76, 93, 97, 102, 115, 135, 137, 138, 140, 148, 159, 160, 173, 174, 182, 201, 207, 216, 226, 236, 237, 238, 242, 243, 255, 258, 262, 265, 267, 269, 271, 276, 285, 295
Phuoc Tuy Province 282, 289
Phuoc Vinh 8
Pieck, 1st Lt. Dennis 58
Pilot Helmets 163
Ping pong 19, 202, 223, 258, 285, 304, 305
Pink (hunter-killer) team 21, 54
Pinups 109, 164
PIO reunion 49
PIO scroungings/junk 228
Plant, Spec 5 Rodney 32, 107
Poker 159
Polaroids 265
Police 33
Political talk 298
Popular Forces (PF) 178
Porthouse, Capt. Harry 149, 150, 151
Postal Exchange (PX) 51, 115
Pot Head Attack 182
Potaozala, SSgt. Kim 308, 309
FSB Powder Ridge 188, 212
Power outage 296
Preece, SSgt. Tom 1, 31, 32, 66, 68, **70**, 84, 126
Press releases 301
Prisoner of war (POW) captured 303
Professional photographer dude 312, 313
Property Disposal Office 204
Promotions 64, 114, 115, 288
Prostitutes (boom boom girls) 49, 50, 177, 225, 252, 291
Psychological operations (Psyops) 16, 36, 107, 199, 200, 211
Psyops Bird 199, 200
Psyops Missions Spread Word 200
Public Information Office (PIO) 49, 96, 138, 216, 228, 235, 240, 244, 256
Putnam, Maj. Gen. George, Jr. 7, 8, 10, 13, 15, **23**, 225, 226, 236
PX hopping in Long Binh 51

Quan Loi 51
Quick Reaction Force 250, 307
Quintes, Sgt. Fernando M. 49

Radio telephone 68, 88, 89, 269
Rally Support Vietnam Personnel (RSVP) 263, 264
Ramlow, PFC Daniel 94, 97, 105
Rangers 54
Rappelling 6, 7
Rarig, Maj. David C. 94
Recon: The Professional's Job 61, 62
Reconstruction from Memory 124
Red hats see FSSE
Reed, Sgt. Jesse 165, 166, 184, 186, 194, 211, 214
Remington, SFC James 318
Republic of Korea (ROK) soldiers 163, 164
Rest & Recreation (R&R) 34, 79, 80, 227, 229, 242, 248
Restful Jungle Day 194
Rewriting stringer's story 250
Reynolds, SSgt. Steven 104
Richmond, Spec. 4 Alan 114
Rienzie, CW2 David 277
Rigby, Capt. Randall L. 55
Riley, Ed 31
Robinson, SSgt. Eddie 221
Roche, Mike 253
Rockets 14, 16, 58, 100, 134
Rome plow 279
Roving Prostitute 250
Runkle, Capt. 218
Runkle, PFC J.B. 98
Runkle, Martha 98
Russo, PFC Ron 94, 110, 173, 241

Saigon 4, 174, 179, 198, 213, 301
FSB Sally 16, 17, 202
Sandbags 4, 244, 245
Sandy Pad 76, 86, **112**, **113**, 114, 145, 292
Sapper Attack Preparations 271, 275
Scared—Couldn't Fight 30
Schlein, WO Joseph 13
Schroader, PFC Robert 126
Scout dogs **11**, 49, 50, 96, 98, 251, 295
Scrounger 26
Scrub Nets $12 Million see Operation Scrub
Self-Declared Heroes 244, 245
Selling First Team books 10, 15, 25, 47
Sending home shirt 262
Sergeant Calls Cobra Protection for Grizzly Affair 186
Sergeant-Lieutenant Flap 281
Shake down inspection 216
Shamming 241

Index

Shaw, SSgt. Troy 300
FSB Sherman 217, 219, 264, 265, 266, 292, 305
Shipp, Carl 184
Shorttimers Plan Ahead 34
Showers 5
Shrinking PIO 240
Shyness 211
Sick call 43
Sidney, Australia 211, 272–274
Siebert, Spec 4 Phil 277
Siegel, Spec 4 Gerald 61
Simpson, Capt. Jerry E. 203
Skin diseases 48, 82, 86
Skycrane Wreck 189, 190, *191*
Skytrooper 151
Skytroopers Say Packages Create Pleasant Problems 80, 81
Sleepless 26, 77
Smith, SSgt. David "Smitty" 73, 75, 84, 126
Smith, WO McDonald 94
Smith, Spec 4 Terry 294
Snakes 29, 92, 132, 158, 224, 225, 227, 288, 290
Sniper rifle 155, 161, 180
Snore Job Lands a POW 303
Snow, Spec 4 Calvin 73, 211
FSB Snuffy 16, 24, 25, 27
Softball 267
Song Be *see* FSB Buttons
Song Dong Nai River 266
Soul brothers 127, 244, 246
Sounds from the Other Side 205
South East Asia Pictorial Center (SEAPC) 216, 239, 256, 262, 267
Stalder, SFC 112
Standdown of 1st Cavalry Division 127, 130, 138, 150, 159, 162, 163, 164, 175, 182, 206, 216, 227, 234, 236, 239, 247
Stars and Stripes, Pacific 42, 80, 93, 123, 124, 129, 130, 140, 141, 152, 158, 169, 182, 233, 248, 265, 269, 270, 271, 289, 295, 299, 303, 310, 313, 314
Steinwandel, SSgt. Norbert 147
Stevenson, Col. 130, 174, 187, 234
Stirling, Spec 4 Ralph 178
Stockman, SFC Thomas 219
Stories 1
Strange bedfellows 265
Streetwalker 274
Stringer, PFC Harvey 99, 100
Stringer's Story 268
Stroman, Spec 5 Willy C. 12
Stuart, SSgt. Charles 35
Stuck on FSB Green 189
Suicide of spouse 312
Sunburns 79, 96, 208, 220, 224, 276, 278, 279, 312

Supply Realities 153
Surfing 232
Swanson, Dick 22, 89
Swanson, Spec 5 Lannie 86, 87
Sweet Sunday 290, 291

Tactical Operation Center (TOC) 11, 14, 27
Taking own pictures 76
Tavasci, PFC John *58*
Telephone call home 312
Telephones 109
Termotto, Capt. Sandy 178
Thomas, Spec 4 Louis 161
Thoughts on Writing Home 99
Tina & Stella 170, 171
Tiner, Spec 5 Garland 181
Tobacco products 77, 95, 96, 158, 161, 267
Ton Son Nhut 77, 301, 307
Top Dog 98
Touring with Battalion Commander 53
Transient hooch 26
Treating addicts 175
FSB Trish 289
Trivia competitions 116, 117
Troubles Gathering Stories 79
Truck rides 127, 128, 218
Trucks log all but H20 277
Trueblood, PFC John 147
Trueblood, SSgt. Ronald K. 50, 51
Tucker, Sgt. James 34
Tucker, PFC James Edward, Jr. *214*
Turtle 270; races 258, 259
Typewriter 11, 16, 123, 148, 171, 180, 214, 256, 262

United Press International (UPI) 301
U.S. Army Vietnam (USARV) 49, 94, 204, 207, 245, 251, 303, 315
Uses Lots of Oil 12

Vasquez, PFC Michael 165, 166, *167*
Vaughn, SFC Loyd "Pappy" 39
Vaxmonsky, 1st Lt. Albert 300
Ventrillio, Spec 5 Jim 255, 260
Vesser, Lt. Col. Dale 53, 91, 93
Vet Needles Pups 59
Veterinarians 59, 320
Victim of His Own Chow 147
Viet Cong 30, 31, 49, 76, 135, 305
Viet K-9 Turns Informer 49
Vietnamese 4, 6, 9, 15, 28, 76, 108, 121, 122, 137, 138, 155, 174, 189, 207, 226, 242, 309, 310; band and strip show 208; interpreter 309, 310; officers tour firebases 108
VIP Center 44
Volleyball 101, *102*, 114, 148, 149, 173
Volunteer army 235

Vonnegut, Kurt: *The Sirens of Titan* 262
Voskuil, SSgt. Ken 73, 74
Vung Tau in-country R&R 224

Walker, SFC Aubrey 126
Walker, Spec 4 Garry 138
Wall, Sgt. Charles 119, 221
Wall Street Journal 239
War Won? 188
Warner, Spec 4 Steve 207
Warren, 1st Lt. Paul T. 32
Watch This, Fellas! 265, 266
Water point 22, 92, 97, 104, 169, 170
Waterlogged Company 38
Webster, John (in Sidney) 273
Wempy, Teddy 298, 299
Werner, Rich 242, 249

Wheeler, PFC Steven J. 90
White, 1st Lt. James 115, 116, 122, 138, 150, 168, 175, 185, 188, 198, 199, 207, 209, 210, 211, 212, 216, 217, 218, 219, 224, 228, 233, 245
Wicked Soldiers 124, 125
Williams, Capt. James L. 20, 21
Wilson, SFC James D. 153, 154, 258
Woodcutter's Area 140
Woods, Sgt. 207
Woodstock 135
Workman, Maj. Ralph C. 38, 39, 201
Writing by Moonlight 194
Wrong Military Occupation Specialty (MOS) 263

Young Americans for Freedom 298

www.ingramcontent.com/pod-product-compliance
Ingram Content Group UK Ltd.
Pitfield, Milton Keynes, MK11 3LW, UK
UKHW041923140426
5217IPUK00014B/282